Cyber Security Politics

This book examines new and challenging political aspects of cyber security and presents it as an issue defined by socio-technological uncertainty and political fragmentation.

Structured along two broad themes and providing empirical examples for how socio-technical changes and political responses interact, the first part of the book looks at the current use of cyberspace in conflictual settings, while the second focuses on political responses by state and non-state actors in an environment defined by uncertainties. Within this, it highlights four key debates that encapsulate the complexities and paradoxes of cyber security politics from a Western perspective – how much political influence states can achieve via cyber operations and what context factors condition the (limited) strategic utility of such operations; the role of emerging digital technologies and how the dynamics of the tech innovation process reinforce the fragmentation of the governance space; how states attempt to uphold stability in cyberspace and, more generally, in their strategic relations; and how the shared responsibility of state, economy, and society for cyber security continues to be re-negotiated in an increasingly trans-sectoral and transnational governance space.

This book will be of much interest to students of cyber security, global governance, technology studies, and international relations.

Myriam Dunn Cavelty is deputy head of research and teaching at the Center for Security Studies (CSS), ETH Zurich, Switzerland.

Andreas Wenger is professor of international and Swiss security policy at ETH Zurich and director of the Center for Security Studies (CSS), Switzerland.

CSS Studies in Security and International Relations

The *CSS Studies in Security and International Relations* series examines historical and contemporary aspects of security and conflict. The series provides a forum for new research based upon an expanded conception of security and will include monographs by the Center's research staff and associated academic partners.

Series Editor: Andreas Wenger

Center for Security Studies, Swiss Federal Institute of Technology (ETH), Zurich

Titles include:

Strategic Culture, Securitisation and the Use of Force
Post-9/11 Security Practices of Liberal Democracies
Wilhelm Mirow

Russia's Security Policy under Putin
A Critical Perspective
Aglaya Snetkov

Negotiating the Nuclear Non-Proliferation Treaty
Origins of the Nuclear Order
Edited by Roland Popp, Liviu Horovitz and Andreas Wenger

Inter-organisational Relations in International Security
Cooperation and Competition
Edited by Stephen Aris, Aglaya Snetkov and Andreas Wenger

The Politics and Science of Prevision
Governing and Probing the Future
Edited by Andreas Wenger, Ursula Jasper and Myriam Dunn Cavelty

Cyber Security Politics
Socio-Technological Transformations and Political Fragmentation
Edited by Myriam Dunn Cavelty and Andreas Wenger

For more information about this series, please visit: https://www.routledge.com/CSS-Studies-in-Security-and-International-Relations/book-series/CSSIR

Cyber Security Politics

Socio-Technological Transformations and Political Fragmentation

Edited by Myriam Dunn Cavelty and Andreas Wenger

First published 2022
by Routledge
4 Park Square, Milton Park, Abingdon, Oxon OX14 4RN

and by Routledge
605 Third Avenue, New York, NY 10158

Routledge is an imprint of the Taylor & Francis Group, an informa business

British Library Cataloguing in Publication Data
A catalogue record for this book is available from the British Library

Library of Congress Cataloging in Publication Data
Names: Dunn Cavelty, Myriam, editor. | Wenger, Andreas, editor.
Title: Cyber security politics: socio-technological transformations and political fragmentation/edited by Myriam Dunn Cavelty and Andreas Wenger.
Description: 1 Edition. | New York, NY: Routledge, 2022. | Series: CSS studies in security and international relations | Includes bibliographical references and index.
Identifiers: LCCN 2021053423 (print) | LCCN 2021053424 (ebook) |
Subjects: LCSH: Information society–Political aspects. | Computer security–Political aspects. | Cyberspace–Political aspects. | Uncertainty.
Classification: LCC HM851 .C957 2022 (print) | LCC HM851 (ebook) | DDC 005.8–dc23/eng/20211108
LC record available at https://lccn.loc.gov/2021053423
LC ebook record available at https://lccn.loc.gov/2021053424

ISBN: 978-0-367-62674-7 (hbk)
ISBN: 978-0-367-62664-8 (pbk)
ISBN: 978-1-003-11022-4 (ebk)

DOI: 10.4324/9781003110224

Typeset in Times New Roman
by Deanta Global Publishing Services, Chennai, India

Contents

Illustrations

Figures

Tables

Note on Contributors

Editors

Myriam Dunn Cavelty is deputy head of research and teaching at the Center for Security Studies (CSS), ETH Zurich. She is the author of *Cyber-Security and Threat Politics: US Efforts to Secure the Information Age* (Routledge 2008).

Andreas Wenger is professor of international and Swiss security policy at ETH Zurich and director of the Center for Security Studies (CSS). The focus of his main research interests lies on security and strategic studies, the history of international relations, and Swiss security politics.

Authors

Farzaneh Badiei (Yale Law School) is the former executive director of Internet Governance Project at Georgia Institute of Technology. For nearly a decade, Farzaneh has been researching and directing projects related to the internet and online platforms.

Marie Baezner works at the Swiss Federal Department of Defense, Civil Protection and Sport. Earlier, she worked as a senior researcher at the Center for Security Studies at the ETH Zurich. Her main publications focused on the use of cyber means in political conflicts and on the use of military reserve forces in cyber security.

Matteo E. Bonfanti is senior researcher at the Center for Security Studies at the ETH Zurich. His research activities focus on the governance implications generated by the development and adoption of new technical, technological, and organizational solutions to enhance cyber security, policing and intelligence cooperation, as well as crisis management.

Aaron F. Brantly is an assistant professor of political science at Virginia Tech and a senior research scientist at the United States Army Cyber Institute at West Point, New York. He is the author of *The Decision to Attack: Military and Intelligence Cyber Decision-Making*.

Sean Cordey is a researcher for the Center for Security Studies at the ETH Zurich. He holds a dual degree from the Fletcher School and the University of St. Gallen. His research has notably focused on national cyber security strategies, cyber-enabled influence operations, and technologies of surveillance.

Jacqueline Eggenschwiler is a doctoral researcher at the University of Oxford. Her research looks at the contributions of non-state actors to global cyber security norm formation processes and corresponding governance implications. Jacqueline holds degrees in international affairs and governance, international management, and human rights from the University of St. Gallen and the London School of Economics and Political Science.

Johan Eriksson is professor of political science at Södertörn University, Stockholm. His research is focused on international relations, particularly the politics of technology and expertise. He is currently leading a project on post-Soviet Russian space policy. Eriksson has published seven books and numerous journal articles.

Giampiero Giacomello is associate professor of political science with the Department of Political and Social Sciences, University of Bologna, Italy, where he teaches cyber security and strategic studies. He has authored and co-edited 12 volumes and published several articles in scholarly journals.

Miguel Alberto Gomez is a senior researcher with the Center for Security Studies at the ETH in Zurich. His current research project investigates the role of cognition and affect on strategic decision-making in response to cyber security incidents. Initial findings of this project are seen in the following publications: *Sound the Alarm! Updating Beliefs and Degradative Cyber Operations* and *Past Behaviour and Future Judgements: Seizing and Freezing*.

Karl Grindal (Georgia Institute of Technology) is a doctoral student and Internet Governance Project collaborator, who previously served as the director of research for Intelligent Cyber Research (ICR), where he developed the Geocyber Risk Index (GCRI), a comparative assessment of the cyber threats.

Jasmin Haunschild is a doctoral student at the research group Science and Technology for Peace and Security (PEASEC) at the Department of Computer Science at Technische Universität Darmstadt, Germany. Her research interests include security institutions, e-government, and digitization in the public domain.

Islam Jusufi is lecturer and head of the Department of Political Sciences and International Relations at Epoka University, Tirana, Albania. His research interests relate to Balkan security politics. Most recently he published on "inclusive security and popular protests" (*Journal of Multicultural Discourses*).

Marc-André Kaufhold is a doctoral student at the research group Science and Technology for Peace and Security (PEASEC) at the Department of Computer

Science at Technische Universität Darmstadt, Germany. His research interests include crisis informatics, emergency management, information overload, and social media analytics.

Brenden Kuerbis (Georgia Institute of Technology) is a research scientist and partner in the Internet Governance Project focused on technical identifier governance and the intersection of national security concerns with forms of internet governance. Kuerbis has published in *Cyber Defense Review*, *International Studies Review*, and *Journal of Cyber Policy*, among others.

Jon R. Lindsay is an associate professor at the School of Cybersecurity and Privacy and Sam Nunn School of International Affairs at the Georgia Institute of Technology (Georgia Tech). He is the author of *Information Technology and Military Power* (Cornell 2020) and edited volumes on deterrence (Oxford 2019) and cyber security (Oxford 2015).

Amir Lupovici is a senior lecturer in the School of Political Science, Government and International Affairs and a research fellow in the Interdisciplinary Cyber Research Center, both at Tel Aviv University, Israel. His book *The Power of Deterrence* was published with Cambridge (2016).

Milton Mueller (Georgia Institute of Technology) is an internationally prominent scholar specializing in the political economy of information and communication and co-founder of the Internet Governance Project. His books include *Will the Internet Fragment?* (Polity 2017), *Networks and States: The Global Politics of Internet Governance* (MIT Press 2010), and *Ruling the Root: Internet Governance and the Taming of Cyberspace* (MIT Press 2002).

Christian Reuter is full professor and holds the chair for Science and Technology for Peace and Security (PEASEC) in the Department of Computer Science at Technische Universität Darmstadt, Germany, with secondary appointment in the Department of History and Social Sciences.

Wolf J. Schünemann is assistant professor at Hildesheim University, Germany, with a focus on internet and politics. He has published on disinformation, cyber security, and internet governance in the *International Review of Information Ethics, New Media and Society* and the *Journal of European Integration.*

Danny Steed is a scholar practitioner and consultant, with experience across academia, government, and the private sector. Danny was a visiting fellow on the Cyber Norms Program at Leiden University, Leiden, Netherlands. His second book, *The Politics and Technology of Cyberspace*, was published with Routledge in 2019.

Stefan Steiger is a research associate at Hildesheim University and a PhD candidate at Heidelberg University, Germany. His research interests include cybersecurity policies, foreign policy analysis, and internet governance.

Christopher Whyte is an assistant professor with the program on Homeland Security and Emergency Preparedness at Virginia Commonwealth University. His research projects focus on dynamics of decision-making during cyber conflict crises, information warfare and the shape of modern cyber-enabled disinformation campaigns, and the impact of artificial intelligence on national security processes. His work is published or forthcoming with a range of scholarly journals and presses.

Acknowledgments

Hard to believe that when the first drafts of the chapters in this volume were presented at an academic conference in Zürich, Switzerland, in 2018, a global pandemic was just an eventuality, one disruptive future scenario among many others.

The world is a different place now.

As we are finalizing the manuscript in the second half of 2021, the pandemic is still in full swing. Uncertainties about the future abound. And yet, there is continuity as well: Cyber security remains an issue of much contention in global politics.

Edited volumes are sometimes faulted for being inevitably uneven in terms of quality or for being nothing more than idiosyncratic collections of chapters. We argue that they are valuable additions to a research field precisely *because* they look at issues from a variety of perspectives. In fact, some issues gain from being addressed in such a manner, with cyber security being a prime example. With this volume, we aim to add to a growing body of literature that looks at how technological developments interact with broader sociopolitical and socioeconomic dynamics and how a changing threat landscape interacts with national and international governance solutions.

We want to express our thanks to the authors and fellow contributors for their enthusiasm and commitment in making this book possible. We are furthermore very grateful for the invaluable editorial assistance provided by Jasper Frei and Oliver Roos and for the support of Andrew Humphrys, Senior Editor at Routledge, and Bethany Lund-Yates, the Editorial Assistant.

1 Introduction

Cyber security between socio-technological uncertainty and political fragmentation

Myriam Dunn Cavelty and Andreas Wenger

In the past decade, cyber security has consolidated its position as one of the top national security issues of the 21st century: The dynamic interaction between technological vulnerabilities and the possibilities of their political misuse creates a problem space with little stability. Due to enduring uncertainties about the scope and tempo of ongoing socio-technological transformations, an increasing willingness to use disruptive cyber tools in the context of great power rivalry, and significant fragmentation of authority and accountability on different levels, managing cyber insecurities continues to be a most challenging governance issue in contemporary politics.

Cyber security is challenging because it is a so-called "wicked problem". Cyber security is "transboundary in nature, occur[s] at multiple levels across sectors, between institutions, and will impact all actors, both public and private, in complex, interconnected, and often highly politicised ways" (Carr and Lesniewska 2020: 392). Wicked problems avoid straightforward definitions and are impossible to solve in simple or final ways because they are composed of many interdependent factors that are often in flux (Rittel and Weber 1973). In addition, involved stakeholders have divergent values, goals, and motivations when it comes to the issue, making it difficult to find solutions that satisfy everyone to a sufficient degree.

As a politically relevant problem, cyber security evolves at the intersection between fast-paced technological development, the political and strategic use of these tools by state and non-state actors, and the various attempts by the state and its bureaucracies, society, and the private sector to define appropriate responsibilities, legal boundaries, and acceptable rules of behavior for this space. Our edited volume sheds light on socio-technical uncertainties and political responses. In 16 chapters, we highlight different facets of this problem space, showing how cyber security challenges states, private actors, and civil society in multiple ways because of dynamic, unforeseeable changes arising from the complex interactions between technical and social systems that have mounting political significance.

DOI: 10.4324/9781003110224-1

Socio-technical uncertainties in complex systems

Cyberspace is a complex socio-technical system. Three points are important in this context: First, cyberspace is brought into being by technologies that are made by humans. What might seem like a somewhat banal statement at first has considerable consequences that are not in the least banal consequences for how to conceptualize cyber security. The intentions, norms, and values of technological developers find their way into the artifacts during the design stage, while existing power structures influence the desirability of specific aspects or forms of technology (Matthewman 2011; Krause 2019). Hence, technologies are to be treated as inseparable from politics and vice versa, which necessitates analytical approaches that are sensitive to how technologies are shaped by political contexts and in turn enable specific political actions in the security domain. Just as importantly, economic forces influence many aspects of technical innovation and shape the availability of products and services to counter cyber risks (Lindsay 2017; Burkart and McCourt 2017). There is no thorough understanding of how economic and political factors interact in the literature yet.

Second, cyberspace is not independent but is closely intertwined with other systems such as the energy network – which in turn depends on communication infrastructure, creating co-dependencies. Important infrastructures and services and their respective interdependencies with digital infrastructures matter in the security discourse because they are crucial for the functioning of society – in fact, cyber security has reached the level of a key national security issue predominantly due to how the topic was interlinked with the critical infrastructure debate in the political process (Collier and Lakoff 2008). In addition, the cyber security discourse has changed considerably over the last 20 years: Cyber security is moving upward in the political agenda and expanding sideways as a problem area to a multitude of additional policy domains with advancing digitalization (Dunn Cavelty and Egloff 2019). As the currently last, important development, the cyber-incidents during the US elections in 2016 – attributed to the Russian government as well as semi-state actors – started a new chapter in the cyber security debate. The hack and leak operations highlighted the issue of strategic manipulation – also called influence operations – as a threat to democratic processes (Whyte 2020). While influence operations are far from new, the current technological environment affords different actors with new opportunities.

Third, cyberspace consists of multiple interactions between the underlying technology and its human users and operators. It is human interaction with technology – and the interaction between humans by means of technologies – that creates cyberspace in the first place. Furthermore, the growing complexity and nonlinear behavior of a complex system, like cyberspace, leads to a growing probability of unexpected disruptive events – from internal accidents to malicious attacks from both inside and outside the system (Hiermaier and Scharte 2019). Growing complexity offers new incentives and possibilities to threat actors to target people and assets in and through cyberspace. These varied interactions with technology introduce a specific type of uncertainty: It is an ontologically intrinsic type of uncertainty linked to human decisions, making us "part of the problem, system and potential solutions" (Sword Daniels et al. 2018: 291).

Political responses and emergent governance arrangements

As a wicked problem, cyber security is notoriously hard to pin down and is contested politically on conceptual and practical grounds in both national and international arenas. This is little surprising, given that security is an essentially contested concept to begin with – one whose proper use "inevitably involves endless disputes about their proper uses on the part of their users" (Gallie 1956: 169). If we consider security politics as "interactions through which values are allocated authoritatively for a society" (Easton 1965: 21), it becomes clear that defining the parameters of any type of security is always about difficult political choices, because the identification of valuable objects in need of protection from particular threats assigns legitimate claims to protection to some security objects and political subjects, but not to others.

In line with this, the "security" in cyber security means fundamentally different things to different communities. On a basic level, the security of digital technologies is grounded in risk management practices developed by computer specialists to make computers and computer networks more secure. Yet, cyber security is more than information security: Rather than just seeking to protect information assets it also extends to humans and their interests (Von Solms and Van Niekerk 2013). Moreover, decisive for the elevation of the issue from a technical to a security political issue was the realization in the 1990s that a set of high-value assets, so-called critical infrastructures, whose disruption or destruction could have severe consequences for a nation, were getting increasingly dependent on digital technologies for a variety of functions (Dunn Cavelty 2008). The related threat discourse that emerged consists of two interlinked factors, linking technical systems to more traditional threat politics: An outward-looking focus that sees an increasing willingness of malicious actors to exploit the weaknesses inherent in our societies without hesitation or restraint. This is coupled with an inward-looking focus on system-inherent vulnerabilities in (computer) systems. Beyond the technical realm, cyber security has become a type of security that refers to offensive and defensive activities of state and non-state actors in cyberspace, serving the pursuit of wider security political goals through the exploitation of various related opportunities (Deibert and Rohozinski 2010).

That said, the right role of the state in cyber security matters remains politically contested because cyber security is *not only* about national security. The question is not whether there *is* a role for the state – but who should have what kind of role and responsibility in different governance arrangements that aim to enhance national and international security (Dunn Cavelty and Egloff 2019). Obviously, states alone cannot ensure an increase of cyber security, not least because many crucial networks are in private hands. Hence, cyber security politics are defined by national and international negotiation processes about the boundaries of the responsibilities of state, economic, and societal actors and the agreement or disagreement over the means these actors use (Dunn Cavelty and Wenger 2020).

Fragmentation of political power can occur through decentralization when government tasks and authority are delegated downward (localization), upward (supranationalization), or sideway (privatization). It also takes place inside the government itself through ever-increasing functional differentiation of the administration. Increasingly, performing tasks requires highly specific expert knowledge. The increasing division of labor, a hallmark of modern societies, blurs the lines between the public and the private sectors. Many tasks that were previously performed by the state are now handled by specialized companies. This reshuffling of responsibility and power is ongoing and probably one of the defining features of cyber security politics.

The objective and structure of the book

The main objective of this book is to portray how technological developments interact with broader sociopolitical and socioeconomic dynamics that call for different national and international political responses. To that end, we bring together innovative, interdisciplinary conceptualizations of a changing threat landscape and explore how national and international governance solutions interact with this environment.

We understand the politics of cyber security as follows: As the interplay between *digital technologies*, their development, their use and misuse by human actors in conflictual economic, social, and political contexts, and the enduring *negotiation processes* between politically relevant actors about their roles and responsibilities in governing this problem space. There is an international security dimension, with state actors trying to shape and use cyberspace in accordance with their strategic goals – while at the same time attempting to stabilize the strategic environment through the development of behavioral norms (Dunn Cavelty and Wenger 2020). In addition, there is a domestic dimension, where states and their bureaucracies negotiate roles and responsibilities with civil society actors and the private sector. Our volume will combine national and international, state and non-state, technical, social, economic, and political perspectives, paying tribute to the complex environment in which cyber security is situated. The book has two main parts: the first focuses on the changing socio-technical environment and its implications for political action, while the second deals with the political responses.

Part I: The changing socio-technological environment and its impact on cyber threats

A first group of chapters focuses on the choice for and effects of cyber influence operations against the backdrop of domestic and international political fragmentation, heightened geopolitical tensions, and international disagreements about accepted political behavior in cyberspace. Though the use of disinformation in conflictual contexts is not a novel phenomenon, it has emerged as a new focal point in contemporary cyber security politics. One of the key questions that the scholarly community should strive to answer is why cyber influence operations have become so interesting of late, what actual impact they have and how we can best study said impact, and what can be done against potentially destabilizing effects. Three chapters in the book give partial answers to these questions.

Marie Baezner and Sean Cordey outline recent trends in cyber operations, showing how different actors in conflictual settings exploit conceptual and legal grey zones (Baezner and Cordey 2022). The chapter thus explores why cyber influence operations have become one of the more interesting tools for both state and non-state actors, even if purposeful strategic impact might be elusive. At the macro level, this trend is due to the overarching political fragmentation, intensification of international rivalries, costly and complex interdependences, relative imbalance in military power/capabilities, and socio-technological vulnerabilities. At the micro and operational-technical level, the relative availability and accessibility of cyber tools coupled with the flexibility, customizability, rapidity, scalability, and limited escalation potential of cyber operations is the main driver for their use. Supported by examples from a range of operations observed in the last few years, the chapter shows the reader that cyber operations, which include cyber influence operations, are efficient and effective tools for disruption and at the same time enhance and transform traditional grey zone activities, such as espionage and influence. It is rather likely therefore that we will see more of this kind of operations in the future. But what are their impacts?

In his chapter, Wolf Schünemann adds to our understanding of the phenomenon and its political impact (Schünemann 2022). Analyzing the existing literature about influence operations, he asks what the contributions and findings are in terms of theory, methods, and empirics and looks at whether there is good empirical evidence that disinformation has a destabilizing effect on democracies. With a three-layered distinction between a micro, a meso, and a macro level of analysis at which distortion and influence can be measured, the chapter includes three perspectives of importance for a solid threat assessment of disinformation campaigns. Moreover, with echo chambers and automation, Schünemann refers to phenomena that are widely associated with the structural transformation of the digital public sphere and are assumed to be facilitating factors for the spread of disinformation. The chapter finds, however, that just like with disinformation in general, their alleged effects are very difficult to prove – thereby adding to the overall uncertainty political actors find themselves in.

Noting that countermeasures need to be drafted carefully since our understanding of the overall challenge is incomplete at best, Schünemann passes the ball to the next chapter in the volume. Based on the notions of cultural violence and cultural peace, the chapter by Jasmin Haunschild, Marc-André Kaufhold, and Christian Reuter shows the potential for political fragmentation through social media, focusing on fake news and terrorist propaganda, and their amplified dissemination through social bots. They show that technology plays an ambiguous role, on the one hand being an amplifier and enabler of effects such as astroturfing and smoke screening, but on the other hand also enhancing social bot detection. However, noting that technology is just one aspect in this issue area, the authors raise the important point that technical interventions cannot address the root causes that make people spread or believe disinformation in the first place. Their findings raise interesting questions about the definition of victims and perpetrators of online structural violence. They ask: “Are people who spread misinformation and propaganda perpetrators of societal fragmentation and structural violence, or victims of a society that has left them with low media literacy and the feeling of being alienated by the society they live in?” (Haunschild et al. 2022: 58). The more digital technologies become interwoven with society and its general functioning, the harder will it be to isolate them from the humans that use them.

The book then moves on to look at new technological developments and their current and future impact on cyber security politics. We look at three technological areas: artificial intelligence/machine learning, quantum computing, and the expansion of cyberspace into space. In his chapter on artificial intelligence and the offense–defense balance in cyber security, Matteo Bonfanti provides an overview over the debate about so-called artificial intelligence in cyber security (Bonfanti 2022). It clarifies the concept of artificial intelligence (AI) and shows in which security-related fields such tools are already used. However, Bonfanti makes clear that future projections are very hard because the actual usage of new technologies depend on too many factors that are highly uncertain. What seems clear, and reinforces the observation made in the previous chapter, is that despite the many uncertainties of how AI will be used in the future, it will benefit both the defense and the offense. Who will benefit more will depend on the capacity of cyber security stakeholders in the private and the public section to master and leverage AI technologies for specific purposes. This usage will be inevitably shaped by the models of governance which will emerge from the formal/informal, fragmented/coordinated, and often unbalanced interactions among public authorities, private organizations, and the civil society.

Following a similar path of reasoning, Jon R. Lindsay evaluates the implications of quantum computing on cyber security and security more generally (Lindsay 2022). The chapter shows that cryptology is shaped by a paradoxical dynamic of cooperation-enabled competition in line with an expanded play of intelligence and covert influence, with ambiguous implications for strategic stability. Using the advent of quantum computing as a thought experiment, the chapter tackles technologically deterministic projections that are rampant in the field of cyber security. In short, if it were true that technology determines politics, then radical changes in technical infrastructure should have important, potentially equally radical political consequences. Focusing on the contest between code makers and code breakers against the backdrop of political logical, strategic context, and organizational implementation, the chapter shows convincingly how such deterministic perspectives neglect the social factors that shape secrecy and intelligence regardless of the type of technology that is involved. Even though quantum computing is making this contest more complex, its political implications are far from predetermined.

In the subsequent chapter, Johan Eriksson and Giampiero Giacomello look at the expansion of cyber infrastructure into the atmosphere and beyond through balloons, satellites, and other bodies in space, spearheaded by private actors (Eriksson and Giacomello 2022). By using fragmentation, vulnerability, and uncertainty as central analytical concepts, the chapter focuses on what this technological change means for the threat landscape, governance, as well as power and accountability. A central point in Eriksson and Giacomello's chapter is how the multiplication of actors and different forms of public-private constellations lead to increasing fragmentation and to more uncertainties. Just like Bonfanti and Lindsay point out in their chapters, new technologies co-create ambiguities because they are embedded in social and political systems that shape the very development as well as the possibilities of use and misuse of these technologies.

Part II: Emerging political responses in a complex environment

Switching to political responses as part of these developments, the book first focuses on the link between an uncertain environment, the role of decision-making in cyber security politics, and academic ways to study them. The uncertainties policy makers face in creating strategies and assessing their effectiveness also become a fundamental challenge for scholars who aim to trace, understand, and explain dynamics in the cyber domain.

Miguel Gomez and Chris Whyte present an analysis of national responses to a cyber security incident in a series of war games involving participants from Taiwan, the Philippines, and the United States (Gomez and Whyte 2022). With the majority of real-world incidents contextualized by geostrategic rivalries involving salient issues and the rise of both cyber capabilities and the willingness to engage in this domain, a better understanding of strategic decision-making becomes all the more crucial. This chapter, in response, applies a pseudo-experimental design to the increasingly popular activity of war gaming to better understand the processes involved in responding to cyber security incidents. By focusing on cognitive heuristics in decision-making and its consequences, the chapter contributes to a "behavioral turn" in the literature. Through war games, the authors observe the value of distinct cross-national perspectives in explaining variation in outcomes across participants. Despite the broad similarities among the participants involved, it is clear that cultural, procedural, and political expectations unique to each national context shape preferences and corresponding actions. As a result, the authors argue for the existence of distinct approaches to cyber security which may or may not reflect prevailing strategic realities but are, instead, rooted in preexisting beliefs among decision-makers. In their chapter, the authors continue the trend of presenting cyber security as a sphere of action that can only be fully understood when we embed it in a much broader context.

Continuing in this vein, Amir Lupovici focuses on Israel's cyber deterrence strategy (Lupovici 2022). He suggests that the Israeli case is puzzling: Despite the prominence of deterrence in Israeli strategic thinking and despite the prominence of cyber technology in Israel, Israel started to incorporate cyberspace into deterrence strategy late and to a limited extent only. How can this be explained? By combining discourse analysis, process tracing, and interviews, the chapter shows what role new constructions of cyber security and political trade-offs played in this evolution. Lupovici makes the point that the uncertainties in the cyber domain not only create difficulties for political actors, but that the same uncertainties also exacerbate scholars' ability to explore the practices, behavior, and strategies of involved actors. His remedy is to focus on the aforementioned embeddedness, namely, to ask, "how technological impetus is embedded in actors' narratives, strategic culture, and identities, and how adopting a certain strategy fits or challenges international norms" (Lupovici 2022: 130). This, so the author, provides new opportunities for studying topics that are defined by uncertainties, rapid changes, and fragmentation of authority. Overall, paying attention to the context of technological change can help us understand how policy makers develop new strategies but also adapt old strategies, such as deterrence, to new domains.

Moving on, we explore how three different states in different geopolitical settings attempt to tackle fragmentation of authority and accountability, outlining both differences and commonalities in their struggles. We show that the integration of cyber security policy into a coherent overall framework involves difficult trade-offs between security and privacy, and that outside influence and policy diffusion do not always translate into effective or legitimate policies.

Stefan Steiger looks at contestation in the formation of the German cyber security policy (Steiger 2022), focusing on the interactions between different actors in their attempts to establish stable and legitimate policies. The chapter analyzes the development of the German cyber security policy in four areas: law enforcement, intelligence services, military, and the protection of critical infrastructure. Drawing on role theory, the chapter proposes a two-level game to account for domestic and international influences on the development of cyber security policies. This approach facilitates a holistic look at the factors that shape cyber security policies. The chapter argues that in order to establish stable cyber security policies the administration's role (in this case "protector") has to be met by complementary counter roles from parliament, judiciary, non-state actors, and international partners. These role plays follow different patterns in the four areas that are studied because of the actors involved and the different kinds of insecurity that have to be addressed. The chapter shows that the government has expanded its protective role, but it also illustrates processes of contestation that limited domestic and international role taking and thereby shaped the cyber security policy.

Aaron Brantly's chapter focuses on Ukraine (Brantly 2022). Ukraine has struggled with the help of European and NATO allies to forge multiple organizational structures capable of facilitating national cyber and information security. The chapter offers a detailed analysis on the construction of national information resilience and cyber capability by a medium-sized state under duress and coercion from an adversary state. The result is an analysis of how the interaction of rapid socio-technological transformation in a highly fragmented political context translated into a hybrid approach to countering propaganda and disinformation, on the one hand, and a centralized approach to addressing cybersecurity challenges, on the other. Overall, Brantly highlights the importance of bureaucratic politics and historical path-dependencies in the shaping of new approaches to cyber threats.

Similarly, Islam Jusufi demonstrates how cyber security is tackled in the Albanian context (Jusufi 2022). Just like Brantly, Jusufi describes the development of the policy approach as a push and pull between different internal and external forces, between cultural contexts and political change, between fears of big attacks and the realities of everyday cyber crime. Standing for other small states transitioning to liberal democracies, Albania can serve as an example for how uncertainties in the cyber realm give more power to non-state actors, especially in the private sector and how these shifts in power translate into the need for states to adapt their ideas of sovereignty and rule. When capacities are low, it seems that international organizations play a big and important role in exporting ideas around multistakeholder models and legitimacy that are then adopted to local contexts.

The last three chapters move inside and beyond the state. Understanding political behavior in cyberspace is difficult at times due to the opaqueness of cyber operations and the limited visibility and ambiguity of many of the involved actors, especially private actors and intelligence agencies. Jacqueline Eggenschwiler focuses on non-state actors in the development of cyber norms (Eggenschwiler 2022). Her chapter examines the contributions of corporate actors to cyber security norm development processes. Specifically, it summarizes and comments on the effectiveness of the norms-based cyber insecurity reduction measures undertaken by technology companies. As a result of political and ideological contentions among governments, and against the background of increasing numbers of threats emanating from cyberspace, corporate entities have started inserting their voices more vocally in debates about rules of the road for the digital domain. The chapter argues that while the norms-based activities carried out by technology firms have been effective in terms of output and outcome, their efforts have borne less fruit apropos decreasing systemic risks and levels of cyber insecurity, respectively. However, this does not mean that their efforts are fruitless: In an environment as malleable as the cyber environment, norm development is messy and often linked to practices.

A concrete set of practices is what Danny Steed looks at in his chapter (Steed 2022) when he examines the impact of cyber security on intelligence practices. He reveals two broad themes: first, that the specific actions and adaptation from intelligence communities are acutely reflective of broader socio-technological transformations presented by the wider information revolution. Secondly, that the actions taken by certain intelligence agencies carry significant political repercussions for the future of cyber security itself. In this vein the chapter shows that in numerous ways the actions taken by intelligence agencies to remain effective instruments of national security actively contributes to exacerbated political fragmentation and an arguable state of increased and increasing cyber *in*security. To Steed, "the impact of intelligence *upon* cyber security carries more significant consequences to political fragmentation and cyber security politics than the impacts of cyberspace upon how the intelligence services conducts their affairs" (Steed 2022: 215).

It is such uneven, invisible power to shape the environment that makes cyber security such a difficult policy topic. In the last chapter, Brenden Kuerbis, Farzaneh Badiei, Karl Grindal, and Milton Mueller offer a view on how the strategic use of cyberspace could be made more governable by examining some of the current practice of cyber attribution, scientific developments in the field, and possibilities for its transnational institutionalization (Kuerbis et al. 2022). Looking at cases from 2016 to 2018, the authors find that new technical approaches reliant on observable artifacts occurring in private networks and behavioral differences of states are upping the need for institutionalizing neutral, transnational attribution where evidence can be assessed and independently reviewed. Most recently, a network of university, civil society, and industry-based researchers have sought to develop attribution capabilities that are considered scientific and credible by the broader community. Numerous challenges remain to this collective action. However, if successful, it could effectively counter state-sponsored or affiliated cyberattacks and the strategic use of attribution, therefore bringing more stability to cyberspace.

In the conclusion, Andreas Wenger and Myriam Dunn Cavelty (Wenger and Dunn Cavelty 2022) highlight four main issues emerging from the individual chapters of this book. The first major point is about the limited strategic utility of cyber operations. Rather than being noticeably escalatory or resulting in visible changes in the existing balance of power between great powers, they are mainly used as tools of subversion and mild sabotage. The second issue deals with the dynamic interrelationship between emerging technologies and the future of cyber security politics, highlighting the role of private actors, tech race dynamics as drivers of cyber threat perceptions as well as the role of institutional factors in shaping the influence that emerging technologies have on the balance between the offense and the defense. A third issue deals with the challenge of upholding strategic stability under multidimensional uncertainty, whereby the chapter discusses the micro-dynamics of decision-making that might drive escalation under uncertainty and ambiguity, the ambiguities of attribution as a precondition for a credible deterrence threat, and the growing role of intelligence in cyberspace. The fourth issue the chapter discusses is how to overcome fragmentation of authority and accountability.

Conclusion

Digital technologies are transforming many aspects of social and political life at a rapid pace while at the same time, they themselves are shaped by political decisions and governance arrangements that seek to balance opportunities and risks in an optimal way. This co-dependency and co-shaping of technology and politics plays a role in all the chapters in this volume. To study it, the authors are sensitive to the complex and non-determined workings of socio-technical systems and assemblages, rather than falling prey to technological determinism that isolates technological artifacts from their societal, economic, and political contexts.

The fact that there is considerable uncertainty regarding the tempo and scope of technological developments creates new demands for research that maps, assesses, models, and forecasts new technological possibilities. As social scientists, we need to understand the increasingly salient political and social aspects of technologies that will affect the patterns of cooperation and conflict in politics and society at the national and international levels. But social scientists also need to become increasingly apt at conversing with a variety of technical disciplines. At the very minimum, we need to familiarize ourselves through expert publications, better even, start a regular dialogue with colleagues in the technical sciences. Even though solutions for wicked problems are elusive, beginning to bridge the gap between different communities is a necessary start.

Bibliography

All links checked on August 20, 2021.

Baezner, M. and Cordey, S. (2022). Cyber in the Grey Zone: Influence Operations and Other Conflict Trends. In: M. Dunn Cavelty and A. Wenger (eds). *Cyber Security: Socio-Technological Uncertainty and Political Fragmentation*. London: Routledge, pp. 17–31.

Bonfanti, M. E. (2022). Artificial Intelligence and the Offence-Defence Balance in Cyber Security. In: M. Dunn Cavelty and A. Wenger (eds). *Cyber Security: Socio-Technological Uncertainty and Political Fragmentation*. London: Routledge, pp. 64–79.

Brantly, A. (2022). Battling the Bear: Ukraine's Approach to National Cyber and Information Security. In: M. Dunn Cavelty and A. Wenger (eds). *Cyber Security: Socio-Technological Uncertainty and Political Fragmentation*. London: Routledge, pp. 157–171.

Burkart, P. and McCourt, T. (2017). The International Political Economy of the Hack: A Closer Look at Markets for Cybersecurity Software. *Popular Communication*, 15(1): 37–54.

Carr, M. and Lesniewska, F. (2020). Internet of Things, Cybersecurity and Governing Wicked Problems: Learning from Climate Change Governance. *International Relations*, 34(3): 391–412.

Collier, S. J. and Lakoff, A. (2008). The Vulnerability of Vital Systems: How "Critical Infrastructure" Became a Security Problem. In: M. Dunn and S. Kristensen (eds). *The Politics of Securing the Homeland: Critical Infrastructure, Risk and Securitisation*. London: Routledge, pp. 17–39.

Deibert, R. and Rohozinski, R. (2010). Risking Security: The Policies and Paradoxes of Cyberspace Security. *International Political Sociology*, 4: 15–32.

Dunn Cavelty, M. (2008). *Cyber-Security and Threat Politics: US Efforts to Secure the Information Age*. London: Routledge.

Dunn Cavelty, M. and Egloff, F. J. (2019). The Politics of Cybersecurity: Balancing Different Roles of the State. *St Antony's International Review*, 15: 37–57.

Dunn Cavelty, M. and Wenger, A. (2020). Cybersecurity Meets Security Politics: Complex Technology, Fragmented Politics, and Networked Science. *Contemporary Security Policy*, 41(1): 5–32.

Easton, D. (1965). *A Systems Analysis of Political Life*. New York: John Wiley.

Eggenschwiler, J. (2022). Big Tech's Push for Norms to Tackle Uncertainty in Cyberspace. In: M. Dunn Cavelty and A. Wenger (eds). *Cyber Security: Socio-Technological Uncertainty and Political Fragmentation*. London: Routledge, pp. 186–204.

Eriksson, J. and Giacomello, G. (2022). Cyberspace in Space: Fragmentation, Vulnerability, and Uncertainty. In: M. Dunn Cavelty and A. Wenger (eds). *Cyber Security: Socio-Technological Uncertainty and Political Fragmentation*. London: Routledge, pp. 95–107.

Gallie W. B. (1956). Essentially Contested Concepts. *Proceedings of the Aristotelian Society*, 56: 167–198.

Gomez, M. A. and Whyte, C. (2022). Cyber Uncertainties: Observations from Cross-National Wargames. In: M. Dunn Cavelty and A. Wenger (eds). *Cyber Security: Socio-Technological Uncertainty and Political Fragmentation*. London: Routledge, pp. 111–127.

Haunschild, J., Kaufhold, M.-A. and Reuter, C. (2022). Cultural Violence and Peace in Social Media: Technical and Social Interventions. In: M. Dunn Cavelty and A. Wenger (eds). *Cyber Security: Socio-Technological Uncertainty and Political Fragmentation*. London: Routledge, pp. 48–63.

Hiermaier, S. and Scharte, B. (2019). Fault-Tolerant Systems. In: R. Neugebauer (ed.). *Digital Transformation*. Berlin: Springer, pp. 285–300.

Jusufi, I. (2022). Uncertainty, International Obligations, Fragmentation and Sovereignty: Cyber Security in Albania. In: M. Dunn Cavelty and A. Wenger (eds). *Cyber Security: Socio-Technological Uncertainty and Political Fragmentation*. London: Routledge, pp. 172–185.

Krause, K. (2019). Technologies of Violence. Myriam Dunn Cavelty and Jonas Hagmann in Conversation with Keith Krause. In: C. Kaltofen et al. (eds). *Technologies of International Relations – Continuity and Change*. Basingstoke: Palgrave Macmillan, pp. 97–106.

Kuerbis, B., Badiei, F., Grindal, K. and Mueller, M. (2022). Understanding Transnational Cyber Attribution: Moving from 'Whodunit' to Who Did it. In: M. Dunn Cavelty and A. Wenger (eds). *Cyber Security: Socio-Technological Uncertainty and Political Fragmentation*. London: Routledge, pp. 220–238.

Lindsay, J. R. (2017). Restrained by Design: The Political Economy of Cybersecurity. *Digital Policy, Regulation and Governance*, 19: 493–514.

Lindsay, J. R. (2022). Quantum Computer and Classical Politics: The Ambiguity of Cryptologic Advantage. In: M. Dunn Cavelty and A. Wenger (eds). *Cyber Security: Socio-Technological Uncertainty and Political Fragmentation*. London: Routledge, pp. 80–94.

Lupovici, A. (2022). Uncertainty and the Study of Cyber Deterrence: The Case of Israel's Limited Reliance on Cyber Deterrence. In: M. Dunn Cavelty and A. Wenger (eds). *Cyber Security: Socio-Technological Uncertainty and Political Fragmentation*. London: Routledge, pp. 128–140.

Matthewman, S. (2011). *Technology and Social Theory*. Basingstoke: Palgrave Macmillan.

Rittel, H. W. and Webber, M. M. (1973). Dilemmas in a General Theory of Planning. *Policy Sciences*, 4(2): 155–169.

Schünemann, W. (2022). A Threat to Democracies? An Overview of Approaches to Measuring the Effects of Disinformation. In: M. Dunn Cavelty and A. Wenger (eds). *Cyber Security: Socio-Technological Uncertainty and Political Fragmentation*. London: Routledge, pp. 32–47.

Steed, D. (2022). Disrupting the Second Oldest Profession: The Impact of Cyber on Intelligence. In: M. Dunn Cavelty and A. Wenger (eds). *Cyber Security: Socio-Technological Uncertainty and Political Fragmentation.* London: Routledge, pp. 205–219.

Steiger, S. (2022). Cyber Securities and Cyber Security Politics: Understanding Different Logics of German Cyber Security Policies. In: M. Dunn Cavelty and A. Wenger (eds). *Cyber Security: Socio-Technological Uncertainty and Political Fragmentation.* London: Routledge, pp. 141–156.

Sword-Daniels V., Eriksen, C., Hudson-Doyle, E. E., Alaniz, R., Adler, C., Schenk, T., Vallance, S. (2018). Embodied Uncertainty: Living with Complexity and Natural Hazards. *Journal of Risk Research*, 21(3): 290–307.

Von Solms, R. and Van Niekerk, J. (2013). From Information Security to Cyber Security. *Computers & Security*, 38: 97–102.

Wenger, A. and Dunn Cavelty, M. (2022). Conclusion: The Ambiguity of Cyber Security Politics in the Context of Multi-dimensional Uncertainty. In: M. Dunn Cavelty and A. Wenger (eds). *Cyber Security: Socio-Technological Uncertainty and Political Fragmentation.* London: Routledge, pp. 239–266.

Whyte, C. (2020). Cyber Conflict or Democracy "Hacked"? How Cyber Operations Enhance Information Warfare. *Journal of Cybersecurity*, 6(1): tyaa013. https://doi.org/10.1093/cybsec/tyaa013

Part I

Socio-technical transformations and cyber conflict trends

2 Influence operations and other conflict trends

Marie Baezner and Sean Cordey

In the past decades, various scholars and politicians have warned about the advent of cyber war and the probable surge of cyber operations[1] of possible catastrophic scale that could lead to the infamous "Cyber Pearl Harbor" (Shanker and Bumiller 2012). As Thomas Rid has pointed out in his book *Cyber War Will Not Take Place*, such operations have not become ubiquitous nor have they escalated into (cyber) war (Rid 2013). While cases in which cyber operations have been conducted to support other military operations in times of war have been observed (e.g. in Georgia or Ukraine), the cybersecurity literature has generally concluded that the majority of such operations takes place below the threshold of armed conflicts, an area that some international security scholars have called the "Gray Zone".

Accordingly, this chapter focuses on the socio-technological logics behind the emergence of gray zone conflicts and more specifically on the use of cyber operations, notably cyber-enabled influence operations, within them. To do so, the first section reviews the theoretical framework and driving factors of gray zone conflicts. The second section reviews some assumptions about cyber operations that make them attractive for gray zone conflicts before discussing, through a comparative analysis of various cases, their use.

As a caveat, this study was conducted on the basis of academic and open source literature. While these sources provided extensive information on cyber operations in gray zone conflicts, they primarily gave a Western point of view on the topic. The lack of literature on Western cyber operations in such conflicts gives the impression that actors targeting Western countries are more numerous and more active, which may not be the case.

Gray zones conflict: A theoretical framework

Geopolitical competition over the last decade has been increasingly played within the space beyond conventional diplomacy and short of conventional war, a space that is commonly referred to in the literature as the "Gray Zone". This concept was developed by scholars linked to the RAND Corporation and the US military (particularly special operations). It rose to preeminence at the same time as

DOI: 10.4324/9781003110224-3

the concept of hybrid warfare (to which it is sometimes equated) following the Crimean and Ukrainian crises.

Gray zone (conflict)[2] is a concept whose utility and definition are still debated. The main conceptual debate revolves around whether it is a new form of competition (Hicks et al. 2019; Hoffman 2007) or just an operational environment (Chambers 2016). The former interpretation is particularly aligned with US military phasing and planning (Pettyjohn and Wasser 2019). Critics, however, have argued that such a denomination has only contributed to conceptual muddling as it is not clear whether there are real boundaries between the phases and to what extent they can be applied in practice (Pettyjohn and Wasser 2019). As a result, part of the scholarship has moved away from it and is instead highlighting the latter understanding, to which the authors subscribe.

According to this strand of literature, gray zone conflicts have the following characteristics (Cantwell 2017; Chambers 2016; Corn 2018; Hicks et al. 2019; Pettyjohn and Wasser 2019; Votel et al. 2016): First, the gray zone is a distinct operating environment between peacetime diplomatic and geopolitical interactions and conventional war where intense political, economic, information, and military competition takes place. Gray zone conflicts thus mostly occur under the threshold of war. The array of techniques and tools used can also be employed once a conflict has escalated. Second, interactions within the gray zone are characterized by operational and strategic ambiguity, thereby allowing some degree of plausible deniability for its actors (Barno and Bensahel 2015; Mazarr 2015b). Third, gray zone conflicts are characterized by the opacity of the parties involved and the relative uncertainty about the relevant policy and legal frameworks that apply to them (Kapusta 2015). Fourth, leveraging the gray zone is (supposedly) mostly the province of revisionist powers,[3] which try to achieve objectives normally associated with victory in war (Chambers 2016; Corn 2018). Finally, within the gray zone, boundaries between the private and public domain are blurred with states using and targeting various affiliated actors – state-owned or private entities (Hicks et al. 2019).

The means and tactics used in gray zones are legion, multidimensional, and span across the full spectrum of state power and capabilities. They are only limited by the bounded threshold (before war) and often not by traditional legal and functional categories (Hicks et al. 2019). As such, operations in gray zone conflicts can be undertaken in all five domains – i.e. air, land, space, sea, and cyber or information – and by any governmental actors (Chambers 2016). These operations are particularly suited for asymmetrical conflicts due to their cost effectiveness, small footprint, low visibility, and covert nature (Votel et al. 2016). Accordingly, Hicks et al. (2019) propose the following categorization of gray zone (non-kinetic) means and tactics: Information operations and disinformation; political coercion; economic coercion; cyber operations; space operations; and proxy support.

While the concept of gray zone conflicts is often presented as relatively new, the types of actions that it describes only reflects what states have been doing for centuries to advance their interests in a competitive international system (Brands

2016; Dostri 2020; Mazarr 2015a, 2015b). Despite this, gray zones are effectively being increasingly leveraged through some new tools (e.g. cyber operations (CO) and cyber influence operations (CIO)) as states look for alternative ways to achieve their goals due to the rising cost of direct aggression (Dostri 2020; Echevarria 2016; Mazarr 2015b). Gray zone conflicts, meanwhile, are growing in saliency, intensity, and scale. This trend is driven by two factors: (1) the dynamics in the international (geo)strategic environments; and (2) the development and diffusion of new socio-technological means and methods (Corn 2018; Echevarria 2016; Mazarr 2015a).

Regarding the former, (1), the rise of gray zone conflicts is symptomatic of larger trends in the international environment such as accelerating geopolitical fragmentation, rising tensions and uncertainty as well as discontinuities in domestic politics around the world. At the domestic level, recent years have seen several nations such as Turkey, Poland, and the United States ravel in internal divisions and grievances, whether ethnical, economic, or political. These coupled with burgeoning illiberal and authoritarian regimes have set the stage and opened avenues for exploitation of the gray zone (e.g. electoral manipulation or influence campaigns).

At the international level, the exploitation of gray zones has become particularly attractive for non-state and state actors due, in part, to the current conventional nuclear superiority of the United States and the extensive economic interdependence, both of which have created a general aversion to major conventional wars (Mazarr 2015a). This is reinforced by the fact that some normative pillars of the international system are increasingly contested or that they simply do not exist (e.g. cyberspace) (Kapusta 2015). This fosters a legal gray zone that encourages bad behavior due to reduced risks of sanctions or escalation. Furthermore, international collaboration to counter this type of exploitation is made difficult by the loss of cohesion and difference in threat perception between like-minded states. These differences, alongside those between the private and public sectors, which are rooted and entangled in economic and political structures, not only complicate the identification of the problem but also the response to it (Dalton et al. 2019).

Regarding the latter, (2), the numerous socio-technical changes of the past decades, such as the widespread use of social media or the democratization of hacking tools, have been another driving cause for this trend. According to Leed (2015), technological advances (i.e. in Information and Communications Technology (ICT)) have allowed an unprecedented level of globalization, which, in turn, has blurred the distinctions between traditional elements of national power (e.g. between the military and commercial technologies) and between state and sub/non-state actors. Moreover, the extensive diffusion of technology – particularly related to space, cyber, and information – coupled with the relative affordability of these allowed a diverse range of actors (from adversaries to partners) to gain new and more effective means for sub-threshold coercion (Hicks et al. 2019). The increasing use of and dependence on technology by all strata of modern society have also opened the door to a plethora of leverageable socio-technical vulnerabilities, such as the fact that most ICTs are not built with a security-first mindset.

Meanwhile, efforts to mitigate these vulnerabilities are "often erratic, dependent on immature and ineffective market forces and regulatory schemes, and consistently outpaced by relatively low-cost exploitation technologies and techniques" (Corn 2018).

Cyber operations in the gray zone

Despite the numerous warnings and scholarship on the issue, the large-scale and systematic use of cyber operations as a means of warfare has remained in the realm of hypothesis unobserved in practice. As a result the literature now advances that cyber operations are instead largely seen as instruments of power, particularly in the gray zone literature (Boeke and Broeders 2018; Buchanan 2020; Fischerkeller and Harknett 2017; Gannon et al. 2021; Nye 2017; Sanger 2018). There are at least two strands within the literature on the strategic role of CO, both echoing the larger debate (Fischerkeller and Harknett 2019; Rovner 2019). The first strand – in line with the view that gray zone conflicts represent a shift away from conventional war – views cyber operations as novel strategic instruments, which are supposedly greatly efficient and effective compared to other instruments, such as economic coercion. The second strand, meanwhile, contests this claim and instead argues that cyber operations are only contemporary instruments of a variety of conventional competition activities, such as espionage, intelligence, or covert operations. In both strands of the literature, however, cyber operations and cyber influence operations play a preeminent role as instruments of power.

To better understand the implications, another strand of the scholarship has focused on the practical use and effects of cyber operations and cyber influence operations in various gray zone conflicts, such as the Americano-Russian influence and espionage campaigns, the Syrian civil war, or the Ukrainian conflict (Al-Rawi 2014; Baezner and Robin 2017a, 2017c, 2018; Barrett 2019; Crowdstrike 2016; DiResta et al. 2018; Galperin et al. 2013; Giles 2016; Grohe 2015; Howard et al. 2018; Nocetti 2015; Ornos et al. 2017). Building upon these, the rest of this section is devoted to assessing, in light of a set of case studies summarized in Table 2.1,[4] three widely shared assumptions that make cyber operations and cyber influence operations attractive in the gray zones.

Accessible and available

The first widely shared assumption is that, apart from highly sophisticated cyber operations (e.g. Stuxnet or Blackenergy II) that require and exploit expensive and rare zero-day vulnerabilities, the majority of cyber technologies and tools for disruptive and cyber influence operations have effectively become widely available and at a relatively low cost. As a result, and as Smeets posits, "the availability of offensive cyber capabilities expands the options available to state leaders across a wide range of situations" (2018: 92), particularly in the gray zone.

Indeed, regarding availability, the underground forums and black markets for malware are today filled with "ready to be used" attack tools and "ready to

Table 2.1 Case study summary

Case study	*Actors*	*Types of cyber operations*
US–Russia	State-sponsored actors	Cyberespionage and cyber-enabled influence
Ukraine	Non-state actors, hacktivists, and state-sponsored actors	Disruption, cyberespionage, sabotage, and cyber-enabled influence
Syria	Non-state actors, hacktivists, and state-sponsored actors	Disruption, cyberespionage, and cyber-enabled influence
US–China	State-sponsored actors	Cyberespionage
North Korea	State-sponsored actors	Cyberespionage, cybercrime, and sabotage
India–Pakistan	Non-state actors, hacktivists, and state-sponsored actors	Disruption, cyberespionage, and cyber-enabled influence
Southeast Asia	Non-state actors, hacktivists, and state-sponsored actors	Disruption and cyberespionage
Iran	State-sponsored actors	Cyberespionage, sabotage, and online influence

be launched" cyber operations, such as Distributed Denial of Service (DDoS). One can also easily contract "hack-for-hire" hacker groups (e.g. Dark Basin) to perform a variety of hacks (Scott-Railton et al. 2020). Meanwhile, the technical knowledge needed to engage in basic cyber operations and cyber influence operations is also relatively low. For the latter, for instance, only a rudimentary understanding of widely available editing software (e.g. meme editors, tweet generators or deepfakes) and social media is necessary (Chesney and Citron 2018).

Regarding costs, David Sanger (2018) advances that cyber weapons necessary for cyber operations are now "so cheap to develop and so easy to hide that they have proven irresistible". Indeed, the cost of entry to engage in cyber operations of low to medium sophistication is also relatively low, notably when compared to other traditional military means. This is particularly the case for cyber influence operations, which only require an internet connection, an internet-enabled device, and access to free account-based applications to engage in disinformation or propaganda. The cost of maintenance of these cyber weapons, however, can vary (Smeets 2018). But at the same time, the cost and time of execution can be further reduced through optimization and the use of more sophisticated tools and techniques, such as automated bots.

Looking at our cases, a first observation is that cyber operations tended to be more disruptive (affecting the logical and/or persona layers of cyberspace) than destructive (affecting the physical layer of cyberspace). This tendency is partly due to the fact that destructive cyber operations are less accessible than disruptive ones. Indeed, destructive cyber operations are more sophisticated and require more resources to be developed and planned, as shown by Stuxnet. Furthermore, destructive cyber operations have more escalatory potential than disruptive ones, making the latter more appropriate for gray zone conflicts. In our case studies, states and state-sponsored actors have shown restraint in their exploitation of cyber operations despite them being increasingly used due to rising international tensions (Gomez 2018; Valeriano and Jensen 2019). Apart from Stuxnet and other cyber operations targeting high-value targets such as Ukraine's electric grid in 2015 and 2016, the effects of cyber operations have remained limited (Cherepanov 2017; Dragos Inc. 2017).

Accordingly, this restraint could derive from the following two points. First, it may simply reflect that states are willing and eager to keep tensions only within the gray zone, even in open conflicts such as in Ukraine. This restraint also indicates that states seem to recognize and respect some "red lines" to avoid escalation (Gomez 2018). Consequently, this restraint shows that states are aware that their behavior in cyberspace can shape discourses on international norms and may want to remain at a level below the threshold of war to avoid precedents. Second, the restraint may simply be linked to inherent difficulties of conducting cyber operations. They require significant costs and time investments, they are difficult to control, their effects are uncertain and difficult to measure, and tools may only be used once in a specific timeframe[5] (Gomez 2018). All these elements make states prefer to reserve their most destructive cyber operations for the time they will most need them (e.g. for war). From a cost-benefit point of view, it is also possible that physical attacks may be simpler, cheaper, and more impressive than cyberattacks.

A second observation derived from our case study is that some states also conduct cybercrime activities in the gray zone, thus reinforcing the fact that cyberspace is well suited for different activities below the threshold of war. The state that best illustrates this particularity is the Democratic People's Republic of North Korea (DPRK). Indeed, the DPRK has been conducting cybercrime activities to finance its regime, its nuclear program, and to circumvent international sanctions (Carlisle and Izenman 2019; Kim 2018; Sanger 2018). A UN report published in 2019 declared that the DPRK's government earned approximately US$2 billion through cybercrime activities (e.g. targeting banks and cryptocurrency exchanges in foreign countries) (Finkle 2017; Guerrero-Saade and Moriuchi 2018; Nichols 2019; Solon 2017).

These DPRK's operations clearly stand out from the other states' that very rarely include cybercrime. In China and Russia, the divide between cybercrime and state-sponsored operations is blurry or at least permeable – a defining characteristic of gray zone conflicts. Indeed, these states often hire contractors that may also conduct cybercrime when they are not under contract with governments. For instance, APT41, working for the Chinese Ministry of State Security (MSS), conducts cyberespionage operations by day and cybercrime activities by night. However, FireEye noticed that the latter were conducted outside regular Chinese office hours and therefore were likely conducted without the state's knowledge or at least with the state's tolerance but likely not under the state's contract (FireEye Inc. 2019). In this example, the state is not the beneficiary of the financial gains perpetrated by these cybercrime operations and might actually suffer from the unwanted attention they generated.

Operationally attractive and effective

A second assumption that renders cyber operations operationally attractive, notably in the gray zone, is that cyber technologies leveraged by cyber operations and cyber influence operations enable rapid and scalable effects, two characteristics which enhance their effectiveness as they lead to the surprise, overload, and paralysis targets (Harknett and Smeets 2020; Warner 2019; Wirtz 2017). In practice, the nearly instantaneous nature of the internet and the interconnectivity of all ICTs have nullified the execution time between the launch and impact of an attack. Regarding cyber influence operations, cyber technologies have drastically reduced the time needed to disseminate information while offering a wide flexibility and range of platforms and formats. Concurrently, cyberspace has – to some degree – removed traditional physical and national barriers, thus providing even more operational scalability, flexibility, and security for its operators. This is also true for cyber influence operations where the new digital means of information dissemination, free from traditional information gatekeepers, have greatly expanded the reach and scale of influence activities.

Accordingly, one observation from our case study is that cyber operations are indeed increasingly used to gain a strategic advantage but particularly through cyberespionage campaigns, as illustrated by the PLA-sponsored Operation Aurora or the hacks of the American military Sea Dragon project (Nakashima and Sonne 2018). As such, this tends to imply that, in accordance with one strand of the literature, cyber operations are more used as a vector for traditional facets of competition in the gray zone rather than a purely novel instrument. In addition to the operational advantages of cyber operations, this can be in part explained by the fact that cyberespionage is not regulated by international law, which allows states to use such operations with relative impunity. However, some states, like the United States, make a distinction between economic espionage and national security espionage. While both types can be used in gray zone conflicts, these states consider the former to be illegal, while the latter is tolerated (Harris 2016; *The Economist* 2013).

A second observation is that cyber influence operations have gained in importance in the past years, as illustrated by the Russian influence campaign during the 2016 US Presidential election. Among others, these operations have used social media and tools to try to influence opinions on specific political topics. Such cyber operations are particularly well suited for gray zone conflicts as they are relatively cost effective, flexible, and easy to organize and limit escalation. As a result of the 2016 US election, some states have even started to mimic Russian influence techniques against, in parts, Western states. This was particularly the case of Iran during the 2018 US midterm elections but with less sophisticated cyber operations than Russia (Barrett 2019; Dave and Bing 2019; Timberg and Romm 2019).

A last observation is that disruptive cyber operations (e.g. DDoS and website defacement) are often opportunistically used following certain political events, such as a protest or a territorial dispute (e.g. Pakistani patriotic hackers targeting Indian websites with DDoS and/or website defacement attacks after a physical clash on the Line of Control in the disputed region of Kashmir) (Balduzzi et al. 2018; Kozy 2015; Mogato 2017). These operations are not specifically sophisticated as they often use old vulnerabilities in websites and are easy and fast to organize (Dewar 2017). However, they particularly attract attention and are tangible. When a website is unavailable because of a DDoS attack, the costs are estimated to be US$22,000 per minute of unavailability (Kenig 2013; NSFocus Inc. 2016). While the economic costs of such cyber operations can be significant, the political consequences of such operations remain rather limited. This limitation reduces risks of escalation and is particularly fitting in the context of a gray zone conflict. Patriotic hackers[6] are the main actors involved in these disruptive cyber operations (Baezner 2018a, 2018c, 2018b, 2018d; Baezner and Robin 2017a, 2017b, 2017d, 2017e).

Limited risk of escalation

The last assumption is that cyber operations present key characteristics that presumably make them highly effective while generating a low risk of escalation, thus particularly suited to use that stays in the gray zone. These are: (1) anonymity and the problems associated with attribution and deniability; and (2) the legal uncertainty surrounding cyber operations, whether for espionage, disruption, or influence (Fitton 2016).

Anonymity being a relatively prevalent feature of cyberspace, the attribution of cyber operations is not only complex and time-consuming at the technical level but also an often delicate, contested, and challenging affair at the political level (Assumpção 2020; Egloff 2019; Rid and Buchanan 2015). Meanwhile, due to the possibility of spoofing and false flag attacks, the chance of perfect technical attribution is low – whether or not this is necessary for political attribution is another debate. This imbalance towards offense is furthermore reinforced by the fact that proponents of cyber operations do not need to achieve perfect unattributable operations; instead, they only need to sow enough confusion and doubt in analysts and policy makers to alter its process (Assumpção 2020). Accordingly, it is unlikely that the resulting verdict of attribution will be so certain (i.e. quality and feasibility) as to justify a traditional military response under the applicable international law regulations (Fitton 2016). This is further reinforced by the fact that cyber operations have – practically and theoretically – a low propensity to lead to deaths, or at least directly attributable death and physical damages (Smeets 2018).

Linked to the issue of attribution, the legality of most cyberattacks and cyber-enabled influence operations remains both uncertain and unsettled normatively under international law (Schmitt 2018). This legal gray zone pertaining to cyber operations is thus ripe for exploitation by states and non-state actors who can avoid consensus and formal condemnation (and thus retaliation) for their use of cyber operations. The lack of international norms, however, is a double-edged sword and can also increase the risk of tensions among states, as shown by the spillover to trade war between the United States and China. The lack of consensus is rooted in diverging understanding and normative behavior – driven by the respective strategic imperatives of each actor – around various types of cyber operations. For instance, on the one hand, cyber-enabled intelligence conducted for the purpose of gathering and processing information for national security is generally tolerated and expected among states across the whole spectrum between peace and war (Harris 2016; *The Economist* 2013). On the other hand, economically driven cyberespionage is denounced and deemed by certain states – e.g. the United States – as illegitimate (Harris 2016).

As for cyberespionage, the debates around cyber influence operations can be rooted in differing conceptual approaches and definitions of cyber security. While Western states understand the concept narrowly and close to its technical definition, other states, including China and Russia, understand the concept more broadly. These states include cybersecurity in the concept of information space (Giles and Hagestad 2013). Therefore, Russia and China consider cyber influence operations as tools available to them for international relations, for instance to project power and advance national interests.

Conclusion

Overall, due to the overarching political fragmentation and intensifying international competition, a number of states, such as Iran, North Korea, the United States, China, or Russia, are increasingly attempting to advance their strategic economic and political interests through other means than war. In an attempt to avoid full-fledged escalations – due, in part, to a logic of cost avoidance as well as the relative imbalance in military power/capabilities – these actors have thus resorted to engaging and competing within the gray zone through the use of tactics of economic or political coercion as well as cyber operations and cyber influence operations. This trend has been particularly reinforced as the various socio-technological transformations of the past years have created plenty of opportunity for exploitation and disruption.

Regarding cyber operations, it is the relative availability and accessibility of cyber weapons and their apparent operational characteristics – flexibility, rapidity, scalability, and limited escalation potential – that help explain why cyber operations have become one of the prevalent instruments of power projection in the gray zone, even when their strategic impact might be elusive. However, despite the widely shared assumption that such operations are a good substitute for conventional military/sabotage operation, their effectiveness and destructiveness should be reconsidered considering the inherent risks, uncertainties, costs, and trade-offs they present.

In practice and according to the analysis of different cases of gray zone conflicts, cyber operations thus seem to be at the same time a novel, efficient, and effective tool for disruption (and to a lesser extent sabotage) while an enhancer and transformer of traditional gray zone activities, such as espionage and influence. Accordingly, it can be reasonably expected that actors operating in the gray zone will continue using, developing, and investing in cyber operations. This is particularly true for cyber influence operations, to which cyber operations have proven to be particularly suited in comparison with traditional sabotage.

Notes

1 There is a whole conceptual debate around the nomenclature pertaining to cyber operations, with numerous scholars differentiating between offensive and defensive cyber operations. In this chapter, it will broadly refer to computer activities by states or state-linked actors that disrupt, deny, degrade, and/or destroy.
2 Gray zone conflicts include variants such as *Gray zone tactics/warfare/competition* and synonyms such as *hybrid/Non-linear/Ambiguous warfare.*
3 An American national security concept, it is defined as those actors seeking to change some or all aspects of the existing international environment and world order.
4 Each of these cases have been analyzed in a respective Hotspot Analysis from the ETH Center for Security Studies (CSS). See *Hotspot Analysis: Cyber Disruption and Cybercrime: Democratic People's Republic of Korea*; *Hotspot Analysis: Regional Rivalry between India-Pakistan: Tit-for-tat in Cyberspace*; *Hotspot Analysis: Use of Cybertools in Regional Tensions in Southeast Asia*; *Hotspot Analysis: Synthesis 2017: Cyber-Conflicts in Perspective*; *Hotspot Analysis: Cyber-Conflict between the United States of America and Russia*; *Hotspot Analysis: Stuxnet*; *Hotspot Analysis: The Use of Cybertools in an Internationalized Civil War Context: Cyber Activities in the Syrian Conflict*; *Hotspot Analysis: Cyber and Information Warfare in Elections in Europe*; *Hotspot Analysis: Strategic Stability between Great Powers: The Sino-American Cyber Agreement*; *Hotspot Analysis: Cyber and Information Warfare in the Ukrainian Conflict Version 2.*
5 Before the adversary has patched his systems.
6 The ties between these individuals and states are, most of the time, blurry and difficult to prove.

References

All links checked on August 20 2021.

Al-Rawi, A. K. (2014). Cyber Warriors in the Middle East: The Case of the Syrian Electronic Army. *Public Relations Review*, 40(3): 420–428. https://doi.org/10.1016/j.pubrev.2014.04.005.

Assumpção, C. (2020, May 6). The Problem of Cyber Attribution between States. *E-International Relations*. Retrieved from: https://www.e-ir.info/2020/05/06/the-problem-of-cyber-attribution-between-states/.

Baezner, M. (2018a). *Hotspot Analysis: Cyber Disruption and Cybercrime: Democratic People's Republic of Korea*. Zurich: Center for Security Studies (CSS). Retrieved from: http://www.css.ethz.ch/content/dam/ethz/special-interest/gess/cis/center-for-securities-studies/pdfs/Cyber-Reports-2018-03.pdf.

Baezner, M. (2018b). *Hotspot Analysis: Regional Rivalry between India-Pakistan: Tit-for-Tat in Cyberspace*. Zurich: Center for Security Studies (CSS). Retrieved from: http://www.css.ethz.ch/content/dam/ethz/special-interest/gess/cis/center-for-securities-studies/pdfs/Cyber-Reports-2018-04.pdf.

Baezner, M. (2018c). *Hotspot Analysis: Use of Cybertools in Regional Tensions in Southeast Asia*. Zurich: Center for Security Studies (CSS). Retrieved from: https://css.ethz.ch/content/dam/ethz/special-interest/gess/cis/center-for-securities-studies/pdfs/Cyber-Reports-2018-05.pdf.

Baezner, M. (2018d). *Hotspot Analysis: Synthesis 2017: Cyber-Conflicts in Perspective*. Zurich: Center for Security Studies (CSS). Retrieved from: http://www.css.ethz.ch/content/dam/ethz/special-interest/gess/cis/center-for-securities-studies/pdfs/Cyber-Reports-2018-06.pdf.

Baezner, M. and Robin, P. (2017a). *Hotspot Analysis: Cyber-Conflict between the United States of America and Russia*. Zurich: Center for Security Studies (CSS). Retrieved from: http://www.css.ethz.ch/content/dam/ethz/special-interest/gess/cis/center-for-securities-studies/pdfs/Cyber-Reports-2017-02.pdf.

Baezner, M. and Robin, P. (2017b). *Hotspot Analysis: Stuxnet*. Zurich: Center for Security Studies (CSS). Retrieved from: http://www.css.ethz.ch/content/dam/ethz/special-interest/gess/cis/center-for-securities-studies/pdfs/Cyber-Reports-2017-04.pdf.

Baezner, M. and Robin, P. (2017c). *Hotspot Analysis: The Use of Cybertools in an Internationalized Civil War Context: Cyber Activities in the Syrian Conflict*. Zurich: Center for Security Studies (CSS). Retrieved from: http://www.css.ethz.ch/content/dam/ethz/special-interest/gess/cis/center-for-securities-studies/pdfs/Cyber-Reports-2017-05.pdf.

Baezner, M. and Robin, P. (2017d). *Hotspot Analysis: Cyber and Information Warfare in Elections in Europe*. Zurich: Center for Security Studies (CSS). Retrieved from: https://css.ethz.ch/content/dam/ethz/special-interest/gess/cis/center-for-securities-studies/pdfs/Cyber-Reports-2017-08.pdf.

Baezner, M. and Robin, P. (2017e). *Hotspot Analysis: Strategic Stability between Great Powers: The Sino-American Cyber Agreement*. Zurich: Center for Security Studies (CSS). Retrieved from: https://css.ethz.ch/content/dam/ethz/special-interest/gess/cis/center-for-securities-studies/pdfs/Cyber-Reports-2017-07.pdf.

Baezner, M. and Robin, P. (2018). *Hotspot Analysis: Cyber and Information Warfare in the Ukrainian Conflict Version 2*. Zurich: Center for Security Studies (CSS). Retrieved from: http://www.css.ethz.ch/content/dam/ethz/special-interest/gess/cis/center-for-securities-studies/pdfs/20181003_MB_HS_RUS-UKR%20V2_rev.pdf.

Balduzzi, M., Flores, R., Gu, L. and Maggi, F. (2018). A Deep Dive into Defacement: How Geopolitical Events Trigger Web Attacks [TrendLabs Research Paper]. Trend Micro. Retrieved from: https://documents.trendmicro.com/assets/white_papers/wp-a-deep-dive-into-defacement.pdf.

Barno, D. and Bensahel, N. (2015, May 19). Fighting and Winning in the «Gray Zone». *War on the Rocks*. Retrieved from: https://warontherocks.com/2015/05/fighting-and-winning-in-the-gray-zone/.

Barrett, P. M. (2019). Disinformation and the 2020 Elections: How the Social Media Industry Should Prepare. Center for Business and Human Rights, New York University STERN. Retrieved from: https://issuu.com/nyusterncenterforbusinessandhumanri/docs/nyu_election_2020_report?fr=sY2QzYzI0MjMwMA.

Boeke, S. and Broeders, D. (2018). The Demilitarisation of Cyber Conflict. *Survival*, 60(6): 73–90.

Brands, H. (2016, February 5). Paradoxes of the Gray Zone. Foreign Policy Research Institute. Retrieved from: https://www.fpri.org/article/2016/02/paradoxes-gray-zone/.

Buchanan, B. (2020). *The Hacker and the State: Cyber Attacks and the New Normal of Geopolitics*. Cambridge and London: Harvard University Press.

Cantwell, D. (2017). Hybrid Warfare: Aggression and Coercion in the Gray Zone. *Insights*, 21(14). Retrieved from: https://www.asil.org/insights/volume/21/issue/14/hybrid-warfare-aggression-and-coercion-gray-zone.

Carlisle, D. and Izenman, K. (2019). Closing the Crypto Gap Guidance for Countering North Korean Cryptocurrency Activity in Southeast Asia (RUSI Occasional paper). Royal United Services Institute. Retrieved from: https://static.rusi.org/20190412_closing_the_crypto_gap_web.pdf.

Chambers, J. (2016). Countering Gray-Zone Hybrid Threats. Modern War Institute. Retrieved from: https://mwi.usma.edu/wp-content/uploads/2016/10/Countering-Gray-Zone-Hybrid-Threats.pdf.

Cherepanov, A. (2017). *TeleBots are back: Supply-chain attacks against Ukraine*. Welivesecurity ESET. Retrieved from: https://www.welivesecurity.com/2017/06/30/telebots-back-supply-chain-attacks-against-ukraine/#:~:text=Conclusions,as%20a%20supply%2Dchain%20attack.

Chesney, R., and Citron, D. (2018). *Deepfakes: A Looming Crisis for National Security, Democracy and Privacy?* Lawfare. Retrieved from: https://www.lawfareblog.com/deepfakes-looming-crisis-national-security-democracy-and-privacy.

Corn, G. (2018). Cyber National Security: Navigating Gray Zone Challenges In and Through Cyberspace. In: W. S. Williams and M. Ford (eds). *Complex Battlespaces: The Law of Armed Conflicts and the Dynamics of Modern Warfare*. Oxford: Oxford University Press, pp. 345–428.

Crowdstrike (2016). Use of Fancy Bear Android Malware in Tracking of Ukrainian Field Artillery Units. Retrieved from: https://www.crowdstrike.com/wp-content/brochures/FancyBearTracksUkrainianArtillery.pdf.

Dalton, M., Hicks, K. H., Donahoe, M., Sheppard, L., Friend, A. H., Matlaga, M., Federici, J., Conklin, M. and Kiernan, J. (2019). By Other Means—Part 2: Adapting to Compete in the Gray Zone. CSIS. Retrieved from: https://csis-website-prod.s3.amazonaws.com/s3fs-public/publication/Hicks_GrayZone_II_interior_v8_PAGES.pdf.

Dave, P. and Bing, C. (2019, June 7). Russian Disinformation on YouTube Draws Ads, Lacks Warning Labels: Researchers. Reuters. Retrieved from: https://www.reuters.com/article/us-alphabet-google-youtube-russia-idUSKCN1T80JP.

Dewar, R. S. (2017). *Trend Analysis: Cyberweapons : Capability, Intent and Context in Cyberdefense*. Zurich: Center for Security Studies (CSS). Retrieved from: https://css.ethz.ch/content/dam/ethz/special-interest/gess/cis/center-for-securities-studies/pdfs/Cyber-Reports-2017-06.PDF.

DiResta, R., Schaffer, K., Ruppel, B., Sullivan, D., Matney, R., Fox, R., Albright, J. and Johnson, B. (2018). The Tactics and Tropes of the Internet Research Agency. *New Knowledge*. Retrieved from: https://disinformationreport.blob.core.windows.net/disinformation-report/NewKnowledge-Disinformation-Report-Whitepaper.pdf.

Dostri, O. (2020). The Reemergence of Gray-Zone Warfare in Modern Conflicts. *Military Review*. Retrieved from: https://www.armyupress.army.mil/Journals/Military-Review/English-Edition-Archives/January-February-2020/Dostri-Gray-Zone/.

Dragos Inc. (2017). *Crash Override Analysis of the Threat to Electric Grid Operations*. Retrieved from: https://www.dragos.com/wp-content/uploads/CrashOverride-01.pdf.

Echevarria, A. (2016). *Operating in the Gray Zone: An Alternative Paradigm for U.S. Military Strategy*. Carlisle: Strategic Studies Institute and U.S. Army War College Press.

Egloff, F. J. (2019). Contested Public Attributions of Cyber Incidents and the Role of Academia. *Contemporary Security Policy*, 41(1): 55–81.

Finkle, J. (2017, April 3). Cyber Security firm: More Evidence North Korea Linked to Bangladesh Heist. Reuters. Retrieved from: https://www.reuters.com/article/us-cyber

-heist-bangladesh-northkorea/cyber-security-firm-more-evidence-north-korea-linked-to-bangladesh-heist-idUSKBN17521A.

FireEye Inc. (2019). Double Dragon APT41, a Dual Espionage and Cyber Crime Operation (Special Report). FireEye Inc. Retrieved from: https://content.fireeye.com/apt-41/rpt-apt41/.

Fischerkeller, M. P. and Harknett, R. J. (2017). Deterrence is not a Credible Strategy for Cyberspace. *Orbis*, 61(3): 381–393.

Fischerkeller, M. P. and Harknett, R. J. (2019, February 19). What Is Agreed Competition in Cyberspace? Lawfare. Retrieved from: https://www.lawfareblog.com/what-agreed-competition-cyberspace.

Fitton, O. (2016). Cyber Operations and Gray Zones: Challenges for NATO. *Connections*, 15(2): 109–119.

Galperin, E., Marquis-Boire, M. and Scott-Railton, J. (2013). Quantum of Surveillance: Familiar Actors and Possible False Flags in Syrian Malware Campaigns. Electronic Frontier Foundation. Retrieved from: https://www.eff.org/fr/document/quantum-surveillance-familiar-actors-and-possible-false-flags-syrian-malware-campaigns.

Gannon, J. A., Gartzke, E., Lindsay, J. R. and Scharm. P. (2021). The Shadow of Deterrence: Why Capable Actors Engage in Conflict Short of War. Retrieved from: https://peterschram.com/wp-content/uploads/2021/01/gray_zone_web.pdf.

Giles, K. (2016). *Handbook of Russian Information Warfare*. Rome: NATO Defence College Research Division.

Gomez, M. (2018, November 6). In Cyberwar, There Are Some (Unspoken) Rules. *Foreign Policy*. Retrieved from: https://foreignpolicy.com/2018/11/06/in-cyberwar-there-are-some-unspoken-rules-international-law-norms-north-korea-russia-iran-stuxnet/.

Grohe, E. (2015). The Cyber Dimensions of the Syrian Civil War: Implications for Future Conflict. *Comparative Strategy*, 34(2): 133–148. https://doi.org/10.1080/01495933.2015.1017342.

Guerrero-Saade, J. A. and Moriuchi, P. (2018). North Korea Targeted South Korean Cryptocurrency Users and Exchange in Late 2017 Campaign. Recorded Future. Retrieved from: https://go.recordedfuture.com/hubfs/reports/cta-2018-0116.pdf.

Harknett, R. J. and Smeets, M. (2020). Cyber Campaigns and Strategic Outcomes. *Strategic Studies*, 1–34. https://doi.org/10.1080/01402390.2020.1732354.

Harris, E. (2016). *Comparing Cyber-Relations: Russia, China, and the U.S.* Toronto: Mackenzie Institute. Retrieved from: https://mackenzieinstitute.com/2016/05/comparing-cyber-relations-russia-china-and-the-u-s/.

Hicks, K. H., Friend, A. H., Federici, J., Shah, H., Donahoe, M., Conklin, M., Akca, A., Matlaga, M. and Sheppard, L. (2019). By Other Means—Part 1: Campaigning in the Gray Zone. CSIS. Retrieved from: https://csis-website-prod.s3.amazonaws.com/s3fs-public/publication/Hicks_GrayZone_interior_v4_FULL_WEB_0.pdf.

Hoffman, F. G. (2007). Conflict in the 21st Century: The Rise of Hybrid Wars. Potomac Institute for Policy Studies Arlington. Retrieved from: https://www.potomacinstitute.org/images/stories/publications/potomac_hybridwar_0108.pdf.

Howard, P. N., Ganesh, B., Liotsiou, D., Kelly, J. and François, C. (2018). The IRA, Social Media and Political Polarization in the United States, 2012–2018 (The Computational Propaganda Project). University of Oxford and Graphika. Retrieved from: https://comprop.oii.ox.ac.uk/wp-content/uploads/sites/93/2018/12/The-IRA-Social-Media-and-Political-Polarization.pdf.

Kapusta, P. (2015). *The Gray Zone [White Paper]*. MacDill Air Force Base: U.S. Special Operations Command.

Kim, S. (2018, February 7). Inside North Korea's Hacker Army. Bloomberg. Retrieved from: https://www.bloomberg.com/news/features/2018-02-07/inside-kim-jong-un-s-hacker-army.

Kozy, A. (2015, June 1). Rhetoric Foreshadows Cyber Activity in the South China Sea. *CrowdStrike Blog*. Retrieved from: https://www.crowdstrike.com/blog/rhetoric-foreshadows-cyber-activity-in-the-south-china-sea/.

Leed, M. (2015). Square Pegs, Round Holes, and Gray Zone Conflicts: Time to Step Back. *Georgetown Journal of International Affairs*, 6(2): 133–143.

Mazarr, M. (2015a). *Mastering the Gray Zone: Understanding a Changing Era of Conflict*. Studies Institute and U.S. Army War College Press.

Mazarr, M. (2015b). Struggle in the Gray Zone and World Order. *War on the Rocks*. Retrieved from: https://warontherocks.com/2015/12/struggle-in-the-gray-zone-and-world-order/.

Mogato, M. (2017, August 15). Philippines Says China Agrees on no New Expansion in South China Sea. Reuters. Retrieved from: https://www.reuters.com/article/us-southchinasea-philippines-china/philippines-says-china-agrees-on-no-new-expansion-in-south-china-sea-idUSKCN1AV0VJ.

Nakashima, E. and Sonne, P. (2018, June 8). China Hacked a Navy Contractor and Secured a Trove of Highly Sensitive Data on Submarine Warfare. *The Washington Post*. Retrieved from: https://www.washingtonpost.com/world/national-security/china-hacked-a-navy-contractor-and-secured-a-trove-of-highly-sensitive-data-on-submarine-warfare/2018/06/08/6cc396fa-68e6-11e8-bea7-c8eb28bc52b1_story.html.

Nichols, M. (2019, August 5). North Korea Took $2 Billion in Cyberattacks to Fund Weapons Program: U.N. Report. Reuters. Retrieved from: https://www.reuters.com/article/us-northkorea-cyber-un/north-korea-took-2-billion-in-cyberattacks-to-fund-weapons-program-u-n-report-idUSKCN1UV1ZX.

Nocetti, J. (2015). Guerre de l'information: Le web russe dans le conflit en Ukraine. *Focus Stratégique*, 62: 1–47.

NSFocus Inc. (2016). *Distributed Denial-of-Service (DDoS) Attacks: An Economic Perspective*. Retrieved from: https://nsfocusglobal.com/company-overview/resources/ddos-economic-perspective-wp/.

Nye, J. S. (2017). Deterrence and Dissuasion in Cyberspace. *International Security*, 41(3): 44–71. https://doi.org/10.1162/ISEC_a_00266.

Ornos, E., Remnick, D. and Yaffa, J. (2017, March 6). Trump, Putin, and the New Cold War. *The New Yorker*. Retrieved from: http://www.newyorker.com/magazine/2017/03/06/trump-putin-and-the-new-cold-war.

Pettyjohn, S. and Wasser, B. (2019). Competing in the Gray Zone—Russian Tactics and Western Responses. RAND Corporation. Retrieved from: https://www.rand.org/pubs/research_reports/RR2791.html.

Rid, T. (2013). *Cyber War Will not Take Place*. Oxford: Oxford University Press.

Rid, T. and B. Buchanan (2015). Attributing Cyber Attacks. *Journal of Strategic Studies*, 38(12): 4–37.

Rovner, J. (2019, July 16). Cyber War as an Intelligence Contest. *War on the Rocks*. Retrieved from: https://warontherocks.com/2019/09/cyber-war-as-an-intelligence-contest/.

Sanger, D. (2018). *The Perfect Weapon: War, Sabotage, and Fear in the Cyber Age*. New York: Crown.

Scott-Railton, J., Hulcoop, A., Razzak, B. A., Marczak, B., Anstis, S. and Deibert, R. (2020, June 9). Dark Basin: Uncovering a Massive Hack-For-Hire Operation. *CitizenLab*. Retrieved from: https://citizenlab.ca/2020/06/dark-basin-uncovering-a-massive-hack-for-hire-operation/.

Shanker, T. and Bumiller, E. (2012, October 11). Panetta Warns of Dire Threat of Cyberattack on U.S. *The New York Times*. Retrieved from: https://www.nytimes.com/2012/10/12/world/panetta-warns-of-dire-threat-of-cyberattack.html.

Smeets, M. (2018). The Strategic Promise of Offensive Cyber Operations. *Strategic Studies Quarterly*, 12(3): 90–113.

Solon, O. (2017, May 15). WannaCry Ransomware Has Links to North Korea, Cybersecurity Experts Say. *The Guardian*. Retrieved from: https://www.theguardian.com/technology/2017/may/15/wannacry-ransomware-north-korea-lazarus-group.

The Economist. (2013, November 2). Rules for spies. *The Economist*. Retrieved from: https://www.economist.com/leaders/2013/11/02/rules-for-spies.

Timberg, C. and Romm, T. (2019, July 25). It's not Just the Russians Anymore as Iranians and Others Turn Up Disinformation Efforts Ahead of 2020 Vote. *The Washington Post*. Retrieved from: https://www.washingtonpost.com/technology/2019/07/25/its-not-just-russians-anymore-iranians-others-turn-up-disinformation-efforts-ahead-vote/?noredirect.

Valeriano, B., and Jensen, B. (2019). *The Myth of the Cyber Offense: The Case for Restraint*. Washington: Cato Institute. Retrieved from: https://www.cato.org/policy-analysis/myth-cyber-offense-case-restraint.

Votel, J. L., Cleveland, C. T., Connett, C. T. and Irwin, W. (2016). Unconventional Warfare in the Gray Zone. *Joint Force Quarterly*, 80(1): 101–109.

Warner, M. (2019). A Matter of Trust: Covert Action Reconsidered. *Studies in Intelligence*, 63(4): 33–41.

Wirtz, J. J. (2017). Life in the "Gray Zone": Observations for Contemporary Strategists. *Defense and Security Analysis*, 33(2): 106–114.

3 A threat to democracies?

An overview of theoretical approaches and empirical measurements for studying the effects of disinformation

Wolf J. Schünemann

Disinformation is everywhere. This short and simple insight does not only hold as a concise summary of the widely perceived fundamental problems with (political) information provision in a digitally transformed public sphere. It is also not meant as a fatalistic reaction to the sometimes alarmist warnings that characterize the relevant debate. Disinformation, understood as deliberately spread false information and rumors, has developed into a major concern in modern, highly connected societies. This phenomenon is very visible and can be studied as under a magnifying glass, albeit at a global scale, given the current so-called "infodemic", i.e. the spread of disinformation regarding COVID-19, its origins, its spread and effects, or suitable treatments (for an overview, cf. Ball and Maxmen 2020). Disinformation even stands out as a widely perceived threat to liberal democracies and their institutions, as these seem particularly vulnerable to manipulative information operations due to their liberal stance toward media freedom and other regime-specific features. Given the unheard-of spread of disinformation – even the emergence of "the disinformation order" (Bennett and Livingston 2018) – induced by the digital transformation, the issue has developed into a widely studied subject in the field of political communication and media studies.

However, disinformation is neither confined to domestic politics nor constrained by disciplinary boundaries in academic discourse. On the contrary, the most intensely debated political information operations in recent years, namely during the Ukrainian crisis in 2014, the British referendum in 2016, and the US presidential election campaign in the same year, were at least partly ascribed to foreign, specifically Russian activity (Maréchal 2017; Pomerantsev 2014). Consequently, the entire problem needs to be viewed in terms of domestic as well as international conflict and has developed into one of the core threats in cyber security discourse and strategy. The current debate on the COVID-19 "infodemic" (Strick et al. 2020), which has seen (dis)information operations seemingly constituting a preferential mode of rivalry between the great powers, is likely to corroborate these trends.

While recent events in international politics have thus raised the awareness of information operations as an essential component of hybrid warfare and produced anxiety among actors in the security and defense sectors (Lanoszka 2019: 228),

DOI: 10.4324/9781003110224-4

there are growing uncertainties about adequate responses, in particular for democratic governments. In international conflict constellations, their "bias against [media] control" (McQuail 2008: 234), applied to the internet, might disadvantage democratic systems compared to autocratic states that protect their so-called information sovereignty by restricting internet freedom (Jamieson 2018: 11; Lanoszka 2019: 228; Omand 2018: 12; Pope 2018: 36) while presumably expending considerable effort on information operations at the domestic and international levels (King et al. 2017). Realistic accounts from international security studies have articulated this asymmetrical vulnerability assessment at the expense of liberal democracies very clearly without deriving any decisive strategy for counteraction (Goldsmith and Russel 2018) or effective deterrence (Goldsmith 2016; Shackelford et al. 2016: 666). In terms of media governance, trends toward more restrictive measures of online control can already be observed even in democratic states (Freedom House 2018).

All in all, disinformation stands out as a major threat to liberal democracies and national security alike. It is likely to appear as one of the crucial ingredients of future securitizing moves by respective political actors across the world. As for cyber security in general, it seems fair to say that threat perceptions in the field are based on a high level of uncertainty. Thus, for disinformation the same critical question needs to be posed as for other cyber threats: Are threat perceptions appropriate or exaggerated? To answer this question, I combine different perspectives: Theoretical reflections mostly developed in the field of cyber security, and empirical insights mainly provided by scholars of political communication and media.

The remainder of the chapter is structured as follows: After giving a basic definition of disinformation in the following section, I present a knowledge-based concept of (dis)information operations, followed by a critical review of threat perceptions as expressed in the core policy documents issued by major democracies and international organizations. Then, I contrast threat perceptions with the evidence as provided by empirical research. In this section, I differentiate three levels of analysis at which effects can be assessed: The micro, meso, and macro levels. Given the lack of knowledge on the actual impact of alleged disinformation and the obvious ambiguities in its interpretation and attribution, I conclude with a call for caution. Increased levels of uncertainty in digital communication must not cause us to stumble into a new phase of international threat politics and the securitization of cyberspace with potentially detrimental effects on liberal democratic values and international peace.

Disinformation as a concept and as a new element of international threat politics

Disinformation is a complex term. After all, in political communication there are probably not many statements made by any strategically motivated actors that would not be depicted as disinformation by any of their adversaries, if only for the sake of casting doubt on the other party's credibility. The somewhat turbulent career of the compelling term fake news, often used synonymously with disinformation (Allcott and Gentzkow 2017), is illustrative in this regard. Following its widespread use in public discourse in the wake of major political events of the year 2016 (Brexit referendum, US elections), and as one of the main terms used to describe the allegedly emergent age of post-truth (Harsin 2015), it has suffered from its ubiquitous use as a weapon in political conflict. Today, it is almost disqualified for use in academic discourse (Vosoughi et al. 2018: 1146; however, used in Lazer et al. 2018).

In contrast, disinformation as preferred in scholarly discourse is a more technical term that refers to information that is misleading by design (European Commission 2018a: 11). Disinformation is classified as such on the basis of the function ascribed to it. Specifically, this means that disinformation needs to have an actor behind it who intentionally produces and disseminates untrue or incorrect information. Therefore, it can be differentiated from all unintentionally misleading information, so-called misinformation, as well as from other forms of distorted facts that are not meant to mislead but to produce amusement or deeper insights such as jokes or satire (Allcott and Gentzkow 2017). Disinformation can also be related to other terms associated with information operations that are more commonly found in strategic studies, such as propaganda or public diplomacy. Disinformation overlaps with propaganda but is not the same. What both terms have in common is purposeful deception in the form of misleading or extremely one-sided information. There is a difference, however, in that propaganda includes other means of strategic communication that are not falsifying. Moreover, propaganda according to a traditional understanding is bound to government actors in totalitarian or authoritarian regimes and mainly oriented toward the domestic population. At the other end of the spectrum, a more traditional, realistic understanding of public diplomacy also focuses on state-led informational activity toward foreign publics. While newer conceptions of public diplomacy include a broader range of actors and the use of digital networks ("public diplomacy 2.0", Tago 2018: 457), communicating false information does not fall under their definition, as this would conflict with the supposed soft power goals also pursued by democratic regimes. However, in the face of current heightened geopolitical tensions, public diplomacy risks being regarded as a euphemism for international disinformation campaigns, similar to its perception as an "*outgrowth* of propaganda" during the Cold War (Tago 2018).

Given the difficulties that arise when categorical distinctions made in abstract terms are applied to real-world phenomena, it is not surprising that disinformation can also become blurry when it is applied to empirical reality. Aside from the question of what is objectively true and what is false (Vosoughi et al. 2018), it remains difficult to attribute information operations and to find evidence for the intent to mislead. While uncertainty has always been a constitutive element of international relations, given the porosity of national borders especially with regard to information flows in cyberspace and the digitally enhanced means of so-called "hybrid warfare", ambiguity stands out even more clearly as a constant feature in discussions on disinformation. As in cyber security more generally, ambiguity extends not only to the attacker and their intent but also to the actual quality and effects of an attack and the appropriate reactions to it.

Overall, it seems fair to assume that the issue of disinformation has caused us to enter a new phase of threat politics (Dunn Cavelty 2008) in which we observe a new quality of securitization in cyber security discourse. Even the notion of cyber war, which is compelling in the use of the "told catastrophes" in cyber security and critically discussed in scholarly discourse, has reappeared in a new form, now fed by anxiety about disinformation as a threat to democracy (Jamieson 2018: 7). With information technology and the allegedly threatened public discourse, two issues of high complexity are combined in the most recurrent threat perceptions around disinformation. In public use, this new version of the told catastrophes in the wider cyber security discourse might serve as the grounds for even more urgent reactions than the stories of earlier days. While those have mostly "remained just that – scenarios" (Dunn Cavelty 2008: 3), the new cyber doom scenarios of disinformation are currently happening or have already become reality, e.g. with Donald Trump in office and the United Kingdom having left the EU.

Disinformation and the question of knowledge

As in cyber security more generally and in current debates about disinformation and its alleged threats to democracy more specifically, actors tend to fill the voids of uncertainty with preexistent elements of knowledge that help produce consistent narratives even without actual empirical evidence. Knowledge is thus an important factor for understanding threat perceptions and political responses toward an alleged attacker and the intentions behind an attack. Moreover, knowledge itself can be seen as under attack by disinformation (Farrell and Schneier 2018). When taking a knowledge-oriented perspective on disinformation, it seems important to avoid two flaws that are frequently evident in extant literature. The first is about attribution, the second about the conception of (relevant) knowledge itself.

First, as for cyberattacks, it is often difficult to know the responsible parties and the original source of a piece of malign disinformation. Even if an act can be traced back to a certain source, it might be impossible to find proof of coordinated activity, e.g. by a foreign power. Thus, attribution often relies on cui bono assessments: "Both domestic and foreign disinformation aim to disrupt the institutional order, undermine politicians, stir anti-refugee sentiments and create confusion around elections" (Bennett and Livingston 2018: 130). Such forms of "meaning-making" – in public and even academic attribution (Egloff 2020) – seem particularly problematic in the field of disinformation, as its effects are so unclear, probably even for a potential malevolent actor (Thornton and Miron 2019: 263, 269–270). But as cui bono does not work for the observer, it maybe does not for the alleged perpetrator either. Moreover, when a cui bono logic is applied, the assumed effects of an information operation become part of the criteria for detection and evaluation (see also Jamieson 2018: 144). Thus, the entire threat assessment risks becoming circular, if the alleged effects are a cornerstone of attribution while the assessment of the effects depends on the attribution.

Second, when assessing the societal effects of disinformation, it seems not very helpful to follow individualistic conceptions of knowledge familiar from electoral studies and major parts of political sociology, where knowledge is understood as personal accumulations of pieces of information an individual is exposed to (Lupia and McCubbins 1998; for a critical discussion see Schünemann 2014, 2018). First, "information by itself usually has no value: it is a raw material that gains value if further processed in specific ways and if meaning and a certain quality are attached to it" (Dunn Cavelty 2008: 15). Knowledge does not belong to the features of an individual (voter) but is produced and processed in discourses. Thus, second, information is "consumed" by individuals only through these collectively built filters of perception. This would necessitate the introduction of more macro-oriented perspectives on political discourse in a target society. From a macro-level knowledge-oriented perspective on disinformation, however, it seems problematic to assume that informational flows are simply discharged into a more or less helpless discourse. In analogy to cyberattacks, it would seem more appropriate to expect successful disinformation campaigns exploiting vulnerabilities already built into the target system (here the discourse), especially if campaigns are steered by a foreign power.

Farrell and Schneier (2018) have introduced a theoretical approach to assessing the vulnerabilities of political systems with respect to information operations from a comparative perspective. Among the various theoretical explorations of the issue, theirs comes closest to the knowledge-oriented macro-perspective, this chapter posits, as it is based on a concept of knowledge orders, namely the distinction between regime-specific stocks of common and contested knowledge, with disinformation campaigns being understood as knowledge attacks. Despite the important re-orientation that the authors present, the underlying conceptual dichotomy of knowledge types seems still too rough so that "common political knowledge" is more or less indistinguishable from other very general categories like trust in institutions or the basic requirement of support for the political system according to functionalist theory, while "contested political knowledge" comprises the broad range of knowledge elements floating around and being processed in public discourse. Consequently, the distinction does not seem truly open to more complex social constructivist conceptions and studies of social knowledge orders. Moreover, the authors do not provide any guidance on how to study the effects of disinformation as knowledge attacks.

Disinformation is all around – the threat perception

Before turning to a discussion of the effects of disinformation, this section sheds light on how the issue has influenced key actors' foreign and security policies on the international scene. How disinformation has developed into a major concern for modern societies can be easily illustrated by examining recent, relevant policy documents published by national state governments and international organizations. Thus, first, I present a critical review of core documents. I selected security strategies and reports published by the governments or dedicated committees of the United States, the United Kingdom, Germany, and at EU level. In accordance with my interest in threat politics, I build on a social constructivist meta-theory and the respective ontology as developed by Dunn Cavelty (2008: 30), which views threat frames as the central analytical concept for identifying the most frequently recurrent interpretive schemes or frames that enshrine ideas and beliefs regarding both the problem definition ("diagnostic framing") and the problem solution ("prognostic framing"). This allows a contrastive picture to be drawn initially that can later be checked against the empirical "evidence" that studies on political communication provide.

Examples from core policy documents

Disinformation has made it into the security strategies of major democracies (Omand 2018: 8). The 2017 "US National Security Strategy" mentions disinformation as one of the primary threats in cyberspace, as "[m]alicious state and non-state actors use cyberattacks for extortion, information warfare, disinformation, and more". Attacks are seen as able to "undermine faith and confidence in democratic institutions" (White House 2017: 31). Germany's Cyber Security Strategy also lists disinformation in its threat analysis and explicitly highlights the potential dangers disinformation poses for liberal societies and the democratic order. In the so-called "White book on Security Policy and the Future of the German Army", the explicit association with "elements of hybrid warfare" (Weißbuch: 37) is illustrative of a prognostic framing, as incidents are interpreted as malicious activity to be countered by security political measures. This notion is even more obvious in the Annual Report 2016–2017 issued by the Intelligence and Security Committee of the British Parliament, which lists the core elements of the foreign disinformation campaigns it discusses ("generally undermining the integrity of the UK's political system", "subverting a specific election or referendum", "poisoning public discourse") as potential objectives of cyberattacks conducted by hostile foreign actors against Great Britain (UK Parliament 2017: 32–33).

At the level of international organizations, the strategic communications units that have been established by NATO and the EU can be seen as telling examples, as they were founded with the explicit goal to counter Russian disinformation, which societies in the Baltic states and Eastern Europe more generally seem particularly vulnerable to. In the EU, relevant efforts were underlined in 2018, when the EU Commission and the EEAS published their "Action Plan against Disinformation" (European Commission 2018b), proposing intensified activities to counter Russian propaganda in Eastern Europe.

Some reflections on recurrent frames

Diagnostic framing is key to understanding threat politics, as it indicates whether disinformation is an element of political threat perception and vulnerability assessment. In this sub-section I want to briefly reflect on some of the most frequently recurrent diagnostic frames in the policy documents examined. At first, it seems particularly important to note that disinformation is mostly not perceived as a standalone activity or incident but is instead seen as one element of a more or less coordinated campaign. Disinformation campaigns – at least the ones that cause most anxiety – are assumed to be led by some kind of a strategically behaving actor, a populist movement or party or a foreign state, with current threat perceptions in Europe and the United States mostly relating to Russia.

Another important element of diagnostic framing is the narrative of national elections being targeted and potentially distorted by disinformation campaigns. This narrative adds to the perceived vulnerability of the target as a national society and polity and to the understanding of what might be the intention behind hostile information operations. Having said this, it is above all this narrative that seems constitutive for the interpretation of disinformation as a threat to national security. Moreover, the narrative extends the threat perceptions of disinformation also to other forms of so-called foreign interference such as foreign propaganda activities, tainted leaks, etc. that do not necessarily contain incorrect information (Jamieson 2018: 144). Finally, another element illustrated by the narrative about threats to national elections is its obvious dependency on supposed agency and attribution as highlighted in the theoretical sections above.

The impact question – the supposed effects of disinformation

In order to accurately assess the appropriateness of current threat perceptions, it is important to look at the empirical evidence presented by academic research so far. Different strands of research have reacted to the recently grown interest in disinformation. Political communication in mediatized environments is a particularly complex subject of social science research. Discerning and measuring the effects of any particular kind of information is difficult, especially in situations of intense political communication like an election campaign, where every bit of (dis-)information is thrown into the troubled ocean of public discourse. However, the attempts made so far can very broadly and superficially be grouped into three major categories that are very unequally populated. Firstly, researchers measure exposure to (dis)information and its audience effects. Secondly, the impact of (dis-)information is assessed by studying its effects on mass media communication. Finally, there is a third dimension often neglected or only incidentally touched upon: the dimension of public discourse. As the three strands address layered dimensions of communicative activity, I refer to them as the micro, the meso, and the macro levels. In addition, research and scholarly debate on disinformation and its effects need to take the dynamic evolvements of digitally transformed information markets and public spheres into account that cut across these different levels. Frequently discussed new phenomena such as echo chambers or the automation of political campaigns are said to induce structural changes that might facilitate the spread of disinformation overall (Vosoughi et al. 2018).

The micro level – individual exposure to disinformation and immediate audience effects

Most studies on the impact of (dis-)information are aimed at the level of individual exposure to information. Scholarly research has relied on survey data, web tracking, other kinds of digital trace data, or – though more seldom – experimental designs in order to study how users were exposed to false information and how this might have affected their attitudes and behaviors (Allcott and Gentzkow 2017; Grinberg et al. 2019; Guess et al. 2018; Keersmaecker and Roets 2017; Pennycook et al. 2018). An influential study on the US presidential elections in 2016 (Alcott and Gentzkow 2017) revealed that fake news – categorized as such by using data from fact-checking sites – indeed played a considerable role in the election campaign regarding the sheer volume of content produced, as fake news was able to attract millions of views and clicks. Moreover, a majority of the detected fake news examined in the study were in favor of Donald Trump. Measured effects, based on a market-based model of media consumption, were rather moderate, though. According to the study, the average US adult had only been exposed to 1.14 fake stories that he/she was able to remember (Allcott and Gentzkow 2017; see also Grinberg et al. 2019).

Vosoughi et al. (2018) also relied on assessments by independent fact-checking websites for categorizing news items as true or false, respectively. The study combined this approach with big data analysis, as approximately 126,000 stories posted or shared by about 3 million individual users on Twitter were included as data. Its findings indicate that, while false stories spread just as rapidly as true ones, they reached far more people and were much more likely to become viral than true stories (Vosoughi et al. 2018: 1148), suggesting that they would have greater potential impact.

Guess et al. (2018) combined an online public opinion survey with web traffic data. By measuring the relationship between selective exposure and disinformation, they were able to reveal the fundamental problems of measuring exposure alone, as exposure by itself does not necessarily equate to impact, at least not in the sense of changing actual political attitudes or behaviors. Instead, the authors found that, while a quarter of US Americans visited so-called fake news websites in the run-up to the 2016 election, most of the measured exposure was "attitude-consistent", suggesting that selective exposure has an attenuating effect on the potential impact of disinformation. With selective exposure, their example makes us aware that broader media logics and discursive predispositions need to be taken into account if a more comprehensive picture is to be obtained.

The meso level – the effects of disinformation on mass media

Digital media have "a complex relationship with traditional media" (Tucker et al. 2018: 4). While they tend to undermine the fundamental structures of traditional mass media (Shirky 2008) on the one hand, they have also "clearly become a tool for traditional media reporting" (Tucker et al. 2018) on the other. Consequently, it is necessary to understand the interactions between so-called new and traditional media (Marwick and Lewis 2017). Among recently published works, Hall Jamieson published the most comprehensive account of how a disinformation campaign allegedly steered by the Russian government had a decisive impact on the US presidential elections by influencing the mass media. Tellingly titled *Cyberwar: How Russian Hackers and Trolls Helped Elect a President*, her book argues that foreign actors successfully influenced, during critical phases of the campaign, the mass media and its most crucial mechanisms for political communication, such as agenda setting, framing and priming, and thereby might have ultimately turned around the public vote in the most decisive battleground states. Thus, her aim is to show how "[t]he legacy media were complicit in this effort" to undermine the US elections (Jamieson 2018: 38). The empirical chapters of her book offer illustrative findings from qualitative analyses of campaign material, analyses of national telephone surveys (oriented toward the micro level but focused on media effects) and ample anecdotal evidence of alleged Russian information operations during the presidential election campaign. All in all, Jamieson concludes that "Russian-hacked content and disinformation not only infected the news agenda but also tilted the balance of discourse in battleground states against the Democratic Party nominee" (Jamieson 2018: 7).

As Jamieson, however, has to admit at the end of her book, the reflections and reported findings cannot provide evidence-based certainty but can only make the conclusions drawn more or less plausible. The fundamental problem of how to distinguish the effects of deceptive information operations from all the other instances of strategic communication that make up a national election campaign and above all seek to achieve the same outcome (namely the victory of a favored candidate) remains unresolved (Jamieson 2018: 208).

The macro level – the effects of disinformation on political discourse and knowledge

Disinformation campaigns in general and foreign meddling in elections in particular are expected to target public discourse. They constitute attempts to move "the discourse in a particular way" (Morgan 2018: 41). It is these presumed effects at the macro level that particularly feed the perception of disinformation as a threat to national security that can, for instance, be put in the context of "a wider Russian operation to disrupt and agitate Western political discourse" (UK Parliament 2017: 52). Discourse is a concept with diverse meanings. Discourse theories, however, tend to converge in the shared assumption of collective knowledge production and processing through symbolic communication. Unfortunately, but not surprisingly, there is particularly little knowledge on the more substantial effects a disinformation campaign might have on public discourse and knowledge (Farrell and Scheier 2018). As seen above, this discourse is often referred to as being threatened by emerging *counter cultural narratives* emanating from Russian information campaigns or on the domestic level by such narratives spread by new radical right movements (Bennett and Livingston 2018: 128). Narratives – being a core concept of discursive structuring – are expected to be inserted or critically manipulated in a deliberate maneuver from the outside (Omand 2018: 5–6). However, these assumptions are mostly made without presenting empirical findings on the actual effects and successes of the presumed maneuvers (for a notable exception from data science, see Bessi et al. 2015).

In contrast, Alexander Lanoszka's work (2019) on "Disinformation in international politics" concentrates on the strategic level and argues that it is unlikely that alleged disinformation campaigns have any substantial effect on policy, as public discourse and public opinion would serve as a "second barrier" for disinformation that would need to be overcome. The most important part of his argument is that the acceptance of disinformation by a target audience is dependent on what he calls the "pre-existing ideological commitments and mindsets" of the people that would make them unlikely to believe and to change their minds on the basis of some novel pieces of information: "[s]haping the information that they receive are ideological commitments and partisan identities in addition to their own experiences, rules of thumb, and the pieces of conventional wisdom that they have acquired over their lifetimes" (Lanoszka 2019: 236). Lanoszka applies his conceptions and empirically tests his assumptions using Russian information operations between 2014 and 2017. All in all, he finds his assumptions and argument confirmed.

Lanoszka's findings are consistent with a discourse theoretical perspective on disinformation, as it seems indeed unlikely that information operations, no matter how sophisticated and coordinated they might be, can disrupt or even turn around public discourse as intended. The idea that it is possible to "give history a nudge" through disinformation campaigns, as Sir David Omand (2018: 5) put it, must thus be regarded as highly questionable from a discourse angle. However, measuring the macro-level effects of disinformation is obviously very difficult, as this requires an all-encompassing view, probably a greater historical distance from the events of interest, and profound knowledge of the sociocultural and political configurations of a given society (Lanoszka 2019: 233).

Facilitating factors of disinformation in the digital public sphere

Disinformation is certainly not a new phenomenon. It has been part of politics throughout the ages. As Omand (2018: 7) rightly states, "there is nothing very new about expecting subversive threats to an established state authority" (see also Morgan 2018: 41). As illustrated above, threat perceptions have, however, changed recently under the impression of the structural changes of the digital public sphere. Indeed, with the attenuation of traditional gatekeepers, everybody can publish content and thus spread information potentially at scale (Allcott and Gentzkow 2017; Keersmaecker and Roets 2017) – albeit without any guarantee that they will be listened to (Hindman 2009; Stier et al. 2018). In addition, Facebook and other social media are accused of serving as "gateway[s] to fake news website[s]" (Guess, et al. 2018). Against this backdrop, more broadly discussed phenomena of online communication such as echo chambers and the high degree of automation through social bots are believed to aggravate polarization (Sunstein 2017) and induce paranoia (Farrell and Schneier 2018: 2). These potentially facilitating factors also need to be checked against the evidence presented by empirical research. What does this mean for the effects of disinformation? While a polarized political system and public might be more vulnerable to the spread of fake news, as hypothesized elsewhere (Zettl 2019), ascribing polarization to digitally enhanced fragmentation (echo chambers) is highly controversial.

As to the *echo chamber*, increasing political polarization is widely perceived as a fertile ground for the spread of disinformation (Jamieson 2018; Lanoszka 2019: 229). Empirical studies have tested the echo chamber hypothesis mainly for the United States, but also for a number of other democracies (Bakshy et al. 2015; Jacobson et al. 2016). The results vary of course, but more recent works have mostly questioned the echo chamber hypothesis (Dubois and Blank 2018; Fletcher and Nielsen 2017; Gentzkow and Shapiro 2011; Guess et al. 2018).

The effects of *automation*, widely observed and discussed in the form of so-called social bots – software-tools that allow for the automated generation of content and/or activity online – are also far from clear. While a number of empirical works have highlighted the potential or factual role social bots have played in political processes, including the spread of (dis-)information as part of information operations based on quantitative measurements (Ferrara 2017; Hegelich and Janetzko 2016; Howard and Kollanyi 2016; Keller and Klinger 2019), their methodology and results have been contested due to the problematic flaws of bot detection (Gallwitz and Kreil 2019) or the hybrid use of automation by real users in actual practice (Grimme et al. 2017).

Even if one accepts the extent to which social bots are active, especially on a micro-blogging service like Twitter, this does not mean that automation is responsible for the substance of manipulation online. Instead, social bots are likely to feed the metrics of the online attention economy; they influence trending topics through following, linking, and sharing, but manipulative content is mostly produced by real users. Moreover, in terms of distribution, Vosoughi et al. (2018: 1150) point out that it is not bots but human users that make "false news spread [...] farther, faster, deeper, and more broadly than the truth". This finding serves as another argument for shifting our attention from alleged attackers and the offensive toolboxes at their disposal to the societies they target and their vulnerability to disinformation. With regard to countermeasures (as discussed in Haunschild et al. 2022), findings emphasize the need to address the attention economics in digital communication and to promote a new ethics of self-regulation in information consumption and provision instead of following restrictive regulatory approaches geared toward the supply side of information.

Conclusion

In this article, I presented an overview of theoretical approaches to and empirical studies of disinformation with a focus on its effects and potential threats to democracy. As to the general debate and current threat perceptions, I argued for a re-orientation toward knowledge-oriented perspectives and social constructivist research strategies. This was followed by an analysis of policy documents that helped identify recurrent threat frames. These were then contrasted with empirical evidence as produced by different strands of empirical research. With a three-layered distinction between a micro, a meso, and a macro level of analysis, at which distortion and influence can potentially be measured, I included two less commonly studied perspectives that might well be at least equally important for threat assessment with regard to disinformation. Moreover, with echo chambers and automation, I also briefly referred to phenomena that are widely associated with the structural transformation of the digital public sphere and are assumed to be facilitating factors for the spread of disinformation. As with disinformation in general, their existence and more importantly their alleged effects are very difficult to prove, thus adding to the overall uncertainty conditions that political actors find themselves in.

Against the backdrop of alarmed publics and politicians, countermeasures need to be drafted carefully with a better understanding of the overall challenge (see Haunschild et al. 2022; Omand 2018; Pope 2018; Thornton and Miron 2019). Empirical research thus needs to be intensified and improved in order to produce a greater body of knowledge on the actual challenge and appropriate solutions. Before reacting to alarmist voices, we should in particular study the long-term effects of alleged campaigns on the macro level of public discourse. Above, I compared the spread of disinformation with the exploitation of certain discursive vulnerabilities. This comparison illustrates that such vulnerabilities cannot – at least not sufficiently – be reduced by conventional regulatory or even security measures, but need to be addressed by political or journalistic means (Omand 2018: 20). Vulnerabilities must be reduced from within. If social media for instance serve as catalysts for the spread of disinformation, the profit-oriented mechanisms of their particular attention economics need to be addressed by regulation (Bakir and McStay 2018) without restricting informational freedom. Civil society engagement as practiced in fact-checking regimes might also be part of more adequate solutions, if designed and implemented with caution and with actors being held accountable.

All in all, a reflective and critical approach to the study of disinformation seems appropriate. For if the most likely and only achievable goal of malevolent actors on the international scene is correctly understood as the generation of paranoia and chaos among democratic publics and the sowing of distrust in democratic institutions (Chen 2016; Farrel and Schneier 2018), alarmist discourses and governmental overreactions might directly lead us into this trap.

References

All links checked on August 20, 2021.

Allcott, H. and Gentzkow, M. (2017). Social Media and Fake News in the 2016 Election. *Journal of Economic Perspectives*, 31(2): 211–236.

Bakir, V. and McStay, A. (2018). Fake News and the Economy of Emotions. *Digital Journalism*, 6(2): 154–175.

Bakshy, E., Messing, S. and Adamic, L. A. (2015). Political Science. Exposure to Ideologically Diverse News and Opinion on Facebook. *Science*, 348(6239): 1130–1132.

Ball, P. and Maxmen, A. (2020). The Epic Battle against Coronavirus Misinformation and Conspiracy Theories. *Nature*, 581(7809): 371–374.

Bennett, W. L. and Livingston, S. (2018). The Disinformation Order: Disruptive Communication and the Decline of Democratic Institutions. *European Journal of Communication*, 33(2): 122–139.

Bessi, A., Zollo, F., Del Vicario, M., Scala, A., Caldarelli, G. and Quattrociocchi, W. (2015). Trend of Narratives in the Age of Misinformation. *PloS One*, 10(8): e0134641.

Chen, A. (2016, 27 July). The Real Paranoia-Inducing Purpose of Russian Hacks. *The New Yorker*. Retrieved from: https://www.newyorker.com/news/news-desk/the-real-paranoia-inducing-purpose-of-russian-hacks.

Dubois, E. and Blank, G. (2018). The Echo Chamber is Overstated: The Moderating Effect of Political Interest and Diverse Media. *Information, Communication and Society*, 21(5): 729–745.

Dunn Cavelty, M. (2008). *Cyber-Security and Threat Politics: US Efforts to Secure the Information Age. CSS Studies in Security and International Relations*. London: Routledge.

Egloff, F. J. (2020). Contested Public Attributions of Cyber Incidents and the Role of Academia. *Contemporary Security Policy*, 41(1): 55–81.

European Commission. (2018a). *A Multi-Dimensional Approach to Disinformation: Report of the Independent High Level Group on Fake News and Online Disinformation. Communications Networks, Content and Technology*. Luxembourg: Publications Office of the European Union.

European Commission (2018b, December 5). *Action Plan against Disinformation: European Commission Contribution to the European Council (No. JOIN(2018) 36 Final)*. Brussels. Retrieved from: https://ec.europa.eu/info/sites/default/files/eu-communication-disinformation-euco-05122018_en.pdf.

Farrell, H. J. and Schneier, B. (2018). Common-Knowledge Attacks on Democracy. *SSRN Electronic Journal*. Advance online publication. https://doi.org/10.2139/ssrn.3273111.

Ferrara, E. (2017). Disinformation and Social Bot Operations in the Run Up to the 2017 French Presidential Election. *SSRN Electronic Journal*. Advance online publication.

Fletcher, R. and Nielsen, R. K. (2017). Are News Audiences Increasingly Fragmented? A Cross-National Comparative Analysis of Cross-Platform News Audience Fragmentation and Duplication. *Journal of Communication*, 67(4): 476–498.

Freedom House (2018). *Freedom on the Net 2018: The Rise of Digital Authoritarianism*. New York/Washington. Retrieved from: https://freedomhouse.org/sites/default/files/FOTN_2018_Final.pdf.

Gallwitz, F. and Kreil, M. (2019). Die Mär von "Social Bots". *Tagesspiegel*. Retrieved from: https://background.tagesspiegel.de/digitalisierung/die-maer-von-social-bots.

Gentzkow, M. and Shapiro, J. M. (2011). Ideological Segregation Online and Offline. *The Quarterly Journal of Economics*, 126(4): 1799–1839.

Goldsmith, J. (2016, 9 October). The DNC Hack and (the Lack of) Deterrence. *Lawfare Blog*. Retrieved from: https://www.lawfareblog.com/dnc-hack-and-lack-deterrence.

Goldsmith, J. and Russell, S. (2018). Strengths Become Vulnerabilities: How a Digital World Disadvantages the United States in Its International Relations. *Aegis Series* (1806): 1–22. Retrieved from: https://www.hoover.org/sites/default/files/research/docs/381100534-strengths-become-vulnerabilities.pdf.

Grimme, C., Preuss, M., Adam, L. and Trautmann, H. (2017). Social Bots: Human-Like by Means of Human Control? *Big Data*, 5(4): 279–293.

Grinberg, N., Joseph, K., Friedland, L., Swire-Thompson, B. and Lazer, D. (2019). Fake News on Twitter during the 2016 U.S. Presidential Election. *Science*, 363(6425): 374–378. https://doi.org/10.1126/science.aau2706.

Guess, A., Lyons, B., Nyhan, B. and Reifler, J. (2018). Avoiding the Echo Chamber about Echo Chambers: Why Selective Exposure to Like-Minded Political News is Less Prevalent than You Think. Knight Foundation. Retrieved from: https://kf-site-production.s3.amazonaws.com/media_elements/files/000/000/133/original/Topos_KF_White-Paper_Nyhan_V1.pdf.

Guess, A., Nyhan, B. and Reifler, J. (2018). Selective Exposure to Misinformation: Evidence from the Consumption of Fake News during the 2016 U.S. Presidential Campaign. Retrieved from: http://www.dartmouth.edu/~nyhan/fake-news-2016.pdf.

Harsin, J. (2015). Regimes of Posttruth, Postpolitics, and Attention Economies. *Communication, Culture and Critique*, 8(2): 327–333.

Haunschild, J., Kaufhold, M.-A. and Reuter, C. (2022). Cultural Violence and Peace in Social Media: Technical and Social Interventions. In: M. Dunn Cavelty and A. Wenger (eds). *Cyber Security: Socio-Technological Uncertainty and Political Fragmentation*. London: Routledge, pp. 48–63.

Hegelich, S. and Janetzko, D. (2016). Are Social Bots on Twitter Political Actors?: Empirical Evidence from a Ukranian Social Botnet. *International AAAI Conference on Web and Social Media*. Retrieved from: https://www.aaai.org/ocs/index.php/ICWSM/ICWSM16/paper/view/13015/12793.

Hindman, M. S. (2009). *The Myth of Digital Democracy*. Princeton, NJ: Princeton University Press.

Howard, P. N. and Kollanyi, B. (2016). Bots, #StrongerIn, and #Brexit: Computational Propaganda during the UK-EU Referendum. Retrieved from: https://papers.ssrn.com/sol3/papers.cfm?abstract_id=2798311.

Jacobson, S., Myung, E. and Johnson, S. L. (2016). Open Media or Echo Chamber: The Use of Links in Audience Discussions on the Facebook Pages of Partisan News Organizations. *Information, Communication and Society*, 19(7): 875–891.

Jamieson, K. H. (2018). *Cyberwar: How Russian Hackers and Trolls Helped Elect a President; What We Don't, Can't, and Do Know*. New York: Oxford University Press.

Keersmaecker, J. de and Roets, A. (2017). 'Fake News': Incorrect, but Hard to Correct. The Role of Cognitive Ability on the Impact of False Information on Social Impressions. *Intelligence*, 65: 107–110.

Keller, T. R. and Klinger, U. (2019). Social Bots in Election Campaigns: Theoretical, Empirical, and Methodological Implications. *Political Communication*, 36(1): 171–189.

King, G., Pan, J. and Roberts, M. E. (2017). How the Chinese Government Fabricates Social Media Posts for Strategic Distraction, not Engaged Argument. *American Political Science Review*, 111(3): 484–501.

Lanoszka, A. (2019). Disinformation in International Politics. *European Journal of International Security*, 4(2): 227–248.

Lazer, D. M. J., Baum, M. A., Benkler, Y., Berinsky, A. J., Greenhill, K. M., Menczer, F., Metzger, M., Nyhan, B., Pennycook, G., Rothschild, D., Schudson, M., Sloman, S., Sunstein, S., Thorson, E., Watts, D. and Zittrain, J. L. (2018). The Science of Fake News. *Science*, 359(6380): 1094–1096.

Lupia, A. and McCubbins, M. D. (1998). *The Democratic Dilemma. Can Citizens Learn What They Need to Know?* Cambridge: Cambridge University Press.

Maréchal, N. (2017). Networked Authoritarianism and the Geopolitics of Information: Understanding Russian Internet Policy. *Media and Communication*, 5(1): 29–41.

Marwick, A. and Lewis, R. (2017). Media Manipulation and Disinformation Online. *Data and Society*. Retrieved from: https://datasociety.net/pubs/oh/DataAndSociety_MediaManipulationAndDisinformationOnline.pdf.

McQuail, D. (2008). *McQuail's Mass Communication Theory* (5th ed., reissued.). London: SAGE Publications.

Morgan, S. (2018). Fake News, Disinformation, Manipulation and Online Tactics to Undermine Democracy. *Journal of Cyber Policy*, 3(1): 39–43.

Omand, D. (2018). The Threats from Modern Digital Subversion and Sedition. *Journal of Cyber Policy*, 3(1): 5–23.

Pennycook, G., Cannon, T. D. and Rand, D. G. (2018). Prior Exposure Increases Perceived Accuracy of Fake News. *Journal of Experimental Psychology. General*, *147*(12): 1865–1880.

Pomerantsev, P. (2014, 5 May). How Putin Is Reinventing Warfare. *Foreign Policy*. Retrieved from: https://foreignpolicy.com/2014/05/05/how-putin-is-reinventing-warfare/.

Pope, A. E. (2018). Cyber-Securing Our Elections. *Journal of Cyber Policy*, 3(1): 24–38.

Schünemann, W. J. (2014). *Subversive Souveräne: Vergleichende Diskursanalyse der gescheiterten Referenden im europäischen Verfassungsprozess. Theorie und Praxis der Diskursforschung*. Wiesbaden: Springer VS.

Schünemann, W. J. (2018). Skad Analysis of European Multi-Level Political Debates. In R. Keller, A.-K. Hornidge, and W. J. Schünemann (eds). *Routledge Advances in Sociology. The Sociology of Knowledge Approach to Discourse: Investigating the Politics of Knowledge and Meaning-Making*. Abingdon, Oxon, New York: Routledge, pp. 91–111.

Shackelford, S., Schneier, B., Sulmeyer, M., Boustead, A., Buchanan, B., Craig, A., Deckard, T. H. and Malekos Smith, J. (2016). Making Democracy Harder to Hack: Should Elections Be Classified as 'Critical Infrastructure?'. *University of Michigan Journal of Law Reform*, 50(3): 629–668. Retrieved from: https://papers.ssrn.com/sol3/papers.cfm?abstract_id=2852461.

Shirky, C. (2008). *Here Comes Everybody: The Power of Organizing without Organizations*. New York: Penguin Books.

Stier, S., Schünemann, W. J. and Steiger, S. (2018). Of Activists and Gatekeepers: Temporal and Structural Properties of Policy Networks on Twitter. *New Media and Society*, 20(5): 1910–1930.

Strick, B., Robinson, O. and Sardarizadeh, S. (2020, May 28). Inside the Pro-China Network Targeting the US. BBC. Retrieved from: https://www.bbc.com/news/blogs-trending-52657434.

Sunstein, C. R. (2017). *#Republic: Divided Democracy in the Age of Social Media*. Princeton, NJ: Princeton University Press.

Tago, A. (2018). Public Diplomacy and Foreign Policy. In C. G. Thies (ed.). *Oxford Encyclopedia. The Oxford Encyclopedia of Foreign Policy Analysis*. New York: Oxford University Press, pp. 453–464.

Thornton, R. and Miron, M. (2019). Deterring Russian Cyber Warfare: The Practical, Legal and Ethical Constraints Faced by the United Kingdom. *Journal of Cyber Policy*, 4(2): 257–274.

Tucker, J., Guess, A., Barbera, P., Vaccari, C., Siegel, A., Sanovich, S., Stukal, D. and Nyhan, B. (2018). Social Media, Political Polarization, and Political Disinformation: A

Review of the Scientific Literature. *SSRN Electronic Journal*. Retrieved from: https://doi.org/10.2139/ssrn.3144139.

UK Parliament (2017, December 20). *Intelligence and Security Committee of Parliament, Annual Report 2016–17 (No. HC 655)*. London. Retrieved from: https://assets.publishing.service.gov.uk/government/uploads/system/uploads/attachment_data/file/727949/ISC-Annual-Report-2016-17.pdf.

US White House (2017, December). *National Security Strategy of the United States of America*. Washington, DC. Retrieved from: https://trumpwhitehouse.archives.gov/wp-content/uploads/2017/12/NSS-Final-12-18-2017-0905.pdf.

Vosoughi, S., Roy, D. and Aral, S. (2018). The Spread of True and False News Online. *Science*, 359(6380): 1146–1151.

Zettl, K. (2019). Lesson Learned? Demokratische Resilienz gegenüber digitaler Wahlbeeinflussung in den USA und Deutschland. *Zeitschrift für Außen- und Sicherheitspolitik*, 12(4): 429–451.

4 Cultural violence and fragmentation on social media

Interventions and countermeasures by humans and social bots

Jasmin Haunschild, Marc-André Kaufhold, and Christian Reuter

Mobile technologies and social media services are among the socio-technological innovations that have an enormous impact transforming modern culture and political processes. Social media are often defined as a "group of internet-based applications [...] that allow the creation and exchange of user-generated content" (Kaplan and Haenlein 2010). Shaping opinions, politics, participation, and protest (Wulf et al. 2013), they are used by citizens for news consumption and social exchange (Robinson et al. 2017); by journalists for reporting, analyzing, and collecting information (Stieglitz et al. 2018a); and by organizations to monitor crises, emergencies, customer feedback, and sentiment, among others (Haunschild et al. 2020). Large-scale international events, such as the 2010 Arab Spring, showcased the potential of socio-technological transformations: Citizens were not passive victims but active and autonomous participants utilizing social media to coordinate protest and for crisis response (Reuter and Kaufhold 2018). However, in other cases, citizens' activities coordinated via social media also increased the complexity of tasks and pressure for formal authorities, since the lack of state control has not had only empowering or benign effects. Instead, on social media, false information spreads fast and it is easy for groups to find an audience there, either to enhance their profit or to target vulnerable groups with dangerous ideology.

To understand the role of social media in contributing to peace and conflict, the conceptions of war, peace, and security from the domains of peace and conflict research and security studies are helpful. They have identified the need to deepen and broaden understandings of the relevant actors, referent objects, and threats (Booth 2007). While traditionally, the state had been the only actor and threatened object, the conflict in former Yugoslavia showed that social groups can also be threatened by their own state and by other groups within the same state (Waever 1993). This is even more the case with regard to cyberspace, where it "is also often unclear whether the actors pursue military-strategic or commercial objectives and whether they have no political, but maybe commercial interests maybe on behalf of the private sector or on behalf of a state or group with political intents" (Reuter 2020: 13). Similarly, the conception of human security shines a light on the potential threats to individuals, which do not only concern security

DOI: 10.4324/9781003110224-5

aspects such as direct attacks, but also safety issues, such as health, development, and environmental threats (Booth 2007). This conception of the potential sources of harm and insecurity helps understand the role of social media as a socio-technological innovation that, along with its emancipatory power, also amplifies existing threats. In this way, social media cannot only contribute to direct, physical violence, e.g. through facilitating the recruitment of terrorists (Weimann 2016), but also to structural and cultural violence by creating, reinforcing, and escalating grievances and political fragmentation, e.g. through the dissemination of fake news and of extremist ideologies (Reuter et al. 2017), partly aided by social bots (Stieglitz et al. 2017). Cultural violence is understood as "all aspects of a culture that are used to justify direct or structural violence" (Galtung 2007: 341), while structural violence describes "unjust economic, social and political conditions and institutions that harm people by preventing them from meeting their basic needs" (Campbell et al. 2010: 390). Accordingly, socio-technological transformations with potential for structural violence can be witnessed (a) in the use and misuse of social media platforms to foster intercultural understanding, but also to disseminate harmful content; and (b) in the use of social bots that can feign widespread support and amplify the spread of harmful content. On the other hand, innovations and regulations are also developed to mitigate socio-technological uncertainties in a way that curbs the misuse while maintaining the positive potential of social media.

In this context, social media are relevant as an important platform for shaping culture, both to foster cultural peace, as well as to be abused for structural and cultural violence. Notions of cyber peace have already recognized the structural dimension, when cyber peace is described as "the peaceful application of cyberspace to the benefit of humanity and the environment [including] the renouncement of all cyberwar activities, but [also the use of] the whole of the communication infrastructure for international understanding" (FifF o.D.). The study of cyber peace should take into account insights from peace and conflict research on conditions that foster peace and conflict in other realms of society, as well as contributions from fields of human–computer iInteractions and IT security, to create designs and modes of interacting with technology that foster peace (Reuter 2019).

In a socio-technological setting, cultural violence might become tangible by the actual *content*, but is also driven by the motives of *actors* and mediated by the capabilities of *technology*. To address these three perspectives with emergent phenomena in cyberspace, the following chapters will examine (1) *fake news* and their exploiting of existing grievances and distrust; (2) *cyber terrorism* showing how actors exploit disadvantaged groups and further alienate them from the society they live in; and (3) the technology of *social bots*, networks of which can be bought by actors to further their political or economic agenda through manipulation and fake news. By conducting a narrative literature review, the chapter identifies challenges and explores socio-technological countermeasures to cultural violence perpetrated on social media, shedding light on the social grievances exploited by technology. It thus shows that both technological and social interventions are fruitful. But it also shows that ultimately the question of how to differentiate the voicing of legitimate grievances and the organization of political opposition from malicious efforts at politically and financially motivated fragmentation remains open and cannot be solved by technology or social media firms who are currently the dominant actors for setting the rules on social media (DeNardis and Hackl 2015).

This chapter illustrates different phenomena that increase societal fragmentation and erode trust in communities and political institutions. First, the case of fake news shows that existing grievances can be nourished by fake news. Secondly, targeted propaganda on social media uses existing grievances to turn individuals against other societies in the process of terrorism recruitment. While social media primarily increases the reach of existing voices, the third case of social bots shows the potential to artificially amplify certain voices, skewing the discourse according to the financial and political agendas of those buying the service of bots. Each case closes by showing socio-technological countermeasures to the exploitation of social media. The chapter concludes by discussing the implications of the socio-technological transformation through social media for legitimacy and regulatory authority.

Fabricated, manipulated, and misinterpreted content: The issue of fake news in social media

By increasing communication among online users, social media can contribute to cultural violence, for instance, by emphasizing religious, ideological, and language divides, including by spreading misinformation and disinformation, commonly known as "fake news". While the term was originally used to mostly refer to comedy news shows, in 2016 the perception changed when many fake stories went viral and started to affect political parties globally and impacted opinions on a larger scale than before (Becker 2016). Although "fake news" is a popular and frequent term, it is often mingled with other phenomena, facilitating misuse of the term to discredit undesired news (Cooke 2017), political opponents, and conspiracy theories.

Dissemination of fake news in social media

Fake news are news articles that are "intentionally and verifiably false and could mislead readers" (Allcott and Gentzkow 2017: 213). The topics of fake news often lead to high emotions and are associated with controversial discussions like migration, child abuse, or war (Ziegele et al. 2014), but prevalent types of fake news differ across states and cultures (Humprecht 2019). Fake news can have serious consequences, e.g. influencing elections, stock markets, or leading to direct violence (Kaufhold and Reuter 2019). In an illustrative case in South Africa, foreign shops were attacked, leading to the deaths of 12 people, mostly nationals, while tensions between South Africans and Nigerians increased with footage on social media from different times and places claiming to portray attacks against

Nigerians (News Afrika 2016). This case shows how already existing xenophobia is exacerbated by social media, leading to retribution for violence that did not actually take place.

Often, political and financial motivations exist for generating fake news. Links from social media posts can result in vast advertising revenues if they are successfully published and shared and fake news have been used to manipulate the public opinion and debate. Well-known incidents are the recent US presidential election (McCarthy 2017) and the UK "brexit" referendum where false information have often been employed in combination with social bots (Mostrous et al. 2017).

Countermeasures against fake news

Three enablers and corresponding response vectors have been identified for countering fake news: To address the susceptibility of the "host" (news readers and social media users), education and clarification is the most promising avenue. Another enabler is a "conducive environment", consisting of toxic and complicit platforms, which can be addressed through regulation. Finally, the various types of fakes acting as "virulent pathogens" can be addressed through auto-detection (Rubin 2019). This leads to four possible approaches to countering fake news (see Table 4.1).

Most social networks have taken measures such as curating, deleting, and censoring. In doing so, even initially independent platforms now take the traditional journalistic role of information gatekeeper (Wohn et al. 2017). Many platforms provide mechanisms for users to flag content that they believe to be false. These annotations are then checked by experts, belonging either to the platform or to national independent fact-checking organizations. This expert-oriented checking of facts is based on human work and deals with the exposure of false statements. The experts check their researched and already created lists with the articles

Table 4.1 Measures against fake news in social media

Gatekeeping	Gatekeeping is the process through which information, including fake news, is filtered for dissemination, e.g. for publication, broadcasting, social media, or some other mode of communication (Barzilai-Nahon 2009).
Media literacy	The purpose of media literacy, which is a multidimensional process allowing people to access, evaluate, and create media, is to help people protect themselves against the potentially negative effects of (mass) media (Potter 2010).
Regulation/Law	Laws assist in fighting fake news and hate speech by forcing platforms to quickly delete illegal content, but potentially threaten freedom of speech (Müller and Denner 2017).
Algorithms/Tools	Algorithmic detection of fake news comprises classification-based, propagation-based, and survey-based approaches (Viviani and Pasi 2017) as well as user assistance tools (Hartwig and Reuter 2019).

flagged by Facebook users. In addition, technological means are used to limit the visibility of fake news on social media by reducing their relevance in news feeds and to limit their spread, e.g. reducing the amount of possible forwarding on messenger apps to five (Hern 2020).

Furthermore, efforts are made to increase the populations' media literacy. People with good media literacy can better navigate today's media and are able to identify and critique false news, but also create fake news themselves (Mihailidis and Viotty 2017). Hancock et al. (2008) show that the style of disinformation often differs from real news: Fraudsters rely more on sense-based, less on self-oriented, and more on other-oriented words. In addition, they use more negatively associated words, which provides guidance for people to detect fake news emotions (Newman et al. 2003). Furthermore, diverse non-state actors and associations are developing tools, such as the app Fake News Check (Neue Wege des Lernens e.V. 2017). Instead of the automatic flagging of fake news, the app aims to sensitize for the critical handling of news by helping users to ask the right questions and identify fake news through guided reflection of a set of 19 questions.

Regarding regulation, in many countries, laws have entered into force that require platforms to quickly delete illegal content, including hate speech. While celebrated for giving support to victims, it has also been widely criticized for threatening freedom of speech. Deleting fake news from social networks may create reactance and thus an even more fertile ground for conspiracy theories (Müller and Denner 2017). Additionally, such laws may incentivize social networks to delete content preemptively if there is any suspicion of fake news.

There are several approaches to use algorithms and tools for fake news detection. Such algorithms use classification-based (including machine learning), propagation-based (including social network analysis), and survey-based (including representative samples) approaches (Viviani and Pasi 2017). This also includes user assistance tools, for instance, *Fake Tweet Buster* helps Twitter users to identify a tweeted image as fake and tools such as *Trusty Tweet* and *Alethiometer* provide indicators and a browser plugin on the trustworthiness of tweets (Hartwig and Reuter 2019; Kaufhold and Reuter 2019).

These approaches place the responsibility for dealing with disinformation on different groups. While media literacy targets the recipients of fake news, regulation demands that either governments or social media platforms make and enforce rules about limiting the availability or spread of fabricated content. Gatekeeping can be performed either by experts employed by social media platforms or by journalists organized in independent fact-checking institutions (Graves 2018). Their results can either prevent fake news from being shown or can be used to inform consumers. Similarly, algorithmic solutions support any of the actors, pointing out identified fake news either to media consumers, to platforms, gatekeepers, or regulators, depending on who is deemed responsible. While citizens are undecided about who should take that responsibility, the majority of Germans supports relevant authorities' swift reaction to fake news, but also transparent journalism (Reuter et al. 2019).

Terrorist actors: Propaganda and recruitment in social media

As indicated, the spread of disinformation is strongly driven by the motivations of different actors. The recent past saw an increase in terrorist attacks across Europe, such as the November 2015 Paris attacks, the 2016 Brussels bombings, or the 2017 London Bridge attack (Stieglitz et al. 2018b). Besides direct violence and extensive media coverage of such events, the internet and especially social media are also used to promote cultural violence, e.g. by disseminating ideologies of terrorism and recruiting new members. Again, radicalization and recruitment into terrorist and extremist organizations is only possible where terrorist propaganda meets experiences or perceptions of injustice and grievances (Al-Saggaf 2016).

Terrorist propaganda and recruitment in social media

Research about terrorist organizations and social media mainly deals with the so-called Islamic State (IS, a.k.a. ISIS, ISIL, DEASH). Neer and O'Toole (2014) emphasize that especially Twitter is used by IS as a strategic tool to gain support from young jihadists, Ba'ath officials, and women. Klausen et al. (2012) stress that the British terrorist group al-Muhajiroun uses its international network of YouTube-channels elaborately for propaganda and the presentation of violent contents. Social media are used to incite phantasies and to normalize extreme views by creating an echo chamber of like-minded individuals (Awan 2017; Torok 2015). This leads to IS developing and disseminating "its central narratives, often by reframing familiar concepts such as jihad and martyrdom" (Torok 2015). In addition to propaganda targeted at vulnerable and like-minded people, terrorists also use tools such as Kik or Skype for "direct, real-time communication between recruiters and their audiences" (Weimann 2016: 82).

The IS propaganda helps in the recruitment not only of potential new fighters, but also of "technically proficient and talented users of social media to sustain the machinery of recruitment" (Gates and Podder 2015: 109). Since May 2014, IS videos or other media have been produced by the al-Hayat Media Center, a special production unit for Western recruitment. Their material exists in many languages and is spread via social media. For example, "IS released a video inciting Muslims to come and participate in jihad, featuring a German chant with an English translation" (Weimann 2016: 80).

Counter-terrorism in social media

A variety of different measures to counter-terrorism have been identified in research (see Table 4.2). Reuter et al. (2017) identify three categories of countermeasures: Clarification, parody/satire, and hacking. They show that private users are more adapt at reaching a wider audience as opposed to institutional accounts aiming to clarify. Satirical content is shown to receive most attention, while the success of hacking scenes is judged as limited due to the ease of reopening accounts and moving content to other platforms.

Table 4.2 Measures against terrorism

Clarification	Countering terrorist propaganda with logic to invalidate false information and simplistic portrayals.
Parody/Satire	Humorous imitation working through distortion and exaggeration (parody), critique and mockery (satire) of serious issues.
Hacking	Illegal "hacktivist" activities like attacking and blocking of pro-IS accounts and websites, supported by crowdsourced reporting of accounts of suspected terrorists. Includes legal activities of multiplying anti-IS parodist content.
Counter-narratives	A narrative that competes with another narrative. Narratives are compelling storylines which can explain events convincingly and from which inferences can be drawn.

Terrorists' activity and dependence on social media propaganda can also be seen as a weak spot that can be attacked with small and quick units that refute IS propaganda, expose untrue aspects, and damage the IS's credibility (Gartenstein-Ross 2015). Jeberson and Sharma (2015) focus on methods to identify terror suspects in social networks. Cheong and Lee (2011) describe that these data could be collected in a knowledge base in connection with intelligent data mining, visualization, and filter methods. They could be used by authorities for quick reaction and control. Furthermore, Sutton et al. (2008) deal with the application of backchannels as a special form of data mining for acquiring information. Instead of a strict censorship of radical contents, "terrorist communication strategies [should therefore be disturbed] by a mixture of technical (hacking) and especially psychological (anti-propaganda) means" (Weimann and Jost 2015). Gartenstein-Ross (2015) concludes that it would be a significant victory to weaken the strategic communication campaign of the IS. Weimann (2016) sees the security community and governments as well as researchers in the role of a counter-terrorism force. For the security community, according to Weimann (2016), it is necessary to include cyberspace in counter-terrorism strategies.

Hussain and Saltman (2014) emphasize that general censorship, similar to that of fake news, can be counterproductive, suggesting positive measures such as counter-narratives (Freedman 2006). Yet, (believable) anti-propaganda does not only come from abroad: Hundreds of Arabic YouTubers transformed an IS-video with religious singing into a funny dance clip after its release (Al-Rawi 2016). Moreover, it is possible to focus on preventive measures in combination with (offline) information at schools, universities, or prisons (Saltman and Russell 2014), focusing on social work and vulnerable populations. An effort that combines social and technological intervention uses machine learning to identify grievances which can then be politically and socially addressed, before radicalization turns into violence (Al-Saggaf and Davies 2019).

Automated technology-driven manipulation: the impact of social bots

When fake news and terrorism propaganda lead to the dissemination of cultural violence across social media, technologies such as social bots and large-scale botnets may be misused as multipliers of cultural violence. "A social bot is a computer algorithm that automatically produces content and interacts with humans on social media, trying to emulate and possibly alter their behavior" (Ferrara et al. 2016: 96). Bots' behavior can establish realistic social networks and produce credible content with human-like patterns. They can be classified along their intent and capacity to imitate human behavior (Stieglitz et al. 2017). The use of bots facilitates the targeted spread of particular ideological content and views on social media, disguised as organic, natural human support, creating new socio-technological phenomena.

Account hijacking and astroturfing by social bots

Bots, in addition to human hackers, can be involved in compromising accounts temporarily or entirely through account hijacking. Login details are received via phishing, malware, or cross-site scripting. Often attackers use compromised accounts for further phishing activities to gain access to additional accounts, misusing trust of befriended users (Stein et al. 2011). Hijacked accounts disseminate malware- or phishing-infected websites with the goal of identity theft (Almaatouq et al. 2016). Account hijacking can be used for political purposes, with compromised accounts abusing the trust of legitimate users within the network, who are then more likely to believe misinformation and propaganda (Trang et al. 2015). The added value of accounts taken over increases when profiles are associated with a popular person or organization. Bots are also used to intervene in online discourse through confusion or misinformation, e.g. by associating a hashtag with non-related content for distraction ("misdirection"), or to hide relevant content amidst unrelated content ("smoke screening").

As a further phenomenon, astroturfing describes the imitation of grassroot movements with the aim of feigning a local, social initiative or organization to influence economic or political conditions (Cho et al. 2011). Using bots to suggest wide-spread support, astroturfing is often conducted by political or economic groups. Similar to lobbying, it aims at manipulating public opinion and political decisions by strengthening its own views and discrediting contrary arguments. However, this type of lobbying is inherently extremely intransparent and involves the payment of individuals to set up the structures and campaigns that suggest a legitimate grassroots organization. In this context, bots can be a cost-effective way of simulating wide-spread support. In addition, illegal or gray area content is frequently distributed, e.g. ad fraud, questionable political statements, or defamatory rumors (Wang et al. 2012). Instead of targeting the outcome of a particular policy, the Russian bot firm "Internet Research Agency" (IRA) was used to manipulate voters in the 2016 US election (Diresta et al. 2019). It had set up accounts across all main social media platforms and used astroturfing to, among other things, encourage and discourage certain voter groups. Research shows that the bot firm co-opted current debates such as the #BlackLivesMatter movement and spread posts both on the extreme spectrum of both the right and left positions, and used existing grievances and distrust to increase fragmentation, societal insecurity, and distrust in the democratic institutions (Stewart et al. 2018).

Algorithmic and crowd-based social bot detection

To counteract social bots, it is first necessary to identify the respective bot accounts. For this purpose, the field of social bot detection has developed various approaches (Ferrara et al. 2016). Social bots may be identified through human engagement or through algorithmic analysis of features and social networks, both complemented by hybrid approaches (see Table 4.3).

To begin with, the approach of crowdsourcing assumes that humans are uniquely able to identify social bot accounts due to their human cognitive skills required to detect human verbal shades of sarcasm, humor, or commitment which cannot be easily imitated by social bots nor recognized by automated bot detection mechanisms. An online platform based on crowdsourcing was thus developed (Wang et al. 2012), with thousands helping to identify bot accounts on Facebook and Renren, a popular Chinese social network. Appling and Briscoe (2017) examine the effectiveness of human identification of social bots and compare it to automated determination of bots. One class of algorithmic detection systems include graph-based approaches which model a respective social network as a finite graph, the participating users constituting vertices and edges illustrating relationships between them. These approaches identify social bots based on analysis of the network topology of the social graph (Yan 2013). Social bots rely on social connections to other accounts for presenting a trustworthy image. It is assumed that bots can only establish a disproportionally small number of social links with legitimate users and are therefore more connected with other bot

Table 4.3 Approaches for social bot detection

Crowdsourcing	Relies on identification of social bots by human actors, assuming humans to be the most able to recognize linguistic nuances like sarcasm, humor, or commitment (Wang et al.2012).
Social graph analysis	Model social networks visually as finite graphs. Nodes illustrate participants of the respective network; edges represent relationships (Yan 2013).
Feature analysis	Identify social bots by determining unique characteristics and behaviors, using machine learning or entropy approaches (Ramalingam and Chinnaiah 2018).
Hybrid approach	Combine different methods, such as adding features to a graph-based approach, to increase the accuracy of social bot detection (Gao et al. 2015).

accounts. This characteristic of close-knit communities of bots within a network is used to identify them through community detection algorithms.

Furthermore, feature-based approaches detect defining characteristics and behaviors of social bot accounts to distinguish them from human users (Ramalingam and Chinnaiah 2018). The examined features are diverse and include the number of followers or tweets, chronological activities of users, content of posts, profile pictures, account names, and friend lists. This group of detection systems may be subclassified into machine learning systems and entropy-based detection systems. Approaches based on machine learning first learn conspicuous training data and subsequently apply a classification algorithm to real data. Entropic-based detection systems do not rely on a prior learning process but identify bots through algorithms searching for anomalies in data sets. Finally, hybrid approaches combine different types of algorithms, for instance, a graph-based approach may be supplemented with features to increase the accuracy of detection (Gao et al. 2018). The simultaneous improvements of both the human-like behavior of bots and of detection systems are leading to an arms race similar to that observed for spam. The experience with spam shows that technical interventions can be powerful, but they must be complemented with social aspects such as knowledge about the mechanisms of abuse to empower users to protect themselves where technical solutions fail.

Conclusion

In this chapter we examined three phenomena that take place in social media where human and (semi-)automatic interventions potentially inflict cultural violence and incite inter-societal conflict through fragmentation. To prevent negative impacts of these phenomena, a variety of different countermeasures are applied which potentially improve cultural peace in social media (see Table 4.4).

In terms of (manual) human interventions, we see that fabricated, misinterpreted, and manipulated content, as well as propaganda and terrorist recruitment,

Table 4.4 Actors and intentions for cultural violence and peace

		Actor	
		Human	*Machine*
Intention	**Malicious interventions**	Fabricated, misinterpreted, manipulated content; propaganda, recruitment	Account hijacking, astroturfing, fake accounts, fake posts, spam
	Countermeasures	Gatekeeping, media literacy, laws, clarification, parody/satire, hacking, counter-narratives	Crowdsourcing platforms, detection algorithms, user assistance tools

may inflict structural or direct violence. Here, countermeasures are similar and include gatekeeping, media literacy and laws, as well as clarification, parody/satire, and hacking. Further research could examine how so far largely neglected actors, such as the crowd and IT-related civil society groups, can contribute to solutions, bringing together IT knowledge and society-level interventions. These can be inspired by established peace interventions from other domains, such as reconciliation. Considering (semi-)automatic machine interventions, we identified account hijacking, astroturfing, fake accounts, fake posts, and spam as potentials for cultural violence exacerbating existing divides and eroding trust in legitimate protest and institutions. Respective countermeasures contain detection algorithms and crowdsourcing for malicious content. Experiences in countering spam show the power of technical arms races, but also spammers' adaptability in using sophisticated social engineering to deceive detection mechanisms and humans by exploiting trust detection mechanisms. Similarly, the Russion bot firm IRA has adapted its strategy to feigning affiliation with established, trusted institutions (Wired 2020). Technical arms races can thus be powerful, but never all-encompassing, leaving the necessity for social interventions. Hybrid forms of intervention include solutions that, without outright censoring posts, limit the visibility or spreading speed of harmful content, or provide technical assistance for users to better judge the truthworthiness of online information, or can identify social media users at risk of radicalization. However, as long as legitimate grievances exist, actors such as terrorists will be able to co-opt these grievances and resistance. Therefore, organizations such as ICT4Peace use communication technology to address community grievances at the root level, helping overcome fragmentation and societal insecurity.

This limit of technical interventions also applies to disinformation and terrorist propaganda: While deletion and flagging of false content are possible, this raises questions about the authority over defining the truth and dangers of censorship. The dominant technical interventions are not addressing the root causes that make people gullible to disinformation and even lead them to potentially sign away their future to join extremist groups. This also raises new questions about the definition of victims and perpetrators of online structural violence: Are people who spread misinformation and propaganda perpetrators of societal fragmentation and structural violence, or victims of a society that has left them with low media literacy and the feeling of being alienated by the society they live in? Similar to fake news, it is difficult to differentiate legitimate protest movements from those instigated by politically and economically motivated bot firms that specialize in feigning public support for radical or partisan opinions. As is in many countries required to start a new political party, for sensitive topics with the potential to fragment society, new organizations could be required to proof their legitimacy through referral by an organization that is trusted by that community. Though a difficult task, such measures may be necessary to save the legitimacy of grassroot protest in the long run. The frame of structural and cultural violence can help to identify issues and populations that are particularly vulnerable to social media incitement of resentment, or topics and corporations that may profitably use disinformation and social bots, suggesting a need for societal interventions.

A promising first step is the social media analytics, which can be used to better understand the social side of social media abuse, e.g. by making situational assessments of specific discourses and events (Kaufhold et al. 2020a), including the identification of fake news or hate speech as potential instances of cultural violence using (supervised) machine learning approaches (Kaufhold et al. 2020b). As an intermediary, technical tools can be developed to flag false content and provide transparency over actors and organizations that fuel the extremes and follow partisan interests. This will require identifying the actors and incentive structures that motivate disinformation and the buying of social bot systems as well as addressing the societal structures, mainly mistrust and grievances, which allow malicious interventions to take devastating effects.

Further research should overcome the limitation of this explorative contribution by first including more socio-technological technological transformations seen in social media that can contribute to structural violence. As this chapter focused on the cultural areas of ideology, a more comprehensive examination should further address issues such as cultural diversity, religion, and economy as factors for cultural violence in social media, e.g. through an apposite mapping to Galtung's (2007) cultural areas of religion, ideology, language, art, and empirical and formal science.

Acknowledgments

Parts of this chapter are based on our previous work (Kaufhold and Reuter 2019). This work has been co-funded by the German Federal Ministry of Education and Research (BMBF) and the Hessen State Ministry for Higher Education, Research and Arts (HMKW) within the SecUrban mission of the National Research Center for Applied Cybersecurity ATHENE and by the LOEWE initiative (Hesse, Germany) within the emergenCITY center.

References

All links checked on August 20, 2021.

Al-Rawi, A. (2016). Anti-ISIS Humor: Cultural Resistance of Radical Ideology. *Politics, Religion and Ideology*, 7689(May): 1–17.

Al-Saggaf, Y. (2016). Understanding Online Radicalisation Using Data Science. *International Journal of Cyber Warfare and Terrorism (IJCWT)*, 6(4): 13–27.

Al-Saggaf, Y. and Davies, A. (2019). Understanding the Expression of Grievances in the Arabic Twitter-Sphere Using Machine Learning. *Journal of Criminological Research, Policy and Practice*, 5(2): 108–119.

Allcott, H. and Gentzkow, M. (2017). Social Media and Fake News in the 2016 Election. *Journal of Economic Perspectives*, 31(2): 211–236.

Almaatouq, A., Shmueli, E., Nouh, M., Alabdulkareem, A., Singh, V. K., Alsaleh, M., … Pentland, A. (2016). If it Looks Like a Spammer and Behaves Like a Spammer, it Must Be a Spammer: Analysis and Detection of Microblogging Spam Accounts. *International Journal of Information Security*, 15(5): 475–491.

Appling, D. S. and Briscoe, E. J. (2017). The Perception of Social Bots by Human and Machine. In: *Proceedings of the Thirtieth International Florida Artificial Intelligence Research Society Conference*, pp. 20–25.

Awan, I. (2017). Cyber-Extremism: Isis and the Power of Social Media. *Society*, 54(2): 138–149.

Becker, B. W. (2016). The Librarian's Information War. *Behavioral and Social Sciences Librarian*, 35(4): 188–191.

Booth, K. (2007). *Theory of World Security* (Vol. 105). Cambridge: Cambridge University Press.

Campbell, P. J., MacKinnon, A. S. and Stevens, C. (2010). *An Introduction to Global Studies*. Hoboken, NJ: Wiley-Blackwell.

Cheong, M. and Lee, V. C. S. (2011). A Microblogging-Based Approach to Terrorism Informatics: Exploration and Chronicling Civilian Sentiment and Response to Terrorism Events via Twitter. *Information Systems Frontiers*, 13(1): 45–59.

Cho, C. H., Martens, M. L., Kim, H. and Rodrigue, M. (2011). Astroturfing Global Warming: It Isn't Always Greener on the Other Side of the Fence. *Journal of Business Ethics*, 104(4): 571–587.

Cooke, N. A. (2017). Posttruth, Truthiness, and Alternative Facts: Information Behavior and Critical Information Consumption for a New Age. *Library Querterly: Information, Community, Policy*, 87(3): 211–221.

DeNardis, L. and Hackl, A. M. (2015). Internet Governance by Social Media Platforms. *Telecommunications Policy*, 39(9): 761–770.

Diresta, R., Shaffer, K., Ruppel, B., Matney, R., Fox, R., Albright, J. and Johnson, B. (2019). *The Tactics and Tropes of the Internet Research Agency*. Report for the United States Senate Select Committee on Intelligence. Retrieved from: https:/digitalcommons.unl.edu/senatedocs/2/.

Ferrara, E., Varol, O., Davis, C., Menczer, F. and Flammini, A. (2016). The Rise of Social Bots. *Communications of the ACM*, 59(7): 96–104. Retrieved February 25 2021, from: http://dl.acm.org/citation.cfm?id=2818717.

Freedman, L. (2006). *The Transformation of Strategic Affairs*. Abingdon: Routledge.

Galtung, J. (2007). *Frieden mit friedlichen Mitteln. Friede und Konflikt, Entwicklung und Kultur*. Münster: Agenda Verlag.

Gao, P., Gong, N. Z., Kulkarni, S., Thomas, K. and Mittal, P. (2018). SybilFrame: A Defense-in-Depth Framework for Structure-Based Sybil Detection. In: *Computing Research Repository*. Retrieved February 25 2021, from: http://arxiv.org/abs/1503.02985.

Gartenstein-Ross, D. (2015). Social Media in the Next Evolution of Terrorist Recruitment. *Hearing before the Senate Committee on Homeland Security and Governmental Affairs*, Foundation for Defense of Democracies, 1–11.

Gates, S. and Podder, S. (2015). Social Media, Recruitment, Allegiance and the Islamic State. *Perspectives on Terrorism*, 9(4): 107–116.

Graves, L. (2018). Boundaries Not Drawn: Mapping the Institutional Roots of the Global Fact-Checking Movement. *Journalism Studies*, 19(5): 613–631.

Hancock, J. T., Curry, L. E., Goorha, S. and Woodworth, M. (2008). On Lying and Being Lied To: A Linguistic Analysis of Deception in Computer-Mediated Communication. *Discourse Processes*, 45(1): 1–23.

Hartwig, K. and Reuter, C. (2019). TrustyTweet: An Indicator-Based Browser-Plugin to Assist Users in Dealing with Fake News on Twitter. In: *Proceedings of the International Conference on Wirtschaftsinformatik (WI)*. Siegen.

Haunschild, J., Kaufhold, M.-A. and Reuter, C. (2020). Sticking with Landlines? Citizens' and Police Social Media Use and Expectation during Emergencies. In: *Proceedings of the International Conference on Wirtschaftsinformatik (WI)*. Potsdam, Germany: AIS Electronic Library (AISel).

Hern, A. (2020, April 7). WhatsApp to Impose New Limit on Forwarding to Fight Fake News. *The Guardian*. Retrieved from: https://www.theguardian.com/technology/2020/apr/07/whatsapp-to-impose-new-limit-on-forwarding-to-fight-fake-news.

Humprecht, E. (2019). Where 'Fake News' Flourishes: A Comparison across Four Western Democracies. *Information, Communication and Society*, 22(13): 1973–1988.

Hussain, G. and Saltman, E. M. (2014). Jihad Trending: A Comprehensive Analysis of Online Extremism and How to Counter It. Report from the Quilliam Foundation. Retrieved from: https://preventviolentextremism.info/jihad-trending-comprehensive-analysis-online-extremism-and-how-counter-it.

Jeberson, W. and Sharma, L. (2015). Survey on Counter Web Terrorism. *COMPUSOFT: An International Journal of Advanced Computer Technology*, 4(5): 1744–1747.

Kaplan, A. M. and Haenlein, M. (2010). Users of the World, Unite! The Challenges and Opportunities of Social Media. *Business Horizons*, 53(1): 59–68.

Kaufhold, M.-A., Bayer, M. and Reuter, C. (2020b). Rapid Relevance Classification of Social Media Posts in Disasters and Emergencies: A System and Evaluation Featuring Active, Incremental and Online Learning. *Information Processing and Management*, 57(1): 1–32.

Kaufhold, M.-A. and Reuter, C. (2019). Cultural Violence and Peace in Social Media. In: C. Reuter (ed.). *Information Technology for Peace and Security - IT-Applications and Infrastructures in Conflicts, Crises, War, and Peace*. Wiesbaden: Springer Vieweg, pp. 361–381.

Kaufhold, M.-A., Rupp, N., Reuter, C. and Habdank, M. (2020a). Mitigating Information Overload in Social Media during Conflicts and Crises: Design and Evaluation of a Cross-Platform Alerting System. *Behaviour and Information Technology (BIT)*, 39(3): 319–342.

Klausen, J., Barbieri, E. T., Reichlin-Melnick, A. and Zelin, A. Y. (2012). The YouTube Jihadists: A Social Network Analysis of Al-Muhajiroun's Propaganda Campaign. *Perspectives on Terrorism*, 6(1): 36–53.

McCarthy, T. (2017, October 14). How Russia Used Social Media to Divide Americans. *The Guardian*. Retrieved from: https://www.theguardian.com/us-news/2017/oct/14/russia-us-politics-social-media-facebook.

Mihailidis, P. and Viotty, S. (2017). Spreadable Spectacle in Digital Culture: Civic Expression, Fake News, and the Role of Media Literacies in "Post-Fact" Society. *American Behavioral Scientist*, 61(4): 441–454.

Mostrous, A., Bridge, M. and Katie, G. (2017, November 15). Russia Used Twitter Bots and Trolls 'to Disrupt' Brexit Vote. *The Times*. Retrieved from: https://www.thetimes.co.uk/article/russia-used-web-posts-to-disrupt-brexit-vote-h9nv5zg6c.

Müller, P. and Denner, N. (2017). Was tun gegen "Fake News"? Eine Analyse anhand der Entstehungsbedingungen und Wirkweisen gezielter Falschmeldungen im Internet. Retrieved from: https://madoc.bib.uni-mannheim.de/50564/.

Neer, T. and O'Toole, M. E. (2014). The Violence of the Islamic State of Syria (ISIS): A Behavioral Perspective. *Violence and Gender*, 1(4): 145–156.

Neue Wege des Lernens e.V. (2017). Fake News Check. Retrieved Februrary 25 2021, from: https://www.neue-wege-des-lernens.de/apps/.

Newman, M. L., Pennebaker, J. W., Berry, D. S. and Richards, J. M. (2003). Lying Words: Predicting Deception from Linguistic Styles. *Society for Personality and Social Psychology*, 29(5): 665–675.

News Afrika. (2016, September). Fake News Fuels Xeniphobic Tensions in South Africa.

Ramalingam, D. and Chinnaiah, V. (2018). Fake Profile Detection Techniques in Large-Scale Online Social Networks: A Comprehensive Review. *Computers and Electrical Engineering*, 65: 165–177.

Reuter, C. (2019). Information Technology for Peace and Security – Introduction and Overview. In: C. Reuter (ed.). *Information Technology for Peace and Security*. Wiesbaden: Springer, pp. 3–9.

Reuter, C. (2020). Towards IT Peace Research: Challenges on the Interception of Peace and Conflict Research and Computer Science. *S+F Sicherheit Und Frieden / Peace and Security*, 38(1): 10–16.

Reuter, C., Hartwig, K., Kirchner, J. and Schlegel, N. (2019). Fake News Perception in Germany: A Representative Study of People's Attitudes and Approaches to Counteract Disinformation. In: *Proceedings of the International Conference on Wirtschaftsinformatik (WI)*. Siegen, Germany: AIS, pp. 1069–1083.

Reuter, C. and Kaufhold, M.-A. (2018). Fifteen Years of Social Media in Emergencies: A Retrospective Review and Future Directions for Crisis Informatics. *Journal of Contingencies and Crisis Management (JCCM)*, 26(1): 41–57.

Reuter, C., Pätsch, K. and Runft, E. (2017). IT for Peace? Fighting against Terrorism in Social Media – An Explorative Twitter Study. *I-Com: Journal of Interactive Media*, 16(2): 181–193.

Robinson, T., Callahan, C., Boyle, K., Rivera, E. and Cho, J. K. (2017). I ♥ FB: A Q-Methodology Analysis of Why People 'Like'' Facebook.' *International Journal of Virtual Communities and Social Networking (IJVCSN)*, 9(2): 46–61.

Rubin, V. L. (2019). Disinformation and Misinformation Triangle: A Conceptual Model for "Fake News" Epidemic, Causal Factors and Interventions. *Journal of Documentation*, 75(5): 1013–1034.

Saltman, E. M. and Russell, J. (2014). *White Paper – The Role of Prevent in Countering Online Extremism*. London: Quilliam Foundation.

Stein, T., Chen, E. and Mangla, K. (2011). Facebook Immune System. *Proceedings of the 4th Workshop on Social Network Systems*, 5: 1–8.

Stewart, L. G., Arif, A. and Starbird, K. (2018). Examining Trolls and Polarization with a Retweet Network. *Proceedings of WSDM Workshop on Misinformation and Misbehavior Mining on the Web (MIS2)*, 6.

Stieglitz, S., Brachten, F., Ross, B. and Jung, A.-K. (2017). Do Social Bots Dream of Electric Sheep? A Categorisation of Social Media Bot Accounts. *Proceedings of the Australasian Conference on Information Systems*, 1–11.

Stieglitz, S., Mirbabaie, M., Ross, B. and Neuberger, C. (2018a). Social Media Analytics – Challenges in Topic Discovery, Data Collection, and Data Preparation. *International Journal of Information Management*, 39: 156–168.

Stieglitz, S., Mirbabaie, M. and Milde, M. (2018b). Social Positions and Collective Sense-Making in Crisis Communication. *International Journal of Human-Computer Interaction*, 34(4): 328–355.

Sutton, J., Palen, L. and Shklovski, I. (2008). Backchannels on the Front Lines: Emergent Uses of Social Media in the 2007 Southern California Wildfires. In: F. Friedrich and B. Van de Walle (eds). *Proceedings of the Information Systems for Crisis Response and Management (ISCRAM)*. Washington, DC, pp. 624–632.

Torok, R. (2015). ISIS and the Institution of Online Terrorist Recruitment. Retrieved February 25 2021, from: https://www.mei.edu/publications/isis-and-institution-online-terrorist-recruitment.

Trang, D., Johansson, F. and Rosell, M. (2015). Evaluating Algorithms for Detection of Compromised Social Media User Accounts. *Proceedings - 2nd European Network Intelligence Conference, ENIC 2015*, 75–82.

Viviani, M. and Pasi, G. (2017). Credibility in Social Media: Opinions, News, and Health Information—A Survey. *Wiley Interdisciplinary Reviews: Data Mining and Knowledge Discovery*, 7(5): e1209.

Waever, O. (1993). Societal Security: The Concept. In: O. Waever, et al. (eds). *Identity, Migration and the New Security Agenda in Europe*. London: Pinter, pp. 17–40.

Wang, G., Wilson, C., Zhao, X., Zhu, Y., Mohanlal, M., Zheng, H. and Zhao, B. Y. (2012). Serf and Turf: Crowdturfing for Fun and Profit. *Arxiv Preprint ArXiv:1111.5654*, 10.

Weimann, G. (2016). The Emerging Role of Social Media in the Recruitment of Foreign Fighters. In: A. de Guttry, F. Capone, and C. Paulussen (eds). *Foreign Fighters under International Law and Beyond*. The Hague: T.M.C. Asser Press, pp. 77–95.

Weimann, G. and Jost, J. (2015). Neuer Terrorismus und Neue Medien. *Zeitschrift Für Außen- Und Sicherheitspolitik*, 8(3): 369–388.

Wired (2020, March 5). Russia Is Learning How to Bypass Facebook's Disinfo Defenses. *Wired*. Retrieved from: https://www.wired.com/story/russia-ira-bypass-facebook-disinfo-defenses/.

Wohn, D. Y., Fiesler, C., Hemphill, L., De Choudhury, M. and Matias, J. N. (2017). How to Handle Online Risks? Discussing Content Curation and Moderation in Social Media. In: *CHI 2017 Extended Abstracts*, pp. 1271–1276.

Wulf, V., Aal, K., Ktesh, I. A., Atam, M., Schubert, K., Yerousis, G. P., … Bank, W. (2013). Fighting against the Wall: Social Media Use by Political Activists in a Palestinian Village. In: *Proceedings of the Conference on Human Factors in Computing Systems (CHI)*. Paris: ACM, pp. 1979–1988.

Yan, G. (2013). Peri-Watchdog: Hunting for Hidden Botnets in the Periphery of Online Social Networks. *Computer Networks*, 57(2): 540–555. https://doi.org/10.1016/j.comnet.2012.07.016.

Ziegele, M., Breiner, T. and Quiring, O. (2014). What Creates Interactivity in Online News Discussions? An Exploratory Analysis of Discussion Factors in User Comments on News Items. *Journal of Communication*, 64(6): 1111–1138.

5 Artificial intelligence and the offense–defense balance in cyber security

Matteo E. Bonfanti

Cyber security is a quickly evolving domain which is constantly shaped by technological, policy, regulatory, economic, and social developments. Homomorphic encryption, quantum computing, and block chain represent some of the latest innovative approaches and applications, which promise to change the practice of cyber security. Nowadays, topping the list is "artificial intelligence" (AI), a variegated suite of concepts, methods, and tools whose transformative capacity is widely celebrated but has yet to be fully seen and understood.

Although researched and developed for some decades, AI has become significantly attractive for cyber security stakeholders only in recent times, when latest advancements in this technological field have shown the potential to impact on cyber security (Cussins Newman 2019: 14 ff.). Such growing attention on AI and its intersections with the security of cyberspace is reflected by the increasing number of dedicated initiatives both governmental and private organizations have promoted over the last few years.

However, the time needed for the outcomes of the AI-induced transformation on cyber security to become more tangible and widespread (the "when" question) is contested. While some are prudent about claiming revolutionary change, others are very enthusiastic. Consider, for example, the statement made by the (former) Commander of US Cyber Command and Director of the National Security Agency, Admiral Michael Rogers, a few years ago: "Artificial Intelligence and machine learning — I would argue — is foundational to the future of cyber security [...] It is not the if, it's only the when to me" (Allen and Chan 2017: 18). Admiral Rogers's thoughts have been seconded by many representatives of the cyber security community across the world (Osterman Research 2018).

As relevant as the "When" question are the "How" and the "To what extent" questions: How and to what extent will AI transform cyber security? How and to what extent will it enhance the protection of individuals, organizations, and their cyber-dependent assets from hostile threat actors? How and to what extent will it introduce novel vulnerabilities and enable additional typologies of actions? How and to what extent will it impact on cyber offense and defense? How and to what extent will cyber security stakeholders be able to deal with AI-induced changing risks and opportunities? This chapter will shed light on the difficulty to answer these questions, especially if one looks for concrete responses that are

DOI: 10.4324/9781003110224-6

valid in the mid-/long term, but at the same time, it will take stock of the contemporary knowledge about when, how, and to what extent AI and cyber security are converging.

A first subsection defines artificial intelligence – then, the chapter introduces recent AI initiatives in the private sector and on the state level. A third subsection moves on to outline the uncertainties of the innovation process, the underlying difficulty to predict the future of AI in cyber security. However, some statements about the future of AI and cyber security are possible. In its subsequent sections, this chapter identifies several trends through the study of selected scientific and technical literature discussing the present – both embryonic and more mature – applications of AI-based solutions, which – from a technical point of view – promise to affect cyber security in the coming few years. The chapter acknowledges that the governance of AI innovation, in general, and with regard to cyber security, in particular, is still at its infancy and fragmented. The governance models that have been emerging so far will develop further under the pressure of the forces which are displayed by the actors mentioned earlier, and their mutual power relations. More initiatives are therefore to be expected; their effects will have to be assessed. At the moment, it seems that the impact of AI innovation on cyber security is still relatively more driven by the achieved, and yet to be achieved but possible, technological advancements than by emerging standards or regulations.

However, there are some early and promising applications of AI to cyber security which allow the making of an informed, although general, guess on what to expect in the near-term future. In particular, they allow to speculate on how the cyber security landscape might look like within the next 3–5 years. AI will enrich the cyber threat landscape – both in quantitative and qualitative terms. It will likely increase the number of cyber threat actors, offer them additional exploitable vulnerabilities and targets, as well as boost their malevolent actions. Conversely, AI will serve the defense from those threats by enabling the discovering of unknown vulnerabilities, the detection of malicious cyber activities, the implementation of countermeasures, and by augmenting the shortage of human professionals available to address imminent challenges.

Simply put, artificial intelligence will integrate and support cyber defensive and offensive activities, which may involve both the logical and the semantic layers of the cyberspace. Most of the features and functionalities which make artificial intelligence appropriate to cyber defense also make it suitable to offense. This is for example the case of the employment of AI to produce targeted cyber intelligence, which can be consumed for both protective and aggressive purposes. It is difficult to establish which application, defensive or offensive, will benefit relatively more from the integration of AI capabilities. It will depend on the capacity of single cyber security stakeholders (governmental or private) to master AI and leverage it for their intended purposes. It will also depend on their overall capacity to identify, understand, and address the risks, threats, and opportunities stemming from the integration of these technologies into cyber defensive or offensive systems.

Looking for a (working) definition of artificial intelligence

There is currently no consensus on what AI exactly is, and often definitions come with controversy. One may claim there is actually no need for any clear-cut, comprehensive, and crystallized definition, given that AI can be seen as a dynamic cluster of several technological concepts and approaches. Furthermore, progresses in this field will make any definition quickly obsolete. On top of that, focusing on notions and definitions might be less important than elaborating on the practical adoptions of AI, whatever this latter is exactly and regardless of any consensus about its core notion.

However, having at least a basic and shared understanding of artificial intelligence seems important because it can help relevant stakeholders to be consistent, transparent, and more effective when they promote programs, initiatives or take actions concerning AI at the policy, legal, operational, and other levels. For the purpose of the present chapter, such understanding is particularly functional to the analysis of the implications of AI research and applications for cyber security (and vice versa).

AI can be loosely defined as the ability, displayed by certain artificial/synthetic systems or "agents", to perform tasks that would require natural (human) intelligence (Coombs 2018; UNIDIR 2018; Russell and Norvig 2016) or, in particular, rationality (AI HLEG 2019).[1] Broadly, it is a field of studies devoted to making artificial systems/agents able to accomplish missions which are commonly thought to require a certain degree of understanding and reasoning (Russell and Norvig 2016).[2]

There are different approaches to provide these agents with intelligence or make them rational, one of which is machine learning (ML). This approach is variously characterized as either a sub-field of AI or a separate field, and refers to the development of systems that improve their performance on a given task over time through experience and learning.[3] The core components of machine learning solutions are learning algorithms, data, and powerful computational capabilities for training algorithms.[4] An advanced approach to machine learning employs deep neural networks, i.e. numerous layers of algorithms (model) – each providing a different interpretation to the data they are fed on (The MITRE Corporation 2017).[5] Such an approach is generally referred to as "deep learning".

It should be noted that to the extent to which an artificial system or agent learns on its own (independently from its designer's constant input) how to compensate for partial or incorrect prior knowledge, it is autonomous. As an attribute of intelligence/rationality, autonomy is the ability of an agent to determine and implement a course of action that is aimed to a certain goal, with no or less external guidance and oversight (Russell and Norvig 2010: 39). Regardless of the specific approach employed to make agents intelligent/rational and autonomous, all AI in existence today and that will be available in the near-term future fall under the broad category of *Narrow Artificial Intelligence* (UNIDR 2018). "Narrow" refers to the fact their intelligence/rationality is limited to a single task or domain of knowledge. Their autonomy is also reduced, meaning that human control is still prevalent. Different from nowadays available narrow AI are futuristic agents commonly labeled *Artificial General Intelligence (AGI)* (or "third wave AI", "transformative AI", "true AI"). "General" refers to the capacity to perform multiple tasks autonomously by employing a degree of intelligence/rationality equal if not superior to the one displayed by human beings.[6]

In the light of the above basic understanding and for the purpose of the present chapter, artificial intelligence can be defined as artificial systems/agents implementing machine and deep learning approaches to perform a given task. In particular, when here discussed with regard to cyber security and cyber-related applications, AI refers to technological solutions integrating machine/deep learning approaches and capabilities to:

> process (*more quickly and efficiently than humans as well as with limited human supervision*) large-constant flows of information and derive insight (*often hidden to humans*) which can inform a course of action relevant for cyber related purposes (*to protect or compromise hardware, software, data or users*).

The provided definition is flawed; it does not have any further ambition than serving the discussion in this chapter. Nevertheless, it integrates the basic properties of AI which have been identified by the relevant literature so far.

Recent AI initiatives

At the forefront of AI innovation there are multinational technology firms and other private corporations. Driven by profit, they keep on investing significant amount of resources (human, technological, organizational, and financial) in the development and commercialization of artificial intelligence. In their capacity of expertise, tools and services providers as well as through political lobbying, they contribute significantly to shape the AI and cyber security ecosystems.

As for governments, they have explicitly sustained AI advancements through multiple policy mechanisms at least since 2016. They have invested in AI infrastructures, encouraged academic education and professional training, funded scientific research, incentivized public-private partnerships and collaborations, as well as promoted standards through procurement or other policies. In consultation with the private sector and the broad civil society, they have in some cases sponsored the adoption of guiding principles or basic norms (*e.g.* fundamental rights, data privacy) to sustain "responsible" or "trustworthy" innovation in this technological field (European Commission 2019). In many countries – *e.g.* China, the United Kingdom, Canada, India, Japan, France – governments orient their actions toward the acquisition of AI capabilities according to wide-scope national AI strategies, most of which address cyber security as one promising field of application (Cussins Newman 2019: 34 ff; OECD.AI).[7] These strategies are then complemented by further policy instruments or other technical documentation tackling sectoral applications of AI.

In general, governmental policies and their implementing actions pursue the threefold objective of encouraging the uptake of AI, maximizing its benefits, and minimizing the associated risks. As far as cyber security is concerned, policies aspire to make AI capabilities available to relevant national cyber security stakeholders (mainly public and private organizations) and ensure they can resort to these capabilities to gain an advantage over their competitors. An advantage which can make the difference in terms of power relations, i.e. in the capacity of such stakeholders to safeguard their assets and promote their interests in or through the cyberspace.

The abovementioned set of initiatives suggests that governments and private corporations largely believe in the transformative capacity of AI and are aware of the importance of mastering it in the coming years. Furthermore, they show there is general consensus on, and expectations for, the role AI will play in shaping future practices of cyber security (and security in general). Many independent experts and academics do also consider AI a sort of game changer for cyber security or, less emphatically, agree on the impact these technologies will have on this domain. The difficulty to tackle the "When?, "How"?, and "To what extent"? questions lies in the inherent uncertainties of the innovation process.

Innovation and uncertainty

Innovation keeps on developing quite fast under the pressure of several forces that are displayed by multiple actors (public/private researchers, developers and providers; policy and regulatory authorities at the domestic or supranational level; security/military agencies; the broad civil society). Making predictions on the mid-/long-term outcomes of such processes is hard. In some ways, it seems to neglect the rapid progress AI research and applications have undergone in the last couple of years only.[8] Progress that will probably continue quite fast, boosted by growing public and commercial investments in the field (Fischer and Wenger 2019). In addition, AI is not the only technological component which promises to change cyber security. There are further technologies displaying a similar transformative capacity. AI will interact with these technologies in a way that can be hardly predicted from now. As a consequence, there are few chances to establish *a priori* the whole spectrum of possible interactions of AI with these technologies and foresee the overall impact on cyber security.

Furthermore, advances in AI should be understood as socio-technical phenomena that are more than the sum of technological capabilities and scientific/technical knowledge (Cussins Newman 2019: 6). Progress made in AI research and applications, and their implications for cyber security, are inevitably shaped by the models of governance which emerge from the formal/informal, fragmented/coordinated, and often unbalanced interactions among public authorities, private organizations, and the civil society. Progresses will be also influenced and driven by the above actors' assessment of the risks and opportunities stemming from the deployment of AI for cyber or other security purposes.

To note, risks and opportunities are not to be understood in narrow technological terms only, e.g. as strictly pertaining to the functioning of AI tools, their safety and efficiency. They are broader and involve further aspects of the communities which are affected by the employment of AI. At the higher level, they involve nations' economic integrity and well-being, social cohesion, diplomatic relations or political stability. The governance of such risks and opportunities will therefore reflect individual and collective assessments, visions, values, interests, and challenges. In sum, given the trajectory of AI innovation remains still uncertain and determined by the interaction of multiple players and forces, it is hard to predict how it will impact on cyber security, especially in the mid-/long term.

The security and cyber security relevance of artificial intelligence

However, a series of elements make artificial intelligence research and application relevant from a broad security perspective (Cussins Newman 2019: 11ff; Brundage et al. 2018: 16–18; 24–29). These are more or less the same elements that raise implications for cyber security. Like many other technologies, AI is "dual-use" meaning that it can be employed for both civil and military purposes, and to do good or harm. It can for example integrate weapon, surveillance, warning, or other types of systems which find military application (defense or offense). It can also upgrade the tools used by civilian security agencies for contrasting threats to public safety and order. Actually, the realm of potential military-security applications and further spillovers are wide and diverse. In principle, such applications can leverage a set of properties/features that are intrinsic to AI technologies or, at least, they aspire to display.

Indeed, these technologies are designed to be both "efficient" and "scalable", as well as "adaptable" to the environment in which they can operate. Efficiency entails that, once deployed, AI can in principle complete a task more quickly or cheaply than humans.[9] Scalability implies that, by increasing one of its underlying components (e.g. computing power), AI may become able to handle a growing amount of work, i.e. complete many more instances of a given task. AI technologies are also designed to be self-adaptable, meaning that they are prone to adjust their behavior/functioning according to changes in the environment they operate or the circumstances they are confronted with. The listed properties make AI appealing to different types of actors (state or non-state) because, among other things, they can be exploited for offensive, defensive, or other security-related goals.

Another element that makes AI relevant from a security standpoint concerns the fact that research and developments in this field lend themselves to rapid diffusion. Algorithms, datasets, processing capabilities – i.e. the basic components of AI – and, in general, relevant scientific findings are available to many research communities across the world. These communities are quite open in terms of knowledge transfer or capabilities sharing. Openness and availability support the so-called process of "democratization" or "commoditization" of artificial intelligence. This implies that there are many and geographically distributed stakeholders who can be empowered by advancements made in AI. Some of them might exploit these advancements for harmful purposes or, in general, to gain a competitive advantage in the security-military domain.

To the above listed elements, one should also add that AI comes with a number of novel, yet unresolved and often unknown vulnerabilities, which may have severe implications from a safety and security perspective. These vulnerabilities might be the cause of incidents or pave the way to both known and unknown malicious forms of exploitation (Patel et al. 2019). Experts are already aware of the risk AI-integrated systems can be subjected to, the so-called "data poisoning attacks" (introducing training data that causes a learning system to make mistakes) or "adversarial examples" (inputs designed to be misclassified by machine learning systems) (Gu et al. 2019). They are also aware there is a wide range of potential malicious exploitations that has still to be fully explored.[10]

What do the above elements – which make AI relevant for security – imply from a cyber-security point of view? To provide a simple answer, it is possible to frame the cyber security implications in terms of the possible threats and risks associated with the use/abuse of AI by cyber (threat) actors (Allen and Chan 2017). Of course, this is only one way to look at the issue. Another way would be to highlight the opportunities that AI may offer in terms of enhanced capacity to pursue cyber security-related goals as well as to cope with emerging threats. Indeed, depending on the adopted perspective, someone's security risks/threats are someone else's opportunities/advantages. Keeping this in mind but looking at the risk side, one may say that, absent the adoption of any substantial preventive measure, the availability and deployment of AI components could (i) expand existing cyber threats (quantity); (ii) alter the typical character of these threats (quality); (iii) introduce new and unknown threats (quantity and quality).

With regard to the first typology of implications, AI could expand the set of actors who are capable of carrying out malicious cyber activities, the rate at which these actors can carry the activities out, and the set of plausible targets/victims. This claim follows the efficiency, scalability, adaptability of AI technologies, as well as the "democratization" of research and development in this field. In particular, the diffusion of AI components among traditional cyber threat actors could increase the number of entities for whom become affordable carrying out particular attacks, especially those that are premised upon advanced social engineering, adversarial vulnerability detection, and spear-phishing.[11] Given that AI applications are also scalable, actors who already possess the resources to carry out the above attacks may gain the ability to do so at a higher rate. It may become worthwhile for them to attack targets who otherwise would not make sense to attack from the standpoint of prioritization or cost-benefit assessment.

From a qualitative point of view, AI-enabled/powered cyberattacks could also feature in more effective, finely targeted, and sophisticated actions than those possible without using AI components. As per the increased effectiveness, it derives from the attributes of efficiency, scalability, and adaptability of these solutions. More finely targeted attacks could be the consequence of the efficient and scalable employment of AI to identifying and scrutinizing potential targets.

Finally, artificial intelligence could enable a new variety of malicious activities and attacks, which exploit the vulnerabilities introduced by these technologies. In other words, the diffusion and integration of AI components in diverse types of cyber-related systems will introduce more hackable things into the virtual and physical world. In this latter regard, it is worth making an important observation. Large part of the public debate on artificial intelligence and cyber security concerns how AI research and applications do or will impact on cyber security, how they will affect the cyber threat landscape and increase risks and opportunities for cyber stakeholders (Loaiza et al. 2019). That is only one dimension of a much broader and articulated interaction between the two domains, however (IEEE and Syntegrity 2017).

Less discussed – except for experts' fora – is how cyber security itself is relevant to, and has a stake in, AI research and applications (I IEEE and Syntegrity 2017). Indeed, to the maximum possible extent, immunity from cyber threats should be an attribute of AI components. In order to preserve their proper functioning, reliability, and integrity, as well as avoid nefarious effects, AI tools should be safeguarded against cyber incidents or attacks. This implies that cyber security is a major and ongoing priority to the development and implementation of AI solutions (Spring et al. 2019: 11). Basically, it means that – when appropriate – relevant cyber security practices need to be applied. Reference is made to a set of actions and procedures aimed at promoting security (ideally "by design") from cyberattacks or incidents that leverage AI or other types of vulnerabilities (Brundage et al. 2018). For example, "red teaming" and "stress testing" should be carried out when AI solutions are at the research or development stage or piloted. Such testing aims at exploring what an actual cyberattack or induced incident might look like. It might help in discovering and fixing potential vulnerabilities.

Testing AI against cyberattacks might also be useful to better assess the skills and capabilities required to carry them out, to draw cyber threat scenarios, and check how defense should work in practice (US NSTC 2020). Another example of cyber security practice which can be beneficial to building secure/safe AI solutions consists in the responsible disclosure of systems' vulnerabilities, especially the so-called "0 days".[12] It consists in disclosing vulnerabilities to the affected parties before disseminating them widely. The goal is to provide these parties with the opportunity to remedy (patching). One could imagine the establishment of shared procedures for confidential reporting on vulnerabilities which are discovered in AI solutions (including potential adversarial inputs, and other types of exploits). Evidently, the adoption of the above or further cyber security practices, as well as the promotion of broad cyber hygiene programs with specific requirements for AI research, development, and application, represent a matter of governance.

To sum up, AI is relevant for cyber security (and vice versa). Depending on the adopted perspective, it may bring additional risks and threats, but also introduces further opportunities. To better understand the origins of such risks, threats, and opportunities, it is useful to look at the potential applications of AI to cyber security from a more practical point of view. This requires examining the notion of AI and framing it within the cyber security context.

Artificial intelligence and cyber security: An overview of defensive/offensive applications

Cyber security is a domain welcoming the deployment of AI-powered solutions by governmental authorities, private organizations, and other non-state actors (criminal organizations, hackers, politically motivated, or other groups), both for offensive or defensive purposes.[13] As mentioned earlier, most of the features and functionalities which make AI appropriate to cyber defense applications are the same that make it suitable to cyber offense (US NSTC 2020). In the near-term future, one should therefore expect organizations adopting and implementing AI-based cyber defense capabilities to safeguard their assets (networks, information, people) from adversaries who might leverage both AI- and non-AI tools for offensive purposes. Similarly, there will be actors employing AI-powered cyber offense capabilities to compromise targets who might engage in AI- or non-AI-integrated cyber defense.

From both the defense and offense sides, AI-based cyber capabilities may support activities involving the logical dimension of the cyber space (software) and/or its semantic dimension (information and data processed therein). As per the former dimension, AI components are expected to be employed either to protecting from or executing computer network operations (CNA, CNE). With regard to the latter, AI will likely support defense from or execution of so-called cyber information and influence operations (Cordey 2019).

AI-powered defense/offense within the logical layer of cyberspace

One promising application of AI concerns the production of targeted cyber intelligence to be consumed for defense or offense purposes, i.e. to enhance or compromise networks, information and users' security. As pointed out by the literature, these technologies are amenable to integrate several functions of the cyber intelligence process, in particular the "collection", "processing", and "analysis" of information (Bonfanti 2018; Galyardt et al. 2019). In particular, they can boost information gathering and widen its scope to multiple sources and several end points. They may also enhance processing operations, i.e. filtering and (probably) the technical validation of collected data. The former concerns the selection of significant items of information; the latter consists in their corroboration with additional data provided by other sources. AI can also support analysis by finding hidden patterns and correlations in the collected and processed data.

By integrating AI capabilities into the listed functions, the cyber intelligence process will probably advance in terms of automation and speed. To avoid misunderstandings, automation will not concern the whole course of actions that can be executed on the basis of the produced (finished) cyber intelligence. To the present date and for the next few years, it seems that no AI solution will be enough efficient and reliable in undergoing "fully" automatic (totally unsupervised) follow-up activities (Ridley 2018; Wirkuttis and Klein 2017). From a defense point of view, it is questionable that AI will support fully unsupervised technical response or remediation (such as automatic patching). It is even more unlikely that it will be in charge of more advanced and articulated forms of unsupervised response consisting in active cyber defense, hacking back, or other forms of automatic retaliation. The latter type of responses would be not only technically inefficient (given the attribution problem) but also undesirable given the political, legal, tactical/operational, or other consequences it may generate. Consequences that need to be carefully pre-assessed by human decision-makers (IEEE and Syntegrity 2017).

The eligibility of AI components to product cyber intelligence will translate into specific applications at the tactical/technical and – to a relatively lesser extent – operational level of cyber security. As per the latter, AI will be probably used for defensive purposes to retrieve and process data gathered from network security analysis programs and correlate them against all known structured and unstructured information available in articles, threat feeds, books, blog posts, and other sources that provide cyber intelligence (Coombs 2018: 35 ff.). With regard to tactical/technical defense, AI will increasingly support cyber threats detection, analysis and, to a limited extent, prevention (Wirkuttis and Klein 2017; Apruzzese et al. 2018).[14] It will integrate and enhance tools for anomaly/intrusion (network-based attacks), phishing, and spam (emails) detection, threat characterization (malicious code), and users behavioral modeling. Another emerging/promising target for tactical defensive application of AI is automated vulnerability testing (Loaiza et al. 2019).

In particular, following a trend which has already started, AI components will upgrade Intrusion Detection Systems (IDS) that are aimed to discover illicit activities within a computer or a network (Buczak and Guven 2016; Apruzzese et al. 2018);[15] spam and phishing detection systems aimed at reducing the waste of time and potential hazard caused by unwanted emails; and, finally, malware detection and analysis tools. As per the latter, AI will probably improve the discovery of modern and emerging malwares, which can automatically generate novel variants to elude traditional rule-based identification approaches. It will help in attributing these variants to the correct malware family thanks to its capacity to recognize some hidden patterns which are invisible to traditional or human-based analysis. AI components will also integrate multifactor authentication or verification systems. In particular, they will be used to detect a pattern of behavior for a particular user in order to identify changes in those patterns. Although promising, the described applications for anomaly and threat detection/analysis are tainted with both false negatives (Zetter 2019) and positives (Xin et al. 2018). As per the former, pilot testing or early deployment show they are still, and keep on being, a main problem. Even a false positive rate of 0.1% could account for hundreds of false alarms which are unbearable for many organizations (Apruzzese et al. 2018).

AI applications will also be used for cyber offensive purposes i.e. to compromise a target organization/user, its networks, and the data therein processed. They will enable more numerous and sophisticated cyberattacks (Brundage et al. 2018). As in the case of defense, AI approaches/components may generate cyber intelligence to prepare and implement attacks. They may improve the selection and prioritization of targets for cyberattacks involving social engineering. Thank to AI, potential victims' online information can be harvested and processed to automatically generate custom malicious websites/emails/links (based on profiling) (Brundage et al. 2018). As AI develops further, convincing chat bots may elicit human trust by engaging people in longer dialogues, and perhaps eventually masquerade visually as another person in a video/audio chat (see also below).

AI components will also enhance adversarial vulnerability discovery and exploitation. They will prompt sophistication in malware designing and functioning, as well as support their obfuscation. AI-powered malware can be able to evade detection and creatively respond to changes in the target's behavior. They will function as an autonomous and adaptive implant – which learns from the host it runs on in order to remain undetected, search for and classify interesting content for exfiltration, search for and infect new targets, and discovers new pathways or methods for lateral movement. Already in 2018, IBM researchers have developed a malware of this type they dubbed "DeepLocker" (Stoecklin 2018).[16] Finally, AI will also be deployed to spoof authentication or verification systems (e.g. those integrating biometric identifiers) (Patel et al. 2019).

AI-powered defense/offense within the semantic layer of cyberspace

From an offensive point of view, artificial intelligence will likely enhance the planning and running of cyber information and influence operations, which are aimed at criminal or other illegitimate goals. By supporting automation, AI will boost digital information/intelligence gathering as well as surveillance of targets/victims' online behavior (Bonfanti 2019). It will add on the set of tools to be employed to inform and influence adversaries through and within the cyberspace (Patel et al. 2019: 22 ff.), especially by leveraging social media platforms. As per the latter, AI can improve bots and social bots management and allow the production of messages to be targeted at those most susceptible to them (similar to behavioral advertisement) (Brundage et al. 2018).

Following an on-going trend, AI-based solutions – especially those integrating deep learning approaches – will be employed to create manipulated digital content to be propagated within online or other media. Such content – known as "synthetic media" or "deepfakes" – consists of hyper-realistic video, audio, imagery or text which cannot be easily exposed as fake through manual or other conventional forensic techniques (Collins 2019).[17] Once generated, synthetic media may be abused, i.e. employed to cause harm to individuals, organizations, and the broad civil society. Harmful employment is already abundant and documented by the media. Mostly, it consists in the deployment of AI-doctored videos (generally of pornographic nature) for targeted cyber bullying/stalking and defamation via/on online media (Chesney and Citron 2018). Less frequent – but probably on the rise in the near-term future – is the weaponization of synthetic media for cyber-enabled blackmailing, scamming, corporate sabotage (via market or other types of manipulative operations), political propaganda, and warfare (Ajder et al. 2019).[18] In these cases, synthetic media will play as add-ons to "individual/organization-oriented" or "communities-oriented" information operations (Bonfanti 2020).[19]

On the one hand, AI will integrate and enable the above activities, and on the other, it will contribute to counter them. Indeed, from a defensive point of view, AI can support the detection of, and response to, cyber influence and information operations. It can be deployed to monitor the online environment (e.g. social media platforms), identify the early signs of malicious operations (e.g. increasing bots or social bots activities) as well as discover altered digital content (e.g. synthetic media) (Knight 2019; Collins 2019).

Conclusions

In light of what has been presented so far, AI will affect cyber security in the coming years. In the short term, it will probably do so along the lines drawn above. It will support both cyber defense and offense. It is difficult to establish which application will benefit more: It will probably depend on the ability of cyber security stakeholders (governmental or private) to sustain, master, and make progresses in artificial intelligence research, development, and applications, as well as leverage AI for achieving specific goals. From a broader perspective, it will also depend on their capacity to identify, understand, and address the risks, threats, and opportunities stemming from the deployment of these technologies for cyber defense or offense.

With regard to governmental cyber security stakeholders, addressing the above risks and opportunities would in principle require them to establish adequate/effective/consistent governance frameworks for AI and cyber security. To the extent possible, frameworks should also be multidimensional and participated/inclusive. It means they should cover a wide array of aspects, ranging from the technological to the policy, regulatory, economic, and diplomatic ones. They could for example integrate standards for validation and certification of AI tools for cyber security, which may include the implementation/adaptation of already existing security/safety best practices to identify and cope with AI vulnerabilities. They could also consist in specific norms and institutions to shape the openness (democratization) of AI research and put additional limits to knowledge/capabilities transfer in this technological domain.

If possible, governance frameworks should be inclusive too. They should be established with the proactive and (possibly) balanced collaboration of relevant domestic or international actors, i.e. representatives and domain experts from different sectors (public, private, the civil society) and disciplines (engineering, computer and data science, human and social science, etc.); they should involve and assign responsibilities to these actors with regard to the factual implementation of the envisaged model of governance.

To a variable extent, the governance frameworks that are emerging nowadays seem – at least in the intentions of their promoters/contributors – aimed at being both multidimensional and inclusive. It has still to be seen whether they will be adequate, effective, and consistent enough to tackle the risks, threats, and opportunities the employment of AI for cyber security raises. Yet little evidence is available to inform such an assessment. As already noted, AI and cyber security governance is still at its infancy. More actions are to be expected; their outcome is uncertain.

Notes

1 The term "agent" has been used with several nuances in AI and related fields (Davis 1999). According to Russell and Norvig (2010: 34 ff.), "An agent is anything that can be viewed as perceiving its environment through sensors and acting upon that environment through actuators". The adjective "artificial" is here used to mark their difference with "human" agents.

2 As a field of study, AI dates back to the 1950s when researchers started creating machines able to accomplish simple and then increasingly difficult tasks in autonomous ways, i.e. with less or no human supervision and control. Since the 1950s AI research has constantly progressed and found applications in different fields. Nowadays, AI is a critical component of widely used devices as automatic speech recognition, machine translation, spam filters, and search engines. Additional promising applications include driverless vehicles, digital assistants for medical diagnosis and treatment, and robotics. One effect of this continuous progress in AI research and applications is that only the most cutting-edge machines are usually labeled "intelligent". In other words, the standard for machines being considered "intelligent" is constantly evolving.

3 Not all AI systems use machine learning. However, for many applications, machine learning can be a powerful method for achieving intelligent behavior.

4 Machine learning can rely on different approaches, the most common are supervised, unsupervised, and reinforced.

5 Neural networks are supposed to work in a fashion similar to the human brain.

6 According to some great futurist minds there will be a point in time they call the singularity, when an artificial agent becomes smarter than humans in nearly every field (Coombs 2018).

7 At the supranational level, intergovernmental organizations like the European Union (EU) or the Organisation for Economic Co-operation and Development (OECD) are also favoring states' cooperation on AI. As far as the EU is concerned, in 2018 it has adopted the European Strategy on AI to address the opportunities and challenges deriving from the development and deployment of AI in different areas.

8 From a technical point of view only, there have been unimaginable improvements in the AI core infrastructures and components, i.e. computing power, algorithms design, standard software frameworks for faster replication of experiments, and the availability of large datasets.

9 This is not to say it is always the best deployable solution; other convenient approaches might better suit for the designated purpose.

10 According to Brundage et al. (2018: 17), there is another feature which makes AI relevant from a security perspective. By supporting automation and less degree of human control and supervision, AI solutions can allow a greater degree of distance of their users from the task to be performed; distance also from the effects/consequences it may have (harm it might cause).

11 Spear-phishing is more effective than regular phishing, which does not involve tailoring messages to individuals, but it is relatively expensive and cannot be carried out en masse. Generic phishing attacks are more profitable than spear-phishing despite their very low success rates but merely by virtue of their scale. Thanks to AI, attackers could conduct more effective spear-phishing attacks with greater frequency and at a larger scale.

12 In the cyber security community, "0-days" are software vulnerabilities that have not been made publicly known (and thus defenders have zero days to prepare for an attack making use of them).

13 As argued by Allen and Chan (2017: 20), "There is no obvious, stable outcome in terms of state vs. non-state power or offense vs. defense cyber advantage. It will depend on the balance of research and development investments by all actors, the pace of technological process, and underlying limitations in economics and technology".

14 At the tactical/technical level, cyber intelligence improves the effectiveness of blocking technologies, helps infrastructure groups prioritize their patching activities, and allows security operations center (SOC) analysts to quickly and accurately decide which alerts require action. Operational cyber intelligence can accelerate incident response by providing rich context (e.g. attackers' modus operandi, tactics, techniques, procedures, capabilities) around an initial indicator.

15 These systems were traditionally based on patterns of known attacks, but modern deployments include approaches for anomaly and threat detection based on machine learning. These approaches can be used for the detection of *botnets* and of *Domain Generation Algorithms* (DGA). As per these latter, they are algorithms which generate domain names automatically, and are often used by an infected machine to communicate with external server(s) by periodically generating new hostnames. They represent a real threat to organizations because they allow to evade defenses based on static blacklists of domain names.

16 This AI-powered malware conceals its intent until it reaches a specific victim. It carries out its malicious action as soon as the AI component identifies the target through indicators like facial recognition, geolocation, and voice recognition. It is virtually impossible to exhaustively enumerate all possible trigger conditions for the AI model. What is unique about DeepLocker is that it uses AI (deep neural network) to unlock the attack. The malicious payload will only be unlocked if the intended target is reached. The AI model is trained to behave normally unless it is presented with a specific input: The trigger conditions identifying specific victims.

17 "Deepfakes" is a neologism (resulting from the merge of "deep learning" and "fake"). They can be generated with a variety of machine/deep learning techniques and approaches. Currently, the most popular is the Generative Adversarial Network (GAN).

18 In 2018–2019, there were already some cases of cybercriminals using AI-generated audio to impersonate a CEO's voice and convince subordinates into transferring funds to a scammer's account (the so-called "CEO-scam").

19 Both types of operations are intertwined and may be executed in combination; they can overlap. The former type of operations points to affect institutional or formal decision-making processes within selected organizations through deception and/or extortion/coercion. The latter target the society as a whole or specific social groups, in particular those groups' ideas, opinions, motivations, and beliefs, and aim at mobilizing them.

References

All links checked on August 20, 2021.

AI HLEG (High-Level Expert Group on Artificial Intelligence) (2019). A Definition of AI: Main Capabilities and Scientific Disciplines. Retrieved from: https://ec.europa.eu/digital-single-market/en/news/ethics-guidelines-trustworthy-ai.

Ajder, H., Cavalli, F., Patrini, G. and Cullen, L. (2019). The State of Deepfakes: Landscape, Threats, and Impact. Retrieved from: https://regmedia.co.uk/2019/10/08/deepfake_report.pdf.

Allen, G. and Chan, T. (2017). *Artificial Intelligence and National Security*. Cambridge, MA: Belfer Center for Science and International Affairs. Retrieved from: https://www.belfercenter.org/sites/default/files/files/publication/AI%20NatSec%20-%20final.pdf.

Apruzzese, G., Ferretti, L., Marchetti, M., Colajanni, M. and Guido, A. (2018). On the Effectiveness of Machine and Deep Learning for Cyber Security. In: T. Minárik, R. Jakschis, and L. Lindström (eds). *10th International Conference on Cyber Conflict CyCon: Maximising Effects*. Tallinn: NATO CCD COE Publications, pp. 371–390.

Bonfanti, M. E. (2018). Cyber Intelligence: In Pursuit of a Better Understanding for an Emerging Practice. *Cyber, Intelligence, and Security*, 2(1): 105–121.

Bonfanti, M. E. (2019). An Intelligence-Based Approach to Countering Social Media Influence Operations. *Romanian Intelligence Studies Review*, 19: 47–67.

Bonfanti, M. E. (2020). *L'impiego offensivo di contenuti digitali "algoritmicamente" manipolati: scenari di minaccia e contromisure*. Gori, U. Information Warfare 2019. Milano: Franco Angeli.

Brundage, M., Avin, S. and Clark, J. (2018). The Malicious Use of Artificial Intelligence: Forecasting, Prevention, and Mitigation. Retrieved from: https://maliciousaireport.com/.

Buczak, A. L. and Guven, E. (2016). A Survey of Data Mining and Machine Learning Methods for Cyber Security Intrusion Detection. *IEEE Communications Surveys Tutorials*, 18 (2): 1153–76.

Chesney, R. and Citron, D. K. (2018). Deep Fakes: A Looming Challenge for Privacy, Democracy, and National Security. *SSRN Electronic Journal*. Retrieved from: https://papers.ssrn.com/sol3/papers.cfm?abstract_id=3213954.

Collins, A. (2019). *Forged Authenticity: Governing Deepfake Risks*. Lausanne: EPFL International Risk Governance Center.

Coombs, T. (2018). *Artificial Intelligence and Cyber Security for Dummies*. Hoboken, NJ: John Wiley and Sons.

Cordey, S. (2019). *Cyber Influence Operations: An Overview and Comparative Analysis*. CSS Risk and Resilience Reports. Zurich: Center for Security Studies (CSS).

Cussins Newman, J. (2019). Toward AI Security. Global Aspirations for a More Resilient Future. *Center for Long-Term Cyber security (CLTC) White Paper Series*. Retrieved from: https://cltc.berkeley.edu/wp-content/uploads/2019/02/CLTC_Cussins_Toward_AI_Security.pdf.

Davis, D. N. (1999). Synthetic Agents: Synthetic Minds? In *SMC'98 Conference Proceedings. 1998 IEEE International Conference on Systems, Man, and Cybernetics*, 11–14 October, 1998, 2658–2663.

European Commission (2019). Communication "Building Trust in Human-Centric Artificial Intelligence". Retrieved from: https://ec.europa.eu/digital-single-market/en/artificial-intelligence.

Fischer, S.-C. and Wenger, A. (2019). A Politically Neutral Hub for Basic AI Research. *CSS Policy Perspective*, 7(2). Zurich: Center for Security Studies (CSS).

Galyardt, A., Gupta, R., DeCapria, D., Kanal, E. and Ettinger, J. (2019). Artificial Intelligence and Cyber Intelligence: An Implementation Guide. Carnegie Mellon University. Retrieved from: https://resources.sei.cmu.edu/asset_files/EducationalMaterial/2019_011_001_548767.pdf.

Gu, T., Dolan-Gavitt, B. and Garg, S. (2019). BadNets: Identifying Vulnerabilities in the Machine Learning Model Supply Chain. Retrieved from: https://arxiv.org/pdf/1708.06733.pdf.

IEEE Industry Engagement Committee and Syntegrity (2017). Artificial Intelligence and Machine Learning Applied to Cyber Security. Retrieved from: https://www.ieee.org/about/industry/confluence/feedback.html.

Knight, W. (2019). Even the AI Behind Deepfakes Can't Save Us from Being Duped. *Wired*. Retrieved from: https://www.wired.com/story/ai-deepfakes-cant-save-us-duped/.

Loaiza, F. L., Birdwell, J. D., Kennedy, G. L. and Visser, D. (2019). *Utility of Artificial Intelligence and Machine Learning in Cyber security*. Virginia: Institute for Defense Analyses.

OECD AI Policy Observatory (2020). National AI Policies and Strategies. Retrieved from: https://oecd.ai/policy-areas.

Osterman Research (2018). *The State of AI in Cyber Security: The Benefits, Limitations and Evolving Questions*. White Paper. Retrieved from: https://info.protectwise.com/osterman-state-of-ai-in-security.

Patel, A., Hatzakis, T., Macnish, K., Ryan, M. and Kirichenko, A. (2019). Security Issues, Dangers and Implications of Smart Information Systems. *Sherpa Project* D1.3. Retrieved from: https://dmu.figshare.com/articles/D1_3_Cyberthreats_and_countermeasures/7951292.

Ridley, A. (2018). Machine Learning for Autonomous Cyber-Defence. *The Next Wave*, 22(1): 8–14.

Russell, S. J. and Norvig, P. (2010). *Artificial Intelligence: A Modern Approach* (3rd ed.). Harlow: Pearson Education Limited.

Spring, J. M., Fallon, J., Galyardt, A., Horneman, A., Metcalf, L. and Stoner, E. (2019). Machine Learning in Cyber Security: A Guide. SEI Carnegie Mellon Technical Report CMU/SEI-2019-TR-005. Retrieved from: https://resources.sei.cmu.edu/asset_files/TechnicalReport/2019_005_001_633597.pdf.

Stoecklin, M. P. (2018). DeepLocker: How AI Can Power a Stealthy New Breed of Malware. Retrieved from: https://securityintelligence.com/deeplocker-how-ai-can-power-a-stealthy-new-breed-of-malware/.

The MITRE Corporation (2017). *Perspectives on Research in Artificial Intelligence and Artificial General Intelligence Relevant to DoD. JSR-16-Task-003*. McLean: The MITRE Corporation. Retrieved from: https://fas.org/irp/agency/dod/jason/ai-dod.pdf.

UNIDIR (2018). The Weaponization of Increasingly Autonomous Technologies: Artificial Intelligence. Retrieved from: https://www.unidir.org/publication/weaponization-increasingly-autonomous-technologies-artificial-intelligence.

US NSTC (National Science and Technology Council) (2020, March). *Artificial Intelligence and Cyber Security: Opportunities and Challenges*. Technical Workshop Summary Report. Retrieved from: https://www.nitrd.gov/pubs/AI-CS-Tech-Summary-2020.pdf.

Wirkuttis, N. and Klein, H. (2017). Artificial Intelligence in Cyber security. *Cyber, Intelligence, and Security*, 1(1): 104–119.

Xin, Y., Kong, L., Liu, Z. and Chen, Y. (2018). Machine Learning and Deep Learning Methods for Cyber Security. *IEEE Access*, 6: 35365–81.

Zetter, K. (2019). Researchers Easily Trick Cylance's AI-Based Antivirus into Thinking Malware Is 'Goodware'. *Motherboard, Tech by Vice*. Retrieved from: https://www.vice.com/en_us/article/9kxp83/researchers-easily-trick-cylances-ai-based-antivirus-into-thinking-malware-is-goodware.

6 Quantum computing and classical politics

The ambiguity of advantage in signals intelligence

Jon R. Lindsay

The discovery of quantum mechanics in the early 20th century transformed our understanding of subatomic reality. A "second quantum revolution" (Dowling and Milburn 2003) in the 21st century is poised to transform our ability to manipulate subatomic reality to process information. It is possible to perform calculations with quantum bits (qubits) that are practically infeasible with classical (digital) bits. Potential applications of quantum computing may improve remote sensing, data processing, and secure networking, all of which might affect global security (Biercuk and Fontaine 2017; National Academies of Sciences, Engineering, and Medicine 2019). These give rise to excited claims about how the "impact of quantum on our national defense will be tremendous" (Hurd 2017) or that "whoever gets this technology first will also be able to cripple traditional defenses and power grids and manipulate the global economy" (Nikias 2018). China's early progress in quantum communication technology has further energized the global race to gain a quantum advantage (Owen and Gorwa 2016; Kania 2018).

How will the second quantum revolution affect global cyber security in particular? A stylized debate has unfolded in the field of international relations (IR) about the relationship between information and communication technology (ICT) and conflict dynamics. One side argues that the nature of cyberspace is strategically destabilizing because it empowers the offense, weakens the defense, or undermines deterrence (Rattray 2001; Lynn III 2010; Kello 2013; Deibert 2013; Buchanan 2017; Schneider 2019). The other side argues that the sociopolitical context of cyber security mitigates the potency of offensive cyber operations and reinforces established power relations (Libicki 2007; Rid 2012; Liff 2012; Gartzke 2013; Lindsay 2014; Valeriano and Maness 2015; Slayton 2017; Kreps and Schneider 2019). In between these extremes scholars highlight variable conditions that influence the difficulty of attribution, offensive advantage, or strategic stability (Rid and Buchanan 2015; Lindsay 2015; Brantly 2016; Smeets 2017; Borghard and Lonergan 2017). Others highlight problems of threat inflation and motivated bias that distort the rhetoric of cyber war (Dunn Cavelty 2008; Lawson 2013).

Because ICT is so vital for everything in the modern world, it is reasonable to expect a new generation of ICT – from bit to qubit – to be particularly consequential. If we believe that technology determines politics, then we might expect

DOI: 10.4324/9781003110224-7

a fundamental change in the underlying infrastructure of cyberspace to have dramatic consequences. If, however, we believe that politics tends to determine technology, then the consequences of the quantum information revolution might not be so profound after all. A more reciprocal or endogenous interaction between them, moreover, could have even more ambiguous implications.

This chapter puts quantum information technology into political context. I focus on the applications for code making (cryptography) and code breaking (cryptanalysis) because they are particularly dramatic. I start with a brief summary of quantum threat narratives. I then explain why all cryptologic phenomena are fundamentally political, no matter the vintage of technology that implements them. Secret communication necessarily depends on cooperation between communicators seeking to exclude another group of competitors. Yet secret eavesdropping also depends on cooperation, since the interloper must adopt the same communicative protocols to gain and maintain covert access. In any practical context, moreover, both sides of the cryptologic contest must deal with organizational and strategic challenges that can either bolster or degrade the security of technical cryptosystems. Scientific innovation in quantum technology will not change, and in many ways will exacerbate, the social interactions that make cryptology a complex and ambiguous practice. I conclude with a few brief remarks on how social scientists can recover quantum technology from the technologists.

Quantum threat narratives

Quantum computing leverages "spooky" quantum phenomena like superposition (the ability for a qubit to be in two states at once), entanglement (the ability for multiple qubits to influence each other from a distance), and indeterminacy (the tendency for measurement to affect the state of reality). Richard Feynman first suggested the idea several decades ago as a promising way to model physical chemistry (Feynman 1982). Experimental progress was slow to catch up, but that is changing quickly. In September 2019, a working quantum computer designed by Google and known as Sycamore achieved a major performance milestone known as "quantum supremacy". Sycamore entangled 53 qubits and ran a quantum algorithm in mere minutes that would take the world's fastest supercomputer thousands of years to complete (Arute et al. 2019).[1]

Quantum computing has important implications for cryptography, which is vital for cyber security, which in turn has become a pressing concern for governments, commercial firms, and civil society around the world. Today, nearly all secure digital communication relies on a small number of cryptographic protocols such as RSA (Rivest–Shamir–Adleman). RSA is the standard used for most implementations of public key infrastructure (PKI), which links real people and organizations to the cryptographic keys they use for secure communications and digital signatures. The categorical compromise of PKI, which would enable a hacker to break encryption, steal data, forge signatures, and install arbitrary code, would be a disaster for global trade, national security, and civil society

(Mulholland, Mosca, and Braun 2017). The security of PKI today is predicated on the computational difficulty of solving (but easily verifying) certain mathematical problems such as factoring large prime numbers. A typical digital computer would need six quadrillion years to crack 2048-bit RSA (DigiCert 2018), but a working quantum computer with 20 million qubits might be able to perform the same feat in eight hours (Gidney and Ekera 2019).

There are major engineering challenges to overcome before it is possible to build such a machine. Quantum error correction is particularly daunting, so a working large-scale universal quantum computer may be decades away. Nevertheless, the cryptanalytic threat posed by quantum computing is plausible enough that the cryptographic community has already moved to develop "quantum safe", "quantum-resistant", or "post-quantum" protocols (Lindsay 2020b). These are mathematical functions that are difficult for both classical and quantum computers, which only provide performance gains if a suitable quantum algorithm can be found. There are several promising classical protocols that are already under review by technical standards setting agencies like the US National Institute of Standards and Technology (Chen et al. 2016; Bernstein et al. 2017). These will almost certainly be available before a working machine powerful enough to break RSA is fielded, but transitioning to the new protocols in practice will be a long and bumpy journey for industry and government (Buchmann, Lauter, and Mosca 2017).

While quantum computing poses an offensive (cryptanalytic) threat to asymmetric encryption, quantum mechanics can also be harnessed to improve defense (cryptography). Quantum encryption protocols are guaranteed secure by the laws of physics rather than just the computational difficulty of particular mathematical problems (Lo and Lütkenhaus 2007; Brassard 2016). There are many other potential applications of quantum communications, all with formidable engineering challenges, to include radically different memory devices and internet architectures (Simon 2017; Wehner, Elkouss, and Hanson 2018). Yet there are also promising signs of progress in this area. China has already built a prototype quantum communication network between Beijing and Shanghai and conducted experiments in quantum entanglement with a satellite link (Kania and Costello 2018).

Progress in communications security seems like a good development, and in general it is. Yet the potential of unbreakable security also gives rise to a different sort of threat narrative. If quantum cryptanalysis augurs the end of confidentiality or, more breathlessly, the "cryptocalypse", then quantum cryptography raises a reciprocal fear that intelligence agencies will be locked out or "go dark". Western governments unable to penetrate the communications of terrorist or state adversaries could be denied warning of surprise attack. Police agencies, similarly, could lose access to forensic data in criminal investigations. All of these concerns feed fears that China, an emerging leader in quantum technology, may become the first to gain a destabilizing cryptologic advantage over the United States and others (Owen and Gorwa 2016; Kenny 2017; Kania and Costello 2018).

It is important to recognize that quantum communications and quantum computing are two different categories of technology. China is making impressive progress in the former but not the latter, where by contrast North America and Europe maintain a strong lead. For the purposes of this chapter, these two technologies have applications on opposite ends of the cryptologic contest between cryptography and cryptanalysis, respectively. I will now set aside the technical mysteries of quantum computing and explore the political context in which any quantum technologies will be employed.

The political essence of cryptology

Quantum mechanics describes the nature of reality at the microscale, but the people who will use quantum computers live at the macroscale. Indeed, political context is so important for information technology that it almost ceases to be context at all. In particular there are political problems lurking at the very heart all cryptography, quantum or otherwise.

As David Kahn points out in his magisterial history, "Cryptology is, by definition, a social activity" (Kahn 1996: 752). Yet it is a paradoxical social activity that combines communication, which enables all manner of political economic interaction, with secrecy, which impedes communication and defines social barriers. According to Kahn, "secrecy is the antithesis of communication, and communication – as that which makes man a social being – encompasses all aspects of cultural behavior. Cryptography combines these antitheses into a single operation; a wag might define it as 'noncommunicating communication'" (Kahn 1996: 753). This stark contradiction is the source of most of the complexities and conundrums in intelligence practice.

Formal theories of communication and cryptography share the same mathematical foundations. It is no coincidence that the author of a seminal paper on information theory (Shannon 1948) also wrote a classified paper for Bell Labs three years earlier on cryptography (Shannon 1945), using nearly identical concepts. Communication and cryptology deal with the same abstract problems of signal and noise. Communicators try to get their signal transmitted through the noise, while cryptographers try to disguise their signals as noise. The goal of the cryptanalyst, on the other hand, is to recover the signal through the noise that the cryptographer creates. Seen from this perspective, cryptanalysts are communicators too. The same communicative protocols used by two notional conspirators, Alice and Bob, can be exploited by Eve the eavesdropper to read their correspondence or inject disinformation. Yet Eve must take pains to keep her cryptanalytic coup hidden to avoid alerting Alice or Bob, who would then take action to lock her out. To paraphrase Kahn, a wag might define cryptanalysis as "communicating noncommunication".

The rival twins of cryptology – cryptography and cryptanalysis – embody a fundamental political paradox. The cryptologic competitors must respect the constraints of a cooperatively produced cryptosystem. They must cooperate to compete. Indeed, this is a general political feature of intelligence and cyber operations, which rely on stealth and duplicity to penetrate and exploit the cultural norms and sociotechnical institutions that enable cooperation within the target organization

(Gartzke and Lindsay 2015). Alice and Bob must be simultaneously concerned with managing the internal interactions within their common group as well as foiling external interactions with rival groups (Eve and her co-conspirators). This makes cryptology a two-level game (Putnam 1988), much as national leaders are simultaneously paying attention to foreign and domestic rivals, but on a smaller scale with tight constraints on communicative interaction.

To communicate in secret, Alice and Bob must agree in advance to use a cryptosystem – practices and technologies that enable them to pass meaningful signals to each other that will look like meaningless noise to Eve. There are three general strategies. First, Alice and Bob might agree to conceal the existence of the messages. This works only if Eve doesn't know where to look or is physically prevented from access. For example, steganography hides text within an image, spies leave messages in hidden dead drops, and "air gaps" isolate computers from the public internet to preclude digital access. Yet Alice and Bob will not be able to hide all messages, especially if they are broadcast over open radio or computer networks. Second, Alice and Bob might agree on a method to disguise the meaning. Alice and Bob can encode messages by substituting letters and phrases according to some prepared translation scheme like a codebook, but all the effort is lost if the codebook falls into Eve's hands. A foreign language can be an effective code (e.g., the Navajo Code Talkers used by the United States in World War II), so long as the enemy has no native speakers or talented linguists. Finally, Alice and Bob can encipher the message using mathematical algorithms or computing machines that systematically scramble the message. This has the advantage that Alice and Bob can communicate anything secretly even if Eve knows what cryptosystem they are using, so long as Alice and Bob keep their cipher key(s) secret. As Shannon points out, "one must expect his system to be found out eventually through espionage, captured equipment, prisoners, etc." (Shannon 1945: 25). Modern digital encryption both encodes text and images into ones and zeros and enciphers the coded data via cryptographic algorithms (Kahn 1996: xv–xviii; Singh 1999).

If Eve can steal or discover Alice and Bob's key(s), then she can participate in their shared communicative institution, but she must do so surreptitiously. If apparent noise or pseudo-randomness is the cryptographer's friend, then non-randomness or redundancy is the cryptanalyst's friend. Indeed, redundancy is any communicator's friend since redundancy enables error correction (Shannon 1951), no matter whether the errors are the result of technical noise or cryptographic obfuscation. To recover the signal from the noise created by Alice and Bob, Eve can study the traffic patterns of their encrypted communications to learn something about the enemy organization (Thirsk 2001). She can perform a brute force attack and try every possible key combination. She can perform frequency analysis across a large volume of intercepted cipher-text to find patterns that narrow the search for keys. She can look for redundant enemy communications or cribs that correlate enciphered messages with known or suspected bits of plaintext (e.g., a morning weather broadcast, a mayday call from a sinking ship, or a lazy operator reusing old keys). She can monitor side-channels in the technical infrastructure of the cryptosystem. For example, a pseudorandom number-generating algorithm may give off detectable signals as computing hardware. The common theme is the discovery of a subtle signal in the subterfuge of noise.

Perfect secrecy is possible if a perfectly random key the same length as the message is used only once for each message (Shannon 1945). Unfortunately, there are practical challenges in generating and distributing a so-called one-time pad, as the Soviet KGB and others found to their detriment (Warner and Benson 1997). Quantum key distribution, interestingly, makes one-time pads practically feasible. Most practical classical cryptosystems, by contrast, use short keys that can be easily stored or remembered, using efficient encryption and decryption processes that can work in arduous field conditions. Because such practical systems cannot produce truly randomized messages, they aim to "maximize the minimum amount of work the enemy must do to break it", as Shannon points out; unfortunately, "in the history of cryptography there have been many ciphers which were at first thought unbreakable but later disclosed weaknesses of their own" (Shannon 1945: 87). The advent of quantum networks appears to be just such a moment, heralding new and unbreakable encryption.

Cryptology as an organizational contest

The logic of cryptology as cooperative competition, or communicating noncommunication, is fundamentally political. The implementation of cryptology piles on additional social factors. Kahn observes that "cryptography and cryptanalysis are sometimes called twin or reciprocal sciences, and in function they indeed mirror one another. What one does the other undoes. Their natures, however, differ fundamentally. Cryptography is theoretical and abstract. Cryptanalysis is empirical and concrete" (Kahn 1996: 737). This has important organizational implications. Alice and Bob and Eve all have to build reliable institutional platforms from which to carry out their complementary yet agonistic activities.

Eve must be both methodical and inventive to break in and collect data. She must collect and analyze her targets' communications, develop programs or build computers that can decrypt them, and find needles of relevant intelligence in haystacks of useless chatter. These usually pose difficult collective problems that require some degree of resourcing and bureaucratic process to accomplish. It generally takes a long time for Eve to prepare her attack, but only a short time for Alice and Bob to lock her out if she is discovered. All of Eve's effort may be undone if Alice and Bob discover that they have been compromised. For this reason, cryptanalytic organizations must also rely on cryptography to cover the internal communications and coordination that makes their exploitation possible – offense plays defense. Figuratively speaking, Eve must encrypt her decryption. Eve must carefully consider the "intelligence gain-loss" trade-offs between acting on intelligence, which may reveal the source to the target, and not acting, so as to keep on collecting in the future. To mitigate this tradeoff, Eve may try to disguise or "sanitize" the source of intelligence, for instance distributing a sensitive signal intercept as if it were a tip from a human agent.

Cryptanalysis increasingly relies on computers. Machines can efficiently search through the pseudo-noise created by Alice and Bob by calculating faster, and with larger memories, than humans working alone. As Kahn points out, "World War II mechanized cryptography and mathematized cryptanalysis" (Kahn 1996: 612). Bletchley Park built electromechanical machines known as Bombes, designed by Bletchley's star cryptographer Alan Turing, to crack the German Enigma machine, a mechanical cipher device used by German forces in the field. Another machine known as Colossus, designed by Turing's mentor Max Newman and the talented engineer Tommy Flowers, was able to defeat the Lorentz teleprinter cipher used by Nazi high command. The world's first programmable, digital, electronic computer was actually Colossus, not the more famous ENIAC (Copeland 2010). Wartime cryptography thus gave rise to both Shannon's information theory and modern digital computers.

One enduring lesson from the history of Bletchley Park is that while cryptology relies on mathematics, intelligence is fundamentally a contest between human organizations (Ratcliff 2006; Grey 2012).

The best signals intelligence (SIGINT) will be useless if Eve and her cronies cannot gain access to, make sense of, and act on Alice and Bob's data. The best cryptosystem is useless, likewise, if Alice and Bob have poor operations security (OPSEC) practices that inadvertently expose data and keys to Eve. We do not have to wait for quantum cryptography to understand why strong cryptosystems might not provide reliable cyber security. Unbreakable asymmetric cryptography like RSA has been available for decades, yet overly complex implementations of PKI and poor "cyber hygiene" among computer users are, nevertheless, responsible for the epidemic of cyber insecurity we experience today. Quantum computing does not change the reliance of cryptology on social factors, and in some ways makes it more complicated (Lindsay 2020a).

The Strategic utility of cryptology

The organizational contest of cryptology is not played for its own sake but in pursuit of more substantive political or economic goals, distributional outcomes, or policy concessions. The political logic of cryptology is implemented by competing organizations in a strategic context of dueling conspiracy. Intelligence collection operations (or criminal theft) is a second-order conspiracy to penetrate a target's first-order conspiracy to gain or preserve the advantages of secrecy. Counterintelligence, likewise, is essentially a third-order conspiracy (i.e., deceiving the deceivers who penetrate deception).

Some of the great success stories in cryptologic history highlight the importance of cryptography for conspiracy and cryptanalysis for defeating it. During her house arrest in 1586, Mary Queen of Scots conspired with a former page to assassinate Elizabeth and foment a Catholic rebellion; they were betrayed by a courier who diverted their enciphered communications to a talented cryptanalyst working for the Crown, and they provided damning evidence for Mary's trial and execution (Kahn 1996: 122–23). A century before the Russian "doxing" of the

US Democratic National Committee in 2016, the British parlayed a cryptanalytic coup into perhaps the greatest diplomatic influence operation of all time. The single most famous cryptogram in history came from German Secretary for Foreign Affairs Arthur Zimmermann proposing a secret alliance with Mexico against the United States; British interception, decryption, and covert delivery of the telegram to the United States helped President Woodrow Wilson persuade Congress to declare war on Germany (Kahn 1996: 266–97). Both of these were ambitious (if reckless) conspiracies to change the balance of power, and cryptanalysis not only defeated but ultimately spelled disaster for the conspirators. If secrecy was potentially destabilizing, had it succeeded, so was revelation, once it failed.

Cryptography is most useful in situations in which secrecy provides some political advantage for a group and the members of that group have to cooperate to gain that advantage. Specifically, secrecy can provide (1) a political bargaining advantage, (2) a military maneuver advantage, or (3) intellectual property protection.

First, cryptography enables a political group to coordinate bargaining strategy while disguising or exaggerating strengths and weaknesses. Political actors have strategic incentives to misrepresent their power to gain a bargaining advantage (Fearon 1995; Slantchev 2010), and cryptography enables them to do so. A group of negotiators will usually want to rehearse their presentation and conceal their potential concessions and reservation price in order to get the best deal. For example, during the 1921 naval disarmament conference in Washington, Japan was publicly demanding a ratio of ten to seven with the United States and Great Britain. The Japanese Foreign Office cabled its negotiator that it was willing to settle for ten to six but should avoid settling if possible. Unfortunately for the Japanese, the US State Department "Black Chamber" had intercepted and deciphered this cable, which enabled US Secretary of State Charles Hughes to demand, stubbornly and successfully, a ratio of ten to six (Yardley 1931).

Second, the secret coordination of operations covertly shifts costs and benefits. A criminal conspiracy, an espionage ring, and a combined arms military unit all have very different material capabilities, to be sure, but they follow a similar political logic in this respect. These groups rely on maneuver and stealth to evade the defenses of an adversary to concentrate at some decisive point to achieve tactical surprise or steal resources. The local advantage achieved through infiltration and maneuver is fleeting. Members of the group must coordinate their efforts before the adversary can reinforce or counterattack the vulnerable areas that the act of maneuver uncovers. The weaker a group is materially, the less able it is to reinforce its vulnerabilities and the more it depends on stratagem (Kahn 2001).

It is notable that many prominent cryptologic successes occur in military domains such as sea and air that emphasize maneuver and surprise. The legendary exploits of Bletchley Park and the Royal Navy's Operational Intelligence Centre in penetrating German U-boat communications enabled convoy rerouting and antisubmarine targeting in the Battle of the Atlantic (Beesly 2000). The US Navy penetration of Japanese codes provided invaluable insight into the order of battle and fleet movements of the Imperial Japanese Navy and was instrumental for victory in the Battles of the Coral Sea and Midway (Parker 2017). Midway is particularly notable as the Japanese intended to fool the Americans with a feint toward the Aleutians and catch them at Midway, but instead the Americans were able to fool the Japanese by appearing at an inopportune moment; the deceivers were deceived (and a deception operation was used to confirm the accuracy of US SIGINT). Cryptography is particularly important in naval warfare, and enemy cryptanalysis particularly dangerous, because the sudden loss of information advantage can be disastrous for expensive "low-density, high-demand" assets. Similarly in air operations, SIGINT can provide valuable targeting data, as Admiral Isoroku Yamamoto found out the hard way in April 1943 after US cryptologists intercepted a report of his travel itinerary (Kahn 1996: 595–601). While land warfare typically depends more on mass and attrition compared to the air and maritime domains, armored warfare relies more on maneuver and surprise, and thus cryptology. German interception of cables from the American military attaché in Cairo reporting on British movements in North Africa "provided Rommel with undoubtedly the broadest and clearest picture of enemy forces and intentions available to any Axis commander throughout the whole war" (Kahn 1996: 473). This, incidentally, is an example of "fourth party" collection, whereby an intelligence service spies on another intelligence service to learn about its targets' communications. The information advantage vanished, however, when the Allies changed attachés and codes, and thus the opening cannonade at Alamein "came as a complete surprise to the Africa Corps" (Kahn 1996: 477).

Third, cryptography protects information resources such as digital money and intellectual property. Information goods are costly to produce and nearly costless to copy, so preventing copying is necessary for creating the scarcity that ensures their value. It is counterintuitive that conspiracies of silence can be stabilizing in this sense. If cryptography can provide advantages in war, it also can be a stabilizing factor in peacetime by protecting the privacy of citizens and legitimate property rights. Most democratic systems of law recognize the sanctity of attorney-client, clerical, and marital privilege, which in effect provide a bargaining advantage to citizens in the courts by protecting their strengths and weaknesses from public scrutiny. Sports teams try to hide their strategies to gain a game time advantage to improve the competitive quality of the game. Some citizens like to protect their personal data from surveillance by advertising firms or cybercriminals. The security of financial transactions and bank accounts from theft and fraud is vital for trust in a system of economic exchange. Cryptography (PKI) provides invaluable protection for all these applications. Legal privacy protections in these examples are provided within an institutional framework that defines property rights and legitimate and illegitimate types of competition. Yet the potential for abuse of legitimate privacy is inherent to the political logic of cryptology. The dilemma of counterintelligence in a democracy is that privacy can both protect citizens and enable traitors (Landau 2010).

Ironically, the availability of strong encryption has contributed to the cyber security epidemic we face today. Robust PKI enables the widespread trust in cyberspace that spies and criminals exploit. For the past two decades, organizations and individuals have been hemorrhaging confidential data, and powerful SIGINT agencies have been enjoying a renaissance in technical collection. This is possible in large part because people fail to use encryption properly. Even worse, the availability of strong cryptography can provide a false sense of security for users. The mathematical strength of encryption protocol effectively shifts the incentives for exploitation to other vulnerabilities in the software, hardware, and organizational implementation of the protocol. Gullible humans are the Achilles Heel of classical cryptology, and they will also be the undoing of quantum cryptology.

In all three cases, there is a fundamentally ambiguous relationship between cryptologic advantage and political advantage. Cryptanalytic success can reveal information that makes bargains more likely than conflict. It can also reveal high value targets that make surprise attack more attractive than bargaining. Cryptographic success can deny either of these advantages, which makes stable bargains less and more likely, respectively. Moreover, while the offensive and defensive sides of cryptology are functionally distinct (i.e., cryptanalytic code breaking and cryptographic code making), they do necessarily correlate with political-military offense or defense. A defensively motivated actor can use cryptanalysis to break into an attacker's networks to figure out where to reinforce defenses to blunt a coming attack. An attacker can use cryptography to protect its military communications and preserve the element of surprise which it needs to overwhelm defenders. Cryptographic success can cover cryptanalysis, and cryptanalytic success can prompt cryptographic innovation. These dynamics are fundamentally political in nature, so they are unlikely to be transformed by quantum technology. On the contrary, quantum technology will be enlisted into the service of cryptologic contests.

Quantum possibility and social reality

The balance between offense and defense in intelligence has always depended more on institutional factors and strategic context than technological architecture. Thus, it will still be possible to collect and protect secrets after the quantum information revolution. In this brief review of the political dynamics of cryptology, we have encountered a broad diversity of actors and applications. The tumultuous relationship between cryptologic technology and political advantage is likely to become even more complex, socially and technically. The overall implications of quantum information technology for strategic stability are profoundly ambiguous, but this ultimately has more to do with the politics of information than the technology of quantum computing.

On the cryptanalytic side (offense), engineers first must overcome formidable challenges such as error correction to build a large-scale universal quantum computer. Quantum computing might then facilitate bulk decryption of intercepted data. It would not, however, improve access and placement to the target's data in the first place, which could still be protected by a smart OPSEC policy. Quantum computing also would not help dramatically with analysis on the back end, although it could help to optimize database searches. It could even complicate the analytical process by vastly increasing the number of decrypts that have to be analyzed.

On the cryptographic side (defense), quantum-safe encryption at best offers a restoration to the status quo, temporarily threatened by the advent of quantum computing, rather than a revolution. On the one hand, quantum communication will cancel out whatever problems quantum cryptanalysis creates for communications security. On the other, quantum cryptosystems will still depend on complex sociotechnical implementations that depend, in turn, on lazy, gullible, selfish human beings. Indeed, if quantum computers marginally improve public trust in information networks and thus the data on them, those networks will simply become more attractive intelligence targets.

New levels of trust will create new opportunities for abusing trust. The golden age of cyber espionage today does not need quantum computing to break into organizations that have access to strong cryptosystems. Cyberspace as we know it today already has robust cryptosystems in modern PKI. Future defenses provided by quantum cryptosystems will, similarly, only be as good as the people who use them.

I would like to conclude on a personal note by discussing how I tackled quantum computing as a social scientist (Lindsay 2020a; 2020b). I am fortunate to have a few advantages in this respect, to include training in physics and computer science as an undergraduate and years serving as an intelligence officer in the US Navy prior to pursuing a doctorate in political science. I have written extensively on cyber security and IR, usually from a skeptical perspective (Lindsay 2013; 2014; 2015; 2017; Gartzke and Lindsay 2015; 2017; Lindsay and Gartzke 2017; 2018). Quantum computing caught my attention because I was starting to hear familiar claims about the deterministic potential of new ICT. I immersed myself in technical sources to gain a basic understanding of quantum concepts (Aaronson 2013; Wilde 2017; National Academies of Sciences, Engineering, and Medicine 2019). However, it quickly became apparent that cryptologic history (Kahn 1996; Singh 1999; Alvarez 2000; Aldrich 2010; Parker 2017) would be just as valuable, if not more.

Technology does not determine politics; often it is the other way round. Scholars of cyber security (or quantum computing) must understand the details of information technology, just as scholars of international political economy need to understand the technical nuances of central banking. But they must then go further to interrogate the social context and constitution of these technologies. Technology can at most alter the value of a variable in some theory about some political outcome, such as conflict onset, escalation, duration, or termination. But that variable will almost always be conditioned on other social factors including organizational doctrine, administrative structure, national culture, or elite politics. Through this project, it became apparent to me that the real problem was not that IR lacked an understanding of quantum computing, but that it had little to say about cryptology of any generation. Likewise for cyber security, I have come to believe that the problem is less that IR does not understand information technology and more that IR has only recently started to seriously study intelligence phenomena (Jervis 2011; Rovner 2011; Carson 2018; O'Rourke 2018; Rid 2020).

The field is wide open for IR to examine the secret side of politics, which increasingly involves the exploitation of information technology. Social scientists can and should reclaim technology from the technologists.

Note

1 IBM scientists argue that the Oak Ridge Summit could complete the same task in three days rather than 10,000 years, but this does not overturn the basic achievement; future quantum computers using more than Sycamore's 53 qubits will be able to outperform Summit or anything else by a huge margin (Aaronson 2019).

References

All links checked on August 20, 2021.

Aaronson, S. (2013). *Quantum Computing Since Democritus*. Cambridge: Cambridge University Press.

Aaronson, S. (2019, October 30). Why Google's Quantum Supremacy Milestone Matters. *The New York Times*. Retrieved from: https://www.nytimes.com/2019/10/30/opinion/google-quantum-computer-sycamore.html

Aldrich, R. (2010). *GCHQ: The Uncensored Story of Britain's Most Secret Intelligence Agency*. London: HarperCollins.

Alvarez, D. J. (2000). *Secret Messages: Codebreaking and American Diplomacy, 1930–1945*. Lawrence, KS: University Press of Kansas.

Arute, F., Arya, K., Babbush, R., Bacon, D., Bardin, J. C., Barends, R., Biswas, R., et al. (2019). Quantum Supremacy Using a Programmable Superconducting Processor. *Nature*, 574(7779): 505–10.

Beesly, P. (2000). *Very Special Intelligence: The Story of the Admiralty's Operational Intelligence Centre, 1939–1945*. London: Greenhill Books.

Bernstein, D. J., Heninger, N., Lou, P. and Valenta, L. (2017). *Post-Quantum RSA*. Cryptology ePrint Archive. Retrieved from: https://eprint.iacr.org/2017/351.pdf.

Biercuk, M. J. and Fontaine, R. (2017, November 17). The Leap into Quantum Technology: A Primer for National Security Professionals. *War on the Rocks* (blog). Retrieved from: https://warontherocks.com/2017/11/leap-quantum-technology-primer-national-security-professionals/.

Borghard, E. D. and Lonergan, S. W. (2017). The Logic of Coercion in Cyberspace. *Security Studies*, 26(3): 452–81.

Brantly, A. F. (2016). *The Decision to Attack: Military and Intelligence Cyber Decision-Making*. Atlanta, GA: University of Georgia Press.

Brassard, G. (2016). Cryptography in a Quantum World. In: *SOFSEM 2016: Theory and Practice of Computer Science*, 3–16. Lecture Notes in Computer Science. Berlin, Heidelberg: Springer.

Buchanan, B. (2017). *The Cyber Security Dilemma: Hacking, Trust and Fear between Nations*. New York: Oxford University Press.

Buchmann, J., Lauter, K., and Mosca, M. (2017). Postquantum Cryptography – State of the Art. *IEEE Security Privacy*, 15(4): 12–13. https://doi.org/10.1109/MSP.2017.3151326.

Carson, A. (2018). *Secret Wars: Covert Conflict in International Politics*. Princeton: Princeton University Press.

Chen, L., Jordan, S., Liu, Y.-K., Moody, D., Peralta, R., Perlner, R., and Smith-Tone, D. (2016). *Report on Post-Quantum Cryptography*. NISTIR 8105. Gaithersburg, MD: National Institute of Standards and Technology.

Copeland, B. J. (ed.). (2010). *Colossus: The Secrets of Bletchley Park's Code-Breaking Computers*. New York: Oxford University Press.

Deibert, R. J. (2013). *Black Code: Inside the Battle for Cyberspace*. Toronto, ON: McClelland & Stewart.

DigiCert (2018). *Check Our Numbers: The Math Behind Estimations to Break a 2048-Bit Certificate*. Archive copy. Retrieved from: https://web.archive.org/web/20181004033325/https://www.digicert.com/TimeTravel/math.htm.

Dowling, J. P. and Milburn, G. J. (2003). Quantum Technology: The Second Quantum Revolution. *Philosophical Transactions. Series A, Mathematical, Physical, and Engineering Sciences*, 361(1809): 1655–74.

Dunn Cavelty, M. (2008). Cyber-Terror – Looming Threat or Phantom Menace? The Framing of the US Cyber-Threat Debate. *Journal of Information Technology & Politics*, 4(1): 19–36.

Fearon, J. D. (1995). Rationalist Explanations for War. *International Organization*, 49(3): 379–414.

Feynman, R. P. (1982). Simulating Physics with Computers. *International Journal of Theoretical Physics*, 21(6/7): 467–88.

Gartzke, E. (2013). The Myth of Cyberwar: Bringing War in Cyberspace Back Down to Earth. *International Security*, 38(2): 41–73.

Gartzke, E. and Lindsay, J. R. (2015). Weaving Tangled Webs: Offense, Defense, and Deception in Cyberspace. *Security Studies*, 24(2): 316–48.

Gartzke, E. and Lindsay, J. R. (2017). Thermonuclear Cyberwar. *Journal of Cyber security*, 3(1): 37–48.

Gidney, C. and Ekera, M. (2019). *How to Factor 2048 Bit RSA Integers in 8 Hours Using 20 Million Noisy Qubits*. arXiv. Retrieved from: https://arxiv.org/pdf/1905.09749.pdf.

Grey, C. (2012). *Decoding Organization: Bletchley Park, Codebreaking and Organization Studies*. New York: Cambridge University Press.

Hurd, W. (2017, December 7). Quantum Computing Is the Next Big Security Risk. *Wired*. Retrieved from: https://www.wired.com/story/quantum-computing-is-the-next-big-security-risk/.

Jervis, R. (2011). *Why Intelligence Fails: Lessons from the Iranian Revolution and the Iraq War*. Ithaca, NY: Cornell University Press.

Kahn, D. (1996). *The Codebreakers: The Comprehensive History of Secret Communication from Ancient Times to the Internet*. Revised. New York: Simon and Schuster.

Kahn, D. (2001). An Historical Theory of Intelligence. *Intelligence and National Security*, 16(3): 79–92.

Kania, E. B. (2018, September 28). China's Quantum Future. *Foreign Affairs*. Retrieved from: https://www.foreignaffairs.com/articles/china/2018-09-26/chinas-quantum-future.

Kania, E. B. and Costello, J. (2018). *Quantum Hegemony? China's Ambitions and the Challenge to U.S. Innovation Leadership*. Washington, DC: Center for a New American Security.

Kello, L. (2013). The Meaning of the Cyber Revolution: Perils to Theory and Statecraft. *International Security*, 38(2): 7–40.

Kenny, R. (2017, November 28). The Quantum Gap with China. *Foreign Policy*. Retrieved from: https://foreignpolicy.com/2017/11/28/the-quantum-gap-with-china/.

Kreps, S. and Schneider, J. (2019). Escalation Firebreaks in the Cyber, Conventional, and Nuclear Domains: Moving beyond Effects-Based Logics. *Journal of Cyber security*, 5(1). https://doi.org/10.1093/cybsec/tyz007.

Landau, S. E. (2010). *Surveillance or Security? The Risks Posed by New Wiretapping Technologies*. Cambridge, MA: MIT Press.

Lawson, S. (2013). Beyond Cyber-Doom: Assessing the Limits of Hypothetical Scenarios in the Framing of Cyber-Threats. *Journal of Information Technology & Politics*, 10(1): 86–103.

Libicki, M. C. (2007). *Conquest in Cyberspace: National Security and Information Warfare*. New York: Cambridge University Press.

Liff, A. P. (2012). Cyberwar: A New 'Absolute Weapon'? The Proliferation of Cyberwarfare Capabilities and Interstate War. *The Journal of Strategic Studies*, 35(3): 401–28.

Lindsay, J. R. (2013). Stuxnet and the Limits of Cyber Warfare. *Security Studies*, 22(3): 365–404.

Lindsay, J. R. (2014). The Impact of China on Cyber Security: Fiction and Friction. *International Security*, 39(3): 7–47.

Lindsay, J. R. (2015). Tipping the Scales: The Attribution Problem and the Feasibility of Deterrence against Cyber Attack. *Journal of Cyber security*, 1(1): 53–67.

Lindsay, J. R. (2020a). Demystifying the Quantum Threat: Infrastructure, Implementation, and Intelligence Advantage. *Security Studies*, 29(2): 335–361.

Lindsay, J. R. (2020b). Surviving the Quantum Cryptocalypse. *Strategic Studies Quarterly*, 14(2): 49–73.

Lindsay, J. R. and Gartzke, E. (2017). Cross-Domain Deterrence and Cyber Security: The Consequences of Complexity. In: D. van Puyvelde and A. F. Brantley (eds), *US National Cyber Security: International Politics, Concepts and Organization*. New York: Routledge, pp. 11–27.

Lindsay, J. R. and Gartzke, E. (2018). Coercion through Cyberspace: The Stability-Instability Paradox Revisited. In: K. M. Greenhill and P. Krause (eds), *Coercion: The Power to Hurt in International Politics*. New York: Oxford University Press, pp. 179–203.

Lo, H.-K. and Lütkenhaus, N. (2007). Quantum Cryptography: From Theory to Practice. *Physics in Canada*, 63(4): 191–96.

Lynn III, W. J. (2010). Defending a New Domain: The Pentagon's Cyberstrategy. *Foreign Affairs*, 89(5): 97–108.

Mulholland, J., Mosca, M. and Braun, J. (2017). The Day the Cryptography Dies. *IEEE Security Privacy*, 15(4): 14–21.

National Academies of Sciences, Engineering, and Medicine (2019). *Quantum Computing: Progress and Prospects*. Washington, DC: The National Academies Press.

Nikias, C. and Max, L. (2018, May 11). This Is the Most Important Tech Contest since the Space Race, and America Is Losing. *Washington Post*. Retrieved from: https://www.washingtonpost.com/opinions/this-is-the-most-important-tech-contest-since-the-space-race-and-america-is-losing/2018/05/11/7a4a4772-4e21-11e8-b725-92c89fe3ca4c_story.html

O'Rourke, L. A. (2018). *Covert Regime Change: America's Secret Cold War*. Ithaca, NY: Cornell University Press.

Owen, T. and Gorwa, R. (2016, September 7). Quantum Leap: China's Satellite and the New Arms Race. *Foreign Affairs*. Retrieved from: https://www.foreignaffairs.com/articles/2016-09-07/quantum-leap

Parker, F. D. (2017). *A Priceless Advantage: U.S. Navy Communications Intelligence and the Battles of Coral Sea, Midway, and the Aleutians*. 3rd ed. Vol. 5. United States Cryptologic History, World War II, IV. Fort George G. Meade, MD: Center for Cryptologic History, National Security Agency.

Putnam, R. D. (1988). Diplomacy and Domestic Politics: The Logic of Two-Level Games. *International Organization*, 42(3): 427–60.

Ratcliff, R. A. (2006). *Delusions of Intelligence: Enigma, Ultra, and the End of Secure Ciphers*. New York: Cambridge University Press.

Rattray, G. J. (2001). *Strategic Warfare in Cyberspace*. Cambridge, MA: MIT Press.

Rid, T. (2012). "Cyber War Will Not Take Place". *The Journal of Strategic Studies*, 35(5): 5–32.

Rid, T. (2020). *Active Measures: The Secret History of Disinformation and Political Warfare*. New York: Farrar, Straus and Giroux.

Rid, T. and Buchanan, B. (2015). Attributing Cyber Attacks. *Journal of Strategic Studies*, 38(1–2): 4–37.

Rovner, J. (2011). *Fixing the Facts: National Security and the Politics of Intelligence*. Ithaca, NY: Cornell University Press.

Schneider, J. (2019). The Capability/Vulnerability Paradox and Military Revolutions: Implications for Computing, Cyber, and the Onset of War. *Journal of Strategic Studies*, 42(6): 841–63. https://doi.org/10.1080/01402390.2019.1627209.

Shannon, C. E. (1945). *A Mathematical Theory of Cryptography. Technical Report MM 45-110-02*. Holmdel: Bell Labs.

Shannon, C. E. (1948). A Mathematical Theory of Communication. *The Bell System Technical Journal*, 27(October): 379–423, 623–656.

Shannon, C. E. (1951). The Redundancy of English. In: *Transactions of the 7th Conference on Cybernetics*. New York: Josiah Macy, Jr. Foundation, pp. 248–272.

Simon, C. (2017). Towards a Global Quantum Network. *Nature Photonics*, 11(11): 678–80. https://doi.org/10.1038/s41566-017-0032-0.

Singh, S. (1999). *The Code Book: The Science of Secrecy from Ancient Egypt to Quantum Cryptography*. New York: Random House.

Slantchev, B. L. (2010). Feigning Weakness. *International Organization*, 64(3): 357–88.

Slayton, R. (2017). What Is the Cyber Offense-Defense Balance? Conceptions, Causes, and Assessment. *International Security*, 41(3): 72–109.

Smeets, M. (2017). A Matter of Time: On the Transitory Nature of Cyberweapons. *Journal of Strategic Studies*, 41(1–2): 6–32.

Thirsk, J. W. (2001). Traffic Analysis: A Log-Reader's Tale. In: M. Smith and R. Erskine (eds), *Action This Day: Bletchley Park from the Breaking of the Enigma Code to the Birth of the Modern Computer*. New York: Bantam Press, pp. 264–77.

Valeriano, B. and Maness, R. C. (2015). *Cyber War versus Cyber Realities: Cyber Conflict in the International System*. New York: Oxford University Press.

Warner, M. and Benson, R. L. (1997). Venona and Beyond: Thoughts on Work Undone. *Intelligence and National Security*, 12(3): 1–13.

Wehner, S., Elkouss, D. and Hanson, R. (2018). Quantum Internet: A Vision for the Road Ahead. *Science*, 362(6412): eaam9288.

Wilde, M. M. (2017). *Quantum Information Theory*. 2nd ed. New York: Cambridge University Press.

Yardley, H. O. (1931). *The American Black Chamber*. Indianapolis, IN: Bobbs-Merrill.

7 Cyberspace in space

Fragmentation, vulnerability, and uncertainty

Johan Eriksson and Giampiero Giacomello

In a novel about World War III, American leaders – confronted with the total collapse of the communication grid caused by Chinese and Russian attacks – call for help from Google and Facebook to restore communications in the United States, since these corporations have wireless infrastructure drones and blimps used in remote locations around the world (Rosone and Watson 2017). This is obviously a fictional scenario, but the fact that Google redirected its "Loon" balloons to Puerto Rico after Hurricane Maria showed that this type of action is possible, and that it was considered by US authorities. It is no longer simply fiction that cyberspace satellites are essential for the functioning of more than social media and email, but also for a vast array of critical infrastructures and societal services, through the "Internet of Things". For instance, despite the challenges to be addressed, the InterPlaNetary (IPN) has long been expected to be the next step in the design and development of deep space networks (Akyildiz et al. 2003). These increasingly space-based infrastructures will likely also be receptive targets in "information warfare" campaigns as well as in physical warfighting (Walsh and Zway 2018).

This chapter addresses the increasing interconnectedness of cyberspace and outer space, a development which opens significant questions for research as well as for strategy. While cyberspace infrastructure is increasingly dependent on space infrastructure, especially satellites, the consequences for politics and security remain uninvestigated. The chapter provides an overview of and introduction to these challenges.

Emphasis herein is on asking important questions rather than providing convincing evidence and conclusions. Further research, including both scenario-based theorizing and systematic empirical inquiry, are needed to improve both knowledge and policy. Hence, this chapter should be considered, to all intents, as a *probe*. Nonetheless, the two questions that will tentatively characterize our exploratory inquire are: (1) What are the consequences of making cyberspace increasingly reliant on satellites and other types of space infrastructure? In addition, (2) what is the meaning and significance of an interplanetary cyberspace? The latter question may seem particularly futuristic and speculative, yet the development of an interplanetary cyberspace is on the agenda within the community of technical experts (Bucur and Iacca 2017; Voosen 2016), and interplanetary

DOI: 10.4324/9781003110224-8

cyberspace is arguably an expected development given the contemporary "new space race" toward the Moon, Mars, and further into deep space.

This chapter suggests that consequences of space-based cyberspace can be analyzed in terms of three categories – fragmentation, vulnerability, and uncertainty. As will be discussed below, the development of satellite-based internet services is spearheaded by private actors, mirroring a general fragmentation and diversification of actors in both cyberspace and space. Moreover, satellite-based cyberspace implies a whole array of new vulnerabilities, as satellites can be targeted by anti-satellite missiles, and that they are vulnerable to new forms of hacking, as well as to space debris, and solar storms. More generally, these new developments are plagued with a great deal of uncertainty, in terms of how governance will be organized, what rules will apply, and whether militarization or peaceful collaboration will prevail. Uncertainty is particularly great regarding the potential development of interplanetary cyberspace, which however should not prevent discussion of what technical experts are claiming.

Cyberspace infrastructure: From Earth to space?

Cyberspace is indeed a virtual space – making real-time communication possible with little or no regard to physical distance. Simultaneously, however, cyberspace has always depended on physical infrastructure in the form of cables, routers, and servers. Moreover, it has long been known that space is a rather vulnerable environment as "[it] poses a number of challenges in providing reliable, end-to-end data communication with a tolerable level of service" (Durst et al. 1997: 389). Undersea cables have been the arteries of the internet, particularly for making global internet communications possible. Until recently, little of cyberspace communication has relied on wireless infrastructure, such as satellites and airwave (mobile communication) technology. This seems to be changing, however.

While satellite-based communication is certainly not new, it was for a long time expensive and unavailable to ordinary people, used mainly by the military, government, maritime traffic, and researchers. With the development of wireless mobile telecommunications (from the 1G to the emerging 5G and eventually 6G networks), cyberspace communication became increasingly integrated with space technology, i.e. satellites. Yet, wireless mobile telecommunications are still dependent on a grid of land-based transmission towers, which explains the prevailing dark patches of an otherwise internet-covered Earth. A complete integration of space and cyberspace has not yet taken place, but efforts are made to make cyberspace available in every part of the world.

Of interest is the "Starlink" project – initiated by multi-billionaire Elon Musk and his rocket company SpaceX. Starlink is advertised as a project to provide the entire globe with Internet access. On 29 March 2018, the US Federal Communications Commission granted SpaceX a license to set up a satellite network for the provision of broadband Internet services available across the globe (Amos 2019; Gross 2018; Choudhury 2019). Two of these satellites were launched already before the license was acquired and another 60 were launched in

May 2019. Toward the end of the 2020s, the Starlink system is expected to consist of up to 12,000 low-orbit satellites, and more will follow.

This initiative makes SpaceX a competitor to UK-based OneWeb (formerly Worldvu), which is a similar project to provide internet service to the entire globe. Other competitors are Amazon's "Project Kuiper", Google's "Project Loon", Samsung, ViaSat, Sierra Nevada Corporation, the UK-based Surrey Satellite Technology Ltd., and the Australian Gilmore Space Technologies. There are several more similar projects, of a public as well as private nature. The EU-operated Galileo satellite system is noteworthy – intended to provide services like the US Global Positioning System (GPS). Several existing and aspiring "space powers" have or are about to set up satellite-based internet services, including Russia, China, Japan, India, Brazil, and the United Arab Emirates. Consequently, the rapid rise of competitors for a satellite-based internet, a first general observation is that diversification in terms of actors involved is increasing. The wide array of entrepreneurs involved, dispersed across the Globe, suggest that fragmentation rather than hegemony will characterize this domain.

With the launch of space-based internet communications, the number of satellites orbiting Earth will increase from today's around 2,000 operative satellites to at least 20,000 satellites. Concerns have been raised that this will dramatically increase the risk of collisions, resulting in vast amounts of "space junk" (out-of-service satellites, debris from crashes, lost equipment from space walks etc.), and also interfere with transmissions, blur the vision of space telescopes, and imply dangers for space launches (Liou and Portman 2007). Undoubtedly, this development implies new vulnerabilities for space companies and their clients (including states and citizens) as well as for the space environment in itself, but also uncertainty in terms of how, when, and with what specific consequences collisions and interference occur. Vulnerability and uncertainty are also exacerbated by, on the one hand, the increasing number and diversity of space entrepreneurs and, on the other hand, the lack of national and international norms and rules adapted to this "new space race". As has often been the case, technological development moves faster than politics.

Moreover, satellite-based cyberspace might make it is easier to bypass censorship and control of access by national governments. How the information age entails a perforation of sovereignty has been suggested before, but that observation must be balanced against the legal and physical capacity of national governments to license and shut down internet service providers and take control of the physical infrastructure. With the transfer of cyber-infrastructure from Earth to space, however, there will still be a need for control centers and dishes on ground, but they can be dispersed across the globe, more easily avoiding the control of national governments. This is particularly the case when internet satellites are provided by multinational space companies, which can simultaneously operate in several countries, and which are also more mobile than any cable junctions.

Indeed, a key driver behind the development of satellite-based cyberspace is that several states have made legal changes opening of for private space projects. According to the 1968 Outer Space Treaty, states are responsible for all space activities emanating from their territories and jurisdictions (Martinez 1998). During the early Space Age, this was hardly an issue, as space was then accessible only by the governments of the United States and the Soviet Union, through NASA and its Soviet counterpart. Liberalization of space access sped up in the United States as NASA faced cutdowns and the Space Shuttle program was cancelled, and both George W. Bush Jr. and later Barack Obama argued that the private space industry must take a bigger role in space exploration, including human space exploration. The United States has spearheaded this development, which opened for companies such as SpaceX, Orbital, Boeing, Lockheed Martin, and others.

Yet other countries, traditionally not associated with space programs, have also changed their laws and opened jurisdictions for private space initiatives, and public-private partnerships. Of this a noteworthy case is Luxembourg, a small European country which over the last 10–15 years has made public-private space programs a key national strategy – specifically regarding satellites. Unlike major space powers such as the United States, Russia, China, India, and Japan – Luxembourg is not working through a national space agency with its own launch capacity but is rather opening jurisdictional space (and low taxes) for multinational space entrepreneurs, with support from the government of Luxembourg, the Planetary Resource center, and the University of Luxembourg (Araxia Abrahamian 2017).

Furthermore, the development of cyberspace in space opens the question of governance. There is clearly no overarching framework or "regime" concerning the governance of space-based cyberspace. By contrast, there is a noteworthy governance gap between the two domains. This is not surprising, however, given the fragmented governance structure regarding cyberspace and space as separate domains. For both domains, national regulation and governance dominate, as both are based on infrastructures that vary greatly between countries. In terms of global governance, the multilateral yet US-based organization ICANN maintains a key role in the governance of cyberspace, with specific authority regarding the basic technical protocols of the internet, and the internet domain name system. ICANN, together with NGOs and national governments, are also crucial in the ongoing global debate on what norms and principles cyberspace should be based upon – a debate that could be simplified as positions on "Internet freedom" and "Internet sovereignty" (Mueller 2017).

Likewise, the global governance of space is limited, with a lack of an overarching "regime" or coordinating organization (Jakhu and Pelton 2017). Yet, of fundamental importance is the Outer Space Treaty from 1967, which states that space belongs to all of humanity, that no state or private entity can claim ownership of any part of space (such as an asteroid or territory on Mars), and that weapons of mass destruction are banned from use in outer space. There are a few other global space treaties, which concern for example the Moon, liability for damages caused by space objects, the sharing of potential dangers in outer space, the use of space-related technologies, and the rescue of astronauts. These treaties are administered by the UN Office for Outer Space Affairs (UNOOSA) and the related Committee on the Peaceful Uses of Outer Space. Thus, there is a global forum for space debate and governance, yet it remains clear that authority remains largely with national governments.

As noted, while there are certain elements of global governance of cyberspace and space, these governance structures are separate. For example, it is unclear how power and authority over cyberspace in space is distributed between ICANN and UNOOSA – or other organizations, such as the International Telecommunications Union.

Moreover, it remains unclear what roles and responsibilities in global governance are held by private internet service providers and private space companies. This includes the emergence of public–private partnerships, many of which are of a transnational character (further discussed below). It is noteworthy that global space law – which is still largely state-centric – is backward in terms of the emergence of private space authority.

In sum, the development of a satellite-based internet implies a fragmentation and diversification of actors involved, the emergence of several new types of vulnerabilities (to space debris, anti-satellite missiles, etc.), and uncertainty in terms of governance (cf. Rothe and Shim 2018; Jakhu and Pelton 2017). In the following sections, we will discuss a few more specific aspects of the cyberspace-in-space development, specifically regarding security and militarization, privatization, and the potential for an interplanetary cyberspace.

Militarization of space/cyberspace?

In 2007, China shot down one of their own satellites with a ground-to-space ABM (anti-ballistic missile), which instantly removed any doubts of their anti-satellite capability. Moreover, in 2010 and again in February 2018, China used ABMs to shoot down one of their own target missiles in space (Lin and Singer 2018). Likewise, although the US "Star Wars" program of the 1980s was cancelled, in the summer of 2018 the Trump administration announced its goal of setting up a new Space Force, expanding the US military forces beyond the Army, Navy, and Air Force. It remains unknown what such a Space Force would look like, but it corroborates the general trend of militarization of space. The development of anti-satellite (ASAT) weapons precedes a potential US Space Force, and it is not limited to the United States and China. These incidents and developments can be interpreted as an indication of a more general militarization of space (Stephens 2017).

What are the implications of this development? To begin with, it means that cyberspace and internet access have become vulnerable to new forms of physical attacks. While anti-satellite weapons previously threatened certain forms of global telecommunications, they are increasingly becoming threats to the very fabrics of cyberspace. Satellite systems for telecommunications and cyberspace seem increasingly worthy of the label "critical information infrastructures" (Dunn 2006; Newlove-Eriksson et al. 2018).

The vulnerability of satellite-based cyberspace is aggravated by the development of dual-use technology, i.e. satellites which can serve both military and non-military purposes, such as a surveillance satellite that can serve the military with observations of troop movements at the same time as it serves climate research with observation of rising sea levels. The development of dual-use technology (which does not prevent the military from operating its own, single-use satellites) has been particularly strong in the United States and in Europe. A noteworthy example is the development of the EU's satellite surveillance system, which for many years bore the acronym GMES. Originally, this acronym stood for Global Monitoring for Environmental Security, which meant it was used only for civilian and scientific purposes, particularly serving climate research. In 2008, however, the EU changed the meaning of the acronym to Global Monitoring for Environment *and* Security. While this may seem as an insignificant change of language, it signaled a major policy change (Newlove-Eriksson and Eriksson 2013). Specifically, the GMES was from then and onward to be used both for civilian and military (and wider security) purposes, providing not only environmental data but also supporting the intelligence services. Later, the EU changed the name of this satellite system from GMES to Copernicus.

There is a twofold consequence of dual-use communications satellites. First, both military and civilian services are endangered if a satellite is attacked or get out of service for some other reason. Second, because of the combination of diverse types of clients – specifically military and business – there will be high demands for encryption and secrecy. Not only the risk of having satellites shot down, but also hacked into, is a new challenge. The integration of space and cyberspace means that the existing militarization of cyberspace – the world of information warfare, strategic hacking, spreading of malware and distributed denial of service attacks – become intermingled with space activities, whether civilian or military (Giacomello 2013). This may lead to an increasing difficulty in satellite-tracking and identification, as previously single-use civilian satellites by necessity are "covered up" because of their new military (and business) functions. In the long run this can be problematic as seen from the perspective of democratic accountability. In sum, the parallel militarization of space and growing dependency on space infrastructure implies great vulnerability, not only for the satellites themselves, but for the many Earth-bound infrastructures and functions they serve.

Given the great deal of uncertainty associated with space in general, it is not surprising that many stakeholders adopt a precautionary or preemptive approach. For example, the EU's approach to space security, specifically the draft International Code of Conduct for Outer Space Activities and the Space Situational Awareness program, is based on a precautionary acknowledgment of risks or threats, considering mostly preemptive measures and elements of prevention (Slann 2016). "Anticipatory security" is the norm in space and thus should be considered when assessing the transition of cyberspace from "Earth-bound" or "Earth-only" infrastructure to space.

Privatization of space/cyberspace?

The significance of private authority in the development, ownership, and operation of internet services has been acknowledged for many years. Indeed, the private sector is the "third" stakeholder in cyberspace, along with governments and users, as it is now established in the literature (Giacomello 2005, 2013: Dunn Cavelty and Suter 2009; Valeriano et al. 2018); hence as the presence of cyberspace in space grows, there will be even more incentive for the private sector to be considered *the* cardinal player. A similar growth of private authority, albeit at a slower rate, seems to be taking place with regard to space technology. As a report by the Center for Strategic and International Studies (Harrison et al. 2017: 1) noted, "commercial companies will likely be the *primary* driver of any significant reduction of the cost access to space" (emphasis added). We have yet to see complete mergers of cyberspace and space companies, and the development of new and already integrated space and cyberspace industries is still in its infancy. But, as noted above, things are changing. The expansion of SpaceX into cyberspace is a notable example.

Given the mix of government/private sector initiatives, lessons learned from past experience with public-private partnership (PPP) in critical infrastructure should be carefully considered, since, as we argued above, the private sector is likely to play the lion's part in these new fields of merging technologies (Newlove-Eriksson et al. 2018). During the privatization "wave" of the 1980s and 1990s, Western governments conformed to the business logic of the private sector in producing and providing goods and services, but also to the PPP doctrine, indicating a long-term contractual agreement between private and public actors to build or manage critical infrastructures or provide services for public utilities.

While PPP has been heralded as a "revolution" for infrastructures (Grimsey and Lewis 2004), results in terms of efficiency and accountability, however, have been mixed at best (Forrer et al. 2010; Andersson and Malm 2006; Hodge and Grebe 2007). Enthusiasm for PPP in critical information infrastructures (CII), including those of outer space, remains strong, however. Public and private actors involved in CII are struggling not only with technological reliability, but also with securing long-term investments, and how to make CII resilient (Wettenhall 2003). Moreover, organizational theories suggest that institutional fragmentation – i.e. too many stakeholders – negatively affects the ability to reliably manage critical systems, with possibly catastrophic consequences (Perrow 2011).

Major disruptions of critical information infrastructures would indeed have serious consequences not only for the public and private actors directly concerned, but also for the well-being and prosperity of possibly millions of people affected. Proper attention to security and safety, however, is sometimes lacking (Bailes and Frommelt 2004), due in part to the dominant techno-optimistic perspective on space and cyberspace technology. Indeed, relevant literature (Dunn Cavelty and Suter 2009; Newlove et al. 2018) shows that the relationship between the private sector and security is, mildly put, "problematic". Unsurprisingly, since security is the archetypical *externality*, economists have been wary about tackling it (Goodwind 1991). Security is a "large state-sector" and a public service for which economic models display an irritating unfitness. Likewise, "cybersecurity is a public good, which implies that without government intervention, it will not be produced" (Van Eeten and Bauer 2009: 230). As cyberspace moves to space, i.e. into another critical security domain, public and private stakeholders should rightly be concerned, particularly if lessons can be learned from the experience of cybersecurity and other critical information infrastructures with the help of the private sector. That public-private partnerships are indeed becoming major nexuses of space infrastructure is undeniable, particularly in Europe and North America (cf. Mörth 2007; Newlove-Eriksson and Eriksson 2013).

Interplanetary cyberspace?

While ideas of space colonization have influenced space policy since the beginning of the space age, they have recently gained new momentum. In 2015 NASA launched a new Mars settlement project, called "Journey to Mars", including the building of a new launch system (SLS), and a new spaceship called Orion. The timeline of NASA's space settlement project, like that of others, seems to have constantly moved forward. In 2015, NASA believed they would send the first crew to Mars sometime in the 2030s. In 2018, the plan has been moved forward, with a first crewed mission taking place in the 2040s, or later. This is partially due to President Trump's recently stated intention to first return to the Moon, and build a base there, before eventually going to Mars.

Among a handful of private initiatives for space colonization, the most well-developed project is that of SpaceX. Since 2011 SpaceX is *inter alia* delivering cargo to the International Space Station on its Dragon vessel. Yet, since the company was founded in 2002, the goal has been much more ambitious, i.e. to make humanity a "multi-planetary race", starting with the colonization of Mars. In 2016, SpaceX declared that it would send a first crew to Mars already by 2024. While the capability of SpaceX to build and launch rockets is undisputed, it is more uncertain if they will be able to send humans to Mars before the end of 2020s, especially as Musk himself has declared that his timelines are sometimes a little optimistic. SpaceX is currently developing a new large and reusable rocket system for interplanetary travel, the so-called Starship. In September 2018, SpaceX announced that the first version of this ship would carry the world's first space tourist – Japanese businessman Yuzaka Maezawa and a small group of friends – on a trip around the Moon in 2023. Other private initiatives for human space exploration include those of Orbital, Boeing, Blue Origins, Lockheed Martin, and Virgin Galactic. Likewise, in co-operation with Lockheed Martin, NASA is building its own rocket for deep space travel, the so-called Space Launch System and the associated Orion capsule.

Moreover, China, which has sent its own taikonauts to a temporary space lab orbiting Earth, has expressed visions of human space exploration far into the galaxy and beyond. Russia – which maintains the Soviet space infrastructure in Kazakhstan – has also stated long-term goals of human presence in space. Likewise, Japan, Canada, India, and a few other states have similar ambitions, although on a smaller scale. The European Space Agency has also stated intentions to join or develop their own human space exploration and has successfully reached far out in the solar system with unmanned probes, including Rosetta – the first human-made object to land on an asteroid. Even the United Arab Emirates – as part of a general mission to become an advanced high-tech country – have stated the goal of building cities on Mars within "the next hundred years".

Whether the exploration of human space continues in the form of settlements or even cities on other planets, or in the form of new free-moving or orbiting space stations – some form of *deep space communications system* is necessary. Space communications technology is rapidly evolving, with experimentation including not only radio signals but also lasers and optical systems. NASA's Jet Propulsion Laboratory, for example, is currently working on systems for internet-like space communication, capable of transmitting high volumes of traffic. This could very well be the first steps toward an interplanetary cyberspace.

The technological aspects of interplanetary cyberspace are discussed in a growing body of scientific and expert literature. This literature has addressed specific problems of deep space communication that have to do with distance, reliability, and versatility (Akyildiz et al. 2003; Bucur and Iacca 2017). For example, while the current internet protocols are built on latency in milliseconds, an interplanetary cyberspace must tolerate latencies or disruptions of up to several hours. This requires creation of so-called Delay-Tolerant Networks (DTN). Also, if space settlements become a reality, space communications *infrastructure* must be developed. In addition to ground stations and satellites orbiting Earth, a network of transmitters and other forms of communications infrastructure needs to be put up in deep space. The currently existing Deep Space Network (DSN), run by NASA, consists of Earth-based radio antennas and dishes, located in California, Spain, and Australia. A similar network has been established in 2013 by the European Space Agency, with antennas in Spain, Argentina, and Australia (Voosen 2016). Earth-based networks are clearly insufficient to support interplanetary settlements.

It is possible that some form of interplanetary internet-like communications system will develop, but it remains to be seen if there will be one or more versions of interplanetary cyberspace, and it is unknown how issues such as connectivity, access, security, privacy, and governance will be dealt with. Will deep space cyberspace be made secure with encrypted communications, or will it be easy to tap? Will there be a new cosmic digital divide? Who or what will govern intergalactic cyberspace? What norms and principles will cyberspace in space be based upon? If anything, the development of an Interplanetary cyberspace is plagued with a great deal of uncertainty –in terms of whether and how it will come about, what capacity and functions it will have, who will build it, and how it will be governed.

To be sure, the making of cyberspace in space requires connectivity also between current internet governance and space governance. ICANN and UNOOSA, for example, currently seem to have very little to do with each other. That might, or even should, be changing.

Conclusion: Fragmentation, vulnerability, and uncertainty

The development of cyberspace in space has two main drivers. The first is obviously the technological advances, which – similar to the development of computers – have made satellites both smaller and cheaper, yet at the same time more powerful and efficient. So-called nano-satellites are rapidly filling the skies, providing an increasing number of services – including cyberspace access – for a wide variety of clients including government, military, business, research, transport, NGOs, and individuals.

The second driver of cyberspace in space is the multiplication of space actors – both private and public, as well as different forms of public-private constellations. Privatization and liberalization of access to space, particularly in the United States but also elsewhere (e.g. Luxembourg) has opened up space for new types of private actors, not only "aerospace" and rocket companies, but also internet and new media companies (e.g. Google), as well as mining corporations, and even NGOs.

The development of cyberspace in space has three major consequences, which sums up the main observations made in this chapter. First, it implies *fragmentation* – particularly in terms of stakeholders and governance. It is likely that "governments will not hold complete control over technology dissemination in the global market" in space, something which is already the case for much of cyberspace (Harrison et al. 2017: 1). The growth of states with space program has gone from the original 2 to around 70 today, and the simultaneous growth of private corporations (and NGOs) in space contributes to an increasingly fragmented field of stakeholders. Fragmentation also applies to governance, which already characterizes the two still separate fields of cyberspace and space. Fragmentation will likely increase as these two fields merge. Comprehensive legal frameworks and mechanisms for conflict management and allocation of accountability are lacking, and the few elements that exist were developed during an earlier period, before privatization of cyberspace and space, the Internet of Things, and the renewed programs for space colonization.

Second, *vulnerability* is increasing. When cyberspace becomes increasingly reliant on space-based infrastructure, it becomes vulnerable to new types of threats (in addition to the more well-known dangers that threaten cyberspace on Earth) – not only deliberate attacks such as the use of anti-satellite weapons and targeted satellite hacking, but also the hazards of space debris and solar storms. Moreover, when some form of cyberspace eventually moves into the galaxy, for example when communications is set up between Earth and a remote space settlement, massive time lags and interruptions are to be expected. Programs for "space situational awareness" and the cleaning up space debris are helpful, but they are limited both in terms of participation and resources.

Third, *uncertainty* will be a prevailing feature for the foreseeable future, particularly concerning norms and principles of space activities, and what "balance of power" (if any) there will be in space. This could of course be said about current developments on Earth as well, yet there it is still possible to discern the relative power and influence of particular stakeholders and positions, for example regarding "Internet freedom" and "Internet sovereignty". With regard to cyberspace in space, however, developments seem even more contradictory and uncertain. Will the contradictory trends of, on the one hand, militarization and, on the other hand, civilian or even utopian visions of peaceful space exploration prevail, or will one type of future dominate – whether dark or bright? Looking beyond the horizon currently yields more questions than answers. Yet that uncertainty makes fertile ground for pioneers and adventurers, and many of them are found at the interface of space and cyberspace.

Finally, in order for social scientists to be able to track the development of cyberspace in space and analyze consequences for politics and security, familiarization with technical development and expertise is essential. Reading of expert articles on satellites and other infrastructures is of importance, as are efforts to bridge the gap between technical and social science expertise, which certainly has its challenges given differences in incentives and epistemic cultures. The latter is a prevailing challenge, which students of STS (Science and Technology Studies) have known for decades. Moreover, case studies and comparative analyses of internet satellite programs are of importance for gaining knowledge about the patterns of change and continuity in this field. In addition, analyses of the linkages and gaps between space governance and internet governance are particularly warranted.

References

All links checked on August 20, 2021.

Akyildiz, I. F., Akan, Ö. B., Chen, C., Fang, J., and Su, W. (2003). InterPlaNetary Internet: State-of-the-Art and Research Challenges. *Computer Networks*, 43(2): 75–112.

Amos, J. (2019). SpaceX Puts Up 60 Satellites. *BBC News*. Retrieved September 26, 2019, from: https://www.bbc.com/news/science-environment-48289204.

Andersson, J., and Malm, A. (2006). Public–Private Partnerships and the Challenge of Critical Infrastructure Protection. In M. Dunn and V. Mauer (eds), *International CIIP Handbook 2006, Vol. II: Analyzing Issues, Challenges, and Prospects*. Zurich: Swiss Federal Institute of Technology, pp. 139–167.

Araxia Abrahamian, A. (2017, September 15). How a Tax Haven is Leading the Race to Privatise Space. *The Guardian*. Retrieved September 26, 2019, from: https://www.theguardian.com/news/2017/sep/15/luxembourg-tax-haven-privatise-space.

Bailes, A., and Frommelt, I. (eds). (2004). *Business and Security Public-Private Sector Relationships in a New Security Environment*. New York: Oxford University Press.

Bucur, D., and Iacca, G. (2017). Improved Search Methods for Assessing Delay-Tolerant-Networks Vulnerability to Colluding Strong Heterogeneous Attacks. *Expert Systems with Applications*, 80(1): 311–322.

Choudhury, S. R. (2019, July 22). Super-Fast Internet from Satellites is the Next Big Thing in the Space Race. *CNBC*. Retrieved September 26, 2019, from: https://www.cnbc.com/2019/07/22/fast-internet-via-satellites-is-the-next-big-thing-in-the-space-race.html.

Dunn, M. (2006). Understanding Critical Information Infrastructure: An Elusive Quest. In M. Dunn and V. Mauer (eds), *International CIIP Handbook 2006, Vol. II: Analyzing Issues, Challenges, and Prospects*. Zurich: Swiss Federal Institute of Technology, pp. 27–53.

Dunn Cavelty, M., and Suter, M. (2009). Public–Private Partnerships Are No Silver Bullet: An Expanded Governance Model for Critical Infrastructure Protection. *International Journal of Critical Infrastructure Protection*, 2(4): 179–187.

Durst, R. C., Miller, G. J., and Travis, E. J. (1997). TCP Extensions for Space Communications. *Wireless Networks*, 3(5): 389–403.

Forrer, J., Kee, J. E., Newcomer, K. E., and Boyer E. (2010). Public-Private Partnerships and the Public Accountability Question. *Public Administration Review*, 70(3): 475–484.

Giacomello, G. (2005). *National Governments and Control of the Internet: A Digital Challenge*. London and New York: Routledge.

Giacomello, G. (ed.). (2013). *Security in Cyberspace: Targeting Nations, Infrastructures, Individuals*. New York: Lexington Books.

Goodwin, C. D. (1991). *Economics and National Security: A History of Their Interaction*. Durham and London: Duke University Press.

Grimsey, D., and Lewis, M. K. (2004). *Public Private Partnerships: The Worldwide Revolution in Infrastructure Provision and Project Finance*. Cheltenham: Cheltenham: Edward Elgar.

Gross, G. (2018, March 30). SpaceX Gets US Approval to Launch Space-Based Broadband Service. *Internet Society Blogpost*. Retrieved September 26, 2019, from: https://www.internetsociety.org/blog/2018/03/spacex-gets-us-approval-launch-space-based-broadband-service/?gclid=EAIaIQobChMIq6Phu97c5AIVhdGyCh36jQFrEAAYAyAAEgKHyfD_BwE.

Harrison, T., Hunter, A., Johnson, K., and Roberts, T. (2017). *Implications of Ultra-Low-Cost Access to Space*. Lanham: Rowman and Littlefield.

Hodge, G. A., and Greve, C. (2007). Public–Private Partnerships: An International Performance Review. *Public Administration Review*, 67(3): 545–558.

Jakhu, R., and Pelton J. (eds). (2017). *Global Space Governance: An International Study*. Cham: Springer.

Lin, J., and Singer, P. W. (2018, February 13). China Shot Down Another Missile in Space. *Popular Science*. Retrieved September 26, 2019, from: https://www.popsci.com/china-space-missile-test.

Liou, J. C., and Portman, S. (2007). Chinese Anti-Satellite Test Creates Most Severe Orbital Debris Cloud in History. *Orbital Debris Quarterly News (NASA)*, 11: 2–3.

Martinez, L. F. (1998). Satellite Communications and the Internet: Implications for the Outer Space Treaty. *Space Policy*, 14(2): 83–88.

Mörth, U. (2007). Public and Private Partnerships as Dilemmas between Efficiency and Democratic Accountability: The Case of Galileo. *Journal of European Integration*, 29(7): 601–617.

Mueller, M. (2017). *Will the Internet Fragment? Sovereignty, Globalization and Cyberspace*. Oxford: Polity Press.

Newlove-Eriksson, L., and Eriksson, J. (2013). Governance beyond the Global: Who Controls the Extraterrestrial? *Globalizations*, 10(2): 277–292.

Newlove-Eriksson, L., Giacomello, G., and Eriksson, J. (2018). The Invisible Hand? Critical Information Infrastructures, Commercialization, and National Security. *The International Spectator*, 53(2): 124–140.

Perrow, C. (2011/1984). *Normal Accidents: Living with High Risk Technologies*. Princeton: Princeton University Press.

Rosone, J., and Watson, M. (2017). *Cyber Warfare and the New World Order: World War III Series*, Book IV. Independently published.

Rothe, D., and Shim D. (2018). Sensing the Ground: On the Global Politics of Satellite-Based Activism. *Review of International Studies*, 44(3): 414–437.

Slann, P. A. (2016). Anticipating Uncertainty: The Security of European Critical Outer Space Infrastructures. *Space Policy*, 35(February): 6–14.

Stephens, D. (2017). Increasing Militarization of Space and Normative Responses. In R. Venkata Rao, V. Gopalakrishnan, and K. Abhijeet (eds), *Recent Developments in Space Law*. Singapore: Springer, pp. 91–106.

Valeriano, B., Jensen, B., and Maness, R. C. (2018). *Cyber Strategy: The Evolving Character of Power and Coercion*. Oxford: Oxford University Press.

Van Eeten, M., and Bauer J. M. (2009). Emerging Threats to Internet Security: Incentives, Externalities and Policy Implications. *Journal of Contingencies and Crisis Management*, 17(4): 221–232.

Voosen, P. (2016). Deep Space Network Glitches Worry Scientists. *Science*, 353(6307): 1477–1478.

Walsh, D., and Suliman, A. Z. (2018, September 4). A Facebook War: Libyans Battle on the Streets and on Screens. Retrieved from: https://www.nytimes.com/2018/09/04/world/middleeast/libya-facebook.html.

Wettenhall, R. (2003). The Rhetoric and Reality of Public-Private Partnerships. *Public Organization Review*, 3(1): 77–107.

Part II

Political responses in a complex environment

8 Cyber uncertainties

Observations from cross-national war games

Miguel Alberto Gomez and Christopher Whyte

Recent years have seen scholars distance themselves from the notion of the revolutionary potential of cyberspace. While the early literature asserted that actions through the domain alter the balance of power between states, evidence over the past decade suggests otherwise (e.g. Valeriano et al. 2018). Instead of serving as an independent transformative instrument, operations in cyberspace are employed alongside established instruments of foreign policy (Gartzke 2013). Consequently, the growing exercise of cyber power is less of a revolution and more of an evolution of state behavior in the 21st century. Yet despite an overall tempering of the exceptionalism attributed to cyberspace, our understanding of domain interactions remains limited with respect to the underlying decision-making processes enacted by policy elites.

Studies that approach the mechanisms of interstate interactions through cyberspace, such as that of Jensen, Valeriano, and Maness (2018), utilize observational data to explore the logic of interactions between states online. These efforts contribute to our understanding of the utility of such interactions. However, the decision-making processes leading up to the use of cyber operations remains relatively obscured. Though the argument that this is an expected limitation of observational studies – particularly in a domain characterized so centrally by covert operation and attribution challenges – is a reasonable one, it is nevertheless the case that a better grasp of the logics that drive decision-making in this domain is critical if scholars are to produce better policy-relevant knowledge about how states harness cyber power.

Despite the surge in both cyber operations and the number of state actors conducting them over the past decade, the utility afforded by actions within the domain remains at least partially unclear. Scholars have, particularly following major incidents like the 2007 digital blockade of Estonia and Stuxnet, questioned the advantages of state operation in cyberspace and have increasingly noted the un-warlike nature of cyber instrument usage.[1] One study, for instance, noted recently that less than 5.2% of publicly disclosed cyber operations resulted in concessions from their intended targets (Valeriano et al. 2018: 23). Given this, it is yet unclear why states continue to invest substantial technical, financial, and organizational resources into using the domain offensively, particularly given the existence of other promising elements of state power.

DOI: 10.4324/9781003110224-10

As the fervor to develop operational capabilities in cyberspace continues unabated and as system-level "logic of the domain" research continues to offer little in the way of new insight as to the utility thereof, it becomes crucial for us to pivot to focus on understanding the motivations and processes that facilitate decisions to operate in cyberspace. This chapter joins an emerging micro-foundational body of scholarship in the field of cyber security research. In the proceeding pages, we discuss the outcome of war games conducted with policy, military, and technical elites from Taiwan, the United States, and the Philippines designed to better understand the significance of decision-maker priors and situational context on key concepts such as "red lines", attribution, and escalation.

The war games discussed in this chapter are pseudo-experimental. Thus, it is important to note that, while it surfaces certain processes, it cannot completely rule out confounding factors as effectively as might conventional experimental studies. Despite this constraint, the cross-national nature of these war games offers crucial insights concerning the commonalities and variations in response to cyber security incidents. Specifically, the war games highlight the importance of priors in the form of preexisting beliefs and policy preferences that shape operation preferences in response to cyber security incidents. Despite the consistency offered by the war games as well as the commonalities shared by the participants (i.e. respective professional backgrounds), we find that their in-game behavior appears motivated by individualized and/or socialized experiences than responding to threats. These, in turn, serve as heuristic mechanisms that guide decision-making behavior throughout gameplay.

While this is by no means a novel finding, it does confirm observations from comparable experimental studies involving non-elites. Theoretically, this demonstrates the existence of common cognitive processes between these two groups, suggesting the existence of a shared perception of cyber security threats. The possibility of this is noteworthy as it establishes the existence of uncertainty toward the domain irrespective of role that is seemingly alleviated by heuristic use. Methodologically, this challenges the criticisms aimed at experimental research that study elite behavior proxied through non-elite participants. If both populations exhibit comparable cognitive processes, then it is fair to argue that the continued use of experimental designs involving non-elites is a worthwhile endeavor.

With the core objectives and overall findings in this chapter established, the following pages are organized as follows. The next section presents an overview of developments in cyber security scholarship that highlights key questions pursued by the war games and sets the theoretical framework that guides our line of inquiry. This is then succeeded by a methodological discussion of wargaming and the design employed. In qualitatively reporting our results, we focus on the unique cross-national variations in response and cognition across different populations. Specifically, the chapter surfaces individual mechanisms resulting in preferred responses that appear to be rooted not in personal experience or strategic assessment so much as they are in shared cultural or institutional-cultural experience. Finally, the discussion concludes by highlighting the primary lessons learned from this study and offers possible avenues of expansion for those wishing to pursue this line of inquiry further.

Evolution of the field

Taking into consideration the emergent nature of cyber security as a field of study, this section provides readers with an overview of how it has evolved. Beginning with a discussion of the inherent vulnerability of the domain, it proceeds into the dominant system-level analysis of decision-making in cyberspace prevalent in the literature. By doing so, it highlights the limitations of this approach by acknowledging inconsistencies such as the emphasis on cyber capability development vis-à-vis the absence of demonstratable strategic utility and the limited prioritization of misperception among disputing parties. Consequently, this permits the discussion to flow naturally into the growing behavioral "shift" in cyber security literature as a means of rectifying these gaps in our understanding of decision-making in cyberspace. Furthermore, it emphasizes the importance of micro-level factors as an important steppingstone toward understanding system-level dynamics.

A vulnerable environment

Since its earliest conception in the writings of Arquilla and Ronfeldt (1999), the exercise of power through cyberspace has often been viewed in the context of interstate relations. Though the literature that has emerged since that time is diverse, most scholars agree that the decision to operate in cyberspace rests on three key aspects that characterized the domain: Increased dependence on cyberspace, vulnerabilities inherent to the domain, and the anonymity granted to actors within cyberspace (see, for instance, Kello 2013). Indeed, alone, these traits typify the *cyber revolution* thesis that was developed during the early 2000s.

That cyberspace sits at the heart of modern society is uncontroversial. Globally, fixed broadband subscription has grown from 0.82 to 14.81 per 100 individuals in just the past 17 years. In that same period, internet usage has ballooned from a mere 8.06% of the global population to nearly 50% (Hoffman and Novak 2001). Declining costs of infrastructure and end-user devices increased the accessibility to cyberspace across the period, permitting societies across the globe to maximize the sociopolitical and economic benefits thereof. As Kuehl (2009) notes, cyberspace is now an enabler of the traditional levers of power employed by states to meet their strategic objectives.

Economically, some states, like Singapore, maximized their potential to find positions of strength by becoming information and communications technology (ICT) service providers (Cyber security Agency of Singapore 2016). Politically, world leaders are increasingly exploiting now-pervasive social media to mobilize support (Bor 2014; Enli 2017). Socially, states like Estonia are turning to ICT to offer faster and more efficient services to their citizens (Kalvet 2012). Finally, and perhaps most relevant to this chapter, the coercive potential of cyberspace has prompted states around the world to develop or improve existing organizational and technological capabilities (see *inter alia* Whyte 2016; Sharp 2017; Borghard and Lonergan 2017).

Juxtaposed to the enabling aspect of cyberspace are the vulnerabilities that are expected of highly complex and interconnected system. As noted by the late Charles Perrow (2014), as systems complexify, it becomes increasingly difficult to correct individual faults. Moreover, it becomes challenging to predict downstream effects of component failure on entire systems. With cyberspace, the features of its components that enable continued expansion also contributes to such pervasive vulnerabilities. Experts estimate that software will typically have between 15 and 50 errors per 1,000 lines of code. To put matters into perspective, systems on the Airbus A380 have around 120 million lines of code (Charette 2009), suggesting at least the existence of approximately 1.8 million errors. Though not all faults will lead to catastrophic failure, the interdependence of systems and their centrality in modern society makes it easy to see how exploitation of single points of failure might have dramatic consequence.

Finally, questions of identity sit at the heart of usage of this man-made domain. While digital forensics allows for the technical identification of malicious actions' origins, attribution of agency or intent remains elusive (Rid and Buchanan 2015). The anonymity offered in cyberspace emboldens malicious actors to exploit the inherent vulnerabilities and growing dependence on cyberspace to meet specific objectives.

A state-centric view of cyber conflict

How does cyberspace actually alter the strategic dynamics of interstate relations? Against the backdrop of the *cyber revolution* thesis's overarching emphasis on domain characteristics, much literature has since focused on the potential of cyber to enable coercion below the threshold of armed conflict. Enabled by expanding utilization, persistent vulnerabilities, and a sense of anonymity, frameworks that account for state activities in this domain build on the notion of the offensive advantage offered by cyberspace (Slayton 2017). Several assumptions underlie this notion, not the least of which is the attribution problem itself. Additionally, attackers rely on secrecy for effectiveness. Their tools have relatively short shelf lives given that even routine defender system updates might nullify technical abilities. And authorization for attacks often does not come from state leaders. Taken together, conflict in cyberspace is characterized by "use or lose" mentalities surrounding capability.

And yet, as convincing as the above logic might be, evidence from this past decade continues to suggest that cyber interactions are not best understood via "logic of the domain"-style arguments. Liff (2012) notes that interstate behavior is governed by the material balance of power, arguing that near-peer adversaries are likely to vigorously engage online while asymmetric relationships may involve more measured responses by the weaker party so as to avoid conventional provocation. Such arguments highlight two key focal points of contemporary cyber security scholarship: Material requirements and escalation avoidance.

In studies of both, it has become apparent that a significant amount of economic, technical, and organizational resources is necessary to effectively employ cyber operations as a coercive instrument (Slayton 2017). In her seminal article, Slayton (2017) argues that substantial organizational capabilities, and corresponding technical skills, are required to successfully infiltrate and threaten secure systems. Furthermore, she challenges the notion that attackers are advantaged in cyberspace by arguing that adversarial success requires knowledge of preexisting defensive mechanisms already in place. Defenders often have the upper hand in shaping the environment such that costs incurred by an adversary are disproportionate to gains (Gartzke 2013). Furthermore, the types of cyber operations popularized by the media and Hollywood are unlikely upon closer inspection. Punishment and risk manipulation strategies are infeasible because of the significant technical and organizational resources required (Valeriano et al. 2018). In these instances, it may be cheaper to rely on conventional means (e.g. a missile).

Recently, scholars such as Lindsay and Gartzke (2016) suggested that in-domain interactions reflect the stability–instability paradox observed during the Cold War. Adversaries interact and exploit one other's vulnerabilities online without necessarily engaging in actions that are likely to trigger escalation. In addition, the covert nature of cyber operations means that digital action can constitute signaling via which adversaries might actively communicate their interests in both long-standing and emergent issues while controlling for domestic pressure that may provoke a less measured response. Similarly, Maness and Valeriano (2015) observe that adversaries limit their interactions within the pre-defined range of the existing adversarial relationship. That is to say, while offensive operations in cyberspace are to be expected, these only occur within the normalized bounds of the existing rivalry.

Although cyber security scholarship continues to prosper as an emergent field of study, the majority of scholars that pursue a structural account of state interactions within cyberspace generally agree on the mechanisms established in the preceding paragraphs. *First, resources constrain the overall utility expected from cyber operations. Second, cyber operations serve as an instrument that signals resolve while minimizing escalation.*

During the third quarter of 2018 the United States issued a new cyber strategy signaling a shift away from a deterrence approach to cyber conflict management. Noting the high tempo of operations and growing capabilities of adversaries online, the new strategy surfaces the concept of persistent engagement and forward defense. In sum, the two concepts argue that cyber security may only be achieved by continually engaging and degrading adversarial capabilities and operations wherever they are found (Department of Defense 2018). These concepts, derived from the work of Harknett and Fischerkeller (2017), align both with the strategic realities faced by the United States and the general trend of cyber security scholarship.

That said, they also ignore the potential unintended escalation. Though it would be correct to note – as many have – that escalation has not taken place in response to cyber operations, the prospect cannot be ruled out entirely. In particular, in debates about the prospective value of persistent engagement, little has been said concerning the possibility of in-domain misperception. Specifically, if the strategy calls for the United States to operate freely in cyberspace, regardless of territorial considerations, what might allies and adversaries interpret from such actions? Although Harknett and Fischerkeller are sanguine about the prospect of continued stability, their dismissal of the possibility for miscommunication is worrisome. Moreover, the limited interest expressed by the field in misperception and other manifestations of cognitive and affective components are problematic given the tendency of decision-makers to rely on these structures given the unique characteristics of the domain.

The behavioral turn in cyber conflict

A groundswell is taking shape with respect to scholarship focusing on the micro-foundational aspects of cyber security. Both Dean and McDermott (2017) support the idea that a growth in the analysis of individual (and organizational) level aspects of cyber security is likely to contribute positively to our understanding of decision-making and state behavior in cyberspace. And while not as consistent as the established structural accounts of behavior in cyberspace, available studies continue to complement existing frameworks as those highlighted in the preceding subsection. Specifically, current research within this level of analysis focuses on the effects of uncertainty on judgment.

For the purpose of this chapter, we treat uncertainty as a function of ambiguity. That is to say, cyberspace is characterized by a significant amount of ambiguity that introduces cognitive constraints on individual decision-makers resulting in sub-optimal outcomes (Rathbun 2007). This is not a novel claim and was proposed by other scholars as a potential source of exceptionalism and hyperbole with respect to cyberspace (Hansen and Nissenbaum 2009; Godman and Arquilla 2014). Ambiguity, in this context, pertains to the uncertainty of meaning given the occurrence of a cyber security incident. That is to say, decision-makers, and the wider polity to the extent that they are aware, are uncertain as to how to interpret malicious actions. In terms of on-going research, interest is centered on how uncertainty impacts judgments concerning intent and consequences (e.g. escalation).

Intent is difficult to gauge when the only evidence available is malicious code. Compared to conventional military instruments, the appearance of tanks at the border sends a clearer signal than the discovery of malware on sensitive systems. Buchanan (2016) argues that this uncertainty of intent may trigger a dilemma between parties. Malicious code used for tolerated espionage activities may also be employed to degrade or disrupt critical infrastructure. Without a clear admission of intent, victims are unable to discern the function of these unwanted discoveries. A similar concern is echoed by Gartzke and Lindsay (2015) who further emphasize that despite discovery and neutralization, victims may feel the need to escalate in order to deter future attempts by potential adversaries.

The lack of certainty with respect to intent provokes a host of heuristic mechanisms to assist in reaching cognitive closure. For their part, both Gartzke and Lindsay (2015) posit that previous behavior may serve as an anchor on which to evaluate the overall intent. This is also shared by Maness and Valeriano (2015) who posit that escalation is minimized in rivalry relationships due to pre-expectations. Both sets of authors indirectly reference the concept of *enemy images* in their arguments. *Enemy images* are cognitive constructs through which other actors are believed to behave in bad faith. These constructs are often formed over time and are molded by another actor's behavior during separate, and possibly unrelated, interactions. As cyber operations are increasingly appearing during emergent or existing disputes, it is likely that these images are formed even before the occurrence of a cyber security incident and lends explanatory weight to the assumptions of the above authors.

Empirically, the influence of *enemy images* on judgments of intent was demonstrated by Gomez (2019) in two separate survey experiments. For the first, the presence of an *enemy image* dissuaded participants from maximizing the available information in order to accurately assess the probability that a suspected adversary was responsible for a given cyber security incident. This implies that behavioral expectations take priority over a rigorous and deliberative assessment of a given situation despite the availability of information. For the second, *enemy images* resulted in participants gravitating toward evidence confirming their preexisting beliefs regarding the behavior of a potential adversary and a refusal to adjust their judgments in the face of evidence.

The reliance of decision-makers on priors, specifically a dependence on preexisting beliefs, is crucial in understanding interstate behavior in cyberspace. While systemic explanations expect restraint as a means of managing escalation, expectations based on past experience may provoke a more forceful response between adversaries. Moreover, these beliefs may also provoke a degree of overconfidence that is unsubstantiated by material realities and may encourage a more hawkish response to an incident (Bar-Joseph and Kruglanski 2003). As such, *the utilization of enemy images as a heuristic mechanism to reduce uncertainty may result in a deviation from expected rational behavior on the part of decision-makers.*

Apart from intent, uncertainty with respect to the consequences of cyber operations may prompt a host of heuristic mechanisms that may prove detrimental to the maintenance of stability in cyberspace. In this case, questions concerning consequences have been approached from the perspective of the general public and that of political elites. And while the results appear to diverge in some areas, these findings add nuance to existing frameworks that explain interstate relations in cyberspace.

With respect to the influence of uncertain consequences on the general public, Gross, Canetti, and Vashdi (2016, 2017) experimentally demonstrate that the physiological and psychological impact of these incidents are comparable to that of conventional terrorist attacks and that the (potential) loss of life provokes a hawkish attitude among participants in the study. This finding is crucial. Despite the lack of ample evidence, the media still continues to promote the idea of cyber operations as an existential threat (Lawson and Middleton 2019). Without the necessary expertise, the public may anchor their beliefs on these narratives that increases pressure on policy elites to act decisively. Elites themselves, however, are not immune to the effects of unknown consequences.

Kreps and Schneider (2019) find that elites participating in a series of war games resort to analogical reasoning to make sense of the uncertain consequences of cyber operations. Over a six-year period, elites participating in a war game sponsored by the US Department of Defense (DoD) drew parallels between cyber operations and nuclear weapons. That is, the use of the former is likely to generate a significant destabilizing effect – even after the militarization of a conflict. The use of analogies as a salve for uncertainty is not unheard of. Political psychologists have long argued that analogies are employed as a heuristic mechanism to simplify complex situations by drawing parallels with previous, though not necessarily similar, cases (Khong 1992). For instance, references to Hitler when certain world leaders are acting in a belligerent manner permit leaders to better communicate their message without having to invest significant cognitive resource to the task. Although this may be an efficient simplifying mechanism, it is not without its issues.

The successful use of analogies depends on the degree to which similarities exist. Suffice to say, applying an analogy to a completely unrelated issue may result in a wholly inappropriate outcome (Khong 1992; Bar-Joseph and Kruglanski 2003) For example, references to cyber operations and the 9/11 attacks find little in common with each other. While the United States is vulnerable through cyberspace owing to the state of its infrastructure, there is no evidence to show that terrorists are capable of launching a similar attack. Moreover, there is no proof that a cyber operation has resulted in the loss of life as a first-order effect. Analogies may also prime the use of stereotypes that further aggravates the situation. Building on the example above, references to 9/11 may provoke anger that, in turn, inhibits further search for information thus resulting in abrupt and rash decision-making (Carver and Harmon-Jones 2009; Weeks 2015).

In the case of the war games conducted by Schneider, participants either refused to exercise or severely curtailed their ability to operate within the domain. This appears to contradict one key aspect of state cyber operations mentioned previously: That these are a function of existing material capabilities. The result of the war games appears to temper this claim. Because of their belief in the destabilizing potential of cyber operations by drawing analogies with nuclear weapons, the participants hesitate to use their capabilities to better influence the situation in their favor. Furthermore, Schneider suspects that apprehension (rather than fear) also served to modulate the exercise of cyber power (2019).

Unlike fear that results in an inhibition of deliberative and thoughtful cognition, apprehension promotes risk-averse behavior among individuals. In this case, apprehension due to uncertainty of effects and how the opposing party would perceive cyber operations resulted in cautious behavior. As with analogies, this limits the ability of participants to maximize their capabilities despite having the balance of power in their favor.

With respect to the uncertainty of consequences, its influence over decision-making and, in turn, state behavior, is twofold. *On the one hand, parallels between real-world violence and cyber operations increases hawkishness among non-elites. On the other, the use of analogical reasoning and a sense of apprehension may temper elite response despite having the capabilities to act more decisively.*

Uncertainty with respect to both intent and consequences has serious implications for our understanding of state behavior in cyberspace. While structural explanations expect adherence to the normative requirements of rational choice, the inclusion of micro-foundational concepts raises questions as to the extent to which one could expect decision-makers to act rationally.

War gaming and cross-national comparisons

A methodological shift

With a growing interest in the micro-foundational components of cyber security, scholars are implementing wargaming as a tool to better understand the phenomenon of decision-making in response to cyber operations (for instance, Lin-Greenberg 2018). Although observational studies provide the means with which to investigate real-world incidents, simulations such as war games offer their own set of advantages.

Unlike observational studies, war games provide researchers with the opportunity to observe the intricacies of decision-making in analogous situations (Kreps and Schneider 2019). While approaches such as archival research may afford scholars the opportunity to dissect these processes after the fact, the nature of cyber security suggests that these artifacts are likely to remain classified in the near future. War games, in contrast, enables scholars to observe (in-game) and probe (post-game) participants on the nuances of their actions. Moreover, the fact that fictitious scenarios are used reduces the reticence of participants to share their opinions.

War games also provide scholars a degree of control. While not as extensive as those afforded to experiments, researchers are able to immerse participants in scenarios that best represent their research objectives. This aspect speaks to the question of controlling for confounding variables that may obscure the mechanisms under investigation. This degree of control also extends to the actual participants of the said game. Scholars are able to select participants based on fundamental attributes (e.g. elites versus non-elites) so as to permit a comparison between groups. For instance, running a simulation between specialists and laymen permits an analysis of the importance of domain expertise.

Finally, war games offer a predictable and plausible environment to conduct research. Cyber security scholars interested in studying novel events are at the mercy of the unpredictability of cyber security incidents. With that in mind, war games permit the immersion of participants into relevant scenarios in order to gauge their respective reactions. And while critics may argue the degree to which observed behavior is aligned with that of real-world cases, it should be noted that absolute realism is not a requirement for participant engagement. Psychological studies note that the suspension of disbelief, or the mere plausibility of the scenario, is enough to encourage realistic behavior from participants (Perla and McGrady 2011). Consequently, the mundane realism of these activities need not be taken to the extreme in order to reap benefits.

War games, however, are not without their disadvantages. Despite the degree of control afforded, these are not comparable with experimental designs that test the internal validity of processes under investigation. Furthermore, experiments are much easier to replicate and thus provide other scholars the opportunity to validate findings. These require other methodologies to complement this particular constraint. War games are also susceptible to developing extreme or unrealistic scenarios. Although nothing prohibits designers from testing behavior at the boundaries of reality, these are less likely to provide useful observations. War games are also best suited to tackling questions concerned with behavior rather than employing it as a means to tease out operations specifics. Phrased differently, a different method is necessary if scholars are after a specific value (e.g. how many tanks will tip the balance of power). Finally, war games are not immune to the problem of accessibility. An accurate assessment of elite behavior still requires the participation of these said elites. The participation of these individuals limits the utility gained from this methodological choice.

Cyber Rubicon wargame

Building on the behavioral turn in cyber security research, a series of cyber security war games were conducted from January to August 2019 involving participants from Taiwan, the Philippines, and the United States.[2] The objective of the war game is to determine the means with which prior beliefs and analogical reasoning are employed to discern intent and consequences. Readers should note that these war games are part of a larger research project which involves a cross-national survey experiment which is not discussed in this chapter.

The war game consists of a scenario involving the fictitious states, Idemore and Vadare (see Figure 8.1). Both are depicted as having comparable military and economic capabilities and share a common border with each other. At the start of the war game, a growing dispute involving natural resources is taking shape between the two states. Overshadowing this issue are disruptive cyber operations that appear to have originated from Vadare. As the game progresses, Vadare appears to be bringing its diplomatic and military instruments to bear in support of its interests. All the while, cyber operations continue to affect Idemore.

Participants, acting in teams of three, play the role of Idemorean policy elites tasked with addressing the growing crisis. Each participant adopts the role of either the Secretary of Foreign Affairs, Secretary of Defense, or the Secretary of Information Technology and Security. The decision to segregate participants into these roles is twofold. First, these represent state organs that are most likely to be involved in an interstate cyber security incident. Second, by assigning participants to leadership roles in different organizations the simulation aims to mimic

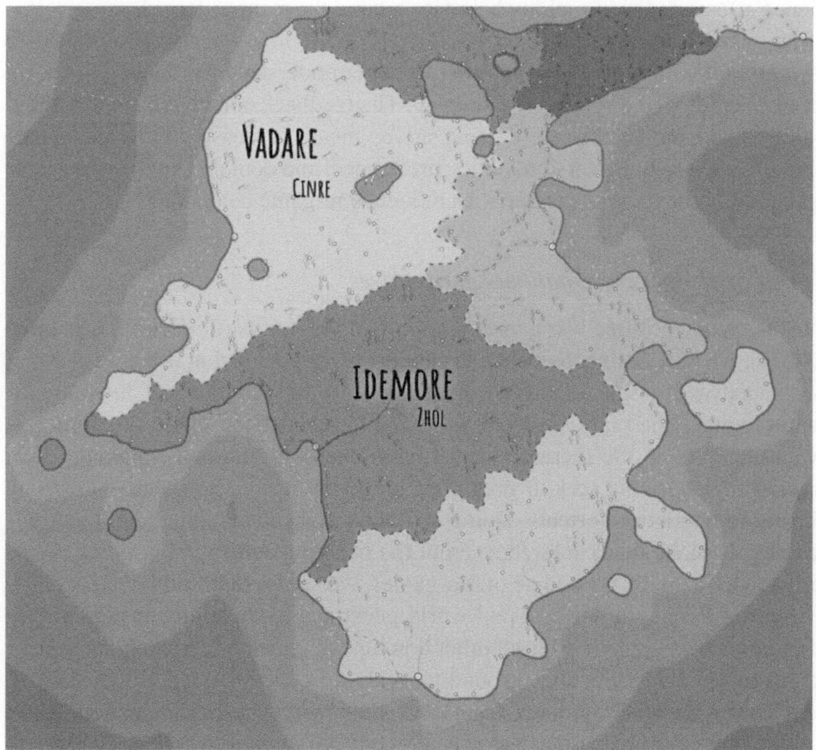

Figure 8.1 Visualization of Vadare and Idemore given to war game participants.

organizational dynamics that may take effect in a real-world setting. It should also be noted that, ideally, participants are recruited from elites that already enact these fictitious roles in one form or another (i.e. military officers are recruited to be the Secretary of Defense). This, however, is constrained by their availability.

The war game is divided into three (3) distinct rounds that simulate growing severity and uncertainty with the situation. At the start of each round, participants are presented with general and role-specific information pertaining to the ongoing crisis. No specific instruction is given whether or not to share or conceal the latter to determine whether or not information-seeking behavior will occur. Other than current developments, participants are also given a list of possible policy responses; one of which needs to be selected by the end of the round. This choice determines the underlying conditions that teams will face in the succeeding round.

It should also be pointed out that this war game is distinct in that it employs a pseudo-experimental component during gameplay. Teams during the second round are either informed that a cyber operation has affected the national healthcare system or the national tax system. Teams are randomly assigned to either condition. This design choice was made to determine the extent to which target salience affects decision-making behavior among the teams.

The entire war game takes approximately 1.5–2 hours to accomplish. After gameplay, teams are debriefed in order to better understand the decision-making processes employed throughout gameplay. The feedback obtained from these sessions are also compared to a pre-game survey meant to measure individual characteristics such as risk aversion, policy preference, and domain expertise to assess whether and how these characteristics influence in-game behavior.

The role of distinct cross-national perspectives

Over the course of three war games involving dozens of participants across three countries, we find distinct evidence in support of the notion that decision-makers, when faced with issues of digital insecurity and the use of cyber instruments, attempt to make their task simpler by looking to parallel non-cyber situations. As is well-observed in the literatures on foreign and domestic policymaking, decision-makers invariably seek to streamline their approach to prospective crises by referring to heuristic shortcuts. Doing so allows stakeholders the cognitive tools necessary to make quick inference about the meaning and significance of events presented to them. In the course of our games, we see, perhaps not unexpectedly, participants frequently look to real-world geostrategic situations, historical episodes, or concepts borrowed from other domains of interstate engagement in their attempt to rapidly assess and respond to evolving cyber-enabled circumstances. Consistent with other findings from preceding survey experimentation, however, the degree to which these efforts affect information processing, confidence in actions proposed and more is variably dependent on preexisting know-how. Simply put, the more individuals know about cyber conflict, the nature of their worldview vis-à-vis international engagement and their educational background – among other things – impacts the manner in which looking for non-cyber parallels is sufficiently grounded in the reality of the scenario being presented.

For the purposes of this chapter, perhaps the most interesting findings from the war games pertain to the clear role of distinct cross-national perspectives in explaining variation in outcomes across participants. Even given the broad similarities in the populations under study as being foreign policy professionals (of one kind or another) in a democratic state, it is clear that cultural, procedural, and political expectations unique to each national context shape decision-maker actions. This is not unique to elites as a similar observation is made with non-elites (Gomez 2019a, 2019b), but it is significant as it confirms the existence of a comparable process among elites.

Perhaps most visibly, there was clear variation across war game participants on numerous instances in how process and procedure made their way into an individual's perception of their assumed role. Across the board, participants communicated clear motivation for their actions based on an operational understanding of the roles given to them. This manifested in two ways – in (1) their understanding of the relationship between roles within their assigned teams and (2) within their understanding of the norms of foreign policy process. On the former point, for instance, one team noted that a unanimous decision was not easy initially because each team member was only willing to accept responsibility for reporting their portfolio. On the latter point, for instance, a US team consistently articulated their logic of approach to cyber intrusions as a potential function of foreign policy gambits being prosecuted in other domains.

Relatedly, this finding that role perception dictated divergent – occasionally dramatically so – decision-making outcomes among participants was clear not only in how procedure made its way into the process of scenario response. Likewise, there was clear variation in how individuals assessed their responsibilities as either policy, military, or cyber experts within a democratic government – i.e. they focused on the normative implications of their potential responses. For several teams, responsibilities assessed toward the civilian side of government or toward the polity at large led to the determination of thresholds for engagement that varied starkly from those whose response emerged more simply – at least as was represented in debriefing – from analysis of the facts being presented. Moreover, such assessments differed across national cases, which we discuss below.

With regard to the details of the foreign policy crisis being experienced, our findings also highlight the fashion in which attribution and blame manifest with some interesting variation across national professional settings. In particular, we found that war game participants diverged around the question of whether or not a foreign country is complicit in aggressive cyber activity *regardless of whether or not that country's government is actually involved.* As one US team noted,

> [s]o, I see that as a little different then Afghanistan harboring Al Qaida forces because they are terrorists, although they are not necessarily linked. Because they are harboring those forces. Because the servers, in this case, were coming from Vadare. The state has some sort of responsibility to react.

This differs from what was generally seen in other country populations (e.g. Taiwan and the Philippines) under study, a team within which, for instance, articulated the consensus position that technical attributes *must* drive calculations above and beyond geographical descriptors. As one officer suggested,

> the fact that there was no traffic, you know, there was no botnet traffic indicating that this was actually fired or, you know, triggered from within the enemy state […] that's probably the key piece of information that attributes the uncertainty into the equation.

Perhaps unsurprisingly, this particular result fits with a broader observation made in post-war game analysis of results and of debriefing materials, that certain specific national narratives dominated the reach for parallels to inform decision-making processes. With respondents in both Philippines and Taiwan, clear reference was made by participants to the overarching threat of Chinese military modernization and perceived assertiveness in regional affairs. Such references occurred both directly and as a lens through which assessments of intent and capabilities were conducted. As one officer in Taiwan noted, "there's an occasion to serve in the military in Taiwan, we know, we are actively prepared for a war, right?" By contrast, respondents in the United States were less willing to cast the scenario being presented as representative of a particular real-world situation and instead resorted on numerous instances to simple categorization of the event (i.e. a contest between "middle powers" such as "Iran and Iraq" or "Pakistan and India") as a means to introduce prospectively useful concepts or precedents. Interestingly, the only two exceptions to this approach with the US population were exchange officers from Australia and the Philippines, both of whom consistently referenced the People's Republic of China in attempting to contextualize in-game cyber actions.

Finally, the debriefing sessions held in conjunction with our war games across three countries demonstrated some variation in the role that death might play in dictating more or less severe response to cyber incidents. In Taiwan, participants generally felt that loss of life throws the question of retaliation to cyber incidents into more assured territory, with one team asserting strongly that the death of a Taiwanese citizen dictates a democratic mandate for the government to affect justice in its chosen foreign policy response. As one official put it, "[c]yber attack against our infrastructure that leads to loss of human life [...] [t]hat would cause astonishing domestic pressure". By contrast, military officers surveyed in the United States again reached for categorical characterizations of the scenario to debate the prospect of death in cyber-enabled incidents versus historical or situational ones. Faced with the question of what level of injury to the American people would require a reasonably severe initial response, American participants variously suggested that low numbers of indirect deaths would, particularly given the relative opacity of cyberattacks, perhaps be seen more as an unfortunate result of infrastructure failure or interference. As one officer put it, problems of foreign source "attribution protects us too with no firm return address". As another noted, "[t]hese things can be slow moving and I don't believe we'd be forced into military force". The severity of initial response would, as they saw it, depend directly on the nature of media coverage and public opinion. In other words, where Taiwanese respondents were quick to assert the principle of severe response to death from cyber incidents, American counterparts suggested that the principle applied in greater or lesser degrees depending on either the fact or scope of negative response by the population. "But sure, it might [...]", one US team described, "[...]become something the president can't ignore".

Conclusion

This chapter supports the premise of the recent behavioral turn in cyber security research that much variation across cyber conflict dynamics and outcomes are best explained at the level of the individual and the institution. Specifically, we suggest that war games are useful tools of research that, particularly when pseudo-experimental designs are employed in support of experiments, can validate findings that often offer greater statistical power and are yet necessarily simple in their construction. Moreover, war games provide the opportunity to better clarify research questions that emerge from such experimental findings.

In our cyber conflict escalation war games, we see evidence that decision-making in this domain works similarly to foreign policy decision-making more broadly insofar as stakeholders reach for shortcuts in past experiences that help them see meaning as quickly as possible. The degree to which such shortcuts interfere with objectivity emerges from a series of factors that constitute individuals' worldview.

Beyond such broad confirmation of well-known decision-making dynamics at work where cyber is involved, however, we also see distinct evidence of cross-national cultural variations influencing response decisions among elite stakeholders. For future research, it seems particularly clear that the socio-institutional correlates of civilian-military relations in a given democracy stand to have a unique impact on decision-making processes, both in terms of the value calculations that individuals bring into their roles and in terms of the strategic cultures that form around unique national circumstance. In our simulations, we see evidence of such context even affecting assessments of the significance of indirect civilian deaths in crisis situations, which suggests that such correlates might ultimately have some effect on the strategic calculations states make around signaling and adversary behavior. As such, scholars and practitioners alike would do well to both encourage and undertake behavioral research that can be scaled to useful inference for the development of doctrine and practical training.

Notes

1 Early examples of which include, among others, Liff (2012), Rid (2013), Lindsay (2013), Gartzke (2013), and Valeriano and Maness (2014).

2 Additional war games are being planned with Singapore, Switzerland, and Israel.

References

All Links checked on August 20 2021.

Arquilla, J., and Ronfeldt, D. (1999). The Advent of Netwar: Analytic Background. *Studies in Conflict and Terrorism*, 22(3): 193–206.

Bar–Joseph, U., and Kruglanski, A. W. (2003). Intelligence Failure and Need for Cognitive Closure: On the Psychology of the Yom Kippur Surprise. *Political Psychology*, 24(1): 75–99.

Bor, S. E. (2014). Using Social Network Sites to Improve Communication between Political Campaigns and Citizens in the 2012E. *American Behavioral Scientist*, 58(9): 1195–1213.

Borghard, E. D., and Lonergan, S. W. (2017). The Logic of Coercion in Cyberspace. *Security Studies*, 26(3): 452–481.

Buchanan, B. (2016). *The Cyber Security Dilemma: Hacking, Trust, and Fear between Nations*. Oxford: Oxford University Press.

Carver, C. S., and Harmon-Jones, E. (2009). Anger is an Approach-Related Affect: Evidence and Implications. *Psychological Bulletin*, 135(2): 183–294.

Charette, R. N. (2009). This Car Runs on Code. *IEEE Spectrum*. Retrieved from: https://spectrum.ieee.org/transportation/systems/this-car-runs-on-code.

Cyber Security Agency of Singapore. (2016). *Singapore Cybersecurity Strategy*. Retrieved from: https://www.csa.gov.sg/news/publications/singapore-cybersecurity-strategy

Dean, B., and McDermott, R. (2017). A Research Agenda to Improve Decision Making in Cyber Security Policy. *Penn State Journal of Law & International Affairs*, 5(1): 29–71.

Enli, G. (2017). Twitter as Arena for the Authentic Outsider: Exploring the Social Media Campaigns of Trump and Clinton in the 2016 US Presidential Election. *European Journal of Communication*, 32(1): 50–61.

Gartzke, E. (2013). The Mth of Cyberwar: Bringing War in Cyberspace Back Down to Earth. *International Security*, 38(2): 41–73.

Gartzke, E., and Lindsay, J. R. (2015). Weaving Tangled Webs: Offense, Defense, and Deception in Cyberspace. *Security Studies*, 24(2): 316–348.

Goldman, E. O., and Arquilla, J. (2014). *Cyber Analogies (No. NPS-DA-14-001)*. Monterey, CA: Naval Postgraduate School.

Gomez, M. A. (2019a). Past Behavior and Future Judgements: Seizing and Freezing in Response to Cyber Operations. *Journal of Cyber Security*, 5(1): tyz012.

Gomez, M. A. (2019b). Sound the Alarm! Updating Beliefs and Degradative Cyber Operations. *European Journal of International Security*, 4(2): 190–208.

Gross, M. L., Canetti, D., and Vashdi, D. R. (2016). The Psychological Effects of Cyber Terrorism. *Bulletin of the Atomic Scientists*, 72(5): 284–291.

Gross, M. L., Canetti, D., and Vashdi, D. R. (2017). Cyberterrorism: Its Effects on Psychological Well-Being, Public Confidence and Political Attitudes. *Journal of Cyber Security*, 3(1): 49–58.

Fischerkeller, M. P., and Harknett, R. J. (2017). Deterrence is not a Credible Strategy for Cyberspace. *Orbis*, 61(3): 381–393.

Hansen, L., and Nissenbaum, H. (2009). Digital Disaster, Cyber Security, and the Copenhagen School. *International Studies Quarterly*, 53(4): 1155–1175.

Hoffman, D. L., Novak, T. P., and Schlosser, A. E. (2001). The Evolution of the Digital Divide: Examining the Relationship of Race to Internet Access and Usage Over Time. In B. M. Compaine (ed.), *The Digital Divide: Facing a Crisis or Creating a Myth*. Cambridge: MIT Press, pp. 47–97.

Kalvet, T. (2012). Innovation: A Factor Explaining e-Government Success in Estonia. *Electronic Government: An International Journal*, 9(2): 142–157.

Kello, L. (2013). The Meaning of the Cyber Revolution: Perils to Theory and Statecraft. *International Security*, 38(2): 7–40.

Khong, Y. F. (1992). *Analogies at War: Korea, Munich, Dien Bien Phu, and the Vietnam Decisions of 1965*. Princeton, NJ: Princeton University Press.

Kreps, S., and Schneider, J. (2019). Escalation Firebreaks in the Cyber, Conventional, and Nuclear Domains: Moving beyond Effects-Based Logics. *Journal of Cyber Security*, 5(1): tyz007.

Kuehl, D. T. (2009). From Cyberspace to Cyberpower: Defining the Problem. *Cyberpower and National Security*, 30. Dulles: Potomac Books.

Lawson, S., and Middleton, M. K. (2019). Cyber Pearl Harbor: Analogy, Fear, and the Framing of Cyber Security Threats in the United States, 1991–2016. *First Monday*, 24(3). https://doi.org/10.5210/fm.v24i3.9623.

Liff, A. P. (2012). Cyberwar: A New 'Absolute Weapon'? The Proliferation of Cyberwarfare Capabilities and Interstate War. *Journal of Strategic Studies*, 35(3): 401–428.

Lin-Greenberg, E. (2018). Game of Drones: The Effect of Remote Warfighting Technology on Conflict Escalation (Evidence from Wargames). SSRN. Retrieved from: https://dx.doi.org/10.2139/ssrn.3288988.

Lindsay, J. R. (2013). Stuxnet and the Limits of Cyber Warfare. *Security Studies*, 22(3): 365–404.

Lindsay, J. R., and Gartzke, E. (2016). Coercion through Cyberspace: The Stability-Instability Paradox Revisited. In K. M. Greenhill and P. J. P. Krause (eds), *The Power to Hurt: Coercion in Theory and in Practice*. New York: Oxford University Press, pp. 179–203.

Perla, P. P., and McGrady, E. D. (2011). Why Wargaming Works. *Naval War College Review*, 64(3): 111–130.

Perrow, C. (2014). *Complex Organizations: A Critical Essay*. Brattleboro: Echo Point Books & Media.

Rathbun, B. C. (2007). Uncertain about Uncertainty: Understanding the Multiple Meanings of a Crucial Concept in International Relations Theory. *International Studies Quarterly*, 51(3): 533–557.

Rid, T. (2013). *Cyber War Will not Take Place*. Oxford: Oxford University Press.

Rid, T., and Buchanan, B. (2015). Attributing Cyber Attacks. *Journal of Strategic Studies*, 38(1–2): 4–37.

Slayton, R. (2017). What is the Cyber Offense-Defense Balance? Conceptions, Causes, and Assessment. *International Security*, 41(3): 72–109.

Sharp, T. (2017). Theorizing Cyber Coercion: The 2014 North Korean Operation against Sony. *Journal of Strategic Studies*, 40(7): 898–926.

US Department of Defense. (2018). *National Cyber Strategy of the United States of America*. Washington: US Department of Defense.

Valeriano, B., and Maness, R. C. (2014). The Dynamics of Cyber Conflict between Rival Antagonists, 2001–11. *Journal of Peace Research*, 51(3): 347–360.

Valeriano, B., and Maness, R. C. (2015). *Cyber War versus Cyber Realities: Cyber Conflict in the International System*. Oxford: Oxford University Press.

Valeriano, B., Jensen, B. M., and Maness, R. C. (2018). *Cyber Strategy: The Evolving Character of Power and Coercion*. Oxford: Oxford University Press.

Weeks, B. E. (2015). Emotions, Partisanship, and Misperceptions: How Anger and Anxiety Moderate the Effect of Partisan Bias on Susceptibility to Political Misinformation. *Journal of Communication*, 65(4): 699–719.

Whyte, C. (2016). Ending Cyber Coercion: Computer Network Attack, Exploitation and the Case of North Korea. *Comparative Strategy*, 35(2): 93–102.

9 Uncertainty and the study of cyber deterrence

The case of Israel's limited reliance on cyber deterrence

Amir Lupovici

Challenges and threats in the cyber domain create many uncertainties for actors – uncertainty about the threat environment as well as about the effectiveness of their means to address these challenges. International relations scholars have long pointed to a number of dynamics that are highly affected by uncertainty, including the security dilemma (e.g. Roe 2004: 9–16; Rathbun 2007). But certain characteristics of the cyber domain can aggravate these difficulties, such as the fragmentation of authority, the lack of accountability, and the tempo and scope of technological developments (Dunn Cavelty and Wenger 2020; Egloff 2020).

The uncertainty policymakers face in crafting strategies and assessing their effectiveness has also become a fundamental challenge for scholars trying to trace, understand, and explain dynamics in the cyber domain. As Dunn Cavelty and Wenger (2020: 20) argue:

> A case in point is the lack in public transparency and trusted knowledge about the perpetrators behind most cyber incidents. Although the number of public attributions of cyber incidents by states and threat intelligence firms has been on the rise, both types of actors have political and economic reasons not to fully disclose their evidence.
>
> (see also Egloff 2020: 61)

The uncertainties around the cyber domain thus exacerbate scholars' ability to explore the practices, behavior, and strategies of the various actors involved. For example, scholars who develop databases of cyber conflicts cannot determine whether their data encompass all the main incidents (Valeriano and Maness 2014: 351).[1] Similarly, scholars exploring the cyber security dilemma are less certain about the means each opponent holds and develops. Scholars (as well as practitioners) are uncertain not only about the capabilities of state actors involved, but also about the means of non-state actors, including advanced technological firms (Dunn Cavelty and Wenger 2020: 23). Furthermore, these uncertainties are aggravated by rapid changes in technology that states and non-state actors alike try to acquire. This arms race is rapid, and the efficiency of the means the actors develop is not fully understood[2] by either the involved actors or scholars. While

DOI: 10.4324/9781003110224-11

how to use an emerging technology is almost always in question (i.e., nuclear weapons as a means of deterrence or of war-fighting), the facts that the changes are rapid and that non-state actors are involved in acquiring and potentially using these technologies make it even more challenging.

These challenges are thus an obvious obstacle to studying specific strategies, such as cyber deterrence.[3] First, studying cyber deterrence is a challenge because scholars have difficulty identifying and tracing situations of deterrence success[4] as well as situations of deterrence failure (Lupovici 2020). Second, many scholars have emphasized the attribution problem as a great challenge for cyber deterrence success, limiting the ability to issue a credible deterrence threat (see in Morgan 2010; Lupovici 2011; Stevens 2012: 149–53).[5] While this challenge is not necessarily unresolvable for deterrence actors[6] – and so should not prevent them from successfully employing cyber deterrence strategies (e.g. Nye 2017) – it may pose an insurmountable challenge for scholars, who have much less access to this kind of information. Given these two problems, scholars who study cyber deterrence have difficulty getting the required empirical information on cyber incidents. Their access to information about deterrence failure and success is limited, and even if they gain knowledge about a case of cyber attack, they may have difficulty attributing the source of the attack. These problems seriously limit the ability to establish arguments about deterrence strategy, especially regarding the conditions under which it works or fails.

It seems from this perspective that the uncertainties created by cyber technology, the rapid changes in technology, and the fragmentation of authority all challenge the scholarly exploration of cyber security. Nonetheless, I argue that these uncertainties should not discourage scholars, but rather might lead them to adapt their research questions, adopt additional methods, and shift their empirical focus. Each of these challenges prompts thinking in directions to minimize or bypass the limitations around studying interactions in the cyber domain. For example, uncertainties and rapid changes in technology mean scholars should focus on shifts over longer segments of time. Even if technology is changing quickly, the impact of this on strategies and doctrines lags. This focus has two important implications. First, it is a more feasible goal: not only does it provide an anchor that decreases uncertainties given the vast amount of information on past strategies and behavior, but it also allows us to limit the challenge of rapid changes. How technology is translated into policy leaves more traces, especially as strategies like deterrence require strategic communication with opponents (i.e., issuing threats). Second, the impact of technologies on strategies and actor behavior is mediated through social attributes.[7] Therefore, scholars can compare new policies and strategies with past ones and explore whether and how they resonate with them.

Focusing on how a new technology enters into doctrines and strategies raises various questions. Some can be developed and answered through interpretative approaches, by looking at the constraints and opportunities the social context creates for actors relying on new technologies. This helps in conducting comparisons, but also in examining specific characteristics of the technology that allow or limit shifts from past types of behavior. For example, rather than exploring how a strategy is effective or not effective (i.e., under what conditions a strategy works) given the limitations of uncertainties and rapid changes, scholars can also direct their research toward questions about the strategy's adoption. Among other things, scholars can explore how actors come to adopt a strategy and adapt it to address challenges of the cyber domain, or alternatively how they refrain from adopting it. Elaborating on these issues leads to questions about how technological impetus is embedded in actors' narratives, strategic culture, and identities, and how adopting a certain strategy fits or challenges international norms.

In order to illustrate this research conduct and its merit, I briefly discuss the Israeli cyber deterrence strategy and the limited extent of its adoption. Focusing on the adoption of the strategy – rather than on the more uncertain questions about deterrence success – demonstrates a way to address key challenges in studying cyber security given the uncertainties and rapid changes discussed above. As I elaborate below, studying Israel's adoption of deterrence strategy directs our attention to how it fits Israel's strategic culture and identities. This, in fact, presents a puzzle. While deterrence is a prominent Israeli strategy, cyber deterrence strategy has so far not been fully adopted. Understanding the social context raises important questions that the rapid technological changes do not prevent us from asking and answering.

Israel (cyber) deterrence

It is beyond the space limits of this chapter to discuss all relevant methodological aspects or fully explore the case. Rather, this discussion aims to demonstrate the methodological solutions presented above by focusing on Israel's cyber deterrence strategy. Despite Israel's reliance on deterrence strategies vis-à-vis various kinds of threats, Israel, unlike for example the United States,[8] has still not adopted an explicit cyber deterrence strategy. However, since the second decade of the 2000s, there has been growing support for adopting such strategy by key Israeli officials.

Deterrence is a prominent strategy in Israel. While this strategy has emerged from different strategic rationales since the 1950s (Yaniv 1987: 72; Levite 1989: 27–35; Bar 1990: 54; Evron 1994: 40, 42–3; Tal 2000: 51; Cohen 2010: 35–6, 77), it continues to be a dominant Israeli strategy, and it is endorsed by both the political and military elites (Yaniv 1987; Evron 1994: 40–1; Levite 1989: 25, 47; Bar-Joseph 2001: 2). Furthermore, over the years the Israeli deterrent strategy has been developed and adapted to address different kinds of threats (Bar-Joseph 1998).

For Israel, practicing deterrence fulfils not just physical security needs, but also identity-related needs. As Lupovici (2016b) suggests, Israel holds a deterrer identity. A deterrer identity is when an actor internalizes a *deterrer role* that it is attached to and through which it perceives how it needs to act in the international arena.[9] The manifestation of the Israeli deterrer identity is evident in how Israel perceives threats, responds to them, and justifies certain policies. From Israel's perspective, lack of violence is deterrence success, while eruption of violence is deterrence failure. Israel prioritizes deterrence strategy and practices over other strategies to the extent that deterrence has become an aim itself: the goal in various situations has been defined (and securitized) in terms of enhancing or restoring the Israeli deterrent posture. Given the high status of deterrence in Israel, policymakers can mobilize support for different policies, pointing to their alleged contribution to the deterrent posture (Lupovici 2016b: 55–8).

However, this discussion on the prominence of Israeli deterrence strategy intensifies the puzzle of the state's limited adoption and employment of deterrence in the context of cyber security challenges. Given the prominence of deterrence in Israel's strategic thinking, one would expect that Israel would be eager to adopt a cyber deterrence strategy to address these challenges. The fact it has not developed a clear cyber deterrence strategy is a phenomenon that requires explanation. While fully explaining this behavior is beyond the scope of this chapter, I argue that focusing on the period of the early 2010s shows how Israel has started to adopt cyber deterrence strategy. This dynamic can be understood as part of a broader strategization of cyber security. On the one hand, Israel gives more attention to these practices; on the other hand, the strategization of cyber security is limited, reflecting the limited adoption of cyber deterrence practices.

The strategization of cyber security in Israel

There are a number of indications of changes in how cyber (in)security is seen in Israel. These highlight the similarities of some aspects of cyber security to traditional security issues. These include changes (1) on an institutional level, (2) in the view of cyber as a strategic domain, and (3) in how cyber insecurities are narrated.

Initial efforts to develop a cyber doctrine at the national level are evident in Israel's attempts to solidify its cyber defense. Especially since the early 2000s, Israel has endeavored to protect and regulate the information security of various bodies, including critical infrastructures, private companies, and financial organizations (Even and Siman-Tov 2012: 76–9; Baram 2013: 28–9; Tabensky and Ben Israel 2015: 35–41). It made further efforts during the 2000s to strategize cyber security. A key development was the attempt in August 2011 to integrate national cyber defense by establishing a new body – the Israeli National Cyber Bureau (INCB) (Adamsky 2017: 115). This body has four departments: security, civilian, intelligence and situation assessment, and organization and policy. In addition, it operates a control room (Baram 2013: 35). According to Even and Siman-Tov, establishing this body was significant in that it was the first strategic organ whose scope of activity is defense at the national level (Even and Siman-Tov 2012: 67–8, see also Government Decision 3611, August 2011). As Tabensky and Ben Israel (2015: 52) further clarify, the main task of the INCB is "drafting comprehensive national cyber strategy". They suggest that evidence of this move to a strategy was hinted in a talk given by Evyatar Matania, who then served as the head of the INCB, in which he emphasized the need of Israel to move from "defense" to "security" (Tabensky and Ben Israel 2015: 52).

Cyber security was further strategized with the establishment of the Israeli National Cyber Directorate (INCD), following a government decision from February 2015. This body is the "highest national authority for strategic cyber policy planning, for the regulation of its operational execution across the government, and for building cyber capabilities for the short, medium, and long term" (Adamsky 2017: 120; see also Government Resolution 2444, 2.15.2015; Even et al. 2016; Orbach 2015; Adamsky 2017: 116, 120).

A brief review of these modifications reveals that Israel went through a process in which policymakers tried to strategize cyber security and centralize the defense of critical infrastructures from cyber threats. Nonetheless, as Baram (2013: 32) suggests, while Israel is a leading cyber power, its capabilities were not reflected in the forming of a cyber strategy or, more specifically, "in the institution of a regular strategy or in a clear statement of an official course of action. It appears that Israel has yet to formulate a strategy in this field".[10] In a similar way, although an increasing number of Israeli policymakers and practitioners acknowledge that cyber is a critical aspect of war, not all institutional changes that aimed to reflect this acknowledgment were employed. Foremost, key officials referred directly to cyber space as a domain of warfare parallel to traditional spaces. For example, in 2009, IDF Chief of Staff Gabi Ashkenazi defined cyber space as "a strategic and operative domain of warfare" (Even and Siman-Tov 2012: 79). Likewise, in 2012 Netanyahu declared, "Today cyber is part of the battlefield ... This is not tomorrow's warfare, it is already here today" (qtd. in Keinon 2013). These views are reflected in a document drafted by IDF's Operations Directorate, which defines cyber space as another battlefield, like land, sea, and airspace (Katz 2012).

Nonetheless, it should also be noted that while key officials ordered the establishment of a new branch – the cyber branch (albeit not a cyber command, as for example in the United States) (Cohen 2015) – it is still not operative (Cohen 2017). Recent years have seen increasing indications not only of attempts to strategize cyber security, but also of seeing it in terms of more traditional security challenges. While there is little public discussion of these issues, some key Israeli political leaders have used analogies clearly demonstrating that they think of cyber security in terms of more traditional security challenges and responses. For example, Prime Minister Netanyahu argued that Israel needs "a cyber Iron Dome".[11] As he claims, "For this purpose, I established the National Cyber Directorate a year ago and it has been working to block these attempts [cyberattacks] by developing what I would call a 'digital Iron Dome'" (qtd. in Hirsch and Gattegno 2012). Netanyahu repeated this analogy several times, including mentioning Iran and its proxy, Hezbollah, as a main source for cyberattacks on Israel that requires this "iron dome" (e.g., Prime Minster Office 2012; see also in Keinon 2013).[12]

While these claims echo the previous assertion that defense was a key aspect in the formation of Israel's cyber security thinking (and strategy), they also provide a clear analogy of the traditional security aspects (Haber and Zarsky 2017: 153–4). As emphasized by Eviatar Matania, who then served as the director general of Israel's National Cyber Directorate, Israel needs to develop a "digital equivalent of the Iron Dome" (Solomon 2017). This analogy reflects both the kind of threat (cyber threat is the same as the "traditional" rocket threat) and how the threat should be dealt with (by the government).

Israel's limited reliance on cyber deterrence

I argue that the limited adoption of cyber deterrence in Israel during the early 2010s reflects and is part of the limited strategization of cyber security in Israel. While there seems to have been increasing acknowledgment of the need for cyber deterrence, it was adopted only to a limited extent. Both the adoption of the strategy and the limited nature of its adoption are evident in two main manifestations of this strategy.

The first can be inferred from the cyber operations Israel conducted against the Iranian and Syrian nuclear programs. In these cases, cyber means were used, albeit in different ways. Experts have pointed to these incidents as Israeli attempts to establish cyber cumulative deterrence based on the actual use of force. For example, Tor (2017: 6) noted regarding Stuxnet that although its effectiveness in damaging the Iranian nuclear program is not entirely clear, "Stuxnet may still have had an effect in demonstrating capability and intent" and thus can be examined in the context of deterrence. Likewise, Tabensky and Ben Israel (2015: 68) refer to these two incidents – Stuxnet and the attack on the Syrian reactor – to suggest that if Israel relied on cyberattacks in these operations, "it attests to the high maturity of technology, doctrine, and organisation of the IDF" and thus had a deterrent effect.

The use of cyber capabilities in attempts to create future deterrence fits the strategy of cumulative deterrence that Israel practices in other domains, and it accords with Israel's reliance on creating deterrence through the actual use of force (Bar-Joseph 1998: 156–7; Almog 2004–5). Nonetheless, not only is the effectiveness of this type of deterrence open to question,[13] but, more importantly, how Israel has used it – if it has used it at all – also demonstrates the limited way Israel has adopted this strategy and adjusted it to cyber space, as it is a deterrent threat only in a very indirect and implicit way.

The second manifestation is the increasing number of Israeli policymakers, including key politicians such as Prime Minster Netanyahu, who make the point that Israel should adopt a cyber deterrence strategy. Netanyahu asserted that cyber warfare is

> cloudy and unknown. The ability to achieve balance in the cyber realm is much harder and is *dependent on combination of defense and deterrence.* The fact that the source of attack is often anonymous challenges the ability to create a balance of deterrence, and we should pay attention to that.
>
> (qtd. in Ben-Yosef 2011, my emphasis and my translation)

This statement clearly demonstrates the limited nature of Israel's adoption of cyber deterrence strategy. While he acknowledges the need to establish such a strategy, Netanyahu's statement emphasizes the strategic challenge of creating it and the need to combine it with another strategy (defense). Nonetheless, he does highlight the need to develop a cyber deterrence strategy, an emphasis that was absent from previous statements in this regard.

This need to acquire a cyber deterrence strategy is evident in statements of other key practitioners, for example, Major-General Amos Yadlin, who then served as the head of IDF's Military Intelligence Directorate. According to him, cyber security poses important questions that should be publicly discussed. These questions concern, among other things, "the essence of deterrence that would prevent war in cyber space" (Yadlin 2009, my translation).

Some have even made more explicit the connection between how they perceive cyber security on the one hand and cyber deterrence on the other. For example, at the beginning of a talk he gave in 2012, Minister of Defense Ehud Barak suggested that cyber is another domain of warfare. According to him, "to the security equation, along with land, sea, air and space we need to add cyber as a new dimension". He concluded his talk by stating that in the vagueness created by cyber capabilities, "leadership is required to show the way as to how to do the right thing for Israel and *to establish a deterrent balance* and act effectively in this new world" (Barak 2012, my emphasis and translation). Barak, thus, connects viewing cyber as a traditional domain of security with adopting cyber deterrence strategy.

Likewise, in January 2012, Deputy Foreign Minister Danny Ayalon called for the adoption of a declared cyber deterrence strategy, justifying it with reference to American cyber deterrence strategy, which is based on an explicit threat of retaliation as presented above. According to him, "[T]he US has announced that any attack on its cybernetic space would be considered a declaration of war and that it would go as far as firing missiles to respond to such an attack. This is a good criterion for us all". Furthermore, as evident with this reference, Ayalon sees cyberattacks as a more traditional means of violence – constituting acts of war (Curiel 2012).

To conclude these points, this discussion demonstrates the limited extent to which Israel has adopted a cyber deterrence strategy. While it marks a shift from the silence on cyber deterrence of previous years, the adoption of this strategy demonstrated by these manifestations is relatively limited. The first emphasizes deterrence through the actual use of cyberattacks but concerns only an implied cyber deterrence strategy. The second – the acknowledgment of the need to develop a cyber deterrence strategy – also demonstrates the limitation, as it mainly concerns the need to adapt Israel's capabilities and doctrine to allow issuing a cyber deterrent threat; it is not about recognizing the existence of this strategy or actually issuing such threats.

Conclusion

This chapter aims to demonstrate the feasibility of addressing the methodological challenges of studying cyber (security) given the uncertainties that surround it. One direction offered is to focus on the adoption and employment of a strategy – and not only on its effectiveness, as most scholars do. I briefly demonstrated these ideas by studying Israel's limited and gradual adoption of a cyber deterrence strategy and how it fits Israel's traditional security practices.

The suggested methodological solutions used in this chapter illustrate that while uncertainties, rapid changes, and fragmentation of authority can constrain the research, they also provide opportunities to develop, think about, and adapt various methods and alternative focuses for research on cyber security. Employing interpretative approaches is another direction that could be developed to explore other aspects of cyber security affected by these challenges.

Furthermore, constructivist research is also highly promising, specifically in studying uncertainties and rapid technological changes (Rathbun 2007: 549–52). Scholars not only can examine whether and how adopted strategies fit states' identities and narratives but can explore the discourse around these strategies: for example, how these strategies are presented, mediated to the public, and justified. These directions provide many opportunities for scholars given both the data and information to which such findings can be compared and given that we can trace such changes evident in the public sphere, despite challenges concerning secrecy.

More traditional methods and directions can also be used to address these challenges in studying cyber security. For example, rapid technological change means that past technologies quickly become obsolete. From a methodological perspective, this means that information about former technologies will become available more quickly than in the past. While the result is that scholars are limited in analyzing the most advanced technologies, scholars can be satisfied with empirical focus on "older technologies" – which, given the rapid changes, may be the advanced technologies of only five years ago.

Similarly, the fragmentation of authority, while enhancing uncertainties in studying different aspects of cyber security, also provides an opportunity. Scholars can focus on non-state actors not only as targets of state actors' strategies but also as strategists themselves. For example, in addition to examining how states attempt to deter non-state actors, scholars can explore how non-state actors issue deterrent threats to different kinds of actors (Wilner 2020: 29; Lupovici 2019).

The discussion of the Israeli case also carries some important implications. One crucial issue is how the understanding of the cyber domain (and the social constructions of it) affects how policymakers develop strategies and adapt old strategies, such as deterrence, to this domain. In explaining this behavior, scholars can contrast this policy with the strategies of other countries that adopt more explicit cyber deterrence strategy, such as the United States (see in Wilner 2020).

Another promising direction concerns tracing changes in the adoption of cyber deterrence over time. A key juncture point is May 2020. As published in the international media, Israel retaliated against targets in Iran following an Iranian cyberattack on water infrastructures in Israel (e.g., Warrick and Nakashima 2020). This case is significant for several reasons. First, Israeli sources officially acknowledged the Iranian attack. Second, and more importantly, the publication of Israeli retaliation as well as other statements made by Israeli officials, such as Minister of Defense Naftali Bennett, was interpreted as the indication of Israel's tendency to send deterrent messages for the Iranians (Siman-Tov and Evan 2020).[14] If this interpretation is correct, this marks a shift in Israeli policy toward deterrence by the actual use of force, which aptly fits traditional Israeli deterrence practices in general, as discussed above. Indeed, there is still some ambiguity in the Israeli policy. Nonetheless, this case may turn out to be a significant point where Israeli cyber deterrence is made more explicit.

These changes also demonstrate the fertility of the suggested methodological solution. The seeming change in Israeli behavior invites various kinds of questions. For example, we can ask whether strategic incentives required Israel to shift its policy, or whether the change was due to perceptions of specific policymakers – such as Bennett, who was about to leave office as a new Israeli government was established. Alternatively, these shifts can be explained by tracing the changes in how the cyber domain is understood or constructed. This is especially important if we acknowledge that messages are delivered not only to international audiences, such as the Iranians, but also to domestic audiences, such as the Israeli public. Targeting domestic audiences may become especially important in the search for legitimacy in how cyber security is understood and in how to address challenges actors face in this domain.

Acknowledgments

The author would like to thank the Interdisciplinary Cyber Research Center at Tel Aviv University for supporting this research.

Notes

1 This, for example, is less of a problem when studying traditional conflicts and attacks, where, while scholars might debate over the details, they face much less difficulty obtaining the information about these incidents.

2 Compare, for example, debates over the degree to which quantum computers challenge international security (e.g., Lindsay 2020; 2022).

3 While there is a debate over what "cyber deterrence" is (see Lupovici 2016a), for the purposes of this project I adopt the view (endorsed by many scholars) that cyber deterrence (by punishment) is a strategy that aims to dissuade a putative challenger from attacking a state's cyber infrastructures or from attacking the state with cyber means by threatening to retaliate should such an event would occur (Stevens 2012: 149–52; see also Lupovici 2016a: 324–6).

4 The traditional assertion is that deterrence success cannot be easily traced because scholars cannot observe it – unlike deterrence failure, where there is an observable incident. The challenge, therefore, is that the scholarship is biased toward studying situations of deterrence failure, where scholars can more easily establish causal arguments (Achen and Snidal 1989: 161; Lebow and Stein 1990: 336, 347; Sauer 2016: 49).

5 Scholars argue that because the putative challenger knows that the defender actor will find it difficult to identify the source of attack, the challenger will estimate that the retaliation cannot be employed.

6 Scholars make three main points about the limitations of this challenge. First, the identity of a challenger can be deduced from the context – for example, in cases of cyberattack during a conflict between two actors or through the use of traditional intelligence capabilities (Kugler 2009: 310, 317–8; Kello 2013: 17–8). Second, as technology pro-

gresses, actors have better tools to identify the source of attack, including better forensic means to attribute cyberattacks (Rid and Buchanan 2015). Third, it is not only cyber technology per se but also international norms that limit retaliation when actors cannot fully identify the source of attack. However, international norms may change over time (Lupovici 2016a: 330–1).

7 Nonetheless, it should be noted that scholars debate to what extent society determines how technology develops and should be used ("social constructivism") or the technology determines actors' behavior ("technological determinism") (e.g., Fritsch 2011; Manjikian 2018).

8 For an excellent review of US cyber deterrence strategy, see Wilner (2019). In this respect, as far as I know Israel has never issued a direct threat as the United States did, according to which any cyberattack against it would lead to a retaliation with all the means it holds – both cyber means and kinetic means (e.g., Department of Defense Cyber Policy Report 2011: 2).

9 Israel's adoption and reliance on this strategy can be also explained by certain Israeli-Jewish narratives and identities, including the Israeli-Jewish victim identity. This narrative provides the context through which Israel interprets and magnifies threats, encouraging the need to use force and take active measures to prevent another Holocaust (Waxman 2006: 49; Bar-Tal 2001: 612–5; Barnett 2013: 37–47; see also Sucharov 2005: 31).

10 This does not mean that Israel lacks any strategic thinking regarding cyber security. A number of issues have gained much attention in the attempt to form a strategy, such as the legal aspect of cyber security and Israel's attempt to shape new global norms of cyber security. However, this is less evident in more "traditional" security aspects that are related to the formation of a strategy, as well as in the operation of the different relevant bodies.

11 Iron Dome is a missile defense system Israel developed to intercept rockets.

12 Interestingly, the former Minister of Defense, Ehud Barak, also implied the connections between cyber threats and the threat of rockets (see in Cohen and Yaron 2012).

13 For critical discussion on the effectiveness of creating deterrence through the actual use of force, see Mercer 1996; Press 2005: 22–4, 147–8; Tang 2005; and Lupovici 2016b, but also see Rid 2012. Furthermore, in the cyber domain this is even more problematic, since revealing capabilities may allow a putative challenger to acquire means to neutralize the defender's capabilities (see also Libicki 2007: 271–2).

14 As emphasized by Siman-Tov and Evan, Bennett stated on May 18, 2020, "We must increase political, economic, military, and technological pressure, and act in other dimensions as well. It can be done" (Bennett, in Siman-Tov and Evan 2020).

References

All links checked on August 23, 2021.

Achen, H. C., and Snidal, D. (1989). Rational Deterrence Theory and Comparative Case Studies. *World Politics*, 42(2): 144–169.

Adamsky, D. (2017). The Israeli Odyssey toward Its National Cyber Security Strategy. *The Washington Quarterly*, 40(2): 113–127.

Almog, D. (2004–5). Cumulative Deterrence and the War on Terrorism. *Parameters*, 25(4): 4–19.

Bar, M. (1990). *Red Lines in Israel's Deterrence Strategy*. Tel Aviv: Ma'arachot (in Hebrew).

Barak, E. (2012, June 6). A Keynote Address by Minister of Defense Yuval Na'man. Workshop for Science, Technology and Security. [Video]. YouTube. Retrieved from: https://www.youtube.com/watch?v=doGiu556ZWQ [in Hebrew].

Baram, G. (2013). The Effect of Cyberwar Technologies on Force Buildup: The Israeli Case. *Military and Strategic Affairs*, 5(1): 23–43.

Bar-Joseph, U. (1998). Variations on a Theme: The Conceptualization of Deterrence in Israeli Strategic Thinking. *Security Studies*, 7(3): 145–181.

Barnett, M. (2013). Cosmopolitanism: Good for Israel? Or Bad for Israel? In E. Adler (ed.), *Israel in the World: Legitimacy and Exceptionalism*. London: Routledge, pp. 32–50.

Bar-Tal, D. (2001). Why Does Fear Override Hope in Societies Engulfed by Intractable Conflict, as It Does in the Israeli Society? *Political Psychology*, 22(3): 601–627.

Cohen, A. (2010). *The Worst-Kept Secret*. New York: Columbia University Press.

Cohen, G. (2015, June 16). Israeli Army Plans to Create Separate Cybercorps, Similar to Air Force or Navy. *Haaretz*. Retrieved from: http://www.haaretz.com/israel-news/.premium-1.661398.

Cohen, G. (2017, January 3). Israeli Military Reorganizing Its Cybersecurity Operations. *Haaretz*. Retrieved from: http://www.haaretz.com/israel-news/.premium-1.762438.

Cohen, G., and Oded, Y. (2012, June 6). Barak Acknowledges Israel's Cyber Offensive for First Time. *Haaretz*. Retrieved from: http://www.haaretz.com/israel-news/barak-acknowledges-israel-s-cyber-offensive-for-first-time-1.434767.

Curiel, I. (2012). Deputy FM Threatens 'Forceful Response' to Cyber Attacks. *Ynetnews*. Retrieved from: http://www.ynetnews.com/articles/0,7340,L-4172329,00.html [in Hebrew].

Department of Defense Cyberspace Policy Report. (2011, November). A Report to Congress Pursuant to the National Defense Authorization Act for Fiscal Year 2011, Section 934. Retrieved from: http://oai.dtic.mil/oai/oai?verb=getRecord&metadataPrefix=html&identifier=ADA552759.

Dunn Cavelty, M., and Wenger, A. (2020). Cyber Security Meets Security Politics: Complex Technology, Fragmented Politics, and Networked Science. *Contemporary Security Policy*, 41(1): 5–32.

Egloff, J. F. (2020). Contested Public Attributions of Cyber Incidents and the Role of Academia. *Contemporary Security Policy*, 41(1): 55–81.

Even, S., and David, S.-T. (2012). Cyber Warfare: Concepts, Trends and Implications for Israel. INSS Memorandum No. 117, May 2012. Tel Aviv: The Institute for National Security Studies. Retrieved from: https://www.files.ethz.ch/isn/152953/inss%20memorandum_may2012_nr117.pdf

Even, S., David, S.-T., and Gabi, S. (2016). Structring Israel's Cyber Defense. *INSS Insight*, 856. Tel Aviv: The Institute for National Security Studies. Retrieved from: https://www.inss.org.il/publication/structuring-israels-cyber-defense/

Evron, Y. (1994). *Israel's Nuclear Dilemma*. New York: Routledge.

Fritsch, S. (2011). Technology and Global Affairs. *International Studies Perspectives*, 12(1): 27–45.

Haber, E., and Zarsky, T. (2017). Protecting Critical Infrastructure from Cyberattacks. *Mishpat UMimshal*, 18(1): 99–155 [in Hebrew].

Hirsch, Y., and Gattegno, I. (2012, October 14). Netanyahu Announces 'Digital Iron Dome' to Battle Cyberattacks. Israel Hayom. Retrieved from: http://www.israelhayom.com/site/newsletter_article.php?id=6070.

Katz, Y. (2012, June 3). IDF Admits to Using Cyber Space to Attack Enemies. *The Jerusalem Post*. Retrieved from: http://www.jpost.com/Defense/IDF-admits-to-using-cyber-space-to-attack-enemies.

Keinon, H. (2013, September 6). PM: Israel Needs 'Digital Iron Dome' to Stop Cyber Attacks. *The Jerusalem Post*. Retrieved from: http://www.jpost.com/Defense/PM-Israel-needs-digital-iron-dome-to-stop-cyber-attacks-315934.

Kello, L. (2013). The Meaning of the Cyber Revolution: Perils to Theory and Statecraft. *International Security*, 38(2): 7–40.

Kugler, L. R. (2009). Deterrence of Cyber Attacks. In F. D. Kramer, S. H. Starr, and L. K. Wentz (eds), *Cyberpower and National Security*. Washington, DC: National Defense University Press, pp. 309–339.

Lebow, N. R., and Stein, J. G. (1990). The Elusive Variable. *World Politics*, 42(3): 336–369.

Levite, A. (1989). *Offense and Defense in Israeli Military Doctrine*. Tel Aviv: Jaffee Center for Strategic Studies.

Libicki, C. M. (2007). *Conquest in Cyberspace*. Cambridge: Cambridge University Press.

Lindsay, J. R. (2020). Demystifying the Quantum Threat: Infrastructure, Institutions, and Intelligence Advantage. *Security Studies*, 29(2): 335–361.

Lindsay, R. J. (2022). Quantum Computer and Classical Politics: The Ambiguity of Cryptologic Advantage. In M. Dunn Cavelty and A. Wenger (eds), *Cyber Security: Socio-Technological Uncertainty and Political Fragmentation*. London: Routledge, pp. 80–94.

Lupovici, A. (2011). Cyber Warfare and Deterrence: Trends and Challenges. *Military and Strategic Affairs*, 3(3): 41–52.

Lupovici, A. (2016a). The 'Attribution Problem' and the Social Construction of 'Violence': Taking Cyber Deterrence Literature a Step Forward. *International Studies Perspectives*, 17(3): 322–342.

Lupovici, A. (2016b). *The Power of Deterrence. Emotions, Identity and American and Israeli Wars of Resolve*. Cambridge: Cambridge University Press.

Lupovici, A. (2019). The Deterrence Strategies of Non-States Cyber Actors. Unpublished manuscript.

Lupovici, A. (2020). Methodology of Cyber Deterrence. Paper accepted for presentation at the Annual Conference of the International Studies Association, March 2020, Honolulu, HI.

Manjikian, M. (2018). Social Construction of Technology: How Objects Acquire Meaning in Society. In D. R. McCarthy (ed.), *Technology and World Politics*. London: Routledge, pp. 25–41.

Mercer, J. (1996). *Reputation and International Politics*. Ithaca: Cornell University Press.

Morgan, M. P. (2010). Applicability of Traditional Deterrence Concepts and Theory to the Cyber Realm. In: National Research Council, J. D. Steinbruner, et al. (eds), *Proceedings of a Workshop on Deterring Cyberattacks*. Washington, DC: The National Academies, pp. 55–76.

Nye, J. S. Jr. (2017). Deterrence and Dissuasion in Cyberspace. *International Security*, 41(3): 44–71.

Orbach, M. (2015, February 15). Government Approved the Establishment of a National Cyber Bureau. Retrieved from: http://www.calcalist.co.il/articles/0,7340,L-3652448,00.html [in Hebrew].

Press, G. D. (2005). *Calculating Credibility: How Leaders Assess Military Threats*. Ithaca: Cornell University Press.

Prime Minster Office. (2012, November 11). At the Weekly Cabinet Meeting. Government of Israel. Retrieved from: https://www.gov.il/en/departments/publications/reports/govmes111112.

Rathbun, C. B. (2007). Uncertain about Uncertainty: Understanding the Multiple Meanings of a Crucial Concept in International Relations Theory. *International Studies Quarterly*, 51(3): 533–557.

Rid, T. (2012). Deterrence Beyond the State: The Israeli Experience. *Contemporary Security Policy*, 33(1): 124–147.

Rid, T., and Buchanan, B. (2015). Attributing Cyber Attacks. *Journal of Strategic Studies*, 38(1–2): 4–37.

Roe, P. (2004). *Ethnic Violence and the Societal Security Dilemma*. London: Routledge.

Sauer, F. (2016). *Atomic Anxieties: Deterrence, Taboo and the Non-Use of U.S. Nuclear Weapons*. New York: Palgrave Macmillan.

Solomon, S. (2017, February 1). Israel Works on 'Digital Iron Dome' for Cyberdefense. *The Times of Israel*. Retrieved from: http://www.timesofisrael.com/israel-works-on-digital-iron-dome-for-cyberdefense/.

Stevens, T. (2012). A Cyberwar of Ideas? Deterrence and Norms in Cyberspace. *Contemporary Security Policy*, 33(1): 148–170.

Sucharov, M. M. (2005). *The International Self. Psychoanalysis and the Search for Israeli-Palestinian Peace*. New York and Albany: State University of New York Press.

Tabensky, L., and Ben Israel, I. (2015). *Cybersecurity in Israel*. Cham: Springer.

Tal, I. (2000). *National Security. The Israel Experience*. London: Prager.

Tang, S. (2005). Reputation, Cult of Reputation, and International Conflict. *Security Studies*, 14(1): 34–61.

Tor, U. (2017). Cumulative Deterrence' as a New Paradigm for Cyber Deterrence. *Journal of Strategic Studies*, 40(1–2): 92–117.

Valeriano, B., and Maness, C. R. (2014). The Dynamics of Cyber Conflict between Rival Antagonists, 2001–11. *Journal of Peace Research*, 51(3): 347–360.

Warrick, J., and Nakashima, E. (2020, May 19). Officials: Israel Linked to a Disruptive Cyberattack on Iranian Port Facility. *Washington Post*. Retrieved from: https://www.washingtonpost.com/national-security/officials-israel-linked-to-a-disruptive-cyberattack-on-iranian-port-facility/2020/05/18/9d1da866-9942-11ea-89fd-28fb313d1886_story.html

Waxman, D. (2006). *The Pursuit of Peace and the Crisis of Israeli Identity. Defining/Defending the Nation*. New York: Palgrave.

Wilner, A. (2020). US Cyber Deterrence: Practice Guiding Theory. *Journal of Strategic Studies*, 36(4): 309–318.

Yaniv, A. (1987). *Deterrence without the Bomb: The Politics of Israeli Strategy*. New York: Lexington Books.

10 Cyber securities and cyber security politics

Understanding different logics of German cyber security policies

Stefan Steiger

The internet has rapidly become an integral part of everyday life in modern societies. While it has helped to facilitate economic growth and cultural exchange, it has also become a new domain for conflict. The increasing sophistication of cyberattacks is politically challenging, as the internet has become the meta-infrastructure of modern societies – a "backbone of backbones" (Choucri and Clark 2012: 151). Today, information technology (IT) influences almost every aspect of social life. Though many states have established cyber security[1] policies, emphasizing their claim to protect the nation and the citizens not only offline but also in cyberspace, the regulation of cyber security is especially complex because of the different actors involved (including both state and non-state) and the international reach of the internet that makes unilateral regulation difficult. Moreover, national decisions regarding cyber security (e.g. the stockpiling of vulnerabilities) can affect actors around the world.

States have dealt differently with these new opportunities and challenges. While some have actively employed offensive cyber capabilities as a substitute for conventional intervention, others have used cyber capacities in complement with more traditional responses to threats. Yet, cyber security policy is not just a military issue that relates to interstate conflict dynamics; it also has the potential to have a lasting impact on the relationship between state authorities and citizens, as well as between states and companies. Therefore, the expansion of state competences in cyberspace has not remained unchallenged. Interventions into the private lives of citizens or entrepreneurial freedom have sparked substantial domestic opposition. Internationally, practices of mass surveillance conducted by intelligence agencies have received considerable criticism. However, it has remained largely unclear which factors, both domestic and foreign, influence different cyber security policies. Since most IR theories tend to focus on either international (i.e. realism) or domestic (i.e. liberalism) dynamics, significant aspects of policies that hinge on the interplay of those two spheres are not accounted for. Thus, scholars have called for approaches that consider both domestic and international influences on cyber security policy, as well as how they interact (Whyte 2018: 12). This chapter employs a role theoretical, two-level game to analyze the

DOI: 10.4324/9781003110224-12

development of German cyber security policy. This approach facilitates a more nuanced view on cyber security policies and considers both the domestic and international dynamics that shape cyber security policies.

This chapter therefore addresses the following question: How did German cyber security policy evolve and what domestic and external factors facilitated its development? The policies under examination will be taken from four areas central to cyber security: Critical infrastructure protection, law enforcement, intelligence services, and the military. Each of these subject areas are significantly shaped by different kinds of uncertainty (for example, evaluating the potential risk of attacks and the benefits of undermining IT security). In addition, responsibility for these domains is often split between state agencies and – especially in the case of critical infrastructure protection – non-state actors. This results in varying policy responses and dynamics between different actors in each field. Furthermore, an examination of German cyber security policies is especially interesting, as a gap exists within the literature concerning the cyber security strategies of states with a cautious foreign policy approach. Most theory-driven studies have focused on developments in the United States and sometimes China or Russia (Dunn Cavelty 2008; Fritz 2017; Maréchal 2017; McCarthy 2018).

To answer the research question, this chapter draws on the symbolic interactionist role of theory in foreign policy analysis (FPA) and traces policy developments relying on a corpus of policy documents from the executive as well as other state agencies and from non-state actors. The chapter proceeds as follows: First, the theoretical premises of role theory are presented, and the concept of a two-level role play is outlined. Following this, essential interactions in the four fields of activity are analyzed. Finally, a short conclusion summarizes the findings.

Role theory

Roles have been increasingly used as analytical concepts for studying foreign policies.[2] Following the symbolic interactionist strain in role theory, roles are understood as social positions that are shaped by ego and alter expectations, and that are associated with a function for a social group (Harnisch 2012: 8). Roles are defined relationally; stable social relationships depend on a role and a complementary counter-role. For example, if an actor claims the role of protector (as the government does in cyber security policy), another actor must fill the role of the one needing protection. However, this relationship does not require any rational complementarity of interests. The motives for assuming role and counter-role may be different and are not immediately relevant for the resulting social structure, as social reality emerges from role interaction (Harnisch 2014: 14).

Though traditional role theory assumes homogeneous and nationally accepted role conceptions, this has changed in recent years. The insight that roles can be disputed domestically between different actors, for example between governments and citizens, has led role theoreticians to develop the concept of role contestation

(Cantir and Kaarbo 2012). Various empirical studies have since traced the influence of domestic role contestation on a nation's foreign policy behavior (Cantir and Kaarbo 2016). However, some analytical blind spots remained. For example, the repercussions of international interactions on the domestic social structure still required more investigation. Therefore, a holistic role theory approach was developed that connects the international process of role and counter-role taking with a domestic role play ("Full-spectrum role-taking"; Harnisch 2014). Examining both levels of role creation is inspired by the two-level game of Robert Putnam (1988), but offers two main advantages: First, it is not limited by a formalistic reference to treaty ratification, but can portray different forms of interaction. Second, the focus is not on balancing two rationalist win-sets, but on the interconnectivity of roles in the different spheres:

> The model suggests that the two role-taking processes are interactive: international role taking and making feeds back into domestic role taking (second image reversed) and domestic role taking enables and/or restrains external role taking.
>
> (Harnisch 2014: 2)

Building on this foundation, this chapter argues that there is a domestic role play between government, legislature, judiciary, the private sector, and other non-state actors, and an international role play concerning other states, institutions, and NGOs. Furthermore, the German government has domestically claimed the role of protector in cyberspace, but still requires a complementary counter-role to facilitate a stable cyber security policy. Although the role of protector is not the only role the German Executive plays domestically (another example might include welfare maximizer), it is the most relevant for cyber security and therefore deserves dedicated analysis. Since there are different significant others involved and the role of protector can apply to different actors in different situations, it should be noted that role interaction patterns vary across the different areas of investigation.

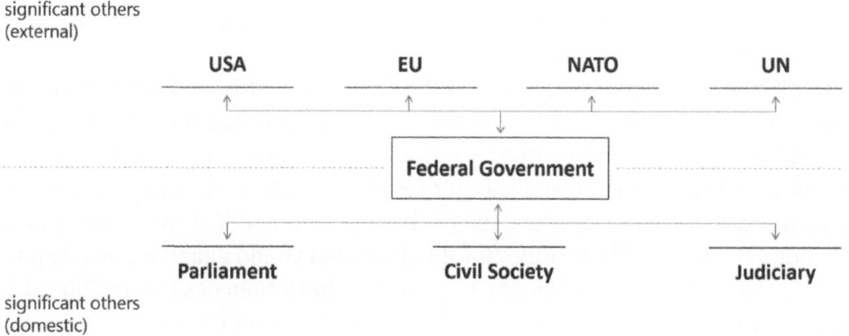

Figure 10.1 Two-level role play.

The development of cyber security policies

The following sections illustrate that the development of cyber security policies differ considerably between the four areas analyzed. This is due to the international and domestic interactions between the government and different significant others. The first section shows that, with regard to critical infrastructure, the role of protector was first delegated to the private sector but has since been reclaimed by the government. The second section illustrates that the government is still struggling to establish a stable protector role regarding cybercrime and is actively embroiled in domestic contestation processes with law enforcement agencies. The third section reveals that, while the conduct of the German intelligence service BND has been criticized following the Snowden revelations, many practices have since been deemed legal due to the value of this information internationally. The final section explores the evolution of the government's role as protector of the military, eventually adopting a more offensive stance toward combating cyber security threats in line with the needs of NATO allies.

From delegation to control: The protection of critical infrastructures

In 1997, the German Federal Government began work on the protection of critical infrastructures. Initially, the government founded a Critical Infrastructures Working Group (Schulze 2006: 155–156), which recommended close cooperation between "business, science and politics" (Ressortarbeitsgruppe KRITIS 1999). Parliamentarians also assessed that this task should be jointly managed by both the state and industry. The operators of critical infrastructures should also be encouraged to establish appropriate security management of the assets (Deutscher Bundestag 1998: 17). However, these findings remained largely inconsequential at first. The policy for the protection of critical infrastructures gained real traction only after the 9/11 terror attacks. Subsequent antiterrorism legislation passed by the government highlighted the vulnerability of critical infrastructures to cyberattacks and strengthened the Federal Office for Information Security (BSI). In addition, the cooperation KRITIS, which was intended to enable the state and economy to exchange information effectively, was founded in 2002. However, experts found the network proved largely deficient (Schulze 2006: 185, 247).

In 2005, the government presented the "National Information Infrastructure Protection Plan", the first strategic document for the protection of critical (information) infrastructures in Germany (Bundesministerium des Innern 2005: 3). Though the plan assigned responsibility for the protection of infrastructures primarily to private sector operators, the German government (in close consultation with industry) would define minimum standards that would guarantee an adequate level of protection against cyberattacks (Bundesministerium des Innern 2005: 13). The KRITIS implementation plan, published in 2007, continued this approach of voluntary cooperation and recommended various measures to be taken by companies. However, the central tenet of the infrastructure protection strategy remained that "the goal should be reached in consensus between the private sector objectives of the operators and the overriding (welfare) interest of the community" (Bundesministerium des Innern 2007: 5). As such, in this first phase of German infrastructure protection, the protector role was delegated to operators of critical infrastructures.

However, cooperation between the state and the private sector fell short of the government's expectations. From the administration's point of view, companies did not comply with their obligation to provide information and neglected their duties to establish suitable standards. In addition, Stuxnet made clear that attacks on industrial targets were no longer just hypothetical scenarios (Bundesministerium des Innern 2011: 3). As a result, the government debated introducing binding regulations that would provide better protection of critical infrastructures. Federal Interior Minister Friedrich said:

> I know that there are voices in the economy that would prefer to cooperate on a voluntary basis. However, experience shows that in the past we have been behind our goals with voluntary measures alone. We need a legal framework for more cooperation and compliance with IT security standards.
>
> (Bundesministerium des Innern 2013)

This marked the departure from the government's reliance on voluntary cooperation and more strongly bound the protector role to state authorities. With the IT Security Act passed in 2015, the government obliged companies to comply with minimum standards and to report substantial cyberattacks. The new law thus significantly strengthened the supervisory competence of the BSI (Bundesamt für Sicherheit in der Informationstechnik 2016: 5). Although the industry associations eco and Bitkom supported the ultimate goals of the law, there was substantial criticism of the government's decision to abandon the previous regulatory arrangement. Companies initially objected to the interference in entrepreneurial freedom and potential overregulation (heise.de 2013; eco 2015: 3). Efforts to stop the IT security law, however, were unsuccessful.

From about 2012, the government increasingly prioritized securing critical infrastructures internationally as well. Following the establishment of the first voluntary principles for the protection of critical infrastructures by the G8 in 2003 (G8 2003), there was increased interest across the EU in regulating the protection of critical infrastructures (European Commission 2009). Yet, discussions on the introduction of EU rules protecting critical infrastructures only started to take shape in 2013. Together with other states also pursuing standards for the handling of critical infrastructures, Germany worked toward the adoption of the Directive on security of network and information systems (NIS Directive). Like the German IT Security Act, the NIS Directive provides for state supervision of critical infrastructures and establishes reporting obligations (European Union 2016). In parallel with developments in the EU, Germany also promoted the protection of critical infrastructures within the OSCE. As early as 2011, the government supported "the obligation to protect critical infrastructures" in a proposed code of conduct, which was also introduced in the UN (United Nations 2011: 9). In 2016, a second round of confidence-building measures related to critical infrastructure protection were adopted within the OSCE under German chairmanship. These additional measures addressed the possibilities for more voluntary cooperation in the protection of cross-border infrastructure (OSCE 2016a).

In Germany's case, international cooperation on the protection of critical infrastructures was only possible after the domestic role of protector was firmly established and clear among all actors. Furthermore, it is no coincidence that this cooperation emerged in regional organizations because of the physical interconnectedness of critical infrastructures. Knowing the minimum standards of other nations and understanding how other actors engaging in the protector role view their position, reduces the uncertainty with regard to cascading effects across borders.

New methods of investigation and domestic contestations: Law enforcement

Germany established the first legal basis to make computer fraud and interference with data integrity criminal offenses in 1986. These changes, supported by the administration's claim that these laws will protect economic well-being, were hardly contested domestically. Yet, as the internet grew into a global phenomenon, it became increasingly clear that a nationally bound protector would be insufficient against the wide scope of threats the internet may introduce. To guarantee effective law enforcement against a transnational force, transnational solutions must be sought (Bundesregierung 1999). Consequently, the government began to engage with like-minded states on the international level. One of the main goals was to avoid conflicts as a result of diverging criminal laws (Brodowski 2015).

As cybercrime represented a significant problem for many states by the late 1990s, legal frameworks for law enforcement agencies were put in place in countries around the world. Much of this legislation shared significant similarities and attempted to address similar problems. Across legislative regimes, both the threat (cyberattacks) and the threatening actor (non-state criminal actors) were typically defined and labeled in similar ways. Early international coordination efforts included the establishment of a committee of experts within the Council of Europe in 1997. The committee was tasked with drafting the first international convention to counter cybercrime. The resulting Budapest Convention was opened for signature in 2001 and outlines a series of criminal offenses that signatories are required to transpose into national law. The compatibility of the national protective roles also enabled the harmonization of criminal law within the European Union. Particular mention should be made of framework decision 2005/222/JHA, and its eventual replacement, directive 2013/40/EU. Despite increasing coordination between states, including the establishment of transnational investigative powers for combating cybercrime, central authority in law enforcement (as well as the responsibility for specific regulations) still rests with individual EU member states (Brodowski 2015: 268; Hilgendorf and Valerius 2012: 36–37; Council of Europe 2001).

The complexities of navigating two levels of cybercrime response, conforming to both international and domestic expectations, is well-illustrated when examining the German case more closely. Two factors have been influential: first, the ongoing domestic debate about which actor is ultimately responsible for ensuring sufficient protections against cybercrime, about who should take on the protector role, makes it difficult to negotiate further international cooperation. Second, a resolution to these debates has been hindered by the reluctance of the government to delegate or share parts of the protector role.

The struggle to establish clear limits, and a clear understanding, of what the protector role of the German government should be intensified after terror attacks in Madrid (2004) and London (2005). To keep pace with technological development, the government provided law enforcement agencies with two tools to enable lawful interception: source telecommunications monitoring (Quellen-TKÜ) and online search (Online-Durchsuchung) (Deutscher Bundestag 2006). The use of these measures created substantial resistance within German society, as many critics considered IT devices to be at the core of private life and thus covert investigations represented a disproportionate invasion of privacy. In July 2007, representatives of civil society and the Left Party filed a constitutional complaint against online search. In February 2008, the Federal Constitutional Court ruled that this measure was admissible only "if there were actual indications of a specific danger to a legally protected interest of paramount importance". The court further defined "the fundamental right to ensure the confidentiality and integrity of information technology systems". In addition, the court requested that an online search could only be conducted with a judicial warrant, restricting its use as a cybercrime prevention tool (Bundesverfassungsgericht 2008). The domestic debate further intensified when, in 2008, the Chaos Computer Club revealed that the software used to conduct lawful interception was much more powerful than it was supposed to be. The software was not limited to intercepting communications prior to encryption as intended, but in fact enabled the complete monitoring of infected devices (CCC 2011). Even though domestic disputes about the appropriate powers of state institutions have been fierce, the German government has repeatedly stressed the importance of the new investigative tools to deal with serious crime and terrorism (Deutscher Bundestag 2017: 24586).

With reference to these challenges, the government reduced the thresholds for using Quellen-TKÜ and online searches in 2017. This step has led to substantial and ongoing criticism (heise.de 2017). Clearly, the scope and powers of the government, the self-appointed protector, in German society is still hotly debated. As long as there is no stable role relationship domestically, it is very difficult to negotiate international rules regarding the same issues. Additionally, the protector role is considered to be at the core of state functionality and therefore has clear limits on how much can be delegated to other actors. Therefore, unlike the protection of critical infrastructure, the establishment of a stable domestic role relationship may not result in substantial international cooperation.

Between criticism and dependency: The German intelligence service

When Edward Snowden revealed the extensive surveillance measures of the NSA and GCHQ in June 2013, Germany found itself in the position of being spied on by some of its closest allies. Chancellor Merkel's initial remarks reflected much of German society's reaction to this reveal: "spying among friends is not at all acceptable" (Spillius 2013). Following the revelations, the government attempted to convince the United States to renounce espionage activities against Germany and proposed a bilateral agreement to this end. However, these efforts were largely ignored by the United States. This alienated Germany and prompted Berlin to initiate increased activities in the field of counterintelligence (Bundesregierung 2015). This introduced a new, and critical, element to the government's protector role; never before did Germany require protection from the actions of its allies.

Since the United States did not respond to bilateral solutions, the German administration resorted to other means to ease domestic outrage. In order to counter the United States' privileged physical access to internet traffic, thereby making espionage more difficult, the construction of a new transatlantic undersea cable was launched in cooperation with Brazil. As a result, less internet traffic would be routed through the United States (Reuters 2014). Germany and Brazil were also responsible for co-sponsoring a UN resolution against excessive surveillance activities in the digital age (United Nations 2013). But even in this context direct confrontation with the United States was avoided. Thus, the text of the resolution was substantially watered down in consultations (Reuters 2013).

As the scope of the allegations became clearer, there was mounting domestic pressure for a thorough investigation of the events. For this reason, the German Bundestag set up a Committee of Inquiry in March 2014. In parliamentary debates and on the part of the government, however, it was repeatedly pointed out that Germany relied on security cooperation with the United States and that this relationship could not be jeopardized by harsh criticism (Bundesministerium des Innern 2014). In particular, Germany could not conduct the intelligence-gathering it required for its security without using data gathered by the United States and other allies (Deutscher Bundestag 2013a, 2013b). For all intents and purposes, Germany had at least partly outsourced its protector role to the United States.

The work of the Committee of Inquiry soon revealed that the practices of the NSA were not the only problem. It became increasingly obvious that the German federal intelligence service (BND) were employing similarly questionable practices in the name of security. The Committee's investigation and the documents disclosed by Edward Snowden revealed, for example, that the BND cooperated with the NSA regularly and substantially, and that data of German citizens were exchanged (Mascolo 2014). As the extent of the government's activities became more widely understood by the public, attention shifted toward the domestic sphere. Members of the political opposition and representatives of civil society accused the government of disproportionate surveillance activities. From a role theoretical perspective, the allegation was that the administration had expanded its role without significant others even knowing.

Domestic criticism in Germany was so intense that the government had to reorganize the legal framework governing foreign intelligence. In 2016, the administration submitted a new law that was meant to bolster the legal justification for the BND. To achieve complementary counter-role taking by parliament and to appease the public, this included new control mechanisms as well as special protections not only for Germans but also for citizens of the European Union. This demonstrates that Merkel's statement about spying among friends may have held weight, and that the protector is only under limited circumstances allowed to act against certain allies. However, the new law also legalized many of the questionable practices uncovered during investigations. Consequently, the law has been subject to considerable criticism from lawyers, the parliamentary opposition, civil society, and even international organizations like the OSCE (OSCE 2016b). Nevertheless, the BND Act was passed by the Bundestag in October 2016. The government had successfully negotiated the expansion of its protector role within an increasingly hostile environment. Furthermore, the experiences of sobering interactions with international partners resonated in the debates (Deutscher Bundestag 2016b: 19625).

Government officials emphasized that for this very reason the legislation was designed not to limit the BND in its operations, but instead to create transparent regulations (Deutscher Bundestag 2016a: 18274). However, the BND and the government's support of the agency continues to attract criticism. In January 2018, an alliance of civil society actors filed a constitutional complaint against the BND Act that has yet to be resolved; it is possible that a ruling by the Federal Constitutional Court might force the government to act again (Reporter ohne Grenzen 2018). At least in part because of ongoing criticism, the government has increasingly outsourced elements of its protector role to its allies, to both capitalize on the efficacy of existing intelligence sources as well as respond to the limits put on its domestic capabilities. This expansion remains contested domestically.

From defense to offense: Military cyber security

In 2007, the German armed forces established a unit assigned to computer network operations (CNO). This marks the first military effort to protect the Federal Republic in cyberspace, and was the first move toward the development of offensive capabilities. The task of this new unit was to operate in computer networks of enemies and, if necessary, complement or replace conventional military operations (Deutscher Bundestag 2014: 1165). The risks of military hostility in cyberspace nonetheless kept the government critical of a militarized cyberspace. Thus, the administration argued for promoting a "culture of restraint" ("Kultur der Zurückhaltung"). This included a prohibition on the development of malware by the German *Bundeswehr* (Deutscher Bundestag 2010: 5). The role of protector thereby remained inconsistent; on the one hand the Bundeswehr should be able to conduct CNOs, but on the other, it should not engage in the practice of developing related tools.

Following this path of self-restraint, the Bundeswehr's responsibilities (largely limited to defense) were described in Germany's first cyber security strategy (Bundesministerium des Innern 2011: 5). While this new role for the protector was not contested, parliamentarians claimed that offensive cyber measures would require a constitutive mandate of the Bundestag – just like conventional deployments. The government subsequently reassured that CNOs were governed by the same rules as more traditional warfare (Deutscher Bundestag 2015b: 4). In addition, the government confirmed that Article 26 of the Basic Law also prohibits a war of aggression in cyberspace (Deutscher Bundestag 2015b: 7).

On the international level, however, efforts to encourage states to exercise self-restraint have found little resonance. Although Germany was substantially involved in UN discussions regarding IT and international security (UN GGE), the government was not able to successfully lobby for a culture of restraint. In fact, despite its posturing for restraint on the international stage, capacities of the German Armed Forces significantly expanded after 2010. Furthermore, early positions regarding the development of offensive technologies were apparently abandoned. Even though the government initially stated that the *Bundeswehr* would not develop malicious software, in 2015 the administration confirmed that the CNO forces had to resort to the exploitation of vulnerabilities to operate in enemy networks (Deutscher Bundestag 2015a: 11–12). While the government argued that vulnerabilities that could have "far-reaching implications for the security of the population or the state" should be disclosed, it nevertheless made clear that such disclosure may not interfere with the government's capability to enact its role as a protector (Deutscher Bundestag 2018: 10). The development of offensive capabilities nevertheless signifies a substantial change in policy and armed the protector with the capabilities necessary to (offensively) act in cyberspace. The growth of capacities was mirrored by expanding claims for protection. While the tasks of the *Bundeswehr* were initially focused on the protection of military infrastructure, cyberspace became an increasingly acceptable domain for military action in the years that followed. The buildup of cyber capacities culminated in 2017 when the German Armed Forces established a new cyber command (Bundesministerium der Verteidigung 2016).

Two processes facilitated the expansion of the military's protector role: first, the German government followed in the footsteps of its international "significant others". In particular, demands and developments in NATO were particularly influential. NATO recognized cyberspace as "a domain of operations in which NATO must defend itself as effectively as it does in the air, on land, and at sea" at the Warsaw Summit in 2016 (NATO 2016). The establishment of a cyber command in 2017 was considered necessary to ensure effective cooperation with allies. Second, the new tools and capabilities were continually justified by the growing number and sophistication of cyberattacks (Bundesministerium der Verteidigung 2016). The Minister of Defense specifically pointed out that cyberattacks were used in complement with conventional forces in Georgia in 2008 and supported hybrid warfare in Ukraine (Bundesministerium der Verteidigung 2015).

The offensive use of cyberspace remains a contentious issue. Critics argue that the peaceful use of the internet is threatened, and that stockpiling vulnerabilities undermined the security of the global system (FIfF 2015; Gesellschaft für Informatik 2015). Against the international pressures, however, the challenges from civil society remain inconsequential.

The ambiguity of the military's protector role is emphasized when the goal of restraint is contrasted with the subsequent buildup of offensive capabilities. It is evident that the process of establishing a more capable protector undermines lofty ideals about restraint in the international system. The actions taken by the German Armed Forces directly contradicted its purported goal, and if other states took similar actions, an international culture of restraint would be made far more difficult to achieve. For example, while international law regulates a visible distinction between combatants and non-combatants for armed forces, the government emphasizes that cyber warfare does not require such a distinction. Although the use of false identities is prohibited (e.g. to direct suspicion onto other actors), the wide acceptance of the use of concealment tactics nevertheless makes it difficult to build a verifiable culture of restraint in cyberspace (Deutscher Bundestag 2015b: 11). Driven by the demands of international significant others and an increasingly dangerous cyberspace, the government's protector role started to undermine the initial goal of restraint.

Conclusion: The different logics of German cyber security policy

This chapter has argued that German cyber security policy is a multifaceted phenomenon characterized by different patterns of interaction in the four areas studied. The analysis has illustrated that the areas of investigation are characterized by different constellations of actors (significant others) that are affected by both domestic and external influences. The approach of a two-level role play takes this into account. The different patterns of international and domestic interactions were found to constitute a variety of "protector roles" the government may attempt to fulfill, though the different spheres were influential to varying degrees. Considering German cyber security policies in total, it is evident that the Government of Germany has successfully and significantly extended the scope of its protective role. It has done so by expanding the competences of different security institutions and by centralizing control of assets like critical infrastructures. But a closer look reveals a more fragmented and nuanced picture.

The most significant source of international cooperation has been related to the protection of critical infrastructures. After unsatisfactory domestic cooperation with companies led to the creation of binding regulations, similar arrangements were pushed for and implemented at the EU level. Reducing the protector's domestic commitments by delegating to the private sector enabled more substantial international cooperation. International coordination also proved useful in relation to law enforcement; the harmonization of criminal law between states is facilitated by the similarities between protector roles in different states. In cases where domestic role contestation is ongoing, for example regarding criminal procedural law, the potential benefits of international cooperation are less clear. In fact, it is this unstable domestic role relationship that impedes useful international cooperation.

Nevertheless, in both areas the protector attempted to regulate the behavior of non-state actors (including companies and criminals). When it comes to self-binding regulations, a different picture emerges. The Snowden revelations illustrate the changing dynamics between domestic and international spheres of role playing. Germany's protector role was simultaneously threatened by the United States' activities, which could not be successfully curtailed, but also bolstered by continued access to the information those questionable practices uncovered.

It was the reluctance of international partners, together with an increasingly dangerous cyber environment and a growing demand for more autonomy domestically, that led the German government to establish a more far-reaching legal basis for foreign surveillance and thereby expand its protector role. The government's success in this matter is even more notable since the Snowden revelations also exposed the BND to substantial criticism, resulting in ongoing role contestation within Germany. With regard to the Armed Forces, the Federal Republic started to work toward an international culture of restraint toward military activities in cyberspace, but here, too, the actions of international partners forced Berlin's hand. In order to fulfill its protector role and meet requirements of NATO, the Federal Republic has set up its own military cyber command and initiated a buildup of capacities after 2010, thereby at least partially undermining the ultimate goal of restraint. Domestic contestations in this area remained largely inconsequential.

Within the larger context of international cyber security, it is clear that even states considered cautious in their foreign policy pursuits can aggravate the challenges of transnational cyber security. Germany's foreign intelligence service is highly capable and is known to analyze internet traffic as it passes German internet exchange points. The government also resorts to stockpiling vulnerabilities and, if necessary, operating covertly in cyberspace. Even though a decision has not yet been made regarding the responsible disclosure of vulnerabilities, it is clear that from a governmental point of view, some vulnerabilities are essential in order to effectively perform the protector role. Resorting to covert action, including purposefully complicating attribution efforts, directly undermines the explicitly stated goal of a verifiable culture of restraint, since even attacks from more cautious states will occur hidden.

Notes

1 The term "cybersecurity policy" refers to political practices aimed at ensuring the confidentiality, integrity, and availability (CIA-triad) of data and data processing systems and to those policies undermining these goals of IT security.

2 For an overview of foreign policy role theory, see Harnisch (2018); Breuning (2017).

References

All links checked on August 23, 2021.

Breuning, M. (2017). Role Theory in Foreign Policy. In *Oxford Research Encyclopedia of Politics*. https://doi.org/10.1093/acrefore/9780190228637.013.334.

Brodowski, D. (2015). Cybersicherheit durch Cyber-Strafrecht? Über die strafrechtliche Regulierung des Internets. In H.-J. Lange and A. Bötticher (eds), *Studien zur Inneren Sicherheit: Band 18. Cyber-Sicherheit*. Wiesbaden [Germany]: Springer VS, pp. 249–276.

Bundesamt für Sicherheit in der Informationstechnik. (2016). Das IT-Sicherheitsgesetz: Kritische Infrastrukturen schützen. Retrieved from: https://www.bsi.bund.de/SharedDocs/Downloads/DE/BSI/Publikationen/Broschueren/IT-Sicherheitsgesetz.pdf?__blob=publicationFileandv=7.

Bundesministerium der Verteidigung. (2015). Keynote der Verteidigungsministerin auf dem Kolloquium des Cyber-Workshop. Retrieved from: https://www.bmvg.de/de/themen/dossiers/weissbuch/perspektiven/keynote-von-ministerin-von-der-leyen-beim-cyber-workshop-11028.

Bundesministerium der Verteidigung. (2016). Abschlussbericht Aufbaustab Cyber- und Informationsraum. Retrieved from: http://docs.dpaq.de/11361-abschlussbericht_aufbaustab_cir.pdf.

Bundesministerium des Innern. (2005). Nationaler Plan zum Schutz der Informationsinfrastrukturen. Retrieved from: https://www.innenministerkonferenz.de/IMK/DE/termine/to-beschluesse/05-12-09/05-12-09-anlage-nr-16.pdf?__blob=publicationFileandv=2.

Bundesministerium des Innern. (2007). Umsetzungsplan KRITIS: des nationalen Plans zum Schutz kritischer Infrastrukturen. Retrieved from: https://www.bmi.bund.de/SharedDocs/downloads/DE/publikationen/themen/it-digitalpolitik/umsetzungsplan-kritis.pdf?__blob=publicationFile&v=4.

Bundesministerium des Innern. (2011). Cyber-Sicherheitsstrategie für Deutschland. Retrieved from: https://www.cio.bund.de/SharedDocs/Publikationen/DE/Strategische-Themen/css_download.pdf?__blob=publicationFile.

Bundesministerium des Innern. (2013). Friedrich stellt Wirtschaft IT-Sicherheitsgesetz vor. Retrieved from: https://www.bmi.bund.de/SharedDocs/kurzmeldungen/DE/2013/03/eco_mmr_itsicherheitsgesetz.html.

Bundesministerium des Innern. (2014). Rede von Bundesinnenminister de Maizière anlässlich des 11. Symposiums des Bundesamtes für Verfassungsschutz am 8. Mai 2014 in Berlin. Retrieved from: https://www.bmi.bund.de/SharedDocs/reden/DE/2014/05/bfv-symposium.html.

Bundesregierung. (1999). Rede des Bundesministers des Innern, Otto Schily, bei der Konferenz der Bertelsmann-Stiftung "International Internet Content Summit 1999": Weltweite Kommunikation - eine neue Kultur gemeinsamer Verantwortung. Retrieved from: https://www.bundesregierung.de/Content/DE/Bulletin/1990-1999/1999/58-99_Schily.html.

Bundesregierung. (2015). Sommerpressekonferenz von Bundeskanzlerin Merkel. Retrieved from: https://www.bundesregierung.de/Content/DE/Mitschrift/Pressekonferenzen/2015/08/2015-08-31-pk-merkel.html.

Bundesverfassungsgericht. (2008). Urteil vom 27. Februar 2008 –1 BvR 370/07. Retrieved from: https://www.bundesverfassungsgericht.de/SharedDocs/Entscheidungen/DE/2008/02/rs20080227_1bvr037007.html.

Cantir, C., and Kaarbo, J. (2012). Contested Roles and Domestic Politics: Reflections on Role Theory in Foreign Policy Analysis and IR Theory. *Foreign Policy Analysis*, 8(1): 5–24. https://doi.org/10.1111/j.1743-8594.2011.00156.x.

Cantir, C., and Kaarbo, J. (eds). (2016). *Domestic Role Contestation, Foreign Policy, and International Relations. Role Theory and International Relations: Vol. 6*. New York: Routledge, Taylor and Francis Group.

CCC. (2011). Analyse einer Regierungs-Malware. Retrieved from: https://www.ccc.de/system/uploads/76/original/staatstrojaner-report23.pdf.

Choucri, N., and Clark, D. D. (2012). Integrating Cyberspace and International Relations: The Co-Evolution Dilemma. *SSRN Electronic Journal*. Advance online publication. https://doi.org/10.2139/ssrn.2178586.

Council of Europe. (2001). Convention on Cybercrime. Retrieved from: https://www.europarl.europa.eu/meetdocs/2014_2019/documents/libe/dv/7_conv_budapest_/7_conv_budapest_en.pdf.

Deutscher Bundestag. (1998). Vierter Zwischenbericht der Enquete-Kommission Zukunft der Medien in Wirtschaft und Gesellschaft — Deutschlands Weg in die Informationsgesellschaft): Sicherheit und Schutz im Netz. Retrieved from: http://dip21.bundestag.de/dip21/btd/13/110/1311002.pdf.

Deutscher Bundestag. (2006). Drucksache 16/3973. Retrieved from: http://dipbt.bundestag.de/dip21/btd/16/039/1603973.pdf.

Deutscher Bundestag. (2010). Drucksache 17/3388. Retrieved from: http://dipbt.bundestag.de/dip21/btd/17/033/1703388.pdf.

Deutscher Bundestag. (2013a). Plenarprotokoll 17/249. Retrieved from: http://dip21.bundestag.de/dip21/btp/17/17249.pdf.

Deutscher Bundestag. (2013b). Plenarprotokoll 18/2. Retrieved from: http://dip21.bundestag.de/dip21/btp/18/18002.pdf.

Deutscher Bundestag. (2014). Plenarprotokoll 18/16. Retrieved from: https://dipbt.bundestag.de/doc/btp/18/18016.pdf.

Deutscher Bundestag. (2015a). Drucksache 18/4286. Retrieved from: https://dip21.bundestag.de/dip21/btd/18/042/1804286.pdf.

Deutscher Bundestag. (2015b). Drucksache 18/6989. Retrieved from: https://dipbt.bundestag.de/doc/btd/18/069/1806989.pdf.

Deutscher Bundestag. (2016a). Plenarprotokoll 18/184. Retrieved from: http://dipbt.bundestag.de/dip21/btp/18/18184.pdf.

Deutscher Bundestag. (2016b). Plenarprotokoll 18/197. Retrieved from: http://dipbt.bundestag.de/dip21/btp/18/18197.pdf.

Deutscher Bundestag. (2017). Plenarprotokoll 18/240. Retrieved from: http://dipbt.bundestag.de/dip21/btp/18/18240.pdf.

Deutscher Bundestag. (2018). Drucksache 19/3420. Retrieved from: http://dip21.bundestag.de/dip21/btd/19/034/1903420.pdf.

Dunn Cavelty, M. (2008). *Cyber-Security and Threat Politics: US Efforts to Secure the Information Age. CSS Studies in Security and International Relations*. London: Routledge.

Eco. (2015). Positionspapier: Zum Kabinettsentwurf für ein Gesetz zur Erhöhung der Sicherheit informationstechnischer Systeme (IT-Sicherheitsgesetz). Retrieved 31 August 2021, from: https://silo.tips/download/positionspapier-zum-kabinettsentwurf-fr-ein-gesetz-zur-erhhung-der-sicherheit-in.

European Commission. (2009). Protecting Europe from Large Scale Cyber-Attacks and Disruptions: Enhancing Preparedness, Security and Resilience. Retrieved from: https://eur-lex.europa.eu/legal-content/GA/TXT/?uri=CELEX:52009DC0149.

European Union. (2016). Directive 2016/1148. Retrieved from: https://eur-lex.europa.eu/legal-content/EN/ALL/?uri=CELEX%3A32016L1148.

FIfF. (2015). Frau von der Leyen, verzichten Sie auf Cyberwaffen für die Bundeswehr!. Retrieved from: https://www.fiff.de/presse/pressemitteilungen/2015_09_30_FIfF_Appell_Cyberpeace.pdf.

Fritz, J. R. (2017). *China's Cyber Warfare: The Evolution of Strategic Doctrine*. Lanham, MD: Lexington Books.

G8. (2003). G8 Principles for Protecting Critical Information Infrastructures. Retrieved from: http://www.cyber securitycooperation.org/documents/G8_CIIP_Principles.pdf.

Gesellschaft für Informatik. (2015). Verteidigungsanstrengungen der Bundesregierung gegen Cyberangriffe aus dem Internet unzureichend - Wirkungsvolle Maßnahmen gegen Angriffe und Angriffskriege im Internet gefordert. Retrieved from: https://gi.de/meldung/verteidigungsanstrengungen-der-bundesregierung-gegen-cyberangriffe-aus-dem-internet-unzureichend-wirkungsvolle-massnahmen-gegen-angriffe-und-angriffskriege-im-internet-gefordert.

Harnisch, S. (2012). Role Theory: Operationalization of Key Concepts. In S. Harnisch, C. Frank, and H. Maull (eds), *Routledge Advances in International Relations and Global Politics: Vol. 90. Role Theory in International Relations: Approaches and Analyses*. London: Routledge, Taylor and Francis Group, pp. 7–15.

Harnisch, S. (2014). Full-Spectrum Role-Taking: A Two-Level Role Theoretical Model. Retrieved from: http://www.uni-heidelberg.de/md/politik/harnisch/person/vortraege/harnisch_2014_-_isa_conference_paper_full_spectrum_role_taking_draft_24_03.pdf.

Harnisch, S. (2018). Role Theory in International Relations. Retrieved from: http://www.oxfordbibliographies.com/view/document/obo-9780199743292/obo-9780199743292-0226.xml?rskey.

Heise.de. (2013). Wirtschaft wettert gegen geplantes IT-Sicherheitsgesetz. Retrieved from: https://www.heise.de/newsticker/meldung/Wirtschaft-wettert-gegen-geplantes-IT-Sicherheitsgesetz-1833835.html.

Heise.de. (2017). Bundesverfassungsgericht: Digitalcourage klagt gegen Staatstrojaner. Retrieved from: https://www.heise.de/newsticker/meldung/Bundesverfassungsgericht-Digitalcourage-klagt-gegen-Staatstrojaner-3785288.html.

Hilgendorf, E., and Valerius, B. (2012). *Computer- und Internetstrafrecht*. Berlin, Heidelberg: Springer Berlin Heidelberg.

Maréchal, N. (2017). Networked Authoritarianism and the Geopolitics of Information: Understanding Russian Internet Policy. *Media and Communication*, 5(1): 29–41. https://doi.org/10.17645/mac.v5i1.808.

Mascolo, G. (2014, October 4). Codewort Eikonal - der Albtraum der Bundesregierung. Retrieved from: https://www.sueddeutsche.de/politik/geheimdienste-codewort-eikonal-der-albtraum-der-bundesregierung-1.2157432.

McCarthy, D. R. (2018). Privatizing Political Authority: Cyber Security, Public-Private Partnerships, and the Reproduction of Liberal Political Order. *Politics and Governance*, 6(2): 5–12. https://doi.org/10.17645/pag.v6i2.1335.

NATO. (2016). Warsaw Summit Communiqué. Retrieved from: https://www.nato.int/cps/ic/natohq/official_texts_133169.htm.

OSCE. (2016a). Decision No 1202: OSCE Confidence-Building Measures to Reduce the Risks of Conflict Stemming from the Use of Information and Communication Technologies. Retrieved from: https://www.osce.org/pc/227281?download=true.

OSCE. (2016b). Surveillance Amendments in New Law in Germany Pose a Threat to Media Freedom, OSCE Representative Says, Asks Bundestag to Reconsider Bill. Retrieved from: https://www.osce.org/fom/252076.

Putnam, R. D. (1988). Diplomacy and Domestic Politics: The Logic of Two-Level Games. *International Organization*, 42(3): 427–460.

Reporter ohne Grenzen. (2018). Verfassungsbeschwerde gegen das BND-Gesetz. Retrieved from: https://www.reporter-ohne-grenzen.de/pressemitteilungen/meldung/verfassungs beschwerde-gegen-das-bnd-gesetz/.

Ressortarbeitsgruppe KRITIS. (1999). Informationstechnische Bedrohungen für Kritische Infrastrukturen in Deutschland. Retrieved from: http://userpage.fu-berlin.de/~bendrath /Kritis-12-1999.html.

Reuters. (2013). U.N. Anti-Spying Resolution Weakened in Bid to Gain U.S., British Support. Retrieved from: https://www.reuters.com/article/us-usa-surveillance-un-idU SBRE9AK14220131121.

Reuters. (2014). Brazil, Europe Plan Undersea Cable to Skirt U.S. Spying. Retrieved from: https://www.reuters.com/article/us-eu-brazil-idUSBREA1N0PL20140224.

Schulze, T. (2006). *Bedingt abwehrbereit: Schutz kritischer Informations-Infrastrukturen in Deutschland und den USA* (1. Aufl.). Wiesbaden: VS Verlag für Sozialwissenschaften/ GWV Fachverlage, Wiesbaden.

Spillius, A. (2013, October 24). Angela Merkel: Spying between Friends is Unacceptable. *The Telegraph*. Retrieved from: https://www.telegraph.co.uk/news/worldnews/europe/ germany/10402570/Angela-Merkel-spying-between-friends-is-unacceptable.html.

United Nations. (2011). Developments in the Field of Information and Telecommunications in the Context of International Security: Report of the Secretary-General. Retrieved from: http://undocs.org/A/66/152.

United Nations. (2013). A/RES/68/167. Retrieved from: https://undocs.org/A/RES/68/167.

Whyte, C. (2018). Dissecting the Digital World: A Review of the Construction and Constitution of Cyber Conflict Research. *International Studies Review*, 80(3). https:// doi.org/10.1093/isr/viw013.

11 Battling the bear

Ukraine's approach to national cyber and information security

Aaron Brantly

Ukraine (Україна, Ukrainian Pronunciation: ukra-jina), derived from its etymology, describes the borderlands between the Kyivan Rus' and Poland. This historical name dating back to the 12th century aptly describes in the modern context a nation that stands as the border between the Russian Federation and the West. The victim of a sustained grey zone conflict since 2014, Ukraine is a case study of both hybrid conflict and the evolution of national informational and cyber conflict between a regional power and a medium-sized weak state. Ukraine's experiences highlight the challenges associated with what is best referred to as a cybered conflict fostered by a new era of socio-technical uncertainty and insecurity. This chapter examines the reality of cybered conflict generated by socio-technical uncertainty originating out of information warfare and cyberattacks between two nations and serves as a testing bed of multiple theories and concepts on deterrence, norms, and security developed over the last 30 years.

Ukraine has been under sustained assault in and through cyberspace both prior to and following the collapse of the Yanukovych regime on February 22, 2014. How Ukraine has addressed the assault on its sovereignty in cyberspace and beyond has been the subject of multiple works on hybrid warfare. Yet few of these works have examined how Ukraine specifically addressed its challenges. Ukraine's approach to cyber and information warfare following the Revolution of Dignity (Euromaidan) serves as a robust case in how to confront a larger aggressive adversary in cyberspace. Ukraine's approach to national cyber security and information security is a work in progress highlighting the challenges of developing organizational structures within contentious political and social environments.

Information warfare and cyberattacks against Ukraine constituting socio-technical assaults occurred in tandem with political fragmentation and reorganization in the face of adversarial activities. Russian news organizations and social media such as Odnaklassniki and Vkontakte rapidly disseminated a narrative of events counter to the perceived realities taking place during Ukraine's Revolution of Dignity (Frum 2014). Beyond sustained information operations, protesters were also subject to a variety of cyberattacks including DDoS[1] and SS7[2] attacks. Attacks on mobile infrastructures targeted the protesters with SMS messages ominously warning "Dear subscriber, you are registered as a participant in a mass disturbance" (Hooton 2014). This form of attack would become prevalent in the

DOI: 10.4324/9781003110224-13

months following Euromaidan and Ukrainian soldiers and their families would be increasingly targeted with similar attacks (Brantly, Cal, and Winkelstein 2017a). Other cyberattacks, mainly DDoS, against opposition websites and protest infrastructures were also common (Pakharenko 2015).

These initial information and cyber operations would become part of a larger and arguably more complicated informational and cyber security environment in the months and years following Euromaidan. Extending well beyond the Ukrainians engaged along a physical contact line with Russian soldiers and their proxies in the East of Ukraine, Ukrainian citizens across the nation have felt the impact of sustained information and cyber operations. These sustained operations create a perpetual siege mentality (Brantly et al. 2017b).

This chapter deconstructs the bureaucratic politics of the state and examines the actions Ukraine has undertaken to address Russian information operations and cyber warfare. Combined, these constitute a change in how Ukrainians address and understand information operations and cyber security. This chapter proceeds in four sections. The first section examines the state of the bureaucracy of Ukraine as it related to information operations and cyber security at the time of the collapse of the Yanukovych government. The second section examines the efforts of Ukraine and her citizens to address information and cyber security challenges. The third section discusses the process of changing the fundamental approach to national cyber and information security in Ukraine. Finally, the chapter concludes with a discussion on the future of Ukrainian approaches to national information and cyber security.

Bureaucratic bits and bytes

Ukraine's woes in cyberspace and information warfare are not solely attributable to external factors. Ukraine's domestic political structures, unitary government, rigid and often ineffectual bureaucracy, and what Paul D'Anieri (2006) refers to as a state of "rule by law rather than rule of law" exacerbate external interventions into the nation and impede efficient responses and the development of effective institutions capable of safeguarding Ukraine. At its most basic, Ukraine is challenged by a consolidation of power within its bureaucracy. This consolidation returns Ukraine to a highly centralized bureaucracy with traditionally embedded criminal–political interests and high levels of corruption. This leads to a situation in which laws are drafted, passed, and institutions are created and staffed but the application of law is inconsistently applied (due to criminal or corruption interests), and institutions are unable to operate effectively without highly centralized control.

Prior to the Revolution of Dignity, Ukraine had a bevy of more than 22 laws on the books associated with information and cyber security. The number and extent of legislation on cyber security and information security in Ukraine prior to 2014 might lead outside observers to believe Ukraine had an effective information security apparatus in advance of Euromaidan. Prior to legislating information and cyber security, the Ukrainian government established, as far back as

1991, the State Special Communications Service of Ukraine (Державна служба спеціального зв'язку та захисту інформації України) and in 2007 established a computer emergency response team (CERT-UA) ("CERT-UA: скорая киберп омощь – PC Week/UE" 2014). Despite all the above laws the state of cyber and information security in Ukraine at the time of Euromaidan was weak. The laws in aggregate deal with many of the conventional challenges associated with information and cyber security.

Despite the robustness and conscientious nature of the laws on the books, the actual enforcement of these laws was subjective at best (D'Anieri 2006). The selective enforcement of legal regimes is in line with highly consolidated power structures. D'Anieri (2006) notes that the consolidation of power does not make the laws inapplicable but creates the conditions under which their application is subject to the discretion of those in political power rather than decentralized administration based on a robust jurisprudence. Taras Kuzio (2015) notes that that the consolidation of power leads to challenges associated with endemic corruption among and within political parties that privileges the interests of an oligarch class. Ukrainian corruption forms a powerful criminal–political nexus of rent-seeking, rent disbursements, and large patronage networks (Kudelia and Kuzio 2015). This criminal–political nexus discourages inconsistencies within political party development and fosters a centralized approach within the frameworks established by party leaders.

Centralized administration limits the autonomy of various state organs. Concurrently, the need to distribute rents associated with a centralization of power and the creation of patronage networks necessitates the construction of a large bureaucracy. In Ukraine during the Yuschenko era the inability to form coalitions or stable governing factions within the Verkovna Rada created a situation in which laws and regulations were on the books but a lack of centralized authority limited their impact. Yet, following the 2010 election and return of Viktor Yanukovych to power, the political structures which under the Yuschenko period were forced to devolve presidential power to the parliament and the prime minister were reversed (Sedelius and Berglund 2016). However, because of the need to maintain patronage and rents the incentive to universally apply legal standards was absent and therefore resulted in an imbalanced and weak utilization of existing legal structures.

Despite having laws on the books, there appears to have been limited enforcement or selective enforcement. Moreover, any resort to prosecution was also likely undermined by substantial penetration by foreign "partners" and a lack of capacity and will within the organs of state to enforce already approved laws. Some reports indicate that under the Yanukovych government Ukrainian security services were penetrated substantially, with up to 30% of the SBU officers being from the FSB (Russia's Security Service) (Galeotti 2014). The foreign officers within the domestic intelligence and security services of Ukraine (FSB) were not solely there due to good case work by Russian FSB officers, rather they were there through a 2010 "cooperation protocol" that explicitly allowed Russian agents in the Ukrainian security services (Galeotti 2014).

The lead-up to Euromaidan Ukraine experienced a shifting media landscape that made accurate, balanced information a rare commodity. As noted by Sergii Leschenko (2014), despite passage of access-to-information legislation, the law was incomplete, never fully implemented and often circumvented on flawed pretenses. This was problematic in a state in which most citizens receive their news through the television (90%) (International Republican Institute 2014), the print news sector is underdeveloped and the major media concerns were controlled by the existing political power brokers including the president. Beyond the challenges associated with a constrained media environment domestically and insufficient legal standards to provide information to the public, almost one-third (30%) of Ukrainians according to a research by the International Republican Institute received their news from Russian media (IRI *Public Opinion Survey Residents of Ukraine* 2014).

To circumvent the controlled media environment online news became increasingly popular. Yet, as the shift away from controlled sources of media occurred, DDoS attacks and false domain attacks on news websites increased (Leshchenko 2014). Glib Pakharenko (2015), in analyzing the increasing number of cyberattacks during the early days of the revolution, noted a distinct cybercriminal nexus and a variety of types of malware directed at everything from social media accounts and websites to phones and financial activities. Pakharenko (2015) also commented on the diversity of IP addresses being used to target Ukrainians during the Euromaidan.

Prior to the overthrow of the Yanukovych regime, Ukraine's cyber and information environments were primed for substantial interference both bureaucratically, with a highly consolidated corrupt, rent-seeking regime that failed to enforce or selectively enforced laws, and an established governance structure in which the institutions tasked with enforcing laws were beholden to political higher-ups. A highly consolidated mass media market with extensive governmental concerns and large foreign presence challenged limited information validity. When Euromaidan began, Facebook and Twitter were not the most popular social networking sites, instead Russian owned Vkontakte and Odnokassniki were. At the basic technical level, Ukraine was heavily dependent on Russian network and information interception capabilities known as SORM[3] and the mobile, terrestrial, and orbital communications firms were owned in part or entirely by entities within the Russian Federation and transnational organized cybercrime organizations (Soldatov and Borogan 2015).

Countering propaganda and disinformation – a hybrid approach

Following the revolution, Ukraine was in political and bureaucratic disarray. The SBU, the state internal security service, experienced major personnel upheavals and its former head was the subject of an extradition request (Interfax 2015) and reports of significant Russian intelligence penetrations were rampant (Miller 2014b). After Euromaidan, more than 325 SBU officers had been removed and

25 had been charged with treason and all regional directors had been replaced (Miller 2014b).

Beyond the SBU, major personnel changes took place across nearly all government ministries. Systemic underfunding of the defense sector combined with rampant corruption set the post-revolutionary status of the military in a perilous position (Oliker et al. 2016). By 2014 out of Ukraine's total military force of 129,950, only 6,000 troops were combat ready and able to counter Russian intentions in Crimea and in Eastern Ukraine (Brantly, Cal, and Winkelstein 2017a). Every organization under the control of Ukraine's National Security and Defense Council (NSDC) was impacted by the change in governance.

The re-establishment of functional governance began when the political controls which fostered a consolidation of power and the existing rent-seeking and distribution networks that left decisions isolated to those at the top of the political hierarchy collapsed. The power vacuum in Ukraine left a large number of mid-tier bureaucrats and the existing bureaucratic culture in place while the temporary government and subsequently the new administration of Petro Poroshenko appointed new leadership to replace the old (Ash et al. 2017). Just as elsewhere, bureaucratic cultures in Ukraine, once entrenched, make change extremely difficult (Wilson 1989). Re-establishing the centralized bureaucracy while possible was challenged organizationally and functionally, as the social norms and practices of state governance developed under the previous government were being rebuilt.

While the Ukrainian leadership was new, change in addressing issues related to cyber security and information security were slow and bogged down in conventional inter-ministry bureaucratic relations that heavily resemble political or bureaucratic fragmentation. The status quo prevailed at the functional level of government. Because of ongoing crises in Crimea and in Eastern Ukraine, little thought was given to unfolding cyber and information warfare activities. Moreover, the new government, in particular nationalist MPs within the Verkovna Rada, failed to grasp the extent of Russian information interference and the impact that their post-revolutionary actions might have on the continuing Ukrainian crisis when they proposed eliminating the status afforded to the Russian language (Kudriavtseva 2016). Although the law never made it past the president, the advancement of a single language, Ukrainian, under the guise of national identity consolidation and security provided substantial fodder for Russian propaganda and information warfare efforts.

After the revolution Ukraine increasingly suffered sustained information operations and limited cyber operations. The pernicious nature of Russian propaganda indicated strong effects with upwards of 80% of the population of the Donbas believing the narrative that Euromaidan was organized by Ukrainian nationalists with substantial assistance from the United States (Kudriavtseva 2016). The impact of propaganda targeted at the Eastern Oblasts was four times as impactful as the same propaganda directed against Western Oblasts (Kudriavtseva 2016). These information campaigns sought to systematically undermine the social and political fabric of the Ukrainian state. These information operations were socio-technical in nature and sought to exploit historical, cultural, linguistic, regional, and religious tensions and grievances via universal technical platforms.

One particularly egregious example of information warfare occurred when a Buk missile (surface-to-air missile) was fired from rebel-held territories in Eastern Ukraine (Toler 2014). The violence of the attack was matched by Russian attempts to seek to pin the blame for the attack on Ukraine (Fitzgerald and Brantly 2017). Eventually BellingCat (2017), an independent investigative journalism organization, provided substantial evidence including photographs and videos of the Buk missile system in rebel-held territories both before and after the attack (missing a missile). A Dutch criminal investigation completed four years later came to the same conclusion.

In May 2017 President Poroshenko, in the face of continued information operations, by presidential decree blocked access to a variety of Russian social media, news, and other technology sites (Freedom House 2017). Every individual or organization I met with while in Ukraine had nearly the same response: "we are under attack; we must protect the nation". Ukrainian academics acknowledged the poor precedent the decree established with regard to the freedom of speech, yet they each in turn commented on the absolute necessity of the implementation. From the time of election until May 2017 Ukraine had no formal decree or legislation to combat information warfare directed against it.

Despite a lack of formal legislation or decrees on information warfare, the Ukrainian government was not passive. Hundreds of signs, television programs, radio programs, and other popular propagandist platforms were being implemented and used nationwide. Many of the signs in Metro stations and around the country encouraged individuals to speak Ukrainian, to take pride in being Ukrainian. Simultaneously, generally positive support, through Facebook groups, civil society organizations, and a variety of newly established NGOs sought to promote national identity and recognition. These efforts were critical in the early months of the Eastern conflict as Ukrainian soldiers and volunteer battalions engaged in sustained conflict operations with limited supply lines and little to no medical assistance (Marten and Oliker 2017).

Information operations were not limited to broad societally based attacks; some of the most aggressive attacks sought to undermine the psychological capacities of the soldiers and their families increasingly engaged in both regular and volunteer units in Ukraine. Information operations on the front lines included SS7 attacks, the use of android hijacking software, the penetration of wireless and fixed line information infrastructures, and other targeted information attacks (Brantly et al. 2017a). Very early in the conflict Russian signals intelligence equipment was placed near the contact line between Ukrainian and separatist forces. Members of the Information Assurance Directorate as well as enlisted personnel from both volunteer and regular Ukrainian battalions engaged on the contact line provided evidence of targeted information operations.

To date the overwhelming response of Ukraine to information warfare has emphasized three distinct categories and styles of approach. First, several organizations engaged in processes of identification and correction of information operations through organizations such as StopFake.org and InformNapalm.o rg and others. Ukrainian and foreign journalists indicate these platforms offer a means of informed counter information warfare using facts and logic.

Second, a variety of government initiatives both legislated and by decree have been undertaken in Ukraine to both foster resilience and combat information warfare. In December 2014 the Verkhovna Rada of Ukraine established the Ministry of Information Policy (MIP) (Matychak 2017). Article 1 of the general provisions of the MIP states: "The Concept purpose is to ensure information sovereignty and determination of approaches to protection and development of national information space for comprehensive information support of Ukrainian society".[4] The creation of the MIP raised concerns that it might transform into an Orwellian information ministry controlling and regulating free speech (Miller 2014a). The MIP was designed to work with journalists, foster national media literacy, emphasize counter information operations in the Anti-Terrorist Operation Zone (ATO), and carry out social media campaigns. The MIP has partnered with NGOs and developed a project, funded by the European Endowment for Democracy Foundation to fund an Open Source Intelligence (OSINT) academy that developed digital courses on information verification (Matychak 2017). The efforts of the MIP have been moderately successful but it lacks funding and suffers from potential reputational challenges.

The Ukrainian government by presidential decree has not only closed access to various web platforms, it has also selectively enforced legal statutes on trans-frontier advertising to shutter Russian broadcast channels. Moreover, Ukraine has also banned some journalists from legally entering the country. Each of these restrictive moves and the introduction of the MIP has raised substantial concerns within the human rights and free speech communities internationally. In Ukraine, however, many see these moves as necessary to safeguard Ukraine against foreign interference.

Part propaganda, part counter information operation, the Ukrainian Ministry of Defense has consistently for the better part of the last four years managed to distribute on a near daily basis maps indicating their assessment of the status of forces along the ATO zone and violations of the Minsk agreements signed between the belligerents. These information operations combined with troop resilience trainings have hardened Ukrainian forces against various forms of information operations.

Third, both domestic civil society NGOs independently and with the aid of foreign governments and IGOs have developed a series of initiatives. One of the most famous of these is the Ukraine World Project sponsored by the European Union, International Renaissance Foundation, Civic Synergy, the Ukrainian government, Open Society Foundation, and Internews.[5] Other organizations such as the Ukraine Crisis Media Center, the OSCE Euromaidan Press and a variety of others have created a variety of engagement platforms to continue to challenge propaganda and disinformation in Ukraine, train civil society and journalists, and provide advice to policymakers. All of these organizations form a counter information operations cacophony that was nonexistent in 2013 and early 2014. While

Ukraine is still susceptible to information operations, its resilience has increased markedly.

Although many of the initiatives undertaken by Ukraine and partners have improved, the status of information balance between the two parties means they face several challenges endemic to a country challenged by corruption and consolidation of power and economic weakness. Concerns about information manipulation in Ukraine are well-founded and recently arose around concerns that the government was manipulating corruption commission reporting and hiding information when it stripped former Georgian President and Former Governor of Odessa Oblast Mikhail Saakashvili of his Ukrainian citizenship and arrested him (Karatnycky 2018). Beyond the challenge of preventing abuses of power by the state in utilizing information operations is a concern about the potential loss of funding from any of the many outside organizations currently financing and providing support to Ukrainian organizations. The successes of counter information and propaganda operations in Ukraine are in large part due to the involvement of the international community and the engagement of civil society, academia, and journalists. These engagements provided a capability that extended beyond the state minimized but did not eliminate the challenges associated with power consolidations and endemic bureaucratic cultures in Ukraine.

The approach to information warfare in Ukraine has been diverse with both bottom-up and top-down developments. Many of the most successful elements of Ukrainian counter information operations have been organic, evolved from civil society or within academia. The story of Ukraine's efforts to counter cyber operations followed a different trajectory.

Addressing Ukrainian cyber security challenges – A centralized approach

Whereas the information warfare situation in Ukraine has been addressed by both decentralized non-governmental and centralized governmental approaches, the cyber conflict in Ukraine has primarily been confined to state bureaucracies. Ukraine has historically been a hotbed of global cybercrime despite its affirmation of the Budapest Convention on Cybercrime and laws on its books dealing with cybercrime (Kostyuk 2015). Ukraine's endogenous cyber capacity is remarkably high. Ukraine produces excellent students with computer science and engineering backgrounds but suffers immensely from economic challenges and a poor political and a burdensome business regulatory environment. Many cyber activities in Ukraine take place under a perception, rooted in social norms, that cybercrime directed against non-Ukrainians constitutes hooliganism rather than a "serious" crime (Kostyuk 2015).[6] Throughout the 1990s and 2000s Ukraine was designated a priority foreign country for its substantial violations of intellectual property rights (IPR) (USTR 2001). Ukraine's adherence to IPR was so poor, that it was sanctioned in the early 2000s and was threatened with denial of its World Trade Organization aspirations if it did not implement reforms (Grassley 2005).

Ukrainian IPR failures might seem an odd starting point, but as of the late 2000s the most common forms of operating systems and software used on devices in Ukraine came from bootleg markets such as Kyiv's famous Petrivka Market. An aging soviet infrastructure, penetrated intelligence services, firms owned in part by Russian interests, and a variety of other market and criminal concerns left Ukraine exposed to potential cyber exploitations. Cyber exploitations came in droves and continue to persist five years after initial hostilities (Baezner and Robin 2017). Over the period of March 2014–June 2018, Ukraine has been the site of some of the most significant cyberattacks ever perpetrated. As noted by Wired reporter Andy Greenberg (2017), Ukraine became the equivalent of a test lab for Russian cyber capabilities. The impact of these attacks was substantial in monetary, reputational, and in the case of attacks against Ukrainian soldiers potentially lives. These attacks impacted access to systems, slowed transport, and reduced or halted services. The attacks are continuous and escalating in both breadth and severity. Actors involved in the perpetration of attacks against Ukraine have been tied through various technical and non-technical analyses to elements of the FSB, GRU, non-state, and criminal groups (ICS-Cert 2016; Zetter 2016; Greenberg 2018).

Ukrainian cyber defense responsibilities reside within the NSDC and encompass the Ministry of Defense (MoD), the Security Service of Ukraine (SBU), Ministry of Internal Affairs (MIA), the Ukrainian Intelligence Community (UIC), and the State Service of Special Communications and Information Protection of Ukraine (SSSCIP) (Kostyuk 2015). In 2017 the coordinating entities of the NSDC related to cyber were managed by a single individual reporting to the NSDC Chairman. In 2017 the NSDC's cyber components were severely understaffed, suffered from personnel turnover, or simply lacked funding to undertake their stated mission.

Ukraine's first cyber security strategy approved by presidential decree and released in 2016 included an acknowledgment that Ukraine's cyber infrastructure has been attacked and that the establishment of a formal cyber security system emphasizing countering cyberterrorism, protection of critical infrastructures, including the military, energy, transportation, and banking spheres, was necessary (Office of the President of Ukraine 2016). The document outlined and proposed that the state would work with NATO and EU members to establish "best practices" within Slightly more than two years after the ousting of the Yanukovych government and following more than 50 severe cyberattacks including those perpetrated against Ukrainian electric infrastructure, Ukraine had a working cyber strategy. The 2-year delay between change of administration and the establishment of a strategy constituted a monumental shift in the bureaucratic and functional approaches to national cyber security in Ukraine. The reorganization codified through presidential decree the organizational structure of cyber defense under the NSDC.

As of 2017 the NSDC Cybersecurity Coordination Center Ukraine followed a legal pathway originating in the constitution of Ukraine, and proceeding through the Law on the National Security of Ukraine (2003, Revised June 21, 2018), the National Security Strategy of Ukraine (2015), the Cybersecurity Strategy of Ukraine (2016), and subsequent annual plans of Cybersecurity Strategy implementation. Ukrainian cyber security was further codified in the October 2017 law on national cyber security. Legally, strategically (based on strategy documents), Ukraine moved very quickly. Yet despite all the improvements it made on paper, its bureaucracy in 2014 was ill-equipped both organizationally and functionally to deal with the challenges it faced.

Ukraine faces significant challenges: First, financial challenges remain a persistent and insurmountable roadblock to the retention of individuals within the military, SSSCIP CERT-UA, police forces, and most other official government positions. Financial remuneration for frontline soldiers and personnel in all of the organizations listed is not competitive with general national nor global market forces. Although this problem is not confined to Ukraine (Wenger et al. 2017), conversations with principles and subordinates indicated extreme pay disparities between individuals in the public sector and those in the private sector. Overall, government service wages constitute a significant matter of concern for Ukrainian security sector reform (Oliker et al. 2016).

Ukraine continues to receive international support for a variety of training initiatives. The United States, NATO and various EU countries, the OSCE, and others provided funding for material resources, the establishment of training centers, equipment for defensive cyber operations, training for police and CERTS, and a variety of affiliated projects (Seals 2017). More than US$1.7 million dollars was committed to Ukraine for cyber defenses by NATO countries (NATO 2016). The United States has sent national guard Units to Ukraine to engage in cyber security training missions. Despite repeated training of Ukrainian military and civilian cyber defense personnel the infrastructure to retain these persons within government service is lacking. Internal documents and conversations with the General Staff of Ukraine indicate that the military services have the most significant retention problem.

Second, although Ukraine lacks the necessary financial resources required for the development and maintenance of cyber defense, the more serious challenge of bureaucratic cultures undermines the ability of Ukraine to systematically establish balanced cyber defenses. All indications both in public and private conversations highlighted the disproportionate control of cyber defense within the SBU.

Despite the bureaucratic challenges, there are some positive changes bureaucratically and financially. Ukraine is presently participating in international training activities such as NATO's Cooperative Cyber Defence Centre of Excellence exercise Locked Shields and even won the 2017 competition (Zilberman and Logan 2018). Each new attack is often followed by a period of increased financial and technical support from European, US, and NATO allies (Paganini 2017). Yet, despite increasing external support, the status quo of cyber security in Ukraine remains inadequate (Williams 2017). Efforts to appropriately distribute resources do appear to be achieving some success, particularly in areas of critical infrastructure (Reuters 2018).

From largely ineffectual beginnings in 2014 until Fall 2018 Ukraine had undergone immense legal and organizational changes. It has revised its national security strategy to include cyber security; it has reorganized and established cyber as a core component of the NSDC. It has written and approved a national cyber security strategy and it recently passed national cyber security legislation. Ukraine has accomplished all of these changes in under four years. Organizationally it has established a rubric for success, but this rubric is still challenged by existing bureaucratic cultures and economic challenges.

Conclusion: Ukrainian cyber and information security in the present and future

Ukraine's bureaucratic cultures are evolving and there have been substantial roadblocks within certain organizations and by certain political figures, but what Ukraine has accomplished over a period of four years, with external help from foreign states, international organizations, and nonprofit assistance has been substantial. It is hard to over-state the challenges Ukraine faced in 2014 and how far it has come. Its approaches to national information security and national cyber security have taken markedly different paths and have achieved fundamentally different outcomes. Ukraine still suffers under sustained information warfare and from cyberattacks. It is growing increasingly resilient to information warfare, yet these same improvements are not carrying over to cyberattacks.

Information security and cyber security require different infrastructural and organizational capabilities. The hybrid development of information resilience through the creation of the Ministry of Information Policy and more importantly through the engagement of civil society to address the challenge of information warfare has proven successful. Fewer capital resources – human and physical – were necessary to achieve resilience in the information space. The sustainment of information warfare resilience is also likely self-perpetuating in ways that cyber security is not. As concepts of national pride and identity, laws on the prevention of disinformation and propaganda come into force, the population of Ukraine is likely to increase rather than decrease its resilience to outside manipulations.

The development of cyber security structures in Ukraine, by contrast, has been highly centralized. The organizations that gained responsibility for cyber security in Ukraine were already in existence prior to 2014 (with the exception of the national cyber police). They each had embedded cultures and relationships within the NSDC and the power structures of Ukraine. Each of these organizations was already familiar with the limited resource environment and generally unable to circumvent it. The laws and processes established look good on paper. They align with European and NATO standards, but they are akin to bolting on new organizational structures and goals to existing frameworks. There are motivated individuals within each of the organizations. Each organization expressed a strong and genuine interest to address cyber security concerns, yet each organization, by necessity had many other priorities that often-superseded cyber security.

The Ukraine case serves as the canary in the coal mine. The likelihood that information operations and cyber operations will become commonplace in conflict is almost assured. Assessing how states under duress address challenges when they are at their most vulnerable provides valuable insights that might hopefully mitigate similar issues in future situations faced by a range of states. Few countries have been so strenuously tested in the information space and in cyberspace as Ukraine. And few countries could reasonably have been expected to reorganize and establish laws and strategies as quickly as Ukraine has. It has done so with external assistance in many cases, but also through a new-found ability to coordinate and work across ministries and divisions of government. Yet, issues of patronage and rent-seeking and rent distribution remain high and often stifle the innovation and aspirations of mid-level bureaucrats. Political and bureaucratic fragmentation, in addition to all the external challenges imposed upon the state by the Russian Federation, remain clear roadblocks to instituting sustained and meaningful reform. If Ukraine is to improve its resilience in cyberspace, commensurate with its advances in resilience to information warfare, it must necessarily address the core issues of financial allocations within the NSDC and the coordination and consolidation of power within certain ministries. Absent a sustained ability to fund the front lines of cyber defense in Ukraine strategy, law and organizational developments will be insufficient to maintain the human capital required for national cyber security. Finally, if Ukraine is unable to foster coordination and cooperation amongst the various NSDC entities then duplication of effort, interagency animosities, and inadequate cyber security outcomes are likely.

Notes

1 Distributed Denial of Service.
2 An SS7 attack is an exploit that takes advantage of a weakness in the design of SS7 (Signaling System 7) to enable data theft, eavesdropping, text interception, and location tracking.
3 SORM – System for Operative Investigative Activities (Система оперативно-разыскных мероприятий,).
4 https://mip.gov.ua/files/documents/Concept.docx
5 http://ukraineworld.org/infowars/
6 These factors were also identified repeatedly in discussions at Kyiv Polytechnic National University and with members of the defense industrial base.

References

All links checked on August 23, 2021.

Ash, T., Gunn, J., Lough, J., Lutsevych, O., Nixey, J., Sherr, J., and Wolczuk, K. (2017). *The Struggle for Ukraine*. London: The Royal Institute of International Affairs.

Baezner, M., and Robin, P. (2017). *CSS CYBER DEFENSE PROJECT Hotspot Analysis: Cyber and Information Warfare in the Ukrainian Conflict*. Zurich: Center for Security Studies (CSS). Retrieved from: http://www.css.ethz.ch/content/dam/ethz/special-interest/gess/cis/center-for-securities-studies/pdfs/Cyber-Reports-2017-01.pdf.

BellingCat. (2017). MH17 - The Open Source Investigation Three Years Later. Retrieved from: https://www.bellingcat.com/wp-content/uploads/2017/07/mh17-3rd-anniversary-report.pdf.

Brantly, A. F., Cal, N. M., and Winkelstein, D. P. (2017a). *Defending the Borderland: Ukrainian Military Experiences with IO, Cyber, and EW*. West Point, NY: U.S. Army Cyber Institute. Retrieved from: https://apps.dtic.mil/sti/pdfs/AD1046052.pdf.

Brantly, A. F., Cal, N. M., and Winkelstein, D. P. (2017b). Don't Ignore Ukraine: Lessons from the Borderland of the Internet. Retrieved from: https://www.lawfareblog.com/dont-ignore-ukraine-lessons-borderland-internet.

CERT-UA. (2014, October 16). скорая киберпомощь. PC Week/UE. Retrieved from: http://www.pcweek.ua/themes/detail.php?ID=147850.

Office of the President of Ukraine (2016) Cybersecurity Strategy of Ukraine. Retrieved from: https://ccdcoe.org/uploads/2018/10/NationalCyberSecurityStrategy_Ukraine.pdf

D'Anieri, P. (2006). *Understanding Ukrainian Politics*. London: M.E. Sharpe.

Fitzgerald, C. W., and Brantly, A. F. (2017). Subverting Reality: The Role of Propaganda in 21st Century Intelligence. *International Journal of Intelligence and Counter-Intelligence*, 30(2): 215–240. https://doi.org/10.1080/08850607.2017.1263528.

Freedom House. (2017). *Ukraine Country Report | Freedom on the Net 2017*. Washington, DC: Freedom House. Retrieved from: https://freedomhouse.org/report/freedom-net/2017/ukraine.

Frum, D. (2014, March 26). Ukraine's Phantom Neo-Nazi Menace. *The Atlantic*. Retrieved from: https://www.theatlantic.com/international/archive/2014/03/ukraines-phantom-neo-nazi-menace/359650/.

Galeotti, M. (2014, October 30). Moscow's Spy Game. *Foreign Affairs*. Retrieved from: https://www.foreignaffairs.com/articles/russia-fsu/2014-10-30/moscows-spy-game.

Grassley, C. (2005, November 18). Grassley Praises Senate Passage of Jackson-Vanik Repeal for Ukraine. United States Senate Committee on Finance. Retrieved from: https://www.finance.senate.gov/chairmans-news/grassley-praises-senate-passage-of-jackson-vanik-repeal-for-ukraine.

Greenberg, A. (2017, June 20). How an Entire Nation became Russia's Test Lab for Cyberwar. *Wired*. Retrieved from: https://www.wired.com/story/russian-hackers-attack-ukraine/.

Greenberg, A. (2018, August 22). The Untold Story of NotPetya, the Most Devastating Cyberattack in History. *Wired*. Retrieved from: https://www.wired.com/story/notpetya-cyberattack-ukraine-russia-code-crashed-the-world/.

Hooton, C. (2014, January 22). Ukraine Protests Demonstrators in Kiev Received Disturbing Mass Text. *Independent*. Retrieved from: https://www.independent.co.uk/news/world/europe/ukraine-protests-demonstrators-in-kiev-receive-disturbing-mass-text-9077327.html.

ICS-Cert, NCCIC. (2016, March 7). IR-ALERT-H-16-043-01BP Cyber-Attack against Ukrainian Critical Infrastructure, 1–17. Retrieved from: https://www.eenews.net/assets/2016/07/19/document_ew_02.pdf.

Interfax. (2015, January 12). Ukraine Accuses Russia of Breaking CIS Agreements over Yanukovych Extradition. Retrieved from: https://en.interfax.com.ua/news/general/243934.html.

International Republican Institute. (2014, April 4) *Public Opinion Survey Residents of Ukraine*. Washington, DC: International Republican Institute.

Karatnycky, A. (2018, February 12). The Rise and Fall of Mikheil Saakashvili. *Politico*. Retrieved from: https://www.politico.eu/article/the-rise-and-fall-of-mikheil-saakashvili/.

Kostyuk, N. (2015). Ukraine: A Cyber Safe Haven? In K. Geers (ed.), *Cyber War in Perspective: Russian Aggression against Ukraine*. Tallinn: NATO Cooperative Cyber Defence Centre of Excellence, pp. 113–122.

Kudelia, S., and Kuzio, T. (2015). Nothing Personal: Explaining the Rise and Decline of Political Machines in Ukraine. *Post-Soviet Affairs*, 31(3): 250–278.

Kudriavtseva, N. (2016). Ukraine: What's a Language for? *Kennan Cable*, 15: 1–9.

Kuzio, T. (2015). *Ukraine, Democratization, Corruption and the New Russian Imperialism*. Santa Barbara, CA: Praeger Security International.

Leshchenko, S. (2014). The Media's Role. *Journal of Democracy*, 25(3): 52–57.

Marten, K., and Oliker, O. (2017, September 14). Ukraine's Volunteer Militias May Have Saved the Country, But Now They Threaten It. *War on the Rocks*. Retrieved from: https://warontherocks.com/2017/09/ukraines-volunteer-militias-may-have-saved-the-country-but-now-they-threaten-it/.

Matychak, T. (2017). David against Goliath: How Ukraine Resists the Kremlin's Information Attacks. In A. Kulakov (ed.), *In Words and Wars: Ukraine Facing Kremlin Propaganda*. Kyiv: Internews-Ukraine.

Miller, C. (2014a, December 2). Ukraine Just Created Its Own Version of Orwell's 'Ministry of Truth'. *Mashable*. Retrieved from: https://mashable.com/2014/12/02/ukraine-ministry-of-truth/#AKpasiKpEOq9.

Miller, C. (2014b, December 30). Ukraine's Top Intelligence Agency Deeply Infiltrated by Russian Spies. *Mashable*. Retrieved from: https://mashable.com/2014/12/30/russian-vs-ukrainian-spies/#y6rqmk6rUOq3.

NATO. (2016, June). *Ukraine Cyber Defence*. Brussels: NATO.

Oliker, O., Davis, L. E., Crane, K., Radin, A., Gventer, C. W., Sondergaard, S., Quinlivan, J. T., Seabrook, S. B., Bellasio, J., Frederick, B., Bega, A., and Hlavka, J. (2016). Security Sector Reform in Ukraine. RAND Corporation. Retrieved from: https://www.rand.org/content/dam/rand/pubs/research_reports/RR1400/RR1475-1/RAND_RR1475-1.pdf.

Paganini, P. (2017, July 12). Following NotPetya NATO Increases Support for Ukraine's Cyber Defenses. *Security Affairs*. Retrieved from: https://securityaffairs.co/wordpress/60941/cyber-warfare-2/nato-support-ukraine-cyber security.html.

Pakharenko, G. (2015). Cyber Operations at Maidan: A First-Hand Account. In K. Geers (ed.), *Cyber War in Perspective: Russian Aggression against Ukraine*. Tallinn: NATO Cooperative Cyber Defence Centre of Excellence.

Reuters. (2018, February 6). Ukraine Power Distributor Plans Cyber Defense System for $20 Million. *Reuters*. Retrieved from: https://www.reuters.com/article/us-ukraine-cyber-ukrenergo/ukraine-power-distributor-plans-cyber-defense-system-for-20-million-idUSKBN1FQ1TD.

Seals, T. (2017, February 2). US Army Funds Cyber-Center for Ukraine Military. *Infosecurity Magazine*. Retrieved from: https://www.infosecurity-magazine.com/news/us-army-funds-cybercenter-for/.

Sedelius, T., and Berglund, S. (2016). Towards Presidential Rule in Ukraine: Hybrid Regime Dynamics under Semi-Presidentialism. *Baltic Journal of Law & Politics*, 5(1): 219–27.

Soldatov, A., and Borogan, I. (2015). *The Red Web: The Struggle between Russia's Digital Dictators and the New Online Revolutionaries*. New York: Public Affairs.

Toler, A. (2014, November 15). Kremlin Has Mastered Propaganda, but not Photoshop: Fake MH17 Photo Lights Up RuNet. *Global Voices Online*. Retrieved from: https://globalvoices.org/2014/11/15/russia-photoshop-kremlin-mh17-ukraine-crash/.

United States Trade Representative. (2001, March 13). USTR - Ukraine Designated as Priority Foreign Country under Special 301. Retrieved from: https://ustr.gov/archive/Document_Library/Press_Releases/2001/March/Ukraine_Designated_as_Priority_Foreign_Country_Under_Special_301.html.

Wenger, J. W., Oconnell, C., and Lytell, M. C. (2017). Retaining the Army's Cyber Expertise. RAND Corporation. Retrieved from: https://www.rand.org/content/dam/rand/pubs/research_reports/RR1900/RR1978/RAND_RR1978.pdf.

Williams, M. (2017, August 1). Ukraine Finally Battens Down Its Leaky Cyber Hatches after Attacks. *Reuters*. Retrieved from: https://www.reuters.com/article/us-cyber-attack-ukraine-idUSKBN1AH35A.

Wilson, J. Q. (1989). *Bureaucracy: What Government Agencies Do and Why They Do IT*. New York: Basic Books.

Zetter, K. (2016, March 3). Inside the Cunning, Unprecedented Hack of Ukraine's Power Grid. *Wired*. Retrieved from: https://www.wired.com/2016/03/inside-cunning-unprecedented-hack-ukraines-power-grid/.

Zilberman, B., and Logan, T. (2018). Increasing U.S.-Ukraine Cyber Cooperation is a Step in the Right Direction. Foundation for the Defense of Democracies (blog). Retrieved from: http://www.defenddemocracy.org/media-hit/boris-zilberman-increasing-us-ukraine-cyber-cooperation-is-a-step-in-the-right-direction/.

12 Uncertainty, fragmentation, and international obligations as shaping influences

Cyber security policy development in Albania

Islam Jusufi

The debate around cyber security has become an area where national authorities seek to (re-)claim parts of their sovereignty in the name of national security. Therefore, cyber security has entered official state planning and policy processes, and departments are being established within national governance structures to deal with cyber security issues more authoritatively. Against this background, it is important to consider how states struggle to adapt to the challenges arising from cyberspace and which factors are particularly influential in shaping their policies. So far, little scholarly attention has been paid to small and medium-sized states that are transitioning toward becoming liberal democracies. This chapter attempts to fill part of this gap.

This chapter analyzes how uncertainties surrounding cyber security and international obligations are shaping cyber security policies in developing parts of the world, more specifically in Albania. On a general level, it shows that a governance regime in response to cyber security threats leads to a fragmentation of authority and a changed conception of how far state sovereignty can extend in cyberspace. Inversely, fragmented authority and accountability establish an open space for multi-actor approaches, leading to a pluralism of relevant actors. The state, this chapter shows, is nudged into sharing responsibilities with other actors, including the private sector, civil society, and individuals.

To make its point, this chapter assembles Albanian public discourses on technological uncertainties and multi-actorness. This is done by analyzing both important public Albanian documents for cyber security discussions and the more general Albanian discourse around cyber security. It will be shown that, with regard to cyber security, the national authorities of Albania have sought to protect different targets, including the state, the private sector, and civil society, which have not been historically or consistently central to the Albanian conception of sovereignty. The main influence, it seems, is international collaborations with NATO and the EU, in which cyber security matters are embedded.

The chapter is organized in three sections. In the first, the chapter reviews literature about how states face cyberspace in general. Section two sets out the cyber

DOI: 10.4324/9781003110224-14

security policies designed and implemented in Albania, particularly as regards the three important aspects of uncertainty, fragmentation of authority, and international obligations. The third section draws conclusions.

States struggle with sovereignty rights in cyberspace: A general view

When it dawned on states that cyberspace was becoming an important aspect of international politics, they initially attempted to assert their sovereignty, traditionally understood as a right exclusive to states and particularly important in the face of national security matters. However, three aspects of cyberspace constrained state actors' coercive behavior in this regard: Uncertainty posed by technology, the presence of many non-state actors staking out their own claims, and, most importantly, international obligations.

Uncertainties arising from cyber technologies

Cyberspace, unlike the air, the space, or the sea, is an entirely man-made realm (Deibert et al. 2008) and as such subject to extensive uncertainties and unpredictability. Thus, a central and longstanding problematic in the practice of cyber security has become the inability to foresee, identify, and act upon threats in time (Dunn Cavelty 2019). The issue of uncertainty is thus an intrinsic part of cyber security, since uncertain threats need to be considered, prepared for, and dealt with continuously by someone who has the capacity to do so.

In addition, societies around the world are growing increasingly dependent on critical infrastructure networks, and risks to critical infrastructure systems are therefore seen as threats to the entire system of modern life and being. There is no place that is safe from an attack; a potential yet imminent threat is now perceived as coming from everywhere, which feeds a permanent sense of vulnerability and inevitable disaster (Dunn Cavelty 2013). Uncertainty about the capabilities and intentions of others also drives a classic security dilemma, boosting incentives for states to build up offensive and defensive cyber capabilities (Dunn Cavelty and Wenger 2020).

A prime issue for law enforcement against cyber threats in this uncertain environment is the "attribution problem", which refers to the difficulty of clearly identifying those responsible for a cyberattack (Dunn Cavelty 2008; Egloff 2019; Dunn Cavelty and Wenger 2020). Also, public attribution of cyber incidents takes place in a heavily contested information environment where multiple truths continue to coexist (Egloff 2019). Despite the expectation that attributional uncertainty may lead to the blame being placed on old enemies more often than not (Schulzke 2018), different actors in this contested environment gain authority to frame the aggressor behind cyber incidents, leading to a fragmentation of authority when it comes to attribution and other important aspects of cyber security.

Fragmentation of authority

The functioning of the Internet is heavily reliant on governance arrangements comprising both state and non-state actors. Many studies have established that the state is just one important player among others, which leads to the inability of states or transnational security organizations to enforce preferred cyber outcomes unilaterally. De facto control over the internet's technical components and the data flowing through them is exercised by private actors. States are adapting to this networked and fragmented governance more or less enthusiastically by attempting to shape standards and practices in a multi-stakeholder environment (Mueller et al. 2013). The use of alternative means to regulate cyberspace has allowed the interference of non-state actors at the expense of state institutions, and this undermines the power of the state in cyberspace (Adams and Albakajai 2016; Gendron 2013), which manifests in most states' inability to control flows of information, capital, and services across cyberspace.

In their efforts to regulate the use of cyberspace within their own borders, states have enacted multiple legislations and instituted new structures and actors (Betz and Stevens 2011). Fundamentally, it has become apparent that states cannot assure the security of information systems alone; instead, responsibility for information security needs to be dispersed across all stakeholders, because the majority of cyberspace is owned and operated by private companies (Bronk 2008). Thus, states will often need to request that private actors operating in their territories take the necessary actions to prevent or terminate detrimental international cyber conduct.

Nevertheless, the state occupies the central role in mobilizing and coordinating responses to the threats caused by cyber security. There is both a symbolic and a practical aspect to this: The role played by the state in responding to actual cyber threats is central in alleviating insecurities. When such threats emerge and are contained within the jurisdiction of a single territory, then the state exercises its traditional role of safeguarding the well-being of its citizens (Thomas 2009). This regards the reproduction of the state as political sovereign and holder of the monopoly of violence (Dunn Cavelty and Jaeger 2015). But, to address cyber threats in a comprehensive manner, states must also cooperate with other stakeholders to achieve mutually beneficial outcomes. Such collaboration implies a degree of policy constraint that goes against the ideal of absolute state sovereignty.

Like many other complex policy issues, cyber security cuts across different areas of responsibility, requiring coordination and cooperation between a wide variety of public actors at different levels of government as well as actors from business and society (Dunn Cavelty and Wenger 2020). In this multi-actor environment, the more the issue is presented as concerning all angles of society, the more natural it seems that the keeper of the peace in cyberspace should be multiple actors (Dunn Cavelty 2014). Thus, governments are embracing a growing "multi-actor-sovereignty" movement to respond to the uncertainties of cyberspace. The different roles of different actors are politically contested, though. Furthermore, states face a series of additional pressures, for example from international obligations.

International obligations

Changes to the understanding of "sovereignty" are common these days. States can sign conventions in which a degree of sovereignty is surrendered in the common interest. The Council of Europe's 2001 Convention on Cybercrime, also known as the Budapest Convention, is a good example of how states have come together to tackle a transnational problem while voluntarily allowing for changes in internal legal frameworks and an increase in cross-border investigative actions (Betz and Stevens 2011; Council of Europe 2001). The cyber security regulations of the EU and NATO, which impose obligations on existing and aspiring member states, are generally considered to constitute a baseline legislative framework for nations seeking to address cybercrime. Thus, international obligations have accelerated the process of embracing the conception of "multi-actor-sovereignty". In the next section, it will be shown how this plays out in the case of Albania.

Albania develops cyber security policies

The development of cyber security policy in the Southeast European country of Albania is very recent. Nevertheless, Albania is increasingly becoming a technology service economy and as such depends more and more on its information infrastructure to run its businesses on a daily basis. This level of reliance on information infrastructure has led to the perception of vulnerabilities (Brechbühl et al. 2010), especially as instances of network and information security breaches are growing rapidly, highlighting the need for action (McAfee 2012).

Albania has increasingly become both the origin and target of cyberattacks, with the first recorded case of cybercrime in 2008. The number of cybercrimes uncovered by police in recent years has grown steadily, with hacking, phishing scams, credit card number theft, identity theft, and malware such as Trojans, which enable criminals to take remote control over thousands of computers, being among the most prevalent crime types. Albania is constantly moving up in the list of countries where users are targeted by harmful software (Arka Telecom 2018). These new security threats challenge Albania's protective capabilities and have put cyber security firmly on the Albanian national agenda. As threats in cyberspace have become abundant, there is rising pressure to take action.

In order to respond to its growing cyber security challenges, Albania has taken steps to enhance both its domestic cyber security capacity and its international cyber security cooperation and partnerships (Begaj 2014). The country's size, combined with its location at the European periphery, has driven Albania to pay attention to strategic alliances and institutional cooperation. Also, the understanding of the term cyber security in Albania has changed over time. Initially, it was understood primarily as a technical risk management issue in critical information infrastructure protection, but it has come to be understood as a key challenge of national security (cf. Dunn Cavelty and Egloff 2019). The three issues outlined above, i.e. technological uncertainties, the fragmentation of authority, and international obligations, all shape Albania's approach to cyber security.

Technological uncertainty and the role of non-state actors as understood in Albanian public discourse

Albania's strategic doctrinal framework regarding cyber security consists of a series of documents, including, among others, the Law on Cyber Security, the Cross-Cutting Strategy "Digital Agenda of Albania 2015–2020", the Cross-Cutting Strategy on the Information Society 2008–2013, the Policy Paper on Cyber Security 2015–2017, the National Security Strategy 2014–2020, the Cyber Defense Strategy 2018–2020, and the Cyber Defense Strategy 2014–2017 (Republic of Albania 2014a, 2014b, 2015a, 2015b, 2017, 2018a, 2018b).

Albania's core cyber security provisions are established by its 2017 Law on Cyber Security (Republic of Albania 2017). When reading important provisions of that law, one finds that uncertainty is a guiding logic for the country's view on how to respond to cyber security incidents. The law defines cyberspace as a "digital environment capable of creating, processing and exchanging information generated by systems" (Article 3, 2017 Law on Cyber Security) and acknowledges that other actors besides the state, such as private legal persons, also have a role to play in cyber security governance, including the "private sector, which administers critical information infrastructure" (Article 3, 2017 Law on Cyber Security).

Another important strategic document is the Cross-Cutting Strategy "Digital Agenda of Albania 2015-2020". It aims to enhance Albania's resilience across sectors against cybercrime, cyber espionage, hacktivism, and terrorist use of the internet. It is an inter-sectoral strategy that establishes public-private collaboration and partnership as well as inter-sectoral, local-central, regional, and international collaboration as part of the basic principles for the development of the digital agenda (Dushi 2016). It is a document with which Albania plans, in a systematic and comprehensive way, the most important activities for protecting all users of modern electronic services, both in the public and economic sectors and among the general population (Bahiti and Josifi 2015). The aim of the Strategy is to achieve a balanced and coordinated response to the security threats of modern-day cyberspace by various institutions representing all sectors of society.

The Strategy is a statement of the cyber security stakeholders' determination to take measures in their respective areas of responsibility, to cooperate with the other stakeholders, and to exchange the necessary information (Galinec et al. 2017). For the Strategy, the internet is a vehicle to "integrate … public administration and private sector services" (p. 9). The Strategy itself commits the government to "cooperate … with businesses, universities, non-profitable organizations and NGOs in Albania, for an efficient development of the information society in the country" (p. 25). For the Strategy, the development of an internet society in Albania

> constitutes a joint objective of all actors, such as the public sector, the academic world, NGOs, civil society and private organizations. The successful completion of this objective is related to the proper coordination and harmonization of developments among all sectors and actors.
>
> (p. 25)

The earlier national strategy was the Cross-Cutting Strategy on the Information Society 2008-2013. Uncertainty was also among the assumptions underlying that strategy: "With the fast-developing information technology and its expansion into almost all areas of activity of society, the need for secure and reliable services becomes ever more obvious" (p. 36). The strategy was also committed to cooperation with different actors, including "other national and international institutions, civil society and the private sector in the Information Society realm" (p. 36), and it stated that the state administration will "cooperate with civil society and private bodies" (p. 39).

Another important public document has been the Policy Paper on Cyber Security (2015-2017), which aims to coordinate the duties and responsibilities of all actors involved in maintaining a secure cyberspace. One of the strategic objectives of this document is the strengthening of partnerships with various responsible stakeholders. This policy paper describes in more detail the fields of collaboration with different stakeholders, such as strengthening the collaboration with internet service providers as regards the treatment of cyber incidents and measures for blocking access to websites with illegal content; collaboration with civil society regarding the online safety of children; collaboration with academia on the opening of specialized study programs about cyber security; and collaboration with the banking sector, which, according to this document, should be represented in any legal or technical initiative taken in the field of cyber security. For this policy paper, the uncertainty of the technology has again been a main assumption: "The fast development of Information and Communications Technology and the extent of its use in almost all areas of activity of society have highlighted the need for safe and reliable services" (p. 8). The uncertainty assumption can also be found in the following sentence of the policy paper: "Developing cyber security under the circumstances of an information technology that is changing daily demands particular attention from the public institutions" (p. 29).

For this policy paper, the private sector is accepted as a referent object besides the state: "The increase in the use of communication represents an added value for the economic and social development of the country, but at the same time it makes it vulnerable to cyber-attacks against state and private actors" (p. 8). For the purposes of this policy paper, cyber security is not a problem that "impacts or belongs to one institution, public institutions, the private sector or citizens. It is a problem that impacts all the areas of life and society. As such, it demands necessary security measures by all users of ICT and the cyber space" (p. 19). It calls for close "cooperation with the public and private sector and cooperation with the academic world" (p. 20). For the policy paper, the private sector is also one of the "owners" of critical information infrastructure: "Due to the fact that these are not only public systems, but could also belong to the private sector, the cooperation and exchange of information with the private sector will be encouraged in order to ensure the basic security of these systems" (p. 24).

The National Security Strategy 2014-2020 classifies cyberattacks as a type one, i.e. highest importance risk. According to the Strategy, threats include "cyber attacks from state or non-state actors" (p. 25). Thus, cyber security is elevated to the national policy level. Albania's perspective on cyber threats has been that cyberspace is a threat to Albania's sovereignty. Hence, the elevation of cyberspace to a national security level is due to the increased risk caused by cyberattacks:

> Increased communication is an added value in the economic and social development of the country, but at the same time it exposes it to the dangers of cyber nature with state and non-state actors. Cyberattacks have the potential to severely damage the exchange of information in public institutions, telecommunications and the financial and banking system, causing disruption of vital services.
>
> (p. 23)

Later publications of cyber security documents and strategies have been consistent in referring to the cyber threat in the national security strategy. The general public supported and did not question the decision to elevate cyber threats to the national threat level because it shared a similar perception of that threat. Given that there have been no large-scale incidents affecting critical information infrastructure in the country, Albania's inclusion of cyber threats in its national security strategy followed a preemptive logic, a fear of possible destructive cyberattacks on its critical infrastructure. Similarly, the upgrade to national threat level was not a result of any prior domestic or national threat event. Therefore, Albania's responses were influenced by events taking place in other countries, such as in Estonia, Georgia, the United Kingdom, and the United States (Guitton 2013). Albania has faced a changing security environment in which threats are increasingly interconnected and national borders are less meaningful, and this has meant Albania is no longer as distant from security threats as it once was (Burton 2013), which resonates in its framing of cyber security.

Another important national strategy regarding cyber security is the Cyber Defense Strategy 2014-2017. Uncertainty is again one of the underlying assumptions of the Strategy. According to that Strategy, "cybercriminals can use computer technology to gain access to personal data or use the Internet for exploitative or malicious purposes" (p. 5). It also states that cyberspace is a space "which anyone can use without time and geographical boundaries, asymmetrically giving advantages to malicious attackers" (p. 9).

The Cyber Defense Strategy also provides space for other actors besides the state being involved in protecting cyberspace, as it states that the efforts

> to reduce cyber security threats and vulnerabilities will include concerted coordinated efforts, which should be carried out by responsible structures in the Ministry of Defense/Armed Forces, in cooperation with other government and private sectors, to identify and rehabilitate serious cyber vulnerabilities and breaches through collaborative activities.
>
> (p. 13)

The previous version of the Cyber Defense Strategy (2018-2020) sees uncertainty extending throughout cyberspace: "The techniques used by attackers are largely similar and designed to exploit the overall vulnerabilities of networks and systems" (p. 11). The Cyber Defense Strategy regards the private sector as a referent object in Albania's cyber security environment:

> Regardless of the achievements in the field of systems and network protection, we must focus on the management of communications and information infrastructure as a whole, on the interconnections between networks, on the control of unauthorized access, and on the continuous control of the transmission capacity of the Ministry of Defense/Armed Forces, which are provided by public and private telecommunication companies.
>
> (p. 7)

Therefore, it highlights that "cyberspace is an area in which both private and public actors, civil and military, national and international, must act at the same time and be mutually dependent on one another" (p. 11).

The driving influence of international obligations

As Albania has sought to overcome shortfalls in its cyber capacity, it has worked with international organizations to mitigate the challenges posed by cyber security threats. Albania has formulated its policy around the promotion of multilateral cooperation through international institutions, particularly the Council of Europe, EU, NATO, OSCE, and the UN, and the adoption and promotion of their norms. This triangular framework (alliances, institutions, and norms) has guided Albania's cyber security policy. Obligations accepted at the national level as part of NATO and OSCE commitments have been met. With regard to the EU, which has developed one of the most comprehensive cyber security agreements of any transnational organization and argued for the establishment of specific cyber security institutions, Albania has responded positively. The EU is the main umbrella providing a comprehensive legal framework in the field, which Albania is adopting in the process of its accession to the EU (DiploFoundation 2016; EEAS 2013).

Both NATO and the EU have placed significantly more weight on a multistakeholder approach rather than on a classic state-centric approach in their cyber security policies. Albanian decision-makers have followed these cues from NATO and the EU and decreased the salience of the classic state-centric idea of sovereignty in protecting vulnerable infrastructure. This in turn increased the importance of "actor neutrality" in defining cyber security. In short, institutional structures have allowed new actors to emerge in the field – the private sector, academia, civil society, international organizations (NATO, EU) – which has caused a shift in the discussion about state sovereignty. The EU's influence in particular has increased the salience of a multi-actor approach and decreased the importance of the norm of strict classic state-based sovereignty.

The cyber security policy promoted by Albania is based on an open internet, as is highlighted by Albania signing the Council of Europe's Convention on

Cybercrime. Albania is pursuing a path toward becoming a liberal democracy and as such does not restrict citizens' access, instead granting relatively open access to web-based materials. Nevertheless, for Albania it has been important to see that a certain type of control can be established over cyber security, with the domestic agenda being heavily influenced by the Council of Europe's Budapest Convention. The entire spectrum of cybercrimes has been criminalized by the Albanian Criminal Code, including hacking (i.e. unauthorized access); denial-of-service attacks; phishing; infection of IT systems with malware (including ransomware, spyware, worms, Trojans and viruses); possession or use of hardware, software, or other tools used to commit cybercrime (e.g. hacking tools); identity theft or identity fraud (e.g. in connection with access devices); electronic theft (e.g. breach of confidence by a current or former employee, or criminal copyright infringement); and any other activity that adversely affects or threatens the security, confidentiality, integrity, or availability of any IT system, infrastructure, communications network, device, or data (ICLG 2018). However, countries such as Albania have weak law enforcement.

On the cyber defense side, there is a strong sense that the NATO alliance, of which Albania became a part in 2009, serves Albania's national interests very well, and that the country is also safeguarded against other influences as a result. Albania has continued to see the broader benefits of the security alliance with NATO, whose enhanced cyber assets may bring considerable benefits to its members. Albania's cyber security benefits extensively from NATO, which provides for consultation and cooperation on cyber security issues as well as for ongoing intelligence sharing. As a member of NATO, Albania signed the Memorandum of Understanding with the NATO Cyber Incident Response Centre on enhancing cyber defense in 2013. The Ministry of Defense plays a role in cyber security via the Computerization and Innovation Directorate and other institutions that are subordinate to the Ministry of Defense.

The result: Networked governance

Both the external influence of international cooperation and the public–private governance necessities that the ownership of infrastructures and capabilities entails have influenced the development of Albania's cyber security policy throughout the years. As in other countries, cyber security institutions in Albania were initially established to protect vulnerable state IT systems. Later, the target community was broadened to include other actors such as the private sector, civil society, and citizens. This occurred as institutions empowered particular actors within certain domains but also opened the potential for new actors to enter the field.

With respect to cyber security institutions in Albania, earlier-generation legislation from the period of 1992–2010 empowered mainly the state. Those laws all held the idea that cyber security was intended to protect only the state. But later, in the 2010s, new legislative acts such as the 2017 Law on Cyber Security empowered new actors to bring cyber security cases from the private sector and civil society into the governance domain for the first time. That was the start of the emergence of the "multi-stakeholder approach" in ensuring control over Albania's cyber security.

The 2017 Law on Cyber Security specifies that private sector operators of critical information infrastructure are obliged to implement certain required safety measures (ICLG 2018; Dushi 2016). As a result, stronger cyber security links are being formed between the Albanian government and private entities, particularly those responsible for providing critical infrastructure. The Albanian government has approved a list of operators of critical and important information infrastructure, the majority of which are private, non-public providers. These operators of critical and important information infrastructure are obliged to implement at least the minimum levels of information security requirements approved by AKCESK (the National Authority on Electronic Certification and Cyber Security), and each of these operators has a contact point responsible for cyber security. Among the most important private operators are OSHEE (electricity distribution operator); Albcontrol (air transport operator); private banks, etc.

AKCESK is responsible for overseeing the enforcement of the Law on Cyber Security and associated implementing legislation. It defines the measures to be undertaken for cyber security at the national level and is a national point of contact and assistance in case of attacks or incidents related to cyber security. The Electronic and Postal Communications Authority (AKEP) in turn regulates and monitors the establishment and operation of ICT service providers. The National Information Society Agency (AKSHI) regulates the IT sector at the national level and provides IT and electronic services to citizens, businesses, and the public administration alike.

In a separate development, the government, together with the private sector and donor agencies, established the Protik Innovation Centre in 2012 as an independent nonprofit information and communication technology center whose primary objectives include increased cooperation between the private sector, educational institutions, and the government. The Centre was established by the combined efforts of the Albanian American Development Foundation (AADF), the Government of Albania, USAID, Microsoft, Albtelecom, and CISCO.

Police authorities are responsible for enforcing the law relating to prescribed activities in cyberspace, such as various forms of cybercrime.[1] Specialist units within the State Police, prosecutors' offices, and the intelligence services as well as elements of the armed forces monitor cyberspace activities that pose threats to Albanian entities and interests. The General Prosecution Office conducts criminal prosecutions against cybercrime offences through the Cybercrime Investigation Units established in eight district prosecution offices in 2014. The State Intelligence Service (SIS/SHISH), via its Cyber Crime Section, is in charge of investigating, detecting, and analyzing cybercrimes that threaten national security (Jica 2013). The Albanian Ministry of Defense has its Inter-institutional Maritime Operational Centre, whose responsibilities include civil emergencies, airspace control, and developing cyber defense capabilities (CSIS 2011).

These public and private organizations have contributed to developing situational awareness of the Albanian cyberspace as a prerequisite for prevention and response actions aimed at controlling some of its aspects. Private industry actors have played a crucial role in promoting cybercrime awareness, and civil society representatives have had input into the drafting of legislation, policy papers, and strategies in Albania. Taken together, the evidence suggests that private and civil society actors have played a substantial role in shaping the Albanian view of cyberspace. In this way, sovereignty has become shared with other actors, and the state has become an aggregator of domestic interests (Guarda 2015). Relevant policies have led to a more fluid conception of sovereignty, i.e. one where non-state actors, social groups, or even individuals as well as state actors are able to materially affect the system's stability and share sovereignty.

Conclusion

As seen in the Albanian case, the state remains a central pillar in cyber security. It is mostly up to the government to decide if a particular issue constitutes a threat or not. However, other actors have increasingly found a wider remit for the self-assessment of cyber and other threats. Yet, technologically less advanced states such as Albania are less capable of preventing or terminating harmful cyber conduct and thus exercise limited control over their territorial cyber infrastructure. Therefore, they rely on other actors as well in order to alleviate cyber-specific threats.

In response to this myriad of influencing factors and actors, Albania has developed a cyber security policy that comprises various institutional elements. Functions of control are delegated to the usual organs of the state, such as the police, prosecutors, security services and the military, and to regulatory bodies such as cyber security and telecommunications regulators. Albania has aligned its cyber security policies to the view that any international policy for cyberspace should be developed using existing multi-actor governance frameworks and processes, and that a "multi-stakeholder" approach is most appropriate, which encompasses governmental, commercial, and non-governmental interests (Cornish 2015). Nontraditional actors such as the private sector, civil society, universities, and others have been networked within the Albanian cyberspace governance.

Even though Albanian legislation on cyber security defines the government as the final arbiter for cyber security cases, the private sector, civil society, and academia have also been assigned additional responsibilities for cyber security. Institutions have thus established opportunities for the unanticipated entry of new actors into the field. This dynamism accounts for shifts in the focus of cyber security and the understanding of sovereignty. In this context, Albania, like many democracies, has developed a fragmented, multi-actor system of cyber and internet regulation (Wagner 2014). The previous exclusively state-controlled governance regime has given way to a mixed governance regime of networks (Collins 2008) and to less hierarchical forms of governance (Héritier 2001), which have empowered other actors besides the state in cyber governance.

In sum, technological uncertainties and international obligations have led to the emergence of a multi-stakeholder approach in the design of laws and institutions in the field of cyber security and thus to a fragmentation of authority and sovereignty among different actors. Exogenous factors such as the dynamics of the cyber security sector; the threats emerging in it; and NATO, the EU, the Council of Europe, and other aspects of international institutional cooperation have encouraged the Albanian government to pursue this multi-stakeholder approach in its state planning and policies. Thus, the new legislation and institutions have provided opportunities for new actors to enter the field.

While this chapter contributes to the understanding of the implications of technological uncertainties with regard to cyber governance in states that have received little attention from the scholarly community so far, further research in other developing countries is needed to understand the relationships between uncertainties, fragmentation, and external factors driving policy development. Comparative studies can explain how multi-actor approaches can help to govern the uncertain space of new technologies.

Note

1 The Computer Crime Division at the General Directorate of the State Police was established in 2009 as part of the Albanian State Police and is Albania's primary cybercrime-combating agency. The State Police, in order to prevent and combat cybercrime, provides a software application for the online reporting of cybercrime, which is located on the official website of the Albanian State Police (Dushi and Bërdufi 2017; ICLG 2018). In 2009, a manual for investigating cybercrime and collecting computer evidence was produced for the State Police. That guide describes in detail the various types of computer evidence and how to deal with them step by step, including actions to be taken since the first moment on the scene, identification of computer evidence and its documentation, collection, packaging, transportation, and storage (Dushi and Bërdufi 2017). Complying with Article 35 of the Budapest Convention, a 24/7 point of contact was established in the Cybercrime Unit of the Albanian State Police.

References

All links checked on August 23, 2021.

Adams, J., and Albakajai, M. (2016). Cyberspace: A New Threat to the Sovereignty of the State. *Management Studies*, 4(6): 256–265.

Arka Telecom (2018). Armenia is Fourth in the World for Frequency of Harmful Software Attacks. Retrieved September 13, 2018, from: http://telecom.arka.am/en/news/internet/armenia_is_fourth_in_the_world_for_frequency_of_harmful_software_attacks_/.

Bahiti, R., and Josifi, J. (2015). Towards a More Resilient Cyberspace: The Case of Albania. *Information and Security*, 32(2): 120–130.

Begaj, E. (2014). *Albania's Vision towards Cyber Security. Paper from DCAF Young Faces 2014 - Cybersecurity Winter School for the Western Balkans*. Geneva: DCAF.

Betz, D. J., and Stevens, T. (2011). *Cyberspace and the State: Toward a Strategy for Cyber-Power*. London: Routledge.

Brechbühl, H., Bruce, R., Dynes, S., and Johnson, M. E. (2010). Protecting Critical Information Infrastructure: Developing Cybersecurity Policy. *Information Technology for Development*, 16(1): 83–91.

Bronk, C. (2008). Hacking the Nation-State: Security, Information Technology and Policies of Assurance. *Information Security Journal: A Global Perspective*, 17(3): 132–142.

Burton, J. (2013). Small States and Cyber Security: The Case of New Zealand. *Political Science* 65(2): 216–238.

Collins, R. (2008). Hierarchy to Homeostasis? Hierarchy, Markets and Networks in UK Media and Communications Governance. *Media Culture and Society* 30(3): 295–317.

Cornish, P. (2015). Governing Cyberspace through Constructive Ambiguity. *Survival*, 57(3): 153–176.

Council of Europe. (2001). *Convention on Cybercrime*. Strasbourg: Council of Europe.

Deibert, J., Palfrey, J., Rohozinski, R., and Zittrain, J. (2008). *Access Denied: The Practice and Policy of Global Internet Filtering*. Cambridge, MA: The MIT Press.

DiploFoundation. (2016). *Cybersecurity in the Western Balkans: Policy Gaps and Cooperation Opportunities*. Geneva: DCAF.

Dunn Cavelty, M. (2008). *Cyber-Security and Threat Politics: US Efforts to Secure the Information Age*. London: Routledge.

Dunn Cavelty, M. (2013). From Cyber-Bombs to Political Fallout: Threat Representations with an Impact in the Cyber-Security Discourse. *International Studies Review*, 15(1): 105–122.

Dunn Cavelty, M. (2014). Breaking the Cyber-Security Dilemma: Aligning Security Needs and Removing Vulnerabilities. *Science and Engineering Ethics*, 20(3): 701–715.

Dunn Cavelty, M., and Egloff, F. J. (2019). The Politics of Cybersecurity: Balancing Different Roles of the State. *St Antony's International Review*, 15(1): 37–57.

Dunn Cavelty, M., and Jaeger, M. D. (2015). (In)visible Ghosts in the Machine and the Powers that Bind: The Relational Securitization of Anonymous. *International Political Sociology*, 9(2): 176–194.

Dunn Cavelty, M., and Wenger, A. (2020). Cyber Security Meets Security Politics: Complex Technology, Fragmented Politics, and Networked Science. *Contemporary Security Policy*, 41(1): 5–32.

Dushi, D. (2016). *Cybersecurity in Albania: A Multistakeholder Approach. Paper from DCAF Young Faces 2016 – Strategic Cybersecurity Policy Development in Southeast Europe*. Geneva: DCAF.

Dushi, D., and Bërdufi, N. (2017). Law Enforcement and Investigation of Cybercrime in Albania. *European Scientific Journal*, 13(12). Retrieved from: https://eujournal.org/index.php/esj/article/view/9228/8769.

Egloff, F. J. (2019). Contested Public Attributions of Cyber Incidents and the Role of Academia. *Contemporary Security Policy*, 41(1): 55–81.

European Union External Action Service. (2013). EU Cyber Security Plan to Protect Open Internet and Online Freedom and Opportunity. Retrieved August 10, 2018, from: http://europa.eu/rapid/press-release_IP-13-94_en.htm.

Galinec, D., Možnik, D., and Guberina, B. (2017). Cybersecurity and Cyber Defence: National Level Strategic Approach. *Automatika: časopis za automatiku, mjerenje, elektroniku, računarstvo i komunikacije*, 58(3): 273–286.

Gendron, A. (2013). Cyber Threats and Multiplier Effects: Canada at Risk. *Canadian Foreign Policy Journal*, 19(2): 178–198.

Guarda, N. (2015). Governing the Ungovernable: International Relations, Transnational Cybercrime Law, and the Post-Westphalian Regulatory State. *Transnational Legal Theory* 6(1): 211–249.

Guitton, C. (2013). Cyber Insecurity as a National Threat: Overreaction from Germany, France and the UK? *European Security*, 22(1): 21–35.

ICLG, The International Comparative Legal Guide. (2018). *Cybersecurity: A Practical Cross-Border Insight into Cybersecurity Work*. London: Global Legal Group Ltd.

ITU, International Telecommunication Union. (2014). *Cyberwellness Profile Albania*. Geneva: ITU.

Jica, H. (2013). Cyber Security and National Security Awareness Initiatives in Albania: A Synergy Approach. *Mediterranean Journal of Social Sciences*, 4(10). Retrieved from: https://www.mcser.org/journal/index.php/mjss/article/view/1236/1265.

Jusufi, I. (2018). Clientelism and Informality in Albania. *Eastern Journal of European Studies*, 9(1): 133–150.

McAfee. (2012). Cyber-Security: The Vexed Question of Global Rules. Retrieved August 10, 2018, from: http://www.mcafee.com/us/resources/reports/rp-sda-cyber-security.pdf.

Mueller, M., Schmidt, A., and Kuerbis, B. (2013). Internet Security and Networked Governance in International Relations. *International Studies Review*, 15(1): 86–104.

Republic of Albania. (2014a). *National Security Strategy 2014–2020*. Tirana.

Republic of Albania. (2014b). *Cyber Defence Strategy 2014–2017*. Tirana.

Republic of Albania. (2015a). *Policy Paper on Cyber Security 2015–2017*. Tirana.

Republic of Albania. (2015b). *Cross-Cutting Strategy 'Digital Agenda of Albania 2015–2020'*. Tirana.

Republic of Albania. (2017). *Law on Cyber Security*. Tirana.

Republic of Albania. (2018a). *Decision on "Approval of the List of Critical Information Infrastructures and List of Important Information Infrastructures"*. No. 222, 26.04.2018.

Republic of Albania. (2018b). *Cyber Defence Strategy 2018–2020*. Tirana.

Schulzke, M. (2018). The Politics of Attributing Blame for Cyberattacks and the Costs of Uncertainty. *Perspectives on Politics*, 16: 954–968.

Thomas, N. (2009). Cyber Security in East Asia: Governing Anarchy. *Asian Security*, 5(1): 3–23.

Wagner, B. (2014). The Politics of Internet Filtering: The United Kingdom and Germany in a Comparative Perspective. *Politics*, 34(1): 58–71.

13 Big tech's push for norms to tackle uncertainty in cyberspace

Jacqueline Eggenschwiler

Reports about large-scale data breaches, critical infrastructure hacks, and malware strikes targeting public and private systems and network infrastructures have become ubiquitous. Given the political and economic ramifications of these malicious activities conducted by both state and non-state actors – global security and prosperity are highly dependent on secure and stable ICTs and networks – governments have sought to stipulate behavior-guiding rules of the road for cyberspace by means of international conferences and expert processes. Progress and agreement on norms of responsible behavior for cyberspace, however, have been slow and unwieldy (Hampson et al. 2017). Disputes among government entities about how and if existing international rules apply to cyberspace have provided flourishing breeding beds for private norm ventures (Väljataga 2017; Henriksen 2019; Korzak 2017). Since the non-consensus outcome of the United Nations Group of Governmental Experts on Developments in the Field of Information and Telecommunications in the Context of International Security (UN GGE) in 2017, corporate as well as other non-state entities have started to more actively insert their voices in debates about rules of the road for the digital domain (Sukumar 2017; Henriksen 2019).[1]

This chapter examines the norms-based cyber insecurity reduction measures initiated by corporate actors. In particular, it summarizes and comments on the effectiveness of the normative strategies pursued by technology companies, including Kaspersky Lab, Siemens, Telefónica, and Microsoft. For the purposes of this chapter, technology companies are understood to denote enterprises engaging in and deriving sizeable percentages of their revenues from the development, manufacturing, and maintenance of technology products and services, including, for instance, hard- and software components and platform services. The selection of the four case studies was informed by geographical (companies displaying different national origins: Russia, Europe, the United States) as well as substantive considerations (companies having made active reference to, proposed, or joined norms-based policy instruments).

Scholarly literatures in the fields of international relations and international law have taken note of the behavior-shaping powers exerted by private entities across different policy areas since at least the early 1990s (Ruggie 2004; Nye and Donahue 2000; Finnemore and Sikkink 1998). In the context of cyber security,

DOI: 10.4324/9781003110224-15

however, performance-oriented assessments of the norms-based activities proposed by non-state actors and their implications for global governance processes have remained sparse. Seeking to address this void, this chapter argues that while the norms-based activities carried out by technology companies have been effective at opening up debates and influencing political processes, their efforts have borne less fruit apropos decreasing systemic levels of cyber insecurity. As long as governments lack the political will to truly follow through on their commitments to make cyberspace more stable and secure, and engage in concerted efforts with private agents, the fact that corporate activities have not managed to reduce systemic levels of cyber insecurity should not come as a surprise.

The lack of systemic change should be even less astonishing if it is accepted that norms constitute what Cristina Bicchieri termed as conditional rules

> such that individuals prefer to conform when they expect a sufficiently large proportion of the population to conform (coordination or "empirical expectation"), and they believe that a sufficiently large proportion of the population might sanction them if they [do not] (fear of sanction or "normative expectation").
>
> (Carbonara 2017: 468)

Arguably, the proportion of conforming agents in cyberspace is not yet sufficiently large enough to invoke shared normative expectations at systemic levels. Cyber operations have provided useful tools for governments and proxy actors "to achieve strategic objectives both covertly and overtly", and have offered much room for maneuver, which they are (now) hesitant to give up (Leuprecht et al. 2019: 402).

Even so, it is critical to appreciate and better understand the normative strategies pursued by non-state actors and resulting consequences. As per Hegemann and others, "[m]any of the core issues and problems of international politics require answers to questions of whether, how, and when certain actors, tools, or policies cause or at least affect specific results" (Hegemann et al. 2012: 15). With a view to supporting critical analyses of the activities undertaken by relevant actors and devising potential alternatives, it is vital to study the consequences of said activities, and the extent to which they have accomplished specified goals (Hegemann et al. 2012: 15). Given the market power of the technology companies flagged above, as well as their economic and political credence, and vocal participation in cyber security norm formation processes, examinations pertaining to the effectiveness of their efforts appear to be particularly pressing.

Methodologically, this contribution relies on secondary sources in the fields of international relations and international law, with a focus on governance-relevant texts, as well as primary sources, including press releases, reports, and audiovisual materials, issued by industry protagonists concerned with promoting norms of responsible behavior in cyberspace.

The remainder of this chapter is organized along three sections. The first section provides contextual information related to the topic under investigation, recaps important developments, and specifies central concepts. The second section examines and appraises the contributions of technology companies to global cyber security norm development processes. Finally, the third section sums up the findings and highlights avenues for further progress.

Cyber security and norms

Early internet pioneers, including John Perry Barlow, regarded cyberspace as a virtual environment not requiring formal rules or external controls (Barlow 1996). However, growing numbers of cyber security events affecting private as well as public information and communication technologies (ICTs) have undermined these non-interventionist positions. Over the course of the past two decades, voluntary norms of responsible behavior "have emerged along with confidence- and capacity-building measures as the principal policy tools of choice to meet the [...] vision of an open, secure, accessible, and peaceful ICT environment" (Kavanagh 2017: 10).

Defined as shared expectations of appropriate behavior, norms can be of regulative (i.e. describing obligations, prohibitions and permissions) or constitutive (i.e. creating categories of actors and actions) nature (Finnemore and Sikkink 1998; Wiener 2017; Björkdahl 2002). "By shaping agents' understandings of their social environments, associated interactions, and possible outcomes", they foster coordination and predictability, and in turn reduce contextual ambiguities to manageable levels (Ferguson 2019: 1). In contrast to formal legal provisions, norms rely on softer means of enforcement and implementation.[2]

According to Finnemore, the move to voluntary cyber security norms can partly be attributed to concerns about the suitability and effectiveness of binding treaties in fast-moving environments, as well as to fears of legal lock-in among leading cyber powers (Finnemore 2017: 3). Abbot and Snidal have argued that

> when circumstances are fundamentally uncertain, that is, when even the range and/or distribution of possible outcomes is unknown, [formal legal agreements] may not be desirable. In particular, if actors are ambiguity-averse, they will prefer to leave agreements imprecise rather than face the possibility of being caught in unfavorable commitments.
>
> (Abbott and Snidal 2000: 442)

Despite perceived needs to reduce threats and corresponding levels of uncertainty, and more than two decades of concerted diplomatic efforts relating to the formulation of norms of responsible behavior for the digital domain, advancement has been slow and political compromise short-lived. In the wake of political contentions among governments surrounding debates about existing and emerging perils emanating from the digital realm and possible normative measures to address them, a number of non-state actors have stepped up and started to more actively make their voices heard (Grigsby 2017; Mačák 2017; Väljataga 2017).

International relations and international law literatures have taken note of the rise of private actors involved in global steering and rule-making processes, and have systematized and subsumed ideational efforts conducted by non-state actors under the umbrella of *norm-entrepreneurship* or *soft-law*, respectively (Finnemore and Sikkink 1998; Risse-Kappen, Ropp, and Sikkink 1999; Abbott and Snidal 2000). Norm entrepreneurs (or protagonists of soft-law instruments) challenge prevailing patterns of behavior, by suggesting normative ideas and mobilizing like-minded stakeholders or networks within and across states to endorse them (Sandholtz 2017: 2). "These alliances [then] bring pressure to bear from above (transnationally) and below (domestically)", and help the standards proposed get more widely accepted (Sandholtz 2017: 2).

Following the non-consensus outcome of the 2017 UN GGE and an accumulation of cyber security incidents of transnational magnitude, including WannaCry and Petya/NotPetya, entrepreneurial activities undertaken by non-state actors in the context of fostering responsible behavior in cyberspace have grown considerably (Hinck 2018; Mačák 2017). The period between February 2017 and November 2018 saw the launch of at least nine different initiatives/proposals.[3] Although noteworthy, in terms of consistency, accountability, and authority, these proposals have contributed to heightened levels of fragmentation (Dunn Cavelty and Wenger 2020). Not only have non-state actors created additional or even competing norm formation processes but they have also set foot in traditionally state-driven domains. Yet, in view of lingering hesitations on the parts of governments apropos meaningfully enforcing existing cyber security norms, trends of fragmentation may be useful in increasing awareness about cyber security norms and widening stakeholder participation across different streams. As per Ruhl and others,

> [d]ifferent processes may be optimised for different kinds of outcomes – in terms of the actors and activities. Norms may be more realistic in some areas than in others, such as peacetime use of cyber capabilities compared with military cyber operations. Having multiple processes can prevent a roadblock in one area from impeding all progress.
>
> (Ruhl et al. 2020: 13)

In order to reap the benefits of these fragmented processes, however, initiators need to deliberately plan for "complementarity" and "cross-pollination".

The next section summarizes leading norms-based efforts launched by Microsoft, Siemens, Telefónica, and Kaspersky Lab, and assesses the effectiveness of their activities along three dimensions: Output, outcome, and impact. Analyzing the effects of regulatory efforts has remained extremely challenging and has incited numerous scholarly debates. There are no unified approaches for assessing the success of norms or regimes. This chapter draws on the work conducted by Flohr et al. and Wolf who have proposed assessments along the dimensions mentioned above (Flohr et al. 2010; Wolf 2010). Only proposals with explicit normative nexus and only proposals launched post-2017 were selected for analysis.

Private cyber security norm development efforts

Non-state actors, in particular technology companies, have been key contributors to the development and expansion of cyberspace.[4] As operators of network infrastructures, designers of products, and suppliers of services, they have made important contributions to the "international [...] architecture for the governance of cyberspace" (Radu 2014: 4). In addition to producing hard- and software, they have come to contribute to the promotion of global cyber security norms and standards. So far, their normative contributions have received little academic attention. This chapter seeks to contribute to richer understandings of the normative parts played by technology companies and unveil the governing qualities of their activities by evaluating them across the dimensions of output, outcome, and impact.[5]

As key providers of ICTs, technology companies have strong incentives to pursue normative strategies to sustain their business models. Through the eyes of technology companies, norms provide useful tools for tackling contextual ambiguities and pre-empt costly changes to legal frameworks, or government-led market interventions. While the reasons for corporate norm-shaping efforts pertaining to the virtual realm may primarily be grounded in commercial considerations, i.e. reducing costs and risks, securing their operations, gaining access to new markets/safeguarding existing customer bases, and strengthening corporate reputation and legitimacy, less self-serving reasons, i.e. upholding good-faith-commitments and values such as user privacy, should not be forgotten (Gorwa and Peez 2018). Not all of the activities undertaken by technology companies in the context of norms of responsible behavior for cyberspace can be explained by rationalist arguments.

Microsoft

One of the first corporate entities to engage in debates about responsible conduct in cyberspace was Microsoft (Microsoft Security Response Center 2010). Valued at over USD 1 trillion (2019), the company ranks among the four largest technology giants globally, the other three being Apple, Alphabet, and Amazon. Following prior norms-oriented ventures between 2013 and 2016, in February 2017, Microsoft President and Chief Legal Officer Brad Smith introduced the idea of a *Digital Geneva Convention to Protect Cyberspace* (Microsoft 2013; McKay et al. 2014; Charney et al. 2016; Smith 2017). Grounded in the belief that deep-rooted collaboration among states, and between states, the private sector, and civil society is needed to curb nefarious doings in the digital realm, the convention as outlined by Smith, asks governments, among other things, to:

- Refrain from attacking critical infrastructures (including civil and financial systems)
- Abstain from engaging in espionage
- Engage in vulnerabilities disclosure processes

- Exercise restraint in developing cyber weapons and engaging in offensive activities, and
- Assist private sector entities in securing cyberspace. (Microsoft 2017)

It also calls on technology companies to behave as neutral actors and recommends the setting up of an independent non-governmental organization capable of investigating and publicly attributing (nation-state) cyberattacks (Smith 2017; Maurer and Taylor 2018). Met with little enthusiasm by governments, Microsoft's call for a Digital Geneva Convention was succeeded by the unveiling of a *Cybersecurity Tech Accord* bringing together "global technology companies committed to protecting their customers and users", 14 months later.[6]

In September 2018, Microsoft unveiled a *Digital Peace Now* campaign, which calls on citizens to protect cyberspace, e.g. through measures of cyber hygiene, and urges governments to refrain from endangering the global digital environment (Microsoft 2018). Only two months later, Microsoft co-sponsored the *Paris Call for Trust and Security in Cyberspace*. Introduced at the 12th Internet Governance Forum (IGF) in Paris, the *Paris Call for Trust and Security in Cyberspace* (short Paris Call) constitutes one of the most widely endorsed multi-stakeholder instruments pertaining to peace and security in the virtual realm to date (Ministère de l'Europe et des Affaires Étrangères 2018).

The Paris Call proposes the development of common principles for securing cyberspace through collaborative efforts across existing international platforms and mechanisms (Ministère de l'Europe et des Affaires Étrangères 2018). Although at first sight a French initiative, the Paris Call was vitally influenced by Microsoft, both in terms of origin and content. According to information presented by Le Monde and WIRED, it was Microsoft's political lobbying that gave rise to the initiation of the Paris Call (Matsakis 2018a; Untersinger 2018). The Paris Call advances nine principles intended to resonate with both state and non-state entities. Specifically, it asks supporters to:

- Prevent and recover from malicious cyber activities that threaten or cause significant, indiscriminate or systemic harm to individuals and critical infrastructure;
- Prevent activity that intentionally and substantially damages the general availability or integrity of the public core of the Internet;
- Strengthen our capacity to prevent malign interference by foreign actors aimed at undermining electoral processes through malicious cyber activities;
- Prevent ICT-enabled theft of intellectual property, including trade secrets or other confidential business information, with the intent of providing competitive advantages to companies or commercial sector;
- Develop ways to prevent the proliferation of malicious ICT tools and practices intended to cause harm;
- Strengthen the security of digital processes, products and services, throughout their lifecycle and supply chain;

- Support efforts to strengthen an advanced cyber hygiene for all actors;
- Take steps to prevent non-State actors, including the private sector, from hacking-back, for their own purposes or those of other non-state actors;
- Promote the widespread acceptance and implementation of international norms of responsible behavior as well as confidence-building measures in cyberspace.

(Ministère de l'Europe et des Affaires Étrangères 2018)

Rather than reinventing the wheel in terms of normative prescriptions, the Paris Call constitutes an attempt at realigning scattered discussions and improving the complementarity of cyber security norm formation processes.

While the Paris Call has seen fairly broad uptake among governments, private industry, the technical community, researchers, non-governmental organizations, and civil society, there have been a number of notable public abstentions, including the United States, Russia, China, Iran, and Israel (Matsakis 2018b).

Siemens

Subsequent to several large-scale cyber security incidents, including WannaCry and Petya/NotPetya, Siemens, together with eight partner corporations issued a *Charter of Trust* for the digital domain at the sidelines of the 2018 Munich Security Conference (Hern 2017; European Commission 2018). Recognizing that cyber security is a critical enabler for further economic growth and transformation, Charter signatories vouched to (re-)instill confidence in digital technologies and services.

Since its launch in February 2018, the number of sponsors has grown from nine to seventeen Charter partners, and four associate members. The list of current (as of May 2020) supporters includes: Siemens and the Munich Security Conference, AES, Airbus, Allianz, Atos, Cisco, Dell Technologies, Deutsche Telekom, Enel, IBM, Infineon Technologies AG, Mitsubishi Heavy Industries, NXP, NTT, SGS, Total and TÜV Süd, as well as the German Federal Office for Information Security (BSI), the CCN National Cryptologic Centre of Spain, the Graz University of Technology, and the Hasso Plattner Institute for Digital Engineering GmbH (HPI) (Siemens 2019a).

Committing to undertake "every effort to protect the data and assets of both individuals and businesses, prevent damage to people, businesses, and infrastructures and build a reliable basis for trust in a connected and digital world", Charter members have called for binding rules and standards, and close collaboration between civil society, governments, business enterprises, and customers (Siemens 2018a: 1).

With the intention of reducing uncertainty in the virtual realm and enabling trusted interactions, the signatories have advanced ten principles, spanning from ownership of cyber and IT security, responsibility throughout the digital supply chain, security by default, user-centricity, innovation and co-creation, to education, certification for critical infrastructure and solutions, transparency and response, regulatory framework, and joint initiatives (Siemens 2018b; Hinck 2018; Kaeser 2018). Multistakeholder in nature, the principles put forward by the Charter signatories are skewed toward key tenets of responsible product development and engineering practices (Horenbeeck et al. 2019).

As part of the ten areas of action identified, Principle 2, i.e. responsibility throughout the digital supply chain, has so far seen most specification.[7] According to a press release issued by Siemens in February 2019, underwriters have committed themselves to devising baseline requirements pertaining to third-party risks in supply chains and have pledged implementation of measures including:

- The protection of data from unauthorized access throughout the data lifecycle
- The enactment and enforcement of identity and access controls and monitoring measures across supply chains
- The putting into place of processes ensuring product and service authenticity and identification, and
- The deployment of regular employee security trainings

With a view to disseminating their efforts, Charter members have engaged in several round table activities, and endorsed related initiatives, including the Paris Call for Trust and Security in Cyberspace.

Telefónica

On 25 June 2018, global telecommunications provider Telefónica published the second edition of its Digital Manifesto.[8] Building on the idea of a social contract, the Manifesto holds that in order to keep reaping the benefits of digital technologies, it is necessary to modernize policies and norms to ensure fair competition and innovation. To that end, a *Digital Constitution*, a new *Digital Bill of Rights* to protect key human values and fundamental rights is required. Such a contract, so Telefónica, needs to be as human-centric as possible and rest on the involvement and support of as many stakeholders as possible (Haas 2018).

Revolving around five core principles, Telefónica's Manifesto for a New Digital Deal maintains that:

- Digitalization should be an inclusive process, in which everyone is able to participate
- Social and fiscal policies have to be adapted to the realities of current market conditions and digital companies
- Users ought to have transparent knowledge of and control over their data and corresponding use thereof
- Global providers of digital services should act responsibly and be committed to social development
- Social policy and citizens' rights have to be modernized. (Telefónica 2018)

In contrast to the normative instruments launched by Microsoft and Siemens, Telefónica's Manifesto for a New Digital Deal is not open to accession by other signatories. Telefónica is, however, a supporter of initiatives, including, for example, the Paris Call for Trust and Security in Cyberspace or the Cybersecurity Tech Accord.

Kaspersky Lab

With a customer base of more than 400 million users, more than 30 subsidiaries, and revenues of over USD 726 million, Kaspersky Lab ranks among the largest privately owned cyber security companies worldwide (Kaspersky Lab 2019a). In recent years, the company has come under scrutiny for alleged collaboration with the Russian government. In response to accusations of collusion with the Kremlin and fading levels of trust as well as operational bans, Kaspersky Lab launched a Global Transparency Initiative in late 2018.

As per Kaspersky Lab's own attestation, the Global Transparency Initiative (GTI) represents

> a reaffirmation of the company's commitment to earning and maintaining the trust of its most important stakeholders: its customers. It includes a number of actionable and concrete measures to involve external independent cyber security experts and others in validating and verifying the trustworthiness of the company's products, its internal processes and business operations, and to introduce additional accountability mechanisms by which the company can further demonstrate that it addresses any security issues promptly and thoroughly.
>
> (Kaspersky Lab 2019b)

In terms of scope and depth, Kaspersky Lab's GTI appears to stand out and differ from comparable benchmarks. Competitor McAfee, for instance, decided to shut down its source-code review programs in 2017 out of fear of foreign interference and vulnerability identification/abuse.[9] In the remit of the GTI, Kaspersky Lab has recently relocated its data processing and storage units from Russia to Switzerland, and has established four transparency centers, located in Zurich (Switzerland), Madrid (Spain), Cyberjaya (Malaysia), and São Paulo (Brazil). The latter serve as dedicated sites for independent reviews of source code, software updates, threat detection rules, and other technical and business processes by external parties, including regulators and government agencies responsible for cyber security, as well as enterprise partners of Kaspersky Lab (Kaspersky Lab 2020).

Rather than advocating a distinct set of norms or action areas, Kaspersky Lab's norms-oriented activities have primarily revolved around three core principles, i.e. transparency (as the most obvious principle named), trust, and independence, which have emerged in close relation to its operations and issued third-party business impediments but, at the same time, appear to reflect larger industry trajectories.[10] Daniel Dobrygowski, Head of Governance and Policy for the World Economic Forum Centre for Cyber Security, for instance, has noted that

> over the last few years, tech-focused companies have begun entering into cyber security alliances and pacts with one another. These alliances are a symptom of the breakdown of trust between policy makers and those they [are] making polices for. Hundreds of companies – some of them, such as Airbus, Cisco, HP, Microsoft, Siemens, and Telefónica, among the largest in the world – have tried to step into this trust gap by forming groups around goals related to the future of the internet and digital networks. Some of these groups (… operational alliances) are mainly practical, sharing intelligence or technical data. Others (… normative alliances) are explicitly aimed at changing the ways companies deal with cyber security vulnerabilities and renegotiating the social contract between states and their citizens.
>
> (Dobrygowski 2019: 2)

In contrast to operational alliances, normative alliances pursue wider political aims and try to "uphold values like trust and accountability in cyber security and to spur collective action in favor of peace and nonaggression – much as agreements between countries do" (Dobrygowski 2019: 2). While important momentum-building elements, the efforts pursued by normative alliances, and norm-promoting technology companies more generally, raise important accountability and legitimacy questions. How are corporate norm leaders held accountable for their proposals and implementation thereof, and where do technology companies derive their normative authority from? Rather than by means of formal democratic legitimacy, corporate actors appear to have relied on combinations of functional (functions executed), epistemic (knowledge brokered), and performance (scale and capabilities available) legitimacy to justify their normative endeavors (Peters et al. 2009; Black 2017).

Effectiveness review

Reviews relating to the effectiveness of the ideational proposals issued by corporate actors concerning cyberspace have remained sparse and difficult to conduct. Nonetheless, such assessments are important yardsticks for making value claims about the contributions of private actors to global steering efforts. This section appraises the consequences of corporate norm formation activities along three dimensions: Output, outcome, and impact (Flohr et al. 2010; Wolf 2010). The three dimensions can be distinguished as follows: Output (category one) refers to identifiable commitments and achievements set by norm entrepreneurs engaging in global steering efforts (Hegemann et al. 2012: 104). They can comprise standards and regulations, programs, as well as institutional structures (Flohr et al. 2010). Performatively linked to category one, category two, outcome, denotes changes in the conduct of participating actors in accordance with the commitments stipulated (Flohr et al. 2010). Impact (category three) relates to contributions to

Table 13.1 Operationalization of the three effectiveness dimensions

	Operationalization	
Output	Adoption of commitments and policies on cyber security-related issues	Accession to collective initiatives
Outcome	Initiation of proactive measures to positively influence the level of cyber security	Change in company-self and the behavior of third parties and implementation of initiatives
Impact	Reduction of global cyber insecurity levels	Far-reaching systemic changes

problem solving or goal attainment resulting from the behavioral alterations of the stakeholders involved.

While categories one (output) and two (outcome) facilitate analyses of non-state actor functions, category three (impact) enables differentiations between commitments and actions on the one hand and their larger effects on the other (Wolf 2010). Although analytically separated, the three categories, "are closely connected and may even be regarded as parts of a causal chain" (Wolf 2010, 4).

The three dimensions can be operationalized as follows:

In terms of analytical complexity, assessing output is relatively unproblematic, while determining outcome and impact is more demanding. Especially with regard to impact, examining effectiveness is complicated by problems of multicausality, shifting baselines, and counterfactual reasoning (Wolf 2010). The results presented in this chapter have to be understood within the context of these limitations.

Output

Apropos output, the norms-based cyber insecurity reduction measures undertaken by technology companies have been rather successful. Since the non-consensus outcome of the 2017 UN GGE, technology companies have released respectable numbers of candidate norms and accompanying advocacy measures. Both in terms of substantive provisions and institutional commitments, firms including Microsoft, Siemens, Telefónica, and Kaspersky Lab have made important contributions to furthering global peace and security in the virtual realm.

The firms' interactions with industry fellows, non-governmental stakeholders, and governments have enabled them to propose widely backed and strategically relevant normative ideas, including, for instance, calls for greater transparency relating to supply chains and products, or widespread protection of critical infrastructures and individuals.

The measures undertaken by the technology firms have also served as important steppingstones for drawing attention to the ideational proposals of non-state actors more generally and opening up conventional structures of debate. Renata Dwan, Director of the United Nations Institute for Disarmament Research (UNIDIR), for example, has aptly noted that

> after being on the UN agenda for over two decades, we are now seeing an expansion on the discussion around what cyber-stability means and for whom. A debate that began focused on state behavior, is now becoming a much wider discussion about the role of the private sector, of regions and of individuals – and how to develop space for rights, for equity, and for access that enhances development for all.
>
> (EastWest Institute 2019)

Outcome

Vis-à-vis outcome, the technology companies analyzed as part of this chapter, have managed to secure seats at political tables, shape policy agendas, and affect ego and alter behavior. They have committed financial and human resources to their norms-based strategies, and have put in place new organizational setups, including brick and mortar structures to substantiate and implement their norms-based pledges. While Kaspersky Lab, for instance, has invested in the building of transparency centers (brick and mortar structures), Microsoft has bolstered its Digital Diplomacy unit (human resources). With a view to implementing its commitments stipulated as part of the Charter of Trust, Siemens has introduced a binding clause in its new contracts, which requests suppliers to comply with minimum binding cyber security requirements. "These requirements will apply primarily to suppliers of security-critical components such as software, processors and electronic components for certain types of control units. […] The goal is to better protect the digital supply chain against hacker attacks" (Siemens 2019c).

Furthermore, Siemens and Microsoft have managed to inject their candidate norms into regional and international policy-making processes.[11] In April 2019, for instance, the Council of the European Union issued a declaration maintaining that

> [t]he European Union and its Member States are strongly committed to the existing consensus [around the norms, rules and principles of responsible state behavior as articulated in the cumulative reports of the UN GGE], and to the further discussions in the United Nations, as well as to the commitments made with regard to the protection of intellectual property against cyber-enabled theft in multilateral fora such as G20, or through the Paris Call for Trust and Security in Cyberspace.
>
> (Council of the European Union 2019)

Through cross-signing initiatives, attending and conducting meetings at the sidelines of major political gatherings, including G7 and G20 meetings, UN-led conventions or major security conferences, technology firms of the likes mentioned above have gained foothold in political arenas and have come to establish themselves as (quasi-)diplomatic actors (Hurel and Lobato 2018b; Gorwa and Peez 2018).[12]

The resonance and uptake of private normative efforts across fora such as the European Union are evidence of their successfully executed roles as norm leaders and also speak to their capacity to promote diplomatic and political changes.

Impact

Despite advocated broader intentions to increase the stability of the digital realm, the efforts conducted by Siemens, Kaspersky Lab, Telefónica, and Microsoft have not (yet) led to substantial changes apropos minimizing levels of cyber insecurity. Over the course of the past years, cyberattacks have risen continuously. The degrees of damage to the global economy as well as the costs for remediation have accelerated from a projected USD 500 billion, or about 0.7% of global income, in 2014, to an estimated USD 600 billion, or 0.8% of global GDP, in 2018. Among others, researchers have quoted the following reasons for the rise in costs:

> quick adoption of new technologies by cybercriminals, [a budding] number of new users online (these tend to be from low-income countries with weak cyber security), … the increased ease of committing cybercrime, with the growth of Cybercrime-as-a-Service, an expanding number of cybercrime centers that now include Brazil, India, North Korea, and Vietnam, [and] a growing financial sophistication among top-tier cybercriminals.
>
> (Lewis 2018: 4)

While the global state of cyber security may have seen little improvement as a consequence of corporate norm development efforts (so far), the activities of global technology companies have at the very least had some broader procedural effects. Their commitment to stipulating responsible behavior in the digital environment has led to greater inclusion of civil society organizations and other private stakeholder in global cyber security problem-solving efforts (Flohr et al. 2010).

Conclusion

As is evident from the remarks above, technology companies have come to execute different roles in global cyber security norm formation processes. Apart from having acted as brokers of technical knowhow and expertise (knowledge brokers), they have stimulated cooperation among like-minded stakeholders (cooperation incubators), championed norms (norm leaders), and filled procedural as well as content-related gaps (gap fillers). In the face of waning levels of trust in digital infrastructures and technologies, it is critical for industry actors to execute their different roles and develop and promote best practices and norms-based interactions in an effort to (re)build confidence and create heightened degrees of predictability in cyberspace.

Against the background of progress-inhibiting discord among governments concerning the enactment of red lines in cyberspace, this chapter has analyzed and appraised the effectiveness of the normative contributions made by technology companies. Exploring the cases of Siemens, Kaspersky Lab, Telefónica, and Microsoft, it has argued that technology companies have come to exert considerable discursive and political power over discussions about responsible behavior in cyberspace. They have generated impressive numbers of candidate norms for increasing the stability and security of the digital realm. Furthermore, they have been successful at signaling their political intentions and promoting/injecting their normative proposals across high-ranking diplomatic venues. While having been fairly effective across the dimensions of output and outcome, technology companies have struggled to effectuate far-reaching systemic changes (impact). However, if incentivized appropriately, and pursued with complementarily in mind, the norms-based endeavors undertaken by technology companies may eventually have the capacity to "have real-world effects on the stability and security of cyberspace" (Ruhl et al. 2020: 19).

As non-state actors continue to be concerned about immediate and future threats to their operations and seek diplomatic engagement, it is important to reconsider existing forms of interaction and cooperation among governmental and non-governmental entities (Melissa Hathaway, in Hampson et al. 2017: 5). In view of the fact that from a formal legal perspective, states are the ultimate enforcers of cyber security norms, it is vital for non-state actors and state actors to work closer together, aid one another in their behavior-shaping efforts, and engage in true cooperation. "[B]roader sets of allies working together to build trust and share responsibility" are more likely to achieve results with systemic effects (Dobrygowski 2019). What appears to be certain at this point is "that the development of cyber security norms [is going to] be a long process", and that persistent engagement on the parts of governments and non-state actors, as well as effective scaling are going to be key factors for success (Nye 2018).

Notes

1 In the remit of the United Nations, discussions about rules of the road to curb malicious behavior in cyberspace began to surface in the late 1990s. In 2003, in reaction to UN General Assembly Resolution 58/32, a Group of Governmental Experts was called to existence to study existing and emerging threats emanating from the digital realm and possible normative measures to address them. The first of a total of six groups met in 2004. While the three UN GGEs meeting between 2009 and 2015 managed to issue non-binding consensus reports, the two groups convening between 2004–2005 and 2016–2017 did not produce corresponding documents (Väljataga 2017). At the time of writing (November 2019), it remains to be seen whether or not the latest iteration of the UN GGE will arrive at a consensus document.

2 Finnemore, for instance, noted that "[a]ctors who may feel nervous about being bound by formal laws may be willing to engage with groups governed by norms. Over time, these initially reluctant states, firms and individuals may become socialized into deeper acceptance of the norms" (Finnemore 2011: 90).

3 The initiatives alluded to include the Tallinn Manual 2.0 (NATO Cooperative Cyber Defence Centre of Excellence), the Digital Geneva Convention (Microsoft), the Global Commission on the Stability of Cyberspace (EastWest Institute & the Hague Centre for Strategic Studies), the Charter of Trust (Siemens), Carnegie Endowment for International Peace's Call for a Global Norm Against Manipulating the Integrity of Financial Data, the Cybersecurity Tech Accord (Microsoft), the Digital Peace Now Campaign (Microsoft), the Paris Call (Microsoft), as well as Kaspersky Lab's Transparency Initiative.

4 Contrary to earlier communication technologies, and despite its emergence in a politically predicated context, sovereign actors initially displayed little inclination toward enacting measures of control over cyberspace. Operation and management of the infrastructure were, for the most part, left to the experts who had contributed to its development, including, among others, Barry M. Leiner, Vinton G. Cerf, David D. Clark, Robert E. Kahn, Leonard Kleinrock, Daniel C. Lynch, Jon Postel, Larry G. Roberts, and Stephen Wolff. Oversight was informal and reflected the academic context within which the digital realm had arisen.

5 Notable exceptions include among others Hurel and Lobato (2018a) and Gorwa and Peez (2018).

6 With a view to defending and advancing the benefits of networked technologies for society, the Cybersecurity Tech Accord calls on private actors to observe four specific principles and behaviors, i.e. to protect all users and customers from nefarious cyber activities, regardless of geographical location, to oppose cyberattacks on civilian and corporate infrastructures, to empower and support users, customers, and developers in their efforts to strengthen cyber security, and to partner with like-minded entities, civil society, and security researchers across proprietary and open source technologies to enhance cyber security.

7 Principle 2 of the Charter of Trust reads as follows: "Companies – and if necessary – governments must establish risk-based rules that ensure adequate protection across all IoT layers with clearly defined and mandatory requirements. Ensure confidentiality, authenticity, integrity and availability by setting baseline standards, such as: Identity and access management: Connected devices must have secure identities and safeguarding measures that only allow authorized users and devices to use them. Encryption: Connected devices must ensure confidentiality for data storage and transmission purposes wherever appropriate. Continuous protection: Companies must offer updates, upgrades and patches throughout a reasonable lifecycle for their products, systems and services via a secure update mechanism".

8 The first edition of the Manifesto was launched in 2014 (Telefónica 2014).

9 In contrast, Kaspersky Lab's Transparency Centres welcome "State agencies and regulators responsible for national cyber security and the protection of information systems (decreed as such by the respective local legislation); Prospective and existing enterprise partners and customers of Kaspersky anywhere in the world. Academia, media and information security community experts are being considered as potential invitees to the Transparency Centre in the future. Under no circumstances whatsoever will Kaspersky provide intelligence or law enforcement agencies that have a mandate and/or capability for cyber-offensive operations with access to the Transparency Centre. The security information and infrastructure in the Transparency Centre are provided by Kaspersky strictly for consultation purposes only. Any actions to modify the company's source code, software updates, or threat detection rules are forbidden and will be prevented by the TC Steering team; any abuse will be reported to the local law enforcement agency" (Kaspersky Lab 2019b).

10 According to Eugene Kaspersky, "[t]ransparency is becoming the new normal for the IT industry – and for the cyber security industry in particular" (Business Wire 2018).

11 In April 2019, for example, Charter of Trust partners met to discuss the latest developments around the EU Cybersecurity Act with Despina Spanou, the responsible representative of the European Commission, and presented their proposals for next steps and further action (see Siemens 2019b).

12 Referring to their endeavors as Charter, Accord, Manifesto, or Convention underscores the underlying political ambitions of these actors.

References

All links checked on August 23, 2021.

Abbott, K. W., and Snidal, D. (2000). Hard and Soft Law in International Governance. *International Organization*, 54(3): 421–456.

Barlow, J. P. (1996). A Declaration of the Independence of Cyberspace. Retrieved from: https://perma.cc/DRJ9-WEGT.

Björkdahl, A (2002). Norms in International Relations: Some Conceptual and Methodological Reflections. *Cambridge Review of International Affairs*, 15(1): 9–23.

Black, J. (2017). "Says Who?" Liquid Authority and Interpretive Control in Transnational Regulatory Regimes. *International Theory*, 9(2): 286–310.

Business Wire. (2018, November 13). Kaspersky Lab Starts Data Processing for European Users in Zurich and Opens Its First Transparency Center. Retrieved from: https://www.businesswire.com/news/home/20181113005169/en/Kaspersky-Lab-Starts-Data-Processing-European-Users.

Carbonara, E. (2017). Law and Social Norms. In F. Parisi (ed.), *Columbia Law Review. Vol. 1*. Oxford: Oxford University Press.

Charney, S., English, E., Kleiner, A., Malisevic, N., McKay, A., Neutze, J., and Nicholas, P. (2016). From Articulation to Implementation: Enabling Progress on Cyber Security Norms. Microsoft. Retrieved from: https://query.prod.cms.rt.microsoft.com/cms/api/am/binary/REVmc8.

Council of the European Union. (2019, April 12). Declaration by the High Representative on Behalf of the EU on Respect for the Rules-Based Order in Cyberspace. Press Releases. Retrieved from: https://www.consilium.europa.eu/en/press/press-releases/2019/04/12/declaration-by-the-high-representative-on-behalf-of-the-eu-on-respect-for-the-rules-based-order-in-cyberspace/.

Dobrygowski, D. (2019, September 11). Why Companies Are Forming Cybersecurity Alliances. *Harvard Business Review*. Retrieved from: https://hbr.org/2019/09/why-companies-are-forming-cybersecurity-alliances.

Dunn Cavelty, M., and Wenger, A. (2020). Cyber Security Meets Security Politics: Complex Technology, Fragmented Politics, and Networked Science. *Contemporary Security Policy*, 41(1): 5–32.

EastWest Institute. (2019, February 7). Global Commission's Cyber Stability Hearings at the UN. *News*. Retrieved from: https://www.eastwest.ngo/idea/global-commissions-cyber-stability-hearings-un.

European Commission. (2018). Charter of Trust for a Secure Digital World. Announcements. Retrieved from: https://ec.europa.eu/commission/commissioners/2014-2019/bienkowska/announcements/charter-trust-secure-digital-world_en.

Ferguson, W. D. (2019). Facing Uncertainty: The Role of Norms and Formal Institutions as Shared Mental Models. SASE Mini-Conference on Uncertain Futures in Economic Decision Making. London. Retrieved from: https://perma.cc/YFD2-39G3.

Finnemore, M. (2011). Cultivating International Cyber Norms. In K. M. Lord and T. Sharp (eds), *America's Cyber Future: Security and Prosperity in the Information Age*. Washington, DC: Center for a New American Security, pp. 87–102. Retrieved from: https://perma.cc/CBZ2-PHT4.

Finnemore, M. (2017). Cyber Security and the Concept of Norms. Carnegie Endowment for International Peace. Retrieved from: https://perma.cc/K7QA-UL6G.

Finnemore, M., and Sikkink, K. (1998). International Norm Dynamics and Political Change. *International Organization*, 52(4): 887–917.

Flohr, A., Rieth, L., Schwindenhammer, S., and Wolf, K. D. (2010). *The Role of Business in Global Governance*. London: Palgrave Macmillan UK.

Gorwa, R., and Peez, A. (2018). Tech Companies as Cyber Security Norm Entrepreneurs: A Critical Analysis of Microsoft's Cyber Security Tech Accord. *SocArXiv Papers*. Retrieved from: https://osf.io/preprints/socarxiv/g56c9/.

Grigsby, A. (2017). The End of Cyber Norms. *Survival*, 59(6): 109–122.

Haas, M. (2018). We Need a New Digital Deal so that Everyone Benefits from Digitalisation. Telefónica. Retrieved from: https://www.telefonica.de/fixed/news/6135/article-by-ceo-markus-haas-we-need-a-new-digital-deal-so-that-everyone-benefits-from-digitalisation.html.

Hampson, F. O., Sulmeyer, M., Hathaway, M., Lewis, J. A., Nye, J. S., Tikk, E., Twomey, P., and Donahoe, E. (2017). *Getting Beyond Norms: New Approaches to International Cyber Security Challenges*. Special Report. Waterloo, ON. https://perma.cc/U8YX-ABDW.

Hegemann, H., Heller, R., and Kahl, M. (eds) (2012). *Studying 'Effectiveness' in International Relations: A Guide for Students and Scholars*. Opladen: Verlag Barbara Budrich.

Henriksen, A. (2019). The End of the Road for the UN GGE Process: The Future Regulation of Cyberspace. *Journal of Cybersecurity*, 5(1): 1–9.

Hern, A. (2017, December 30). WannaCry, Petya, NotPetya: How Ransomware Hit the Big Tme in 2017. *The Guardian*. Retrieved from: https://perma.cc/CNC7-ZSCR.

Hinck, G. (2018, June 25). Private-Sector Initiatives for Cyber Norms: A Summary. Lawfare. Retrieved from: https://perma.cc/MR4K-VR4K.

Horenbeeck, M. Van, Kumar, S., Van Aardt, F., Mohr, S., Birarda, C., Hurel, L. M., Hering, J., Hollis, D., and Kulesza, J. (2019). Cyber Security Agreements. Internet Governance Forum Background Paper. Retrieved from: http://www.intgovforum.org/multilingual/filedepot_download/4904/1658.

Hurel, L. M., and Lobato, L. (2018a). Unpacking Cybernorms: Private Companies as Norms Entrepreneurs. *SSRN Electronic Journal*. Retrieved from: https://doi.org/10.2139/ssrn.3107237.

Hurel, L. M., and Lobato, L. (2018b). Unpacking Cyber Norms: Private Companies as Norm Entrepreneurs. *Journal of Cyber Policy*, 3(1): 61–76.

Kaeser, J. (2018, May 22). Working Together for More Security in the Digital World. *LinkedIn Pulse*. Retrieved from: https://www.linkedin.com/pulse/working-together-more-security-digital-world-joe-kaeser.

Kaspersky Lab. (2019a). About Us. Retrieved from: https://www.kaspersky.com/about.

Kaspersky Lab. (2019b). Transparency Centres. Retrieved from: https://perma.cc/F826-R4TY.

Kaspersky Lab. (2020). Kaspersky's Global Transparency Initiative Status Updates. Blog. Retrieved from: https://perma.cc/Q47K-HMUS.

Kavanagh, C. (2017). The United Nations, Cyberspace and International Peace and Security: Responding to Complexity in the 21st Century. *UNIDIR Resources*. Geneva. Retrieved from: https://perma.cc/ZT92-6GEA.

Korzak, E. (2017, July 31). UN GGE on Cybersecurity: The End of an Era? *The Diplomat*. Retrieved from: https://thediplomat.com/2017/07/un-gge-on-cybersecurity-have-china-and-russia-just-made-cyberspace-less-safe/.

Leuprecht, C., Szeman, J., and Skillicorn, D. B. (2019). The Damoclean Sword of Offensive Cyber: Policy Uncertainty and Collective Insecurity. *Contemporary Security Policy*, 40(3): 382–407.

Lewis, J. (2018). Economic Impact of Cybercrime – No Slowing Down. CSIS/McAffee Report. Retrieved from: https://perma.cc/J987-TUS8.

Mačák, K. (2017). From Cyber Norms to Cyber Rules: Re-Engaging States as Law-Makers. *Leiden Journal of International Law*, 30(4): 877–899.

Matsakis, L. (2018a, November 12). The US Didn't Sign the Paris Call for Trust and Security in Cyberspace. *Wired*. Retrieved from: https://www.wired.com/story/paris-call-cybersecurity-united-states-microsoft/.

Matsakis, L. (2018b, November 12). The US Sits Out an International Cyber Security Agreement. *Wired*. Retrieved from: https://perma.cc/6F5B-V24W.

Maurer, T.and Taylor, K. (2018, March 2). Outlook on International Cyber Norms: Three Avenues for Future Progress. *Just Security*. Retrieved from: https://perma.cc/XY32-6PEX.

McKay, A., Neutze, J., Nicholas, P., and Sullivan, K. (2014, December 3). International Cybersecurity Norms. Microsoft Blog. Retrieved from: https://blogs.microsoft.com/cybertrust/2014/12/03/proposed-cybersecurity-norms/.

Microsoft. (2013). Five Principles for Shaping Cyber Security Norms. Digital Geneva Convention White Paper. Retrieved from: https://perma.cc/G6RJ-883W.

Microsoft. (2017). A Digital Geneva Convention to Protect Cyberspace. Digital Geneva Convention Policy Paper. Retrieved from: https://perma.cc/698H-84P5.

Microsoft (2018). Digital Peace Now. Retrieved from: https://perma.cc/88RC-N8ZX.

Microsoft Security Response Center. (2010, July 22). Announcing Coordinated Vulnerability Disclosure. TechNet. Retrieved from: https://blogs.technet.microsoft.com/msrc/2010/07/22/announcing-coordinated-vulnerability-disclosure/.

Ministère de l'Europe et des Affaires Étrangères. (2018). Cyber Security: Paris Call of 12 November 2018 for Trust and Security in Cyberspace. *French Foreign Policy*. Retrieved from: https://perma.cc/8P82-X5JU.

Nye, J. S. Jr. (2018, March 12). How Will New Cyber Security Norms Develop? Belfer Center for Science and International Affairs. *Analysis & Opinion*. Retrieved from: https://perma.cc/9NLG-HZJC.

Nye, J. S. Jr., and Donahue, J. D. (2000). *Governance in a Globalizing World*. Washington, DC: Brookings Institution Press.

Peters, A., Förster, T., and Koechlin, L. (2009). Towards Non-State Actors as Effective, Legitimate, and Accountable Standard Setters. Non-State Actors as Standard Setters. In A. Peters, L. Koechlin, T. Förster, and G. Fenner Zinkernagel (eds), *Non-State Actors as Standard Setters*. Cambridge: Cambridge University Press, pp. 492–562.

Radu, R. (2014). Power Technology and Powerful Technologies: Global Governmentality and Security in the Cyberspace. In J.-F. Kremer and B. Müller (eds), *Cyberspace and International Relations*. Berlin, Heidelberg: Springer, pp. 3–20.

Risse-Kappen, T., Ropp, S. C., and Sikkink, K. (1999). *The Power of Human Rights: International Norms and Domestic Change*. Cambridge: Cambridge University Press.

Ruggie, J. G. (2004). Reconstituting the Global Public Domain - Issues, Actors, and Practices. *European Journal of International Relations*, 10(4): 499–531.

Ruhl, C., Hollis, D., Hoffman, W., and Maurer, T. (2020). Cyberspace and Geopolitics: Assessing Global Cyber Security Norm Processes at a Crossroads. Carnegie Endowment for International Peace Working Paper. Washington, DC. https://perma.cc/WXC3-JAEP.

Sandholtz, W. (2017). International Norm Change. In *Oxford Research Encyclopedia of Politics*. Oxford: Oxford University Press. https://doi.org/10.1093/acrefore/9780190228637.013.588.

Siemens. (2018a). Charter of Trust: For a Secure Digital World. Retrieved from: https://perma.cc/ZNQ6-UCZ5.

Siemens. (2018b). Time for Action: Building a Consensus for Cyber Security. *Research & Technologies*. Retrieved from: https://perma.cc/P23M-BGE3.

Siemens. (2019a, February 19). Mitsubishi Heavy Industries Signs LoI to Join Charter of Trust for Cyber Security. Press Release. Retrieved from: https://assets.new.siemens.com/siemens/assets/api/uuid:9ad7dc01-843c-453d-99f4-17634babd8c0/PR2019020163COEN.pdf.

Siemens. (2019b). One Year Charter of Trust: Important Milestones for More Cybersecurity. Retrieved from: https://perma.cc/8CTL-NEQD.

Siemens. (2019c, February 15). Siemens Establishes Binding Cyber Security Requirements for Suppliers. Press Release. Retrieved from: https://assets.new.siemens.com/siemens/assets/api/uuid:1886b34e-bd26-4c3c-be8b-98f1b346dbb3/PR2019020139COEN.pdf.

Smith, B. (2017, February 14). The Need For a Digital Convention. Microsoft. Microsoft Blog. Retrieved from: https://blogs.microsoft.com/on-the-issues/2017/02/14/need-digital-geneva-convention/#sm.0001hkfw5aob5evwum620jqwsabzv.

Sukumar, A. M. (2017, July 4). The UN GGE Failed. Is International Law in Cyberspace Doomed as Well? *Lawfare*. Retrieved from: https://www.lawfareblog.com/un-gge-failed-international-law-cyberspace-doomed-well.

Telefónica (2014). A Digital Manifesto: An Open and Safe Internet Experience for All. Retrieved from: https://www.telefonica.com/documents/341171/362460/20140410_A_Digital_Manifesto_ING_FINAL_reviewed.pdf/978031f0-d352-4f65-9c3c-b7d70fddf407.

Telefónica (2018). A Manifesto for a New Digital Deal. Retrieved from: https://perma.cc/9RXC-JE3D.

Untersinger, P. M. (2018, November 8). La France Veut Relancer Les Négociations Sur La Paix Dans Le Cyberespace. *Le Monde*. Retrieved from: https://www.lemonde.fr/pixels/article/2018/11/08/la-france-veut-relancer-les-negociations-sur-la-paix-dans-le-cyberespace_5380571_4408996.html.

Väljataga, A. (2017). Back to Square One? The Fifth UN GGE Fails to Submit a Conclusive Report at the UN General Assembly. NATO CCDCOE Insider Articles. Retrieved from: https://ccdcoe.org/incyder-articles/back-to-square-one-the-fifth-un-gge-fails-to-submit-a-conclusive-report-at-the-un-general-assembly/.

Wiener, A. (2017). A Theory of Contestation: A Concise Summary of Its Argument and Concepts. *Polity*, 49(1): 109–25.

Wolf, K. D. (2010, July). Output, Outcome, Impact: Focusing the Analytical Lens for Evaluating the Success of Corporate Contributions to Peace-Building and Conflict Prevention. Peace Research Institute Frankfurt Working Paper No. 3. Retrieved from: https://perma.cc/STL2-35UH.

14 Disrupting the second oldest profession

The impact of cyber on intelligence

Danny Steed

The practice of intelligence has undergone numerous challenges throughout its history, particularly since the 12th century when permanently standing, professionalized intelligence services were established. The challenge posed by the rise of cyberspace has, however, arguably proved one of the most severe against which intelligence would have to adapt. The end of the Cold War served to present intelligence with a dual challenge. First, the end of the Cold War also ended the known international order, removing the primary *raison d'être* for the intelligence services itself. This raised the legitimate, but of course ultimately incorrect, concern that intelligence itself "is a dying business" (Adams 1994: 316).

Second, and most important to this chapter, was the maturation of three key technologies – the personal computer (PC), email, and the World Wide Web – that served to, if not invent, then certainly to catalyze the information revolution exponentially. By coinciding with the end of the Cold War, the maturation of these technologies laid the foundations for cyberspace as we now know it, thereby presenting a new challenge for intelligence communities to consider: How to maintain their craft during the change from the analog world in which they had become so proficient, to the vastly more open, connected, and intrusive digital one.

This is the motivating concern behind this chapter, how the intelligence world adapted to the challenges presented by the digital age. In doing so, it will be revealed how the actions taken by those very actors in order to retain their relevance to the pursuit of security not only pioneered (Buchanan 2020: 329) the methods for intelligence in the digital age but have disproportionately disrupted cyber in turn. This disruption from intelligence is playing a leading role in the transformation of cyber security politics, driving socio-technological uncertainties through their practices, perhaps so far as to exacerbate the fragmentation of geopolitical interests themselves, as this author will argue.

The chapter will proceed first by detailing the nature of the digital challenge that was presented to the intelligence world at the end of the Cold War, before detailing the specific actions of American and British intelligence agencies to "master the internet". The main focus of the chapter will then move on to the consequences of intelligence actions on the politics of cyber security itself. By examining three core areas of socio-technological uncertainty that are impacted – the evolution of secrecy, intelligence as agents of proliferation, and intelligence as

DOI: 10.4324/9781003110224-16

shapers of norms – it will be demonstrated that the second oldest profession has in fact disrupted and fragmented cyber security politics far more than the arrival of cyber did the intelligence profession.

The intelligence world, who were once the invisible actors constituting the "missing dimension" (Andrew and Dilkes 1985) in the international system, through their exploitation of disruptive cyber tools and adapting to the socio-technological transformation of the digital age, have very much become central, perhaps even dominant, actors in the international system driving the fragmentation of cyber security politics. For better or for worse, the spies have migrated from the shadows into the very code and fiber that everyone worldwide uses.

The transformation: Challenge, fear, and opportunity

Whyte and Mazanec are right to declare that there has been an "unbreakable marriage between computers and espionage" (Whyte and Mazanec 2019: 61), so closely aligned has been the development of the technology with the practice of spying. The origins of the computer itself lie at the heart of the Allied successes in breaching Nazi codes during the Second World War, Enigma the most famous among them (Whyte and Mazanec 2019; Andrew 2018). The sternest challenge to be posed by the technologies that espionage has been "intimately connected" (Lowenthal 2018: 34) with would only truly emerge in the post-Cold War years, when those very technologies challenged the entire infrastructure on which intelligence had been built for decades, the shift from the analog to the digital world.

The challenge became one of migrating intelligence skillsets from the analogue expertise centered on cryptography for decades, to one that could penetrate digital codes and infrastructures. That shift was to take the intelligence world away from an infrastructure it had come to know well, that of listening outposts, telegraph stations, and transmitters that enabled passive gathering. During this time in the early 1990s, the American National Security Agency (NSA) – then led by Rear Admiral William Studeman – had commissioned an internal "Global Access Study" (Kaplan 2017: 41–44), aimed at projecting long-term access to the information the NSA required to fulfil its functions. It offered a vision of a world migrating to the digital age, where the intelligence gathering infrastructure, which had been established over many decades, would gradually decrease in relevance as the world's information flows left the electromagnetic spectrum and migrated into fiber optics as ones and zeros instead.

The motivating fear behind intelligence community evolution was clear, to avoid the situation of "going dark" and being cut off from essential sources of necessary information. Where global information and communications flow migrate, so too must the eyes of the intelligence community. As the 1990s progressed, the NSA study was being proven correct; a clear shift in reality was observed across the world where traditional radio receivers and antennas were no longer picking up signals, or certainly they were picking up far reduced traffic (Kaplan 2017: 35). The actions taken to change with the evolving world presented a potentially golden opportunity to the intelligence community, summed up best by the inventor of the World Wide Web himself, Tim Berners Lee: "to allow links to be made to *any information anywhere*" (Berners-Lee 1991).

Numerous practical challenges needed to be navigated, that included a closer alignment with the private sector, as the private sector owned much of the infrastructure that needed accessing (Clemente, in Goodman and Hillebrand 2014: 259). Speed was also a key factor; Degaut illustrates this well in stating that the information revolution changed the dynamic where policymakers were once almost entirely reliant on the intelligence community for insights. Intelligence "now has to compete for policymakers attention" (Degaut 2016: 510) with the multitudes of sources, both traditional and new, who have also been enabled by the vast data flows on offer. A mission statement from former NSA Director Keith Alexander to solve this is very illustrative:

> Let's collect the whole haystack ... Collect it all, tag it, store it ... And whatever it is you want you go searching for it.
> (Alexander in Nakashima and Warrick 2013)

The old intelligence adage – to find the needle in the haystack – very simply cannot take place without access to the haystack in the first place (Kaplan 2017: 262). The intelligence solution to this problem relied on exploiting, above all, sovereign geographic access to the submarine cables on which the bulk of the internet traffic traverses. Specifically, the cables that land from the American east coast – Apollo North, TAT-8, TAT-14, and AC-2 (Harding 2014: 214) – to the British South West Coast. In combination with Britain's key geographic position, these landing points become a unique communications hub due to the sheer percentage of global traffic pushed between these two points. Estimates can vary, but perhaps up to 25% of global internet traffic traversed the cabling infrastructure that lands in Cornwall (Harding 2014: 215) by the start of the 2010s.

What matters here is less an exhaustive counting of where traffic is intercepted, but rather in how the data is processed. For what is essentially the world's largest ever phone tap, the British Government Communications Headquarters (GCHQ) and the NSA had indeed "mastered the internet" (MacAskill, Borger, Hopkins, Davies and Ball 2013) through their TEMPORA and PRISM programs. Regarding TEMPORA, GCHQ's key breakthrough lay less in tapping the cables themselves than in innovating a buffer system, whereby internet information could be cached for automated analysis for up to three days, with broader metadata held for up to 30 days (Gill and Phythian 2018: 150). "Analysts and data miners would then retroactively be able to sort through this vast pool of digital material" (Harding 2014: 220). The operation, known under the code name Tempora, would intercept "all forms of online activity" (Greenwald 2014: 116) for this method of retrospective analysis.

PRISM, meanwhile, operated in partnership with numerous big technology corporations to facilitate access and sharing. In his leaks, Snowden specifically named Microsoft, Yahoo!, Google, Facebook, Paltalk, YouTube, Skype, and

Apple as willing participants to enable the NSA to gather browsing data as an "upstream collection" strategy (Snowden 2019: 347). Snowden then details two further tactical tools, TURMOIL and TURBINE. TURMOIL was a passive tool to filter all traffic. "Seeing your request, it checks its metadata for selectors … that mark it as deserving for more scrutiny" (Snowden 2019: 347). If flagged, that data is referred to TURBINE, designed to actively engage the user by determining which software exploits to send to the user and deploy them with the objective of surveiling that user (Snowden 2019: 348).

In tandem, the NSA and GCHQ had provided the prerequisite for competing in the digital age, *to have the information to begin with.* Mastering the internet required, first and foremost, collecting the entire haystack. Or, as another now well-known phrase describes the dynamic: "Getting information from the internet is like taking a drink from a fire hydrant".[1] American and British intelligence had solved how to fully absorb that information, subject it to automated analytics, and prioritize the findings for further action.

The consequences of intelligence actions on cyber security politics

While the intelligence community may have mastered the internet and developed strategies to remain effective, their actions bring with them wider consequences that must be considered. There are three consequences of socio-technological uncertainty causing political fragmentation that intelligence community actions highlight which are worthy of consideration here: Secrecy, proliferation, and norms.

First is secrecy, or rather the evolving meaning of secrecy. Secrecy, as Tucker argues well, enjoys a strange relationship in liberal nations, he notes that in early modern Europe "before the rise of liberalism, secrecy was synonymous with advantage and greater power" (Tucker 2014: 31). Liberalism, however, reversed the dynamic fundamentally in favor of the individual, developing a presumption against secrecy in politics, favoring privacy for the people instead. "Government became public, open; the people gained a right to privacy" (Tucker 2014: 35). This reversal was, of course, imperfect, carrying with it an inherent tension between the needs of the state to ensure security, versus the need to intrude upon the liberties enjoyed by the people. Privacy versus liberty is thus eternally in tension with regard to the work of intelligence agencies; it is a dynamic that is forever susceptible to the uncertainties brought by new innovations and technologies, and one that is always liable to fragmentation and rebalancing.

Until recent decades, intelligence agencies in the Western nations have mostly operated by avoiding this tension as far as possible through a series of means intended to conceal their operations. In the UK, this included not basing the intelligence agencies on any statutory footing at all until the 1980s and, even when they were codified in law, those laws afford significant protections and exemptions from other laws. For example, the UK Intelligence Community is afforded blanket exemption from the Freedom of Information Act (2000) and Public Records Act

(1958). Lustgarten's conclusion still remains very much valid in explaining the meaning of such approaches, that the "brevity of British statute reflects the fact that it is largely a cloak draped over an unchanged figure, not intended to disturb existing working relationships" (Lustgarten and Leigh 1994: 424).

The Information Revolution has, however, disturbed and fragmented those relationships, by forcing intelligence agencies to operate in the same environment as everyone else. The arrival of disruptive cyber tools increased the scope of uncertainty faced by intelligence actors. In this regard Peter Swire's assessment is most apt in arguing that there is now a "declining half-life" (Swire 2015) to secrets in intelligence. Swire argues convincingly that intelligence can no longer enjoy the "Cold War luxury" of operating in geographically distinct infrastructures, because civilian and intelligence targets alike "use the same operating systems, encryption protocols, apps, and other software" (Swire 2015: 4).

In a congested and constantly contested environment, spies carry increased risk that reduces their ability to keep secrets in two ways, intrusion detection and the leaking of methods. First, intelligence is rarely a purely passive activity, active intrusive methods are also needed. Indeed, as Whyte and Mazanec rightly point out, there is little technical difference between access and exploitation, the difference lying in "the intentions of those who hack for intrusive or disruptive purposes and the kinds of effects they are able to cause" (Whyte and Mazanec 2019: 76). Fundamentally the risk is as Swire states, that "intrusion carries with it the risk of intrusion detection" (Swire 2015: 5) and nowhere more so than online where monitoring occurs constantly and by automation; intelligence intrusions can simply be exposed far faster than before, bringing with it unwelcome levels of transparency. Access can also be lost with incredible speed, as Michael Hayden states, months spent gaining privileged access "can be lost with a casual upgrade of the targeted system" (Hayden 2016: 210). Such decreased windows of opportunity only incentivize intrusive measures, to use exploits before they expire, which of course increases the risk of regular operational compromise.

Not only are intelligence activities at greater risk of frequent detection, their sources and methods are now harder to keep secret, which is the second area of reduced capability. Leaks are of course the primary vehicle of exposing intelligence methods, as seen through leaks perpetrated by WikiLeaks, Chelsea Manning, and Edward Snowden throughout the 2010s. Snowden, in particular, has brought to the fore methods that may have remained unearthed for many years otherwise, raising questions about the legitimacy of intelligence actions and responsible behavior. Yet intelligence methods are also exposed via the nature of cyber tools themselves, specifically their code. Unlike traditional weaponry, code is not destroyed after use and can be forensically analyzed, reverse-engineered, or simply copied and deployed by other actors.

This leaking of methods is closely linked to the second consequence of socio-technological uncertainty, which is that intelligence agencies have become a source of proliferation in cyberspace. Exposure of intelligence methods educates other users how to act in the same vein, but for entirely different purposes. This is because, revisiting Swire's note, when everybody uses the same platforms, protocols, operating systems, and applications, methods are immediately transferable. The proliferation of intelligence tools (regardless of the means by which they were acquired) arms, for lack of a better phrase, other actors throughout cyberspace, and can only be approached as a significant consequence of socio-technological uncertainty that contributes to greater political fragmentation in this space.

This is because while there are always concerns regarding the legitimacy of intelligence actions, certainly in the liberal nations great efforts are expended to ensure levels of transparency on their work. For those who are the beneficiaries of intelligence tools and methods proliferation, there can be no such assurance of responsible or legitimate use in the eyes of the law, as well as an almost zero possibility of ensuring oversight. After all, how can legitimate authorities ensure transparency over a multitude of enabled actors outside the security space who have been armed anonymously? The more who become armed and enabled in this fashion, arguably only adds to an increased environment of cyber insecurity, thereby serving to further fragment cyber security politics.

Before offering a tangible example of this proliferation, however, it is necessary to briefly address the debate as code classifying as a cyber "weapon" or not. Analogizing code to weapons proves useful particularly in an illustrative function relating to proliferation, but it is wise to note the resistance to such classification by Thomas Rid. Rid bases his position on the view that computer code does not carry the same coercive power (the power to kill), that weaponry as traditionally viewed does, and risks being no more than a category error (Rid and McBurney 2012). The lack of proof in coercive abilities is a view shared and developed by Valeriano, Jensen, and Maness, who remain unconvinced by the empirical scorecard of cyber operations to achieve more than limited political objectives (Valeriano et al. 2018). Lucas Kello, by contrast, finds the "absence of death and the intangibility of most direct effects are not convincing grounds" and offers the term "virtual weapon" centrally in his argument (Kello 2017: 61).

Ground between these two positions is being established, however. Lin and Zegart offer a series of unique characteristics in order to think in a strategic context, specifically: Tools to gain intelligence versus those inflicting damage are difficult to distinguish; offensive cyber operations act on intangible targets; the target's characteristics themselves greatly impact the effectiveness of the attack; prior interaction with a target is often a prerequisite ahead of an actual cyberattack; and that cyberspace targets are often fleeting, liable to disappear in ways unlike physical targets (Lin and Zegart 2018: 607). Van Puyvelde and Brantly, meanwhile, are wise to have adopted a compromise position between the above camps, carrying the general classification of cyber "capabilities", noting that as capabilities expand and develop, so too will the debate itself (Van Puyvelde and Brantly 2019: 74).

Proliferation of this type is exactly what happened in 2017 when the hacker group "Shadow Brokers" compromised an NSA staging server, taking possession of a large cache of tools reportedly developed by the NSA's secretive Tailored Access Operations unit (Herrington, in Andrew et al. 2020: 578–579). Among these tools was an exploit named "EternalBlue", which worked against a vulnerability in all Windows systems prior to Windows 8, specifically the Server Message Block (SMB) function that could enable remote code execution (Greenberg 2019: 301–302). Following a wider release of the exploit by the Shadow Brokers, it was appropriated and deployed in two global ransomware attacks, WannaCry and NotPetya in 2017. In the UK, the WannaCry attack became notable for its impact on the National Health Service – arguably the attack's most famous victim – paralyzing 35% of all hospital trusts in the UK (80 out of 236) among many hundreds of other health organizations (NAO 2018: 11). NotPetya meanwhile, became the first cyberattack to cost more than US$10 billion in losses worldwide, costing global corporations *Maersk* and FedEx at least US$300 million each (Greenberg 2019: chapter 27).

The global ransomware attacks of 2017, armed at their core with exploits developed by the NSA, must be regarded as a seminal example of intelligence agencies becoming inadvertent proliferators in cyberspace. As Greenberg states, instead of any hypothetical fear of inspiring non state or hostile state actors to behave in certain ways and develop their own tools, "America's hacking arsenal had fallen, suddenly and directly, into enemy hands" (Greenberg 2019: 290). Sanger is in agreement in arguing that some levels of secrecy are no longer required among nation-states because "after Snowden and the Shadow Brokers, there is not much mystery left" (Sanger 2018: 566). By occupying the same infrastructure on cyberspace as other users, intelligence agencies are also vulnerable to thefts and data breaches, carrying consequences that WannaCry and NotPetya proved are not hypothetical in their ability to cause harm, and perhaps lending greater credence to Kello's position that code is increasingly a weapon.

The third and final consequence of socio-technological uncertainty is that intelligence agencies have become, as Georgiva argues, unexpected norm-setters (Georgiva 2020). Noting the previously established history of intelligence agencies enjoying significant statutory protections domestically, Georgiva establishes well that this ambiguity also extends into international law, with precious little consensus on whether it is legal or illegal (Georgiva 2020: 42). This is also reflected in the *Tallinn Manual*, stating that "International law does not directly address peacetime espionage as such" (Schmitt 2017: 25). This is a legal ambiguity that is increasingly becoming a concern because "many of the exposed cyber operations set alarming precedents" (Broeders et al. 2019: 2) that are more and more difficult to ignore.

This legal ambiguity, combined with the reality that in the information age those whose craft is information itself should be primary actors, contributes to a security dynamic. This dynamic is that intelligence holds a legitimate purpose as security actors in the pursuit of their objectives. At the same time, however, the digital "unpeace" (Kello 2017: 249) is exacerbated by their actions and behaviors, setting normative precedents that encourage – and through inadvertent proliferation, both educate and arm – multitudes of other actors, whether state or non-state in their various guises. Making a judgment on whether such normative setting behavior is correct or in need of redress is beyond the scope of this chapter's focus. Suffice to say however one must question Georgiva's call that intelligence behaviors be incorporated into the calculus of norm-building agendas, whether at the UN or otherwise (Georgiva 2020: 48).

The history of intelligence practice to date has largely been one of crafting deliberate ambiguity in as many arenas as possible – domestic and international law being the most tangible – to enable the spies to operate. Generally, the logic has rested on the Cold War era reasoning, which hopes involuntary intrusion into the sovereign affairs of actors serves to provide sufficient enough transparency among other actors and avoid escalations. In this vein, intelligence is to be seen as a form of steam valve to help depressurize the international order from movements toward large-scale confrontation and war. It is a view that, so far, can be argued as having been effective enough following the Total Wars period. Altering the state of deliberate ambiguity that intelligence has enjoyed so far may address *some* aspects of cyber security, but it is also highly likely to carry unforeseeable consequences that extend far beyond the affairs of cyberspace into other arenas of geopolitics. Intelligence actions in the digital age certainly contribute to increased insecurity in cyberspace, but their overall mission is likely to still yield a net positive impact on depressurizing global security tensions.

Cyber disrupting intelligence, or intelligence disrupting cyber?

What is clear from this exploration and the argument by Georgiva that intelligence agencies are not only shaping, but *driving* normative behavior in cyberspace, is that the disruption that intelligence is having on cyberspace is arguably larger and more politically significant than those that cyberspace wrought on the practice of intelligence itself. Policymakers and lawmakers face acute difficulties in navigating the challenges posed by this reality; the Snowden revelations have served to arm actors such as China, and even American allies, with the charge of hypocrisy at Western nations who preach a "rules-based order". Similarly, American complaints at Intellectual Property theft online can easily be met with reminders that espionage is not expressly prohibited in international law. As Dunn Cavelty rightly points out, when intelligence agencies are expected to operate "unfettered and without restraint" internationally, they present themselves as the biggest issue (Dunn Cavelty 2018a: 118).

In an international system where security is a legitimate pursuit, a cyberspace where "everyone favors insecurity" becomes in fact desirable (Schneier 2018: 83). This creates a problem in the pursuit of security, as established by Dunn Cavelty that "the security *of* cyberspace and security *by (or through)* cyberspace are often diametrically opposed" (Dunn Cavelty 2018b: 27). In this case, the pursuit of security through the exploitation of cyberspace as a means to an end significantly impacts the security of cyberspace itself. The fear ultimately becomes that while some actors become skilled at the pursuits of security through cyberspace for their own objectives, in doing so they continue to make that very cyberspace ever more the "wild, wild West" that President Obama described it as in 2015 (Obama 2015).

With these points in mind, a fruitful avenue for scholarship to consider is to revisit a seminal Cold War concept in international relations theory, the security dilemma. Here, the traditional concept established by Robert Jervis is considered, that one state's actions to increase its security inherently decreases that of the others (Jervis 2007). Much of Jervis' conceptual framework applies well to considerations of cyber security, especially the difficulty in determining defensive tools and behaviors from offensive ones, and the relative cost and balance between the offence and defense in its centrality to decision-making (Jervis 2007: 145–146). Yet although these are eminently valid considerations for scholars to use, it is instead the environmental, structural element of Jervis' thesis that matters most to this argument.

Specifically, it is the consideration that the dilemma results primarily not from the actions of actors, but instead from the structure of the international system itself (Griffiths et al. 2002: 295), which locks and incentivizes security-seeking behavior from the outset. Brantly has previously established the place of the security dilemma within cyber security politics, highlighting how the characteristics of cyberspace lends itself as being a place of anarchy and order at the same time. "There are rules defined by code and architecture, and at the same time the current of information and ideas has historically been considered a realm free of governance" (Brantly 2014: 133). Cyberspace, therefore, with a governance structure originally intended only for its technical, architectural considerations, was a natural fit for a security dilemma to ultimately unfold, with intelligence agencies the natural actors to lead it. As Carlin notes, when it comes to geopolitics, cyberspace has become "an extension of the real world" (Carlin 2018: 79).

The exploitation of cyberspace by intelligence actors is undoubtedly leading to socio-technological uncertainties. That uncertainty, however, lies not in the actions or issues themselves, but rather the uncertainty of the outcome for the future of cyber security politics. Ultimately, the risk that is carried is that the behaviors of intelligence actors in the pursuit of security do indeed develop cyberspace into a true security dilemma, one that is fully entwined with the rest of the geopolitical world. This carries the potential for political fragmentation in two arenas that are already well known, that from within – the balance between security and liberty – and that from without – the fundamental geopolitical architecture on which espionage is grounded.

From within, this fragmentation greatly impacts a perennial issue among liberal societies, which is the balance between liberty and security, how far the state's power should justifiably extend into the rights of individuals. The Snowden leaks are the primary culprit in precipitating renewed public debate in how far the powers of the security state should extend, a debate that was renewed for the digital age. This is a battleground already joined worldwide, highlighting significant political fragmentation in the fundamental values by which states govern themselves. Are domestic laws seeking to assert their sovereignty, or protect their citizens' liberal values? Farrell and Newman are entirely correct in stating that "Questions of privacy, security, and information will be at the heart of many political battles over the next century as information *has at last been politicized*" (Farrell and Newman 2019: 63, italics added).

The clearest battleground where this can be seen worldwide is the imposition of various data localization laws, all aimed to establish sovereign authority over information itself. In the UK, the controversial Investigatory Powers Act, 2016 – commonly dubbed "The Snoopers Charter" – provides the British intelligence services a new legal framework to enable bulk collection practices, while mandating that internet service providers retain records for 12 months, to facilitate law enforcement investigation where needed. Many similar statutory acts worldwide mandate data storage in-country, ensuring access by legal authorities. Russia's Federal Law No. 242-FZ carries the most expansive position, however, in declaring authority over the data of all Russian citizens regardless of where in the world both the individual and their data resides.

Fragmentation in cyber security politics is already happening worldwide, with efforts to establish sovereign authority over data itself a raging battleground of competing legislation claiming legitimacy, but across a spectrum of interpretations on where one's own sovereignty extends to. These acts also enable intelligence and law enforcement intrusion with varying, if any, transparency over the methods and legal practices permitting access. The fragmentation of cyber security politics within states is made clearest by the current creation and establishment of data localization laws worldwide; this is an arena that should be researched carefully in order to better understand how the uncertainty of the balance between security and liberty will play out.

From without, Inkster is right to state that a "battle for the soul of the Internet" is being waged (Inkster 2016: chapter 4), where political fragmentation is threatened over the fundamental mechanics to govern the internet itself. As this author has previously argued, cyberspace grew in an "apolitical honeymoon" (Steed 2019: 32) period in the immediate post-Cold War years, providing a form of incubator to protect its nascent growth from significant geopolitical challenge that it no longer enjoys. Kello has argued that a "sovereignty gap" exists in cyberspace (Kello 2017: 254), which has become the scene for political fragmentation as a new geopolitical battle begins to be waged for control of it; that gap itself is not the source of fragmentation, it is the growing competition to fill the gap that is. The resulting socio-technological uncertainty that is faced is simple, which geopolitical vision wins this battle for the soul of the internet?

For authoritarian nations, cyberspace and the internet have always been viewed as threats to their national security, for the liberal West, they were seen as tools of liberation for the individual and a mechanism for prosperity to the market-driven state. These perspectives are reflections of respective strategic cultures adapting to the presence of cyberspace, cultures which are "deeply rooted in history, economics, and strategic challenges" (Segal 2016: 361) that extend far beyond the experience of only the internet. Hughes Wilson rightly, although incompletely, identifies the key issues facing these core protagonists in the future of cyber security politics. "For China and other autocratic governments, the priority is to control citizens" access to information; whereas for the more liberal West, the key concern is the struggle to protect intellectual property rights and technological supremacy" (Hughes Wilson 2017: 635). Hughes Wilson's view is incomplete in failing to identify the West's battle to protect the balance between security and liberty as an additional key domestic concern. It should be clear, however, that the trajectory of cyber security politics has extended far beyond the original concerns of intelligence actors, who sought simply to adapt to the digital age and ensure continued access to information. Their actions have arguably contributed to creating one of the biggest geopolitical battlegrounds of the 21st century.

Conclusion

This chapter began with the intent of mapping some of the impacts and changes that cyberspace and cyber security brought to the business of intelligence actors. Throughout, however, it has become clear that the socio-technological challenges posed by cyberspace to those in the intelligence world, and the adaptations taken by those actors to maintain their value as national security instruments, have resulted in a more significant conclusion. This is that the impact of intelligence *upon* cyber security carries more significant consequences to political fragmentation and cyber security politics than the impacts of cyberspace upon how the intelligence services conducts their affairs.

There are three broad conclusions to offer underneath this overarching position. First, the socio-technological transformations brought with cyberspace have fundamentally affected, if not altered entirely, the meaning of secrecy in the modern world, carrying with it significant effects on the intelligence profession. It has been seen that with a "declining half-life" of secrecy affecting even those intelligence services with historically excellent records at keeping secret even their existence, the meaning and value of both secrecy and secrets themselves is evolving in ways clearly not anticipated.

Broeders is right to note that, unlike in the past, the collection of information itself is "less the issue than keeping secret the fact you are collecting it" (Broeders 2016: 302), which has also been made increasingly difficult by the exposure of intelligence methods and tools. Combined with the rise of the post-trust world, where accepted realities are subject to distortion and challenge, and "virality can overwhelm truth" (Singer and Brooking 2019: 46), increased pressure is placed on an old challenge. This is whether it is the duty of intelligence to *remove* or *assess* uncertainty itself. Intelligence Studies may need to revise its traditional view that the latter is to be sought (Friedman and Zeckhauser 2012: 845) in light of continued concerns around election interference and the resurgence of disinformation campaigns.

Second, that intelligence has become a dominant source of proliferation, enabling the multitudes of diverse actors that also share and use cyberspace. A form of "collateral damage" now accompanies intelligence work that must sift through the stacks of data gathered from the civilian population at large. If the "whole haystack" must be collected, then it becomes surely inevitable that some kind of impact will be felt among those within the haystack. Additionally, and closely linked to the declining half-life of secrecy, is the exposure of intelligence sources and methods more routinely. By moving from passive to ever more proactive gatherers of information, intelligence services pioneer methods in intrusion, exploitation, and analysis that proliferate.

This proliferation, which has ranged from code exploits such as EternalBlue, through to understanding of OSINT methodology and big data analytics, has been adopted and reverse engineered elsewhere. This includes innovations by adversary nations also pursuing their geopolitical ambitions, but also to large corporates, hacktivist groups, organized crime, journalistic bodies, and even technically capable individuals. The linkages behind the intelligence agency that (allegedly) developed Stuxnet attack to the recycled variant of the Flame virus unleashed widely, and the EternalBlue exploit compromise being used in both the WannaCry and NotPetya attacks, should not be underestimated.

With intelligence agency sources, methods, and tools now subjected to greater exposure than ever before, the final conclusion should not be surprising. That conclusion is that intelligence agency behavior is incentivized by traditional security perspectives, but that very pursuit is also strongly contributing to ever increased cyber insecurity, creating a new manifestation of the security dilemma in the 21st century. Kello's view that every advancement "invites its dangers" (Kello 2017: 256) and contributes to a dynamic of deceasing security accompanies not only advances in technology, but so too in the path of intelligence community behavior. Dunn Cavelty's observation that information operations blur not only the boundaries between civilian and military objectives, but those between war and peace itself (Dunn Cavelty 2008: 142), serve to illustrate the uncertainty and accompanying insecurity such activities bring. This is a point that Singer and Brooking also insist upon in stating that "*war and politics have never been so intertwined*" in an environment where all are participants, making us "*all part of the battle*" (Singer and Brooking 2019: 493–494, italics original).

The intelligence community, in their search for answers to the questions of how to remain relevant, operate within, and exploit cyberspace in pursuit of national security objectives, have become disproportionate influencers of norms in the international system. Georgiva is entirely correct in arguing that the intelligence community in their deployment of disruptive cyber tools have become "unexpected norm-setters" (Georgiva 2020), yet it must be realized that their behavior carries more significant consequences related to political fragmentation. These are all dynamics worthy of further scholarly attention, both from Intelligence Studies to better consider the impact of cyber security upon both the practice and study of intelligence, but also from international relations scholars too. For if a key geopolitical battleground of the 21st century is the fragmentation of cyber security politics, then the impact of intelligence actor behavior has already proven to be a dominant consideration for researchers. Through its actions to adapt to the digital age, the second oldest profession has disrupted the politics of cyber security in ways that carry great consequences to the geopolitics of the 21st century.

Acknowledgment

The author wishes to thank Dennis Broeders and the Cyber Norms Program at the University of Leiden. Their Visiting Fellowship Program I was fortunate enough to be part of was invaluable in the development of this chapter.

Note

1 Typically credited to Mitchell Kapor, but acknowledged as being without definitive source and a variation on a similar phrase from generations past. https://cyber.harvard.edu/archived_content/people/reagle/inet-quotations-19990709.html

References

All links checked on August 23, 2021.

Adams, J. (1994). *The New Spies: Exploring the Frontiers of Espionage*. London: Pimlico.

Andrew, C. (2018). *The Secret World: A History of Intelligence*. New Haven, CT: Yale University Press, Apple iBooks edition.

Andrew, C., and Dilkes, D. (eds). (1985). *The Missing Dimension: Governments and Intelligence Communities in the Twentieth Century*. Basingstoke: Macmillan.

Berners-Lee, T. (1991, August 6). Tim Posting to the Newsgroup alt.hypertext. Retrieved from: https://www.w3.org/People/Berners-Lee/1991/08/art-6484.txt.

Brantly, A. F. (2014). The Cyber Losers. *Democracy and Security*, 10(2): 132–155.

Broeders, D. (2016). The Secret in the Information Society. *Philosophy and Technology*, 29(3): 293–305.

Broeders, D., Boeke, S., and Georgiva, I. (2019). *Foreign Intelligence in the Digital Age: Navigating a State of 'Unpeace'*. Leiden: The Hague Program for Cyber Norms Policy Brief, September.

Buchanan, B. (2020). *The Hacker and the State: Cyber Attacks and the New Normal of Geopolitics*. Cambridge, MA: Harvard University Press, Apple iBooks edition.

Carlin, J. P. (2018). *Dawn of the Cold War: America's Battle against Russia, China, and the Rising Global Cyber Threat*. New York: Public Affairs, Apple iBooks edition.

Clemente, D. (2014). Cybersecurity. In R. Dover, M. S. Goodman, and C. Hillebrand (eds), *The Routledge Companion to Intelligence Studies*. Abingdon: Routledge, pp. 256–263.

Degaut, M. (2016). Spies and Policymakers: Intelligence in the Information Age. *Intelligence and National Security*, 34(1): 509–531.

Dunn Cavelty, M. (2008). *Cyber-Security and Threat Politics: US Efforts to Secure the Information Age*. Abingdon: Routledge.

Dunn Cavelty, M. (2018a). Aligning Security Needs for Order in Cyberspace. In H. W. Maull (ed.), *The Rise and Decline of the Post-Cold War International Order*. Oxford: Oxford University Press, pp. 104–119.

Dunn Cavelty, M. (2018b). Cybersecurity Research Meets Science and Technology Studies. *Politics and Governance*, 6(2): 22–30.

Farrell, H., and Newman, A. L. (2019). *Of Privacy and Power: The Transatlantic Struggle over Freedom and Security*. Princeton, NJ: Princeton University Press.

Friedman, J. A., and Zeckhauser, R. (2012). Assessing Uncertainty in Intelligence. *Intelligence and National Security*, 27(6): 824–847.

Georgiva, I. (2020). The Unexpected Norm-Setters: Intelligence Agencies in Cyberspace. *Contemporary Security Policy*, 41(1): 33–54.

Gill, P., and Phythian, M. (2018). *Intelligence in an Insecure World* (3rd ed.). Cambridge: Polity Press.

Griffiths, M., O'Callaghan, T., and Roach, S. C. (2002). *International Relations: The Key Concepts Second Edition*. Abingdon: Routledge.

Greenberg, A. (2019). *Sandworm*. New York: Doubleday, Apple iBooks edition.

Greenwald, G. (2014). *No Place to Hide: Edward Snowden, the NSA and the Surveillance State*. New York: Penguin Books, Apple iBooks edition.

Harding, L. (2014). *The Snowden Files: The Inside Story of the World's Most Wanted Man*. New York: Vintage Books, Apple iBooks edition.

Hayden, M. V. (2016). *Playing to the Edge: American Intelligence in the Age of Terror*. New York: Penguin, Apple iBooks edition.

Herrington, L. (2020). The New Frontier: Cyberespionage and Cyberwar. In C. Andrew, R. J. Aldrich, and W. K. Wark (eds), *Secret Intelligence: A Reader* (2nd ed.). Abingdon: Routledge, pp. 566–83.

Hughes Wilson, J. (2017). *The Secret State: A History of Intelligence and Espionage*. New York: Pegasus Books, Apple iBooks edition.

Inkster, N. (2016). *China's Cyber Power*. London: IISS.

Jervis, R. (2007). CooperationUnder the Security Dilemma. In B. Buzan and L. Hansen (eds). *International Security, Volume I: The Cold War and Nuclear Deterrence*. London: SAGE Publications.

Kaplan, F. (2017). *Dark Territory: The Secret History of Cyber War*. New York: Simon and Schuster, Apple iBooks edition.

Kello, L. (2017). *The Virtual Weapon and International Order*. London: Yale University Press.

Lin, H., and Zegart, A. (2018). Introduction. In H. Lin and A. Zegart (eds), *Bytes, Bombs and Spies: The Strategic Dimensions of Offensive Cyber Operations*. Washington, DC: Brookings Institution Press, pp. 1–17.

Lowenthal, M. M. (2018). *The Future of Intelligence*. Cambridge: Polity, Apple iBooks edition.

Lustgarten, L., and Leigh, I. (1994). *In from the Cold: National Security and Parliamentary Democracy*. Oxford: Clarendon Press.

MacAskill, E., Borger, J., Hopkins, N., Davies, N., and Ball, J. (2013, June 21). Mastering the Internet: How GCHQ Set Out to Spy on the World Wide Web. *The Guardian*. Retrieved from: https://www.theguardian.com/uk/2013/jun/21/gchq-mastering-the-internet.

Nakashima, E., and Warrick, J. (2013, July 14). For NSA Chief, Terrorist Threat Drives Passion to 'Collect it All'. *The Washington Post*. Retrieved September 16, 2018, from: https://www.washingtonpost.com/world/national-security/for-nsa-chief-terrorist-threat-drives-passion-to-collect-it-all/2013/07/14/3d26ef80-ea49-11e2-a301-ea5a8116d211_story.html?noredirect=onandutm_term=.3846af9dab73.

National Audit Office. (2018, April 25). Investigation: WannaCry Cyber Attack and the NHS, HC 414. Retrieved from: https://www.nao.org.uk/report/investigation-wannacry-cyber-attack-and-the-nhs/.

Obama, B. (2015, February 13). Remarks by the President at the Cybersecurity and Consumer Protection Summit. Retrieved from: https://obamawhitehouse.archives.gov/the-press-office/2015/02/13/remarks-president-cybersecurity-and-consumer-protection-summit.

Rid, T., and McBurney, P. (2012). Cyber-Weapons. *RUSI Journal*, 157(1): 6–13.

Sanger, D. E. (2018). *The Perfect Weapon: War, Sabotage, and Fear in the Cyber Age*. New York: Crown, Apple iBooks edition.

Schmitt, M. N. (ed.) (2017). *Tallinn Manual 2.0 on the International Law Applicable to Cyber Operations*. Cambridge: Cambridge University Press.

Schneier, B. (2018). *Click Here to Kill Everybody: Security and Survival in a Hyper-Connected World*. New York: W. W. Norton and Company, Apple iBooks edition.

Segal, A. (2016). *The Hacked World Order: How Nations Fight, Trade, Maneuver, and Manipulate in the Digital Age*. New York: Public Affairs, Apple iBooks edition.

Singer, P. W., and Brooking, E. T. (2019). *Like War: The Weaponisation of Social Media*. New York: Houghton Mifflin Harcourt, Apple iBooks edition.

Snowden, E. (2019). *Permanent Record*. New York: Macmillan, Apple iBooks edition.

Steed, D. (2019). *The Politics and Technology of Cyberspace*. Abingdon: Routledge.

Swire, P. (2015). The Declining Half-Life of Secrets and the Future of Signals Intelligence. *New America Cybersecurity Fellows Paper - Number 1*, July. Retrieved from: https://www.newamerica.org/cybersecurity-initiative/policy-papers/the-declining-half-life-of-secrets/.

Tucker, D. (2014). *The End of Intelligence: Espionage and State Power in the Information Age*. Stanford, CA: Stanford University Press.

Valeriano, B., Jensen, B., and Maness, R. C. (2018). *Cyber Strategy: The Evolving Character of Power and Coercion*. Oxford: Oxford University Press.

Van Puyvelde, D., and Brantly, A. F. (2019). *Cybersecurity: Politics, Governance and Conflict in Cyberspace*. Cambridge: Polity.

Whyte, C., and Mazanec, B. (2019). *Understanding Cyber Warfare: Politics, Policy, and Strategy*. Abingdon: Routledge.

15 Understanding transnational cyber attribution

Moving from "whodunit" to who did it

Brenden Kuerbis, Farzaneh Badiei, Karl Grindal, and Milton Mueller

Like the broader field of cyber security, cyber attribution is a socio-technical endeavor. Accordingly, we can expect that any transformation of cyber attribution will "be co-constituted by technological possibilities, political choices, and scientific practices" (Dunn Cavelty and Wenger 2020). This chapter examines some of the current practices of attribution, scientific developments in the field, and possibilities for its transnational institutionalization.[1]

First, we provide some background on the role of attribution in deterrence and accountability, and the challenges of attributing, particularly to nation-state actors. We then analyze attributions made from 2016 to 2018. We characterize the actors involved and types of attributions, finding a shift toward private actor attributions and mix of approaches by states. Next, we explore some technical advances in attribution. Better algorithmic-driven attribution, seemingly possible by the collection and analysis of numerous artifacts left on networks by threat actors, could certainly help push attribution forward although it raises issues of how state and non-state actors cooperate. We also look at attempts to understand behavioral aspects of attribution, exploring one game-theoretic attempt to model when states will or will not attribute an attack to another state, and use our dataset to explore certain predictions of the model. This exercise allows us to understand more clearly which state and non-state actors make or avoid making attributions, and the institutional conditions under which their agreement on attribution might occur.

In light of the above analysis, it is unlikely that attribution made by a nation-state (or even allied states) will be accepted as neutral and authoritative by another state, especially if those states are rivals or hostile. Given political fragmentation and socio-technical uncertainty around the current practice of attribution, we review proposed models for institutionalizing transnational attribution. The initial models offered have dramatically different structures and actor participation. Recognizing the shortcomings in them and the strategic use of attribution by states, a group of university-based and independent researchers are seeking to build independent, transnational attribution capabilities grounded in scientific method. Such a collective approach, if recognized, could address credibility

DOI: 10.4324/9781003110224-17

issues and result in more stable outcomes and ultimately help with accountability. We conclude with a brief agenda for future research.

The role of cyber attribution in deterrence and accountability

One can defend against a cyberattack, but without attribution, attackers lack a deterrent. At best, secure systems increase the time needed to find a vulnerability to a point beyond that which the attacker is willing to spend. Without proper incentives to restrain malicious attacker behavior, be they state or non-state, it's unreasonable to expect the present situation to change. As a deterrent, attribution has several advantages over other responses: Unlike strategies such as hack backs, it might not result in the militarization of the internet and it might even prevent it (Dunn Cavelty 2012).

Accurate attribution requires experienced threat intelligence and digital forensics experts. While governments and threat intelligence groups will attribute attacks to specific intrusion sets, sometimes even linking these to specific actors, there is no internationally recognized forensic process with an evidentiary based level of confidence. Rather, attribution is more often than not based on limited evidence and the reputation of the attributing entity. Considering that both attributing groups and attackers could be based anywhere in the world, without a recognized standardized and institutionalized process for attribution, can we expect a global coalition to implement sanctions or otherwise deter the attacker?

There is an important distinction between identifying intrusion sets and assigning them to an adversary or "threat group" on the one hand and linking this adversary with a known state or non-state actor on the other. Robert Lee refers to the latter as "true attribution" (Lee 2016). This two-part distinction can be compared to Herb Lin's model, developed in the article "Attribution of Malicious Cyber Incidents", which uses three levels of attribution: Machines, human operators, and the ultimate party responsible (Lin 2016). In Mandiant's 2013 attribution of an Advanced Persistent Threat (i.e., "APT-1") to the China PLA Unit 612398 all three levels of Lin's model are described (Wittes 2013). At the lowest level would be IP addresses associated with command and control (C&C) servers. Next, is attribution to a human operator; the Mandiant report identifies a persona who went by the alias "ugly gorilla", but associated this with the real person, Wang Dong. Ultimately though, the report is attributing APT-1 to China's People's Liberation Army and hence the Chinese state.

Defining an ultimate responsible party can be particularly challenging when it comes to state involvement. Even when a person is clearly identified as being in the attributed country, it is not necessarily clear from the forensics whether that person was a contractor or an employee, or whether they were operating under express instructions or on their own. Jason Healey's Spectrum of State Responsibility acknowledges that states employ hackers, contract out hacking, encourage hacking, or permit its use within their jurisdiction, each level representing a different degree of state responsibility (Healy 2013).

The challenge of attribution to nation-state actors

The practice of attribution can be cumulative, grouping information from incidents to create intrusion sets. Intrusion sets are adversarial behaviors, what is sometimes abbreviated as "tactics, techniques, and procedures (TTPs)", and technical resources with common properties from previous attacks that are grouped together (e.g., a "campaign") and associated with a common actor (e.g., a "threat group"). This process has some general standardization by convention and predictive success, but there is no one correct method. Accordingly, SANS in 2010 noted:

> There is no rule of thumb or objective threshold to inform when linked intrusions should become a campaign. The best measure is results: if a set of indicators effectively predict similar intrusions when observed in the future, then they have probably been selected properly.
>
> (Cloppert 2010)

This predictive modeling creates important questions about degrees of confidence, and how the practice of threat intelligence responds to novelty. Assuming an incident is correctly associated with an intrusion set, how is this intrusion set linked to a specific actor? Information like common language, activity during specific hours, the choice of targets, and level of complexity are often used to associate an incident group with a specific responsible threat actor. But this type of attribution extends beyond a purely technical association. The reuse of certain TTPs can complicate this attribution. For example, the vulnerability EternalBlue is reported to have been developed by the NSA, but was later exploited by Russia, North Korea, and Iran (Segal 2018).

Attribution conceptual frameworks help digital forensics to structure collected information and compare it to known intrusion sets. Examples of these include, the Diamond Model of Intrusion Analysis developed by Caltagirone and Pendergast (2013), and the "Q-model" developed by Rid and Buchanan (2015). Both the Diamond Model and Q-model acknowledge the need for a nontechnical dimension to attribution. In the Diamond Model, the nontechnical dimension is described by the relationship between the victim and adversary. The strategic dimension of the Q-Model is described as a "function of what is at stake politically" (Rid and Buchanan 2015).

While the political dimension of attribution might be quantified, it is necessarily relational, a product more of political science or intelligence studies than computer science. As sanctions or other disincentives are used to punish offensive cyber operations, we might expect cyber operations to adjust by taking steps to disguise their identity. The CIA's leaked Marble Framework, for example, has been described as providing the capability to change the language of the source code from English to another language like Russian or Farsi (Burgess 2017). Meanwhile, cyber tools invented by one country are being reused by another. This suggests a technical race between forensic experts and counter-forensic obfuscation. While obfuscation might serve powerful states well in the short term, it does little to mitigate the long-term damage of offensive cyberattacks. There is also the inequity of state attribution capability. This is said to have played a role in the breakdown of the UN Group of Governmental Experts on Developments in the Field of Information and Telecommunications in the Context of International Security (UN GGE) (Schmitt and Vihul 2017).

Attribution processes today

Our preliminary research has started to categorize the origin and characteristics of publicly attributed incidents. This work builds on the Council on Foreign Relations (CFR) dataset of state-sponsored cyber incident[2] (Segal and Grigsby 2018). Reviewing 82 incidents identified by CFR between 2016 and the first quarter of 2018 (Table 15.1), we coded each case, identifying whether states and/or private actors made a public attribution, as well as details related to the attribution,[3] including timing and outcome.

We understand that publicly disclosed incident databases can be criticized as being just the tip of the iceberg, and that two years of data based on a single dataset is not conclusive. However, this data, which has been supplemented with some of our own observations, is one of the most complete data sources available, and is superior to the anecdotal treatment attribution usually gets. Several interesting initial observations can be made. First, the vast majority of incidents, 70 (85%), resulted in some form of public attribution, with only 12 incidents (15%) not being attributed to a perpetrator. A small number of incidents, 7 (9%), included attributions involving both government(s) and private actor(s). These public attributions may have involved coordinated action between states (e.g., NotPetya) or states and non-state actors (e.g., WannaCry), or attributions published by non-state actors citing anonymous government sources, or what appeared to be separate attributions made independently by private actors and states (e.g., Democratic National Committee hacks).

Table 15.1 Incident attributions made by actor type

	Year			
Actor type	*2016*	*2017*	*2018 1Q*	*Grand Total*
No attribution made	6	5	1	12
Both government(s) and private actor(s)	4	3		7
Government(s)	7	7	1	15
Private actor(s)	12	26	10	48
Grand Total	**29**	**41**	**12**	**82**

Fifteen incidents (18%) were attributions made by government(s), including where identified government officials informally "named and shamed" alleged perpetrators, or formally accused them in official statements, reports, sanctions, or indictments. The largest number of attributions have been made by private actors, a category that includes threat intelligence organizations, network security companies and news media organizations. The importance of these actors in attribution is evident from the number of attributions made by them, which seems to be nearly doubling over the past three years. It also highlights the need for a standardized attribution process.

The incident data also allow important distinctions to be made. Table 15.2 shows attributions made to threat group(s) or state sponsor(s) by the actor type making the attribution. The total number of attributions made differs from the number of incidents (Table 15.1) as more than one entity may be implicated per incident by one or more actor type. Consistent with the incident observations above, private actors made substantially more attributions to both threat groups (31 versus 5) and state sponsors (38 versus 13) than governments. The majority of attributions made by government(s) were made to a state sponsor. These attributions included the United States and allied countries accusing Iran, Russia, and North Korea, as well as the United States implicating itself. As noted previously in Table 15.1, governments made attributions in 15 incidents. Table 15.2 shows that governments attributed those incidents to state sponsors 13 times. Governments (in this case, the United States) attributed an attack to a threat group five times; three of those times the attribution was to both a threat group (APT28, APT 29, Lazarus) *and* an alleged state sponsor (Russia, North Korea). Only twice did a government (in this case, Switzerland) not attribute to a state sponsor, but limited its accusation to a threat group (Turla) although a state sponsor was suspected. However, despite the appearance, a Chi-Square test concludes there is no significant difference between actor type (i.e., governments or private actors) with regard to whom (threat group or state sponsor) they attribute incidents. Neither actor type is more likely, or perhaps better suited, to make attributions to a threat group or state sponsor.

An evaluation of the collected attribution documents, namely Executive Orders (in the United States), criminal complaints, indictments, sanctions, and government statements, reveals that the United States' current attribution practice is possibly the most elaborate compared to other countries, using various attribution methods and judicial processes. Table 15.3 shows states use the judicial system and forensic

Table 15.2 Attributions made by actor type to actor type

Attribution made by (actor type)	*Incidents attributed to threat group*	*Incidents attributed to state sponsor*
Both government(s) and private actor(s)	4	7
Government(s)	5	13
Private actor(s)	31	38
Grand Total	**40**	**58**

Table 15.3 Attribution documents

	Year			
Document type	*2016*	*2017*	*2018 1Q*	*Grand Total*
Criminal complaint			1	1
Executive order	1			1
Indictment	1	2	2	5
Sanction	1		2	3
Statement		3	7	10
Media report	5	6	6	17
Press release	1	1		2
Technical report	14	30	11	55
Grand Total	**23**	**42**	**29**	**94**

technical evidence to carry out the attribution. All the collected indictments (5) are issued by the United States. The US government's approach is different from other countries when issuing official statements (such as White House Press Secretary announcements). It usually collaborates with the Department of Justice (DoJ); after the DoJ receives the indictment, the Office of Asset Control (OFAC) imposes sanctions on the indicted individuals (US Department of Treasury 2018). While other countries such as New Zealand, Australia, the United Kingdom, and Canada have special agencies that might get involved with attribution, the outcome of attribution is usually announced by government agencies and ministries and no national court is involved in charging the attackers.[4]

Various actors including the private sector and government agencies issue technical reports containing indicators of compromise or threat intelligence that attribute cyberattacks. These reports are more common than other forms of attribution documents. This might be due to the fact that issuing technical reports might be easier than going through complex and lengthy judicial processes and issuing alerts based on technical reports by government agencies might prevent further damage and stop the cyberattack from scaling.

The evolution of the US approach

Until recently, the US approach to attribution was as follows: The prosecutor gathered technical and circumstantial evidence about the identity of the adversary and as well as their direct or indirect links to the responsible state. Then the prosecutor would file an indictment against the alleged attacker(s) in the federal court, which grants indictments through the grand jury. This process was lengthy, and documents would not be unsealed until many months after the filing of the indictment. The grand jury would then issue the indictment and the Department of Justice would release a statement along with sanctions being imposed on the alleged attackers through OFAC.

Over time, US prosecutors' filings have become more complex, relying on more evidence to receive the indictment. However, a "complaint" was filed against the alleged perpetrator of WannaCry and not an indictment. A complaint is different in that it is not issued by a grand jury and the prosecutor can decide to file the complaint, naming the individual to be arrested. It should include an affidavit by a prosecutor or a law enforcement official familiar with the case (US Department of Justice 2014, 2018). The prosecutor in the criminal procedure decides to file a complaint if a crime is imminent and it proves "probable cause". After the arrest is made based on a criminal complaint, the federal prosecutor must secure an indictment (with a limited amount of time) to proceed with the felony charge(s).

In an indictment, a grand jury hears evidence and testimony from witnesses presented by the prosecution. It also has the power to subpoena witnesses. But grand jury proceedings are closed to the public and secret, the defense has no opportunity to present evidence or challenge the prosecution evidence. The probable cause standard is one of the lowest in criminal law; only enough evidence that convinces a reasonable person to believe that a crime has been committed must be established. Once an indictment is issued, there is a very small chance that it will be dismissed. Hence it provides higher certainty in the case of attribution that the charges are based on strong grounds.

Despite the procedural pitfalls of an indictment relative to a complaint, it is stronger and might be procedurally more just. The US Treasury's quick reaction to the conspiracy complaint that was filed against the WannaCry alleged attacker and North Korea and the imposition of immediate sanctions based on that and not an indictment reduces the procedural standards of attribution even further.

Other national approaches to attribution

Countries other than the United States also attribute cyberattacks to nation states, either by supporting another state's statement or action or by carrying out their own cyber attribution through their national cyber security agencies. New Zealand's National Cyber Security Center is a government center that has been involved with attribution, and its most common target of attribution is to states:

> The NCSC's most common form of attribution occurs when an incident is detected or discovered that contains indicators or technical artefacts previously associated with a state-sponsored actor. These indicators and artefacts come from numerous sources including the NCSC's own analysis and partner and open source reporting.
>
> (National Cyber Security Center of New Zealand 2016)

The UK's National Cyber Security Centre (NCSC) similarly gets involved with attributing cyber-attacks to states actors. It issues technical alerts in collaboration with other countries' government agencies, for example the US DHS and FBI in the case of NotPetya (UK National Cyber Security Centre 2018), as well as the assessment of whether a state actor has been involved with a cyberattack. The UK Foreign Office minister relies on those assessments to issue statements condemning such cyberattacks (UK Foreign Office 2018).

New developments in advancing attribution

Within the private sector and academia, research into attribution has advanced on technological and behavioral fronts. Promising technologies are emerging to significantly improve the forensic confidence in attribution. New areas of research include improved monitoring of infrastructure and application of machine learning to identify anomalous network traffic possibly indicative of adversaries (e.g., Radford et al. 2018). Our colleagues at Georgia Tech's Institute for Internet Security & Privacy are also investigating attribution as part of the Rhamnousia project (Toon 2016). The work is sponsored by the United States' Defense Advanced Research Project Agency's Enhanced Attribution program, which seeks to "develop technologies to associate the malicious actions of cyber adversaries to individual cyber operators and then to enable the government to reveal publicly the malicious actions of individual cyber operators without damaging sources and methods" (DARPA 2018). At a high level, the Rhamnousia project seeks to connect large sets of disparate data artifacts to fuel new algorithmic attribution methods that will expedite the process of attribution. As such, the process of conducting a cyberattack leaves numerous observable data artifacts on adversary-controlled and victims' networks, as well as on networks in-between. Data includes, but is not limited to, behavioral biometrics from user devices, network traffic, and intrusion detection logs, as well as Domain Name System (DNS) use and registrations (Keromytis 2016).

In some cases, this data can be used to help identify what are presumably nation-state adversaries. For instance, researchers at ETH Zurich were able to reliably determine C&C infrastructure used by APT campaigns by examining web query data (Lamprakis et al. 2017). Applying machine learning techniques to detect and cluster data observed across multiple networks and associate it with APT threat actors continues to advance (Ghafir et al. 2018; Rubio et al. 2020). As mentioned earlier in the case of APT-1, these technical data, when merged with other data like open source and other intelligence can be linked to adversary personas, real-world identities, and in some cases, responsible state entities. The above research efforts represent steady improvements that will continually evolve in response to changing adversarial tactics, and may increase the speed, confidence, and breadth of attribution. But these efforts also raise questions about data collection and sharing between private actors and/or governments, methodological transparency and reproducibility of analysis, effective public communication, and interaction with other legal and political attribution processes.

Behavioral understanding of when and how actors engage in public attribution of nation-state attacks is also advancing. Edwards et al. (2017) study the strategic aspects of attribution and blame in the context of cyber conflicts between attacking and victim states. They present a Bayesian game-theoretic model,[5] in which the decision to blame an attacker "depends on the vulnerability of the attacker, the knowledge level of the victim, payoffs for different outcomes, and the beliefs of each player about their opponent". In their model, vulnerability refers to an attacking state being technically susceptible to counterattack (e.g., in the case of states with low cyber capabilities, or large attack surface) or being in a tenuous geopolitical position, where it would be detrimental if a high-profile cyberattack that it conducted came to light (e.g., in the case of states with offensive capabilities). Knowledgeable victims are able to distinguish the type of its attacker (vulnerable or not) and have the requisite technical capability and understanding of the nature of the attack as well as geopolitical context to know whether blaming will hurt the attacker. Unknowledgeable victims cannot determine its adversary's type or convincingly attribute an attack.

While their analysis focuses on states, it draws several interesting conclusions which we relate to our dataset. First, Edwards et al. recognize it may be rational for a victim state to tolerate attacks rather than risk escalation through blaming (i.e., attribution), especially when attacks are mild, and no appropriate response is available. Citing the case of Chinese-sponsored economic espionage against US industry, they note the US government's inability to respond with in-kind attacks and refusal to blame China publicly given the importance of the countries' broader relationship, instead pursuing diplomacy resulting in the US–China 2015 cyber agreement (US White House 2015). While this strategy apparently worked initially, analysis suggests the underlying intergovernmental negotiation has been unsuccessful in stemming China's PLA-backed espionage (Segal et al. 2018).

Moreover, the USG did eventually also file an indictment, publicly attributing espionage activity to individuals affiliated with China's PLA (US Department of Justice 2014). So, it may be more precise to describe the strategy as one that evolves over time. Tolerance of attacks in the near-term may be explained by Edwards et al.'s logic, but restraint allows the opportunity for sufficient evidence to be marshaled. Perhaps more importantly, the substantially higher number of attributions made by private actors to state sponsors observed in our data suggests that the extent of state's use of the strategy may be dramatically understated. States may be knowingly refraining from blaming other states far more often and for more reasons than are evident.

Second, Edwards et al. "somewhat surprisingly" conclude that it is rarely beneficial for a victim to increase its own attribution capability. Why? They suggest that a non-vulnerable state will attack regardless of the victim's capability to blame. And if an attacking state is vulnerable, a knowledgeable victim's confidence in its ability to accurately attribute an attack will increase its incentive to counterattack. In both cases, the equilibrium outcome is unstable (i.e., attack, no blame). To the contrary, they argue the likelihood of stable equilibrium(s) (i.e., no attack; attack, blame) increases if both attackers and victims become knowledgeable through improved symmetric technical attribution capabilities. As explained below, the data illustrate the limited usefulness of individual attribution capability, and how collectively determined attribution methods and outcomes have evolved and arguably encourage restraint but also suffer from shortcomings as currently conceived.

A clear example of the former is Ukraine's public attribution of numerous incidents to Russia. Subject to so many attacks allegedly from Russia that Ukrainian officials have called their country "Russia's cyber-attack testing ground". The Ukrainian government "has managed to directly link Russia to most cyberattacks, citing the characteristics of the attacks and their timing; many occur on historically significant dates in Ukraine, or just before or during holidays, thus maximizing the effect" (Miller 2018). But, despite condemning Russia publicly for the alleged attacks in addition to substantial financial and other support from the United States and NATO to bolster its cyber security, attacks have persisted.

Another example is the Democratic National Committee incident. In December 2016, the White House and US Dept. of Treasury separately leveled sanctions against five Russian entities (including two Russian intelligence organizations) and six Russian individuals in response to attacks on the Democratic National Committee (Federal Register 2017). They were based in part on a technical report issued by the Dept. of Homeland Security and Federal Bureau of Investigation that provided many already reported indicators of compromise (e.g., IP addresses, domain names), as well as classified USG intelligence information (US Department of Homeland Security 2016; Office Director of National Intelligence 2017). There was no detail supporting attribution in the White House statement, and the DHS/FBI report was criticized by a former NSA security expert for failing to provide any evidence of attribution (Lee 2016). In short, the veracity of the attribution suffered, given the absence of publicly available evidence (or explicit linkages to evidence which had already been published by a threat intelligence company). Moreover, while the sanction and indictment processes clearly attributed alleged activities to individuals and organizations, questions remain as to their enforceability and effectiveness as a deterrent.

To the contrary, the WannaCry and NotPetya incidents were followed by attribution efforts coordinated between multiple allied states, and seemingly to a lesser degree, private actors. The coordination of public attribution among the states took place through various means. States that support other states' attribution results have been mainly subjected to the same cyberattack or are allies of the attributing and attacked countries.[6] Some states that have supported US attribution announcements clarify that they have done their own investigation. For example, in the case of WannaCry, New Zealand endorsed the US claims of attribution to the North Korean government, while relying on its own evidence.

The United Kingdom also assessed that WannaCry was carried out by North Korea, not directly mentioning the assessment of the United States but saying: "we are committed to strengthening coordinated international efforts to uphold a free, open, peaceful and secure cyberspace" (UK Foreign Office 2017). Multiple states also supported attribution of NotPetya to Russia, including Australia, Estonia, Ukraine, the United Kingdom, Denmark, Lithuania, Japan, and Canada. Again, the United Kingdom carried out its own investigations and condemned the attack (UK Foreign Office 2018). Canada was not attacked by NotPetya, but condemned the attack to show its support for other allies. Australia declared that

Russia was behind NotPetya, based on advice from its own intelligence agencies and consultations with the United States and the United Kingdom.[7]

The apparent success of these efforts was institutionalized, with a ministerial and communique expressing that the states "would coordinate on appropriate responses and attribution" (Department of Homeland Affairs Australian Government 2018). However, this agreement was only among the Five Eyes, which raises the question whether or not collective attributions made by those states will be accepted more broadly. Moreover, this initiative focuses on "coordinating technical attribution and operational response policies to mitigate significant cyber incidents" and does not discuss the attribution process.

Not all states are willing to participate in collective public attribution. Germany, one of the most affected countries by NotPetya, surprisingly did not join the collective action of states condemning Russia. Some relate Germany's inaction to its close ties to Russia or its lack of a capability to coordinate a response (Koch 2018). But it was clear that Germany was not willing to publicly attribute the attack. The European Union has also followed a similar approach and does not engage with public attribution. In response to a question from the Council of the European Union as to why it has not joined its allies to publicly attribute NotPetya to Russia, the Council said:

> In its conclusions on malicious cyber activities of 16 April 2018, the Council expressed the EU's serious concern about the increased ability and willingness of third states and non-state actors to pursue their objectives by undertaking malicious cyber activities, [...] It is not for the Council to comment on national governments' decisions, based on all-source intelligence, to publicly attribute cyber-attacks to a state actor.
>
> (Council of European Union 2018)

The European Union also in the conclusions on malicious cyber activities emphasized the importance of cyber norms.

Institutionalizing transnational attribution

Both technological developments and better understanding of how states act strategically highlight the need for institutionalizing neutral, transnational attribution. At some point, the evidence has to be assessed and independently reviewed, and that cannot be carried out through technological means alone. A decision to blame a responsible party has to take place through a recognized collective attribution process. Such a process has not been implemented, nor have current processes been studied in detail.

Proposals for institutionalizing transnational attribution

A transnational attribution institution could serve as a neutral global platform to evaluate and perform authoritative public attributions. It would be an independent entity or set of processes whose attribution decisions would aspire to be widely perceived as *unbiased*, *legitimate*, and *valid*, even among parties who might be antagonistic (such as rival nation-states). Various proposals have been put forward with different scopes of activity, organizational structures, levels of stakeholder involvement, and evidentiary standards to potentially achieve such a process. Four of the leading attribution proposals have markedly different descriptions. Microsoft describes their proposal as "a public-private forum to address attribution" (Charney 2016); the Atlantic Council called for a multilateral "attribution and adjudication council for cyber-attacks rising to the [legal] level of 'armed conflict'" (Healy et al. 2014); a RAND study called for a "Global Cyber Attribution Consortium" of non-state actors (Davies et al. 2017); a Russian think tank called for an "independent, international cyber court or arbitrage method that deals only with government-level cyber conflicts" (Chernenko et al. 2018). A more recent initiative builds on two of these proposals.

The International Attribution Organization proposed is one such proposal that has been widely touted in the Microsoft Digital Geneva Convention, and in its subsequent articulation (see Charney 2016, also Charney et al. 2016), This proposal included language that suggested that an independent attribution organization should (1) span the public and private sectors while including civil society and academia, (2) both investigate and serve an information sharing role, and (3) resemble the International Atomic Energy Agency (IAEA). The initial proposal contained significant ambiguity as to whether or not this is describing a multistakeholder or multilateral model.

The Atlantic Council's 2014 *Confidence Building Measures in Cyberspace* report proposes a multilateral "attribution and adjudication council for cyberattacks rising to the [legal] level of 'armed conflict'" (Healy et al. 2014). While the scope is only limited to incidents that rise above an international legal threshold, Healey et al. suggest that these assessments should result in the application of an enforcement mechanism. The organization, like the Digital Geneva Convention draws on the IAEA for inspiration, but also the Biological Weapons Convention and Nuclear Nonproliferation Treaty.

RAND's Stateless Attribution Report draws on both the Atlantic Council's and Microsoft's work, but suggests that "an attribution organization should be managed and operated independently from states". Their report also differs from the Atlantic Council report in suggesting that an enforcement role is not needed. While the RAND Report classifies the Atlantic Council proposal as including non-state actors in collaborative investigations, this seems to confuse organizational management and support. As the Atlantic Council's proposal makes use of private sector data and expertise as a multilateral entity, the RAND proposal does not explain how non-state actors would assist targeted states without their involvement.

The work by Chernenko et al. paper presents an interesting contrast to the IAEA model for attribution. While not denying the significance of private sector actors, the Chernenko et al. proposal is explicitly state based, recommending an "independent, international cyber court ... that deals only with government-level cyber conflicts" (Chernenko et al. 2018). This scoping is less expansive than the Microsoft proposal, but more inclusive than the Atlantic Council's, covering government-level cyber conflict which would include those below the threshold of armed conflict.

Each proposal offers different scopes of activity for a cyber attribution organization and pushes for dramatically different structures (e.g., multilateral vs. nongovernmental, or hierarchical vs. networked). And while the RAND Report makes powerful arguments as to why states have conflicting incentives to participate in an attribution organization and cautions against their membership in any Consortium, none of the above proposals explicitly consider the incentives for private actors to participate in the forensic process. The authors are tracking the aforementioned proposals and critiquing their viability, but believe more research is needed before a consensus can form.

Over the past two years, a handful of organizations, including the Internet Governance Project (with which the authors are affiliated) and Swiss-based ICT4Peace, have built upon the ideas presented in both Microsoft and RAND proposals. After socializing the idea of transnational, independent cyber attribution in fora like RightsCon, the UN Internet Governance Forum and the North American Network Operators Group, an initial workshop bringing together university-based and independent researchers took place in May 2020 (Internet Governance Project 2018). Together the workshop participants continue to develop a global network of researchers based in academia, civil society, and business who want to cooperate to develop attribution capabilities that are considered scientific and credible by the broader community. If successful, this could effectively counter state-sponsored or state-affiliated cyberattacks and the strategic use of attribution, and complement other efforts like the CyberPeace Institute (https://cyberpeaceinstitute.org/) to build and enforce cyber norms through accountability.

Challenges of collective action in attribution

Three major challenges are likely to present themselves in institutionalizing transnational attribution; these include geopolitical conflict, building independent capability, and private sector participation. These challenges overlap with, but are more institutional than, the challenges identified by the RAND study: Effective attribution and persuasive communication. Efficacy and communication will be contingent on the breadth of participation of public and private entities and their willingness to be transparent with the evidence. As with any political challenge, getting collective action from actors with competing interests presents a challenge.

Adversarial geopolitical relationships are likely to extend to any attribution organization. The advantage of such an organization is that by joining it participants agree to adhere to the constitutive as well as procedural rules, even when they disagree over the particulars. Neutrality of international bodies is often established through the professionalism of participants: Either a technical independence as described in the RAND study or a judicial independence might claim to embody this ethos. Should states as political actors be involved, as described by the Atlantic Council proposal, a majoritarian ethos might be needed to result in collective action. A consensus-based solution proposed in the Microsoft Digital Geneva Convention research could certainly face challenges acquiring unanimity.

In addition to the geopolitical challenges of managing an organization are those of creating trustworthy assessments. The Organization for the Prohibition of Chemical Weapons (OPCW) manages to maintain global trust in its forensics with an independent laboratory, whose work it supplements with a network of over 20 certified laboratories distributed across numerous national jurisdictions. While the same strategy might help to supplement the capability of an attribution-based organization, building this capability will require financial resources. Finding dedicated financial resources for transnational attribution might create its own challenges. Would a government finance an organization tasked with rooting out its espionage operations, what incentives are there for the private sector, particularly those who sell services to multiple governments?

The cyberspace domain is uniquely defined by private sector participation and ownership of the core infrastructure. In this respect, Microsoft's Digital Geneva Convention is served well by including the private sector but creates a potential contradiction by drawing on the example of the International Atomic Energy Agency. It is possible to imagine an independent, member state-funded international organization, like that of the IAEA. Or by empowering the private sector, academia, and civil society is Microsoft suggesting a multistakeholder model? At face value, it appears that governments will set the rules, while private actors will lend their services and data, but nothing is stated about how these interests might be aligned. If a subset of private sector cyber security firms has advanced forensic capability equaling or exceeding that of most states, why would they participate in a monopsony attribution organization? Presumably, benefits to them would need to outweigh costs. Alternatively, if access to the internet's infrastructure allows an investigation to backtrack the origins of an attacker, what process should enable the acquisition of relevant evidence? Should this layer of attribution include partnerships with national law enforcement or permit international inspections? Either way, this potentially burdens the private sector and has implications for global privacy.

Conclusion

This chapter has briefly described the state of play in cyber attribution and number of competing visions for its future. At present, threat intelligence firms and national security agencies are the primary producers of forensic data and attributions. While reliance on algorithms to cluster observed data and identify infrastructure and adversaries is advancing this introduces socio-technical uncertainties around how data is collected, shared, and analyzed. Coupled with political fragmentation and strategic behavior by states there is need to focus on the institutionalization of credible, independent attribution. While ideal models for making attribution were described, too little is known about the current state of affairs.

As Edwards et al. (2017) suggest, understanding behavior in attribution clearly needs to incorporate the role and incentives of private actors. A research agenda going forward should attempt to better understand the practice of attribution and provide novel institutional designs and processes grounded in scientific method that go beyond merely replicating international organization approaches in other fields. To achieve this further exploration is needed around research questions like:

- How does the public and state response to attribution differ based on whether the forensic assessment comes from the private sector, state intelligence, law enforcement, or secondhand media reporting?
- How can scientific concepts and practices of empirical data and methodological transparency, reproducibility, and falsifiability be incorporated into and improve the practice of attribution?
- What data and methods are used in attribution to threat actors and ultimately to responsible parties?
    - When it comes to findings, are there different accepted levels of confidence?
    - How do geopolitical rivalries undermine the confidence placed in attribution?
- Is a hierarchically organized institution really needed to align participant incentives, or can a more loosely organized form of networked governance suffice?
- How would different visions for attribution address the concerns and incentives of stakeholders, distribute costs, and get off the ground?

Future work should continue to seek a better understanding of how governance models, including an independent network of researchers based in academia, civil society, and business might help resolve the issues flagged above so that responsible parties can be held accountable. Despite the capacity of advanced and persistent threat actors, the need to protect intelligence sources and methods, and conflicting nationalistic approaches we believe that movement toward transnational, independent, credible attributions to "who did it" is possible.

Notes

1. This chapter is based in part on an earlier work by the authors, "Cyber Attribution: Can a New Institution Achieve Transnational Credibility?", *Cyber Defense Review*, 4(1), 2019.
2. The Council on Foreign Relations is not the only entity collecting and publishing cyber incident data. Another example is the Dyadic Cyber Incident and Dispute Dataset by Valeriano and Maness (2015), as well as incident data collected by the New America Foundation. Methodological questions can be raised where differences occur between these datasets, e.g., in what is considered a state-sponsored "incident", or an attribution to a specific perpetrator.
3. For example, we have linked technical reports published for each incident from the APT Notes repository available at https://github.com/aptnotes/data/blob/master/APTnotes.csv

4 Other countries make statements and announcements through their cyber security centers or foreign ministries. See, e.g., Canada's announcement condemning NotPetya (Communications Security Establishment 2018) and UK's Foreign Office announcement on WannaCry (UK Foreign Office 2017). One factor that might explain the difference in approach between the United States and the rest of the world is that the United States is mainly the main target of the attacks while others might indirectly suffer.

5 A game in which the players have incomplete information on the other players (e.g. on their available strategies or payoffs), but, they have beliefs with known probability distribution.

6 For example, Estonia and Canada condemned cyberattacks that did not harm their countries; see Estonian Ministry of Foreign Affairs (2018).

7 "Based on advice from Australian intelligence agencies, and through consultation with the United States and United Kingdom, the Australian Government has judged that Russian state sponsored actors were responsible for the incident". Statement by Minister of Law Enforcement and Cyber security (no longer available online).

References

All links checked on August 23, 2021.

Burgess, M. (2017, May 7). WikiLeaks Drops 'Grasshopper' Documents, Part Four of Its CIA Vault 7 Files. *Wired*. Retrieved from: https://www.wired.co.uk/article/cia-files-wikileaks-vault-7.

Caltagirone, S., Pendergast, A., and Betz, C. (2013). The Diamond Model of Intrusion Analysis. Working Paper. Retrieved from: https://www.activeresponse.org/wp-content/uploads/2013/07/diamond.pdf.

Charney, S. (2016, June 23). Cyber Security Norms for Nation-States and the Global ICT Industry. *Microsoft on the Issues* (Blog). Retrieved from: https://blogs.microsoft.com/on-the-issues/2016/06/23/cyber security-norms-nation-states-global-ict-industry/.

Charney, S., English, E., Kleiner, A., Malisevic, N., McKay, A., Neutze, J., and Nicholas, P. (2016). From Articulation to Implementation: Enabling Progress on Cyber Security Norms. Microsoft Corporation Working Paper, June. Retrieved from: https://query.prod.cms.rt.microsoft.com/cms/api/am/binary/REVmc8.

Chernenko, E., Demidov, O., and Lukyanov, F. (2018, February 23). Increasing International Cooperation in Cyber Security and Adapting Cyber Norms. Council on Foreign Relations (Blog). Retrieved from: https://www.cfr.org/report/increasing-international-cooperation-cybersecurity-and-adapting-cyber-norms.

Cloppert, M. (2010, June 21). Security Intelligence, Defining APT Campaigns. *SANS* (Blog). Retrieved from: https://www.sans.org/blog/security-intelligence-defining-apt-campaigns/.

Communications Security Establishment [CSE]. (2018, February 15). CSE Statement on NotPetya Malware. Retrieved from: https://www.cse-cst.gc.ca/en/media/2018-02-15.

Council of European Union. (2018, April 16). Council Conclusions on Malicious Cyber Activities – Approval. Retrieved from: https://data.consilium.europa.eu/doc/document/ST-7925-2018-INIT/en/pdf.

Davis II, J. S., Boudreaux, B., Welburn, J. W., Aguirre, J., Ogletree, C., McGovern, G., and Chase, M. S. (2017). *Stateless Attribution*. Santa Monica: RAND Corporation.

Defense Advanced Research Project Agency [DARPA]. (2018). Department of Defense Fiscal Year (FY) 2018 Budget Estimates. Retrieved from: https://www.darpa.mil/attachments/DARPA_FY18_Presidents_Budget_Request.pdf.

Department of Homeland Affairs Australian Government. (2018). Five Country Ministerial 2018 Official Communiqué. Retrieved from: https://www.homeaffairs.gov.au/about-us/our-portfolios/national-security/security-coordination/five-country-ministerial-2018.

Dunn Cavelty, M. (2012). Militarizing Cyberspace: Why Less may Be Better. In C. Czosseck, R. Ottis, and K. Ziolkowski (eds), *Proceedings of the 4th International Conference on Cyber Conflict*. Tallinn: NATO CCD COE Publications, pp. 141–153.

Dunn Cavelty, M., and Wenger, A. (2020). Cyber Security Meets Security Politics: Complex Technology, Fragmented Politics, and Networked Science. *Contemporary Security Policy*, 41(1): 5–32.

Edwards, B., Furnas, A., Forrest, S., and Axelrod, R. (2017). Strategic Aspects of Cyberattack, Attribution, and Blame. *Proceedings of the National Academy of Sciences of the United States of America*, 114(11): 2825–2830.

Estonian Ministry of Foreign Affairs. (2018, February 19). Estonia Foreign Minister Condemns NotPetya Attacks against the Ukraine. Retrieved from: https://vm.ee/en/news/foreign-minister-mikser-condemns-russia-notpetya-attacks-against-ukraine.

Federal Register: The Daily Journal of the United States. (2017). Taking Additional Steps to Address the National Emergency with Respect to Significant Malicious Cyber Enabled Activities, Executive Order 13757 of December 28, 2016.

Ghafir, I., Hammoudeh, M., Prenosil, V., Han, L., Hegarty, R., Rabie, K., & Aparicio-Navarro, F. J. (2018). Detection of Advanced Persistent Threat Using Machine-Learning Correlation Analysis. *Future Generation Computer Systems*, 89: 349–359.

Healey, J. (ed.). (2013). *A Fierce Domain: Conflict in Cyberspace, 1986 to 2012*. Vienna, VA: Cyber Conflict Studies Association.

Healey, J., Mallery, J. C., Jordan, K. T., and Youd, N. V. (2014). *Confidence-Building Measures in Cyberspace: A Multistakeholder Approach for Stability and Security*. Report. Washington, DC: Atlantic Council. Retrieved from: https://www.atlanticcouncil.org/in-depth-research-reports/report/confidence-building-measures-in-cyberspace-a-multistakeholder-approach-for-stability-and-security/.

Internet Governance Project. (2018, April 13). Defusing the Cyber Security Dilemma Game through Attribution and Network Monitoring. Retrieved from: https://www.internetgovernance.org/2018/04/13/defusing-cybersecurity-dilemma-game-attribution-network-monitoring//.

Internet Governance Project. (2020, June 15). Workshop Synopsis: Building Transnational Attribution (Day 1). Retrieved from: https://www.internetgovernance.org/2020/06/15/workshop-synopsis-building-transnational-attribution-day-1/.

Keromytis, A. (2016, April 25). Enhanced Attribution, Proposers Day Briefing. DARPA. Retrieved from: https://www.enisa.europa.eu/events/cti-eu-event/cti-eu-event-presentations/enhanced-attribution/.

Koch, M. (2018, February 22). Germany is Just Fine with the NotPetya Cyberattack but Its Allies Aren't. *Handelsblatt*. Retrieved from: https://www.handelsblatt.com/english/politics/state-secrets-germany-is-just-fine-with-the-notpetya-cyberattack-but-its-allies-arent/23581222.html.

Lamprakis, P., Dargenio, R., Gugelmann, D., Lenders, V., Happe, M., and Vanbever, L. (2017). Unsupervised Detection of APT C&C Channels Using Web Request Graphs. In M. Polychronakis and M. Meier (eds), *Detection of Intrusions and Malware, and Vulnerability Assessment. DIMVA 2017. Lecture Notes in Computer Science, vol 1032*. Cham: Springer, pp. 366–387.

Lee, R. (2016, March 4). The Problems with Seeking and Avoiding True Attribution to Cyber Attacks. *SANS DFIR* (Blog). Retrieved from: https://www.sans.org/blog/the-problems-with-seeking-and-avoiding-true-attribution-to-cyber-attacks/.

Lin, H. (2016, September 2). Attribution of Malicious Cyber Incidents: From Soup to Nuts. *SSRN Scholarly Paper*. Retrieved from: https://papers.ssrn.com/abstract=2835719.

Miller, C. (2018). What's Ukraine Doing to Combat Russian Cyberwarfare? "Not Enough." Radio Free Europe/Radio Liberty. Retrieved August 21 2020, from https://www.rferl.org/a/ukraine-struggles-cyberdefense-russia-expands-testing-ground/29085277.html.

National Cybersecurity Center of New Zealand. (2016). *Unclassified Cyber Threat Report*. Retrieved from: https://www.ncsc.govt.nz/assets/NCSC-Documents/NCSC-2016-17-Unclassified-Cyber-Threat-Report.pdf

Office of the Director of National Intelligence, United States Government. (2017). Background to "Assessing Russian Activities and Intentions in Recent US Elections": The Analytic Process and Cyber Incident Attribution. Retrieved from: https://www.dni.gov/files/documents/ICA_2017_01.pdf.

Radford, B. J., Apolonio, L. M., Trias, A. J., and Simpson, J. A. (2018). Network Traffic Anomaly Detection Using Recurrent Neural Networks. Prepared for the 2017 National Symposium on Sensor and Data Fusion. Retrieved from: http://arxiv.org/abs/1803.10769.

Rid, T., and Buchanan, B. (2015). Attributing Cyber Attacks. *Journal of Strategic Studies*, 38(1–2): 4–37.

Rubio, J. E., Alcaraz, C., Rios, R., Roman, R., and Lopez, J. (2020). Distributed Detection of APTs: Consensus vs. Clustering. In *European Symposium on Research in Computer Security*. Cham: Springer, pp. 174–192.

Schmitt, M., and Vihul, L. (2017, June 30). International Cyber Law Politicized: The UN GGE's Failure to Advance Cyber Norms. *Just Security*. Retrieved from: https://www.justsecurity.org/42768/international-cyber law-politicized-gges-failure-advance-cyber norms/.

Segal, A. (2018, June 19). The Theft and Reuse of Advanced Offensive Cyber Weapons Pose a Growing Threat. Council on Foreign Relations (Blog). Retrieved from: https://www.cfr.org/blog/theft-and-reuse-advanced-offensive-cyber weapons-pose-growing-threat.

Segal, A., and Grigsby, A. (2018, April 23). New Entries in the CFR Cyber Operations Tracker: Q1 2018. Council on Foreign Relations (Blog). Retrieved from: https://www.cfr.org/blog/new-entries-cfr-cyber operations-tracker-q1-2018.

Segal, A., Hoffman, S., Hanson, F., and Uren, T. (2018, September 25). Hacking for ca$h: Is China Still Stealing Western IP? Australian Strategic Policy Institute. Retrieved from: https://s3-ap-southeast-2.amazonaws.com/ad-aspi/2018-09/Hacking%20for%20cash_0.pdf?FHTEXSif5qZDfwPoxnAAhTliEw45dMR1.

Toon, J. (2016, November 29). $17 Million Contract Will Help Establish Science of Cyber Attribution. Georgia Tech Research, *Horizons* (Blog). Retrieved from: http://www.rh.gatech.edu/news/584327/17-million-contract-will-help-establish-science-cyber attribution.

UK Foreign Office. (2017, December 19). Foreign Office Minister Condemns North Korean Actor for WannaCry Attacks. Retrieved from: https://www.gov.uk/government/news/foreign-office-minister-condemns-north-korean-actor-for-wannacry-attacks.

UK Foreign Office. (2018, February 15). Foreign Office Minister Condemns Russia for NotPetya Attacks. Retrieved from: https://www.gov.uk/government/news/foreign-office-minister-condemns-russia-for-notpetya-attacks.

UK National Cyber Security Center. (2018, April 16). Russian Sponsored Cyber Actors Targeting Network Infrastructure Devices. Retrieved from: https://www.ncsc.gov.uk /news/russian-state-sponsored-cyber actors-targeting-network-infrastructure-devices.

US Department of Homeland Security. (2016, December 29). GRIZZLY STEPPE – Russian Malicious Cyber Activity (JAR-16-20296A). Retrieved from: https://us-cert .cisa.gov/sites/default/files/publications/JAR_16-20296A_GRIZZLY%20STEPPE -2016-1229.pdf.

US Department of Justice. (2014, May 19). U.S. Charges Five Chinese Military Hackers for Cyber Espionage against U.S. Corporations and a Labor Organization for Commercial Advantage. Retrieved from: https://www.justice.gov/opa/pr/us-charges-five-chinese -military-hackers-cyber-espionage-against-us-corporations-and-labor.

US Department of Justice. (2018). Criminal Procedures. Retrieved August 1, 2018, from: https://www.justice.gov/usao-mn/criminal-procedures.

US Department of Treasury. (2018, September 6). Treasury Targets North Korea for Multiple Cyber Attacks. Retrieved from: https://home.treasury.gov/news/press-releases /sm473.

US White House. (2015, September 25). FACT SHEET: President Xi Jinping's State Visit to the United States. Retrieved from: https://obamawhitehouse.archives.gov/the-press -office/2015/09/25/fact-sheet-president-xi-jinpings-state-visit-united-states.

Valeriano, B., and Maness, R. C. (2015). *Cyber War versus Cyber Realities: Cyber Conflict in the International System*. Oxford: Oxford University Press.

Wittes, B. (2013, February 20). Mandiant Report on 'APT1'. Lawfare (Blog). Retrieved from: https://www.lawfareblog.com/mandiant-report-apt1.

16 Conclusion

The ambiguity of cyber security politics in the context of multidimensional uncertainty

Andreas Wenger and Myriam Dunn Cavelty

In a world of rapid socio-technical transformation and increasing fragmentation of political power and authority, cyber security has firmly established itself as one of the top national security issues of the 21st century. Managing cyber insecurities will most likely further increase in complexity and political significance in the next decade, co-produced by an acceleration of the ongoing socio-technical transformations, on the one hand, and the changing dynamics of the related political responses, on the other. The first part of the book recorded the ongoing geographic expansion of cyberspace into outer space, anticipated how emerging technologies will increase the interconnectedness of infrastructures and services, and projected how in a context of ever tighter coupled and integrated socio-technical systems cyber threat narratives will inevitably expand to more policy fields at both the national and international levels. The second part of the book discussed how in cyberspace state actors need to find the right balance between restraint and exploitation, why they need to uphold their efforts to control the risk of escalation, and why governments increasingly share responsibility with actors from economy and society.

The current state of cyber security politics is very much a reflection of the interplay between the underlying forces of great power competition and the dynamics of socio-technical and socio-economic globalization processes. From the interplay of these two processes emerge the two key factors – multidimensional uncertainty and socio-political ambiguity – that characterize the current context of cyber security politics at both the national and international levels, as highlighted in Figure 16.1. Multidimensional uncertainty plays a key role in the emergence of cyber insecurity as a wicked problem and shapes – and is shaped by – the ambiguity of cyber security politics.

The ambiguity of cyber security politics encompasses the two dimensions of cyber security outlined in the introductory chapter (Dunn Cavelty and Wenger 2022): First, the international dimension of cyber *security politics* concentrates on how state actors shape and use cyberspace in accordance with their strategic goals, while at the same time struggling to uphold the stability of their strategic relationships. In Figure 16.1, the interactive search for an acceptable balance between

DOI: 10.4324/9781003110224-18

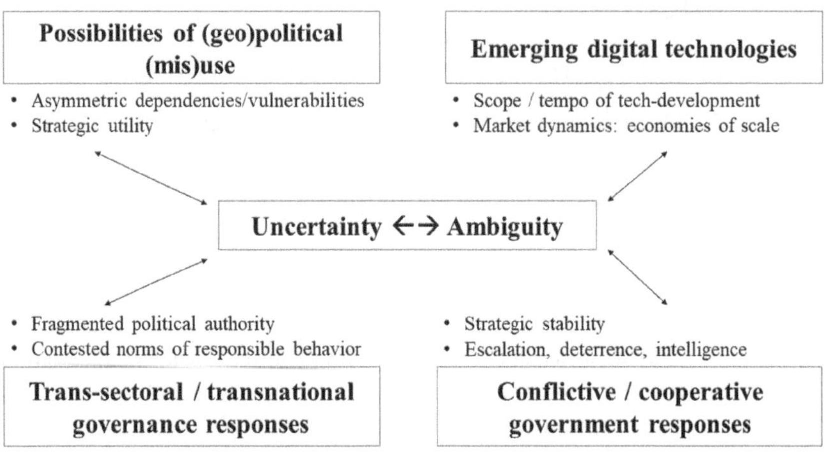

Figure 16.1 The dimensions of cyber security.

the strategic utility of and the strategic stability in cyberspace is represented in the upper left (possibilities of (geo)political (mis)use) and lower right (conflictive / cooperative government responses) corners. Second, the broader dimension of cyber security *politics* focuses on how state, industry, and societies negotiate their respective roles in governing cyberspace, while at the same time competing in the tech innovation process that affects the continued transformation of cyberspace. In Figure 16.1, the interactive search for norms of responsible behavior in an uncertain and ambiguous socio-technical and sociopolitical context is represented in the lower left (fragmented trans-sectoral/transnational governance responses) and upper right (emerging digital technologies) corners.

This concluding chapter, building on the individual contributions to this book, highlights four key debates that together encapsulate the complexities and paradoxes of the current thinking about the future of cyber security politics from a Western perspective. The first section asks how much political influence states can achieve via cyber operations and what context factors condition the (limited) strategic utility of such operations. A second section discusses the role of emerging digital technologies in cyber security politics and notes how the dynamics of the tech innovation process reinforce the fragmentation of the governance space around them. A third section asks how states attempt to uphold stability in cyberspace, and in their strategic relations more general, highlighting three interconnected challenges – escalation, deterrence, and intelligence – of this interactive quest. A fourth and final section focuses on the shared responsibility of state, economy, and society for cyber security and calls attention to the continuing re-negotiation processes about their respective roles in an increasingly trans-sectoral and transnational governance space.

The strategic utility of cyber operations

The debate about the strategic utility of cyber operations arises in a context characterized by the interplay between the rapid emergence of new digital technologies and the politics of their use and misuse. Over time, the debate evolved considerably, as cyber security issues transformed from a technical risk management issue discussed by a limited circle of experts into a key challenge of national security debated at the highest level of governments (Dunn Cavelty 2008; Dewar 2018). In its early stages, the debate focused on "doomsday" cyberattack scenarios that centered on the strategic exploitation of increasingly interconnected and vulnerable infrastructures (Clarke and Knake 2010). As out-of-the-blue cyber war failed to make its expected appearance, experts began to shift their attention to the political and strategic implications of low-level cyber conflict (Baezner 2018; see also Rid 2012; Lindsay 2014/15), on the one hand, and to the increase of computer network attack campaigns linked to covert state involvement (Dunn Cavelty 2015), on the other.

At the current point in time in the history of cyber security politics the empirical picture is characterized by "dogs that did not bark" at the high end of conflict and persistent cyber operations and instability at the low end of conflict (Schulze 2020; Harknett and Smeets 2020; Lupovici 2021). Within this context, the chapters in this volume point to three interconnected aspects of the enduring debate about the strategic utility of cyber operations: A first subsection concentrates on the difficulty of achieving a controlled strategic effect under multidimensional uncertainty. The focus here is on explaining why most cyber operations so far seem not very escalatory and appear unlikely to result in visible changes in the existing balance of power between great powers. A second subsection focuses on the utility of cyber operations as a tool of subversion and mild sabotage. Here the focus is on understanding how the ambiguity of involved actors and the opaqueness of cyber operations can be manipulated in specific strategic contexts by some powers for asymmetric influence. A third subsection deals with the assumed asymmetrical vulnerability of democracies to disinformation as the latest cyber threat focus in Western (security) politics. Here the debate centers on the question if a strategic effect can be achieved via cyber influence operations that aim at undermining social cohesion and trust in democratic political institutions.

The difficulty of achieving a controlled strategic effect under multidimensional uncertainty

Several chapters in this volume engage with the notion that cyber operations are of limited strategic utility in terms of transforming the balance of economic and military power at the level of interstate relations or, more specifically, in terms of an adversary changing its rival's political goals (Gomez and Whyte 2022; Baezner and Cordey 2022). The authors do not explicitly dispute the conclusion of the strategic studies literature that a strategic impact of cyber operations might be elusive (Smeets 2018; Borghard and Lonergan 2017: 477; Kostyuk and Zhukov 2017;

Valeriano and Maness 2015: 183; Gartzke 2013). Yet they are concerned, albeit for different reasons, that the insights of this literature might translate into policies that underestimate the escalatory risk of persistent engagement and defend forward (see also Devanny 2021; Healey and Jervis 2020; Healey 2019; Cavaiola et al. 2015). We will come back to the problem of upholding strategic stability under multidimensional uncertainty below.

Operating strategically in cyberspace, so much seems to be clear, is far more technically and operationally demanding than the "cheap and easy" metaphor suggests (Lindsay 2013; Slayton 2017; Lewis 2018). "Causing a specific, targeted cyber effect, at a designated point in time, which achieves a strategic purpose, and outweighs the impact of negative consequences, is hard", Max Smeets notes in a forthcoming book (Smeets forthcoming). Resources constrain the overall utility expected from cyber operations. This is a point reinforced by the economic logic of cyber influence, as Jon R. Lindsay has argued (Lindsay 2017). He holds that setting up cyber exploitations is generally more expensive than countering them, which increases the incentive to keep the target at risk over longer periods of time, turning cyber conflict into primarily an intelligence game (cf. Chesney and Smeets forthcoming; Chesney and Smeets 2020; Rovner 2019). These technical, organizational, and economic challenges all reflect the structural features of cyberspace.

Achieving a controlled strategic impact via cyber operations is challenging because cyberspace as an operating environment is characterized by multidimensional uncertainty and sociopolitical ambiguity. On the one hand, cyberspace is marked by a high degree of interconnectedness. This very feature makes it very difficult to fully control the strategic effects of cyber operations, since some unintended side-effects in the sense of collateral damage beyond the intended target seem almost unavoidable (Smeets 2018). On the other hand, cyberspace is characterized by constant political contestation. This makes it very difficult to achieve a stable political outcome in which an adversary changes their political goals. According to the same logic, attribution of cyber operations to specific political actors remains time-consuming and often inconclusive (Rid and Buchanan 2015). Neither states nor cyber intelligence firms have enough of an incentive to fully share the data, methods, and tools behind their attribution claims (Egloff 2020a, Egloff and Wenger 2019). As a consequence, many attribution processes lack transparency and credibility, making it difficult to build broad and stable political support for response strategies based on inherently contested attribution claims (Egloff and Dunn Cavelty 2021).

In the context of political competition, cyber operations lack strategic utility as a stand-alone tool to gain an enduring political or military advantage. In actual practice, however, they are linked to and integrated with a broad range of other foreign and security policy instruments. The covert nature of cyber operations means that elites use them as instruments that signal resolve while minimizing escalation risks (Poznansky and Perkoski 2018). The second subsection turns to the question how certain actors attempt to manipulate cyber operations in certain strategic contexts for limited asymmetric influence.

The power to subvert: manipulating "gray zones" while minimizing the risk of escalation

Most cyber operations take place below the threshold of war, Marie Baezner and Sean Cordey (2022) note in their chapter. Mapping the practical use of such operations in a series of cyber conflict case studies, they confirm that especially influence operations fall into a zone which goes beyond conventional diplomacy and stops short of conventional war, which Lucas Kello describes as "unpeace" (Kello 2017). Taking this empirical puzzle as a starting point for their analysis, the chapter asks why some actors see such operations as attractive and efficient tools of power projection and influence. The (limited) strategic utility of cyber (influence) operations, the two authors conclude, depends on the characteristics of the strategic context and the operational environment in which they are employed and on the nature of the strategic actor employing such operations.

At a strategic level, the increasingly pervasive use of cyber (influence) operations in international affairs reflects the current dynamics of great power competition. Together, the increasing costs of conventional war and the realities of economic interdependence create incentives, especially for great powers, to gain asymmetric influence through cyber operations, in particular in their spheres of interest, without however unduly undermining the strategic stability of great power relations. At an operational level, the use of cyber influence operations reflects an operational environment that is characterized by legal ambiguity and political contestation, opacity of the parties involved and blurred boundaries between the private and public domains. Referring to the concept of and literature on "gray zones", Baezner and Cordey argue that revisionist powers use cyber operations as tools to operate below the threshold of armed combat to gain an asymmetric advantage in their relationship with other political actors, especially in view of the global (military) dominance of the United States.

Based on a series of case studies, Baezner and Cordey note that the following operational assumptions about cyber (influence) operations seem to make them attractive tools for many to intervene in gray zone conflicts. First, the majority of the cyber technologies used in such contexts are widely available at relatively low cost. Patriotic hackers or opaque criminal groups with ties to domestic or foreign elites use them opportunistically for disruption and mild sabotage rather than for destruction. Second, cyber espionage and influence operations are increasingly used to influence the information environment of a conflict and gain an asymmetric advantage. They work in tandem with a wider set of economic, political, and military coercive tools. Third, the legal uncertainty surrounding intelligence operations allows state actors to avoid formal condemnation and uphold a posture of plausible deniability. The opaqueness of actors and operations makes it unlikely that a verdict of attribution would be as transparent and credible as to justify a military response.

The importance of the strategic context and the nature of the strategic actor employing cyber (influence) operations are confirmed by Aaron Brantly (2022) in his chapter on Ukraine. He analyzes Ukraine as a case of how to confront a larger aggressive adversary employing cyber and information warfare in its considered sphere of influence at a time of extreme domestic vulnerability amid violent regime change. Before the 2014 Euromaidan revolution, widespread rent-seeking behavior of criminal–political patronage networks and extensive penetration of Ukraine's state structures by Russia's intelligence service made Ukraine vulnerable to foreign cyber and influence operations. The revolution reversed Ukraine's foreign policy alignment from Russia to the West and began a slow process of domestic legal, organizational, and policy transformation that however remains contested by entrenched elites. Both the relative success of Russia's cyber and information warfare as well as the relative success of Ukraine's response to Russian cyberattacks and disinformation campaigns, Brantly notes, must be assessed in the context of broader patterns of domestic political contestation, on the one hand, and the countries' international orientation and dependence, on the other.

Cyber operations in "gray zone" strategic contexts should be conceptualized less as a means of warfare and more appropriately as a tool of political power projection, Marie Baezner and Sean Cordey conclude. The two authors see such operations as both a novel, efficient and effective tool for disruption (and, to a lesser extent, sabotage) and an "enhancer and transformer" of traditional espionage and covert intelligence operations (Baezner and Cordey 2022: 25). Although their strategic utility will remain elusive, they argue, actors operating in the "gray zones" of modern conflict will likely continue to invest into cyber operations and use them in order to gain an asymmetric advantage. Yet the widely shared assumption that cyber (influence) operations carry a limited risk of escalation might be misplaced and should be reconsidered, the two authors argue. As long as there is a lack of consensus among great powers about norms of acceptable espionage and as long as their definitions of cyber security diverge, the risks of unintentional escalation remain worrisome.

Disinformation as a new threat focus: Asymmetrical vulnerability of democracies?

In cyberspace "the power to subvert seems to trump both the power to coerce and the power to attract" (Dunn Cavelty and Wenger 2019: 15). Subversive power is especially relevant in strategic contexts in which the perceived spheres of interest by rising powers overlap with the geopolitical interests of ruling powers that uphold the status quo (Maschmeyer 2021). But to what degree can revisionist powers use cyber influence operations also as effective tools to undermine the social cohesion and the political stability of democracies? This concern has turned into one of the most relevant cyber threat narratives in Western policy circles, ever since US authorities have attributed the cyber campaigns targeting the US election in 2016 to Russia (Egloff 2020b).

Western policymakers increasingly perceive disinformation and cyber influence campaigns by Russia and China as a major threat to liberal democracies, Wolf J. Schünemann (2022) notes in his chapter. Analyzing the threat frames used in Western policy documents, he shows that Western policymakers conceptualize disinformation campaigns that target democratic elections as strategic tools used by Russia and China in the context of great power competition. According to the threat narrative that emerges from these policy documents, foreign actors are actively exploiting the bias of liberal democracies against media control. They actively manipulate the ambiguities between public diplomacy and coordinated disinformation campaigns to target and potentially distort national elections. Such a threat narrative is often connected to a policy response that aims at strengthening the state's strategic communication capacities. This, however, Schünemann cautions, might have unintended side-effects. Expanding the control of the state over the information sphere might weaken a democracy's best barriers against disinformation: public discourse and public opinion.

The political context of the alleged asymmetrical vulnerability of democracies is characterized by uncertainty and a lack of knowledge about the actual impact of disinformation. There is very little robust empirical evidence, Schünemann notes, that foreign disinformation campaigns have a substantial long-term effect on public discourse and public policy. The potential macro effects on political discourses are very difficult to understand and to prove, not least because the digital public sphere and the mass media system are themselves in the middle of a structural transformation. Several phenomena associated with this transformation – for example, echo chambers and automated social bots – are seen as facilitating factors for the spread of disinformation. Yet there is little robust evidence about how they influence the processes of political opinion formation at the macro level (also see Maschmeyer et al. forthcoming). Understanding how the attack surface – the public sphere and public discourse – is changing in the context of digitalization is a precursor for the study of the impact that disinformation might have on political discourse and electoral processes at the national level.

New digital tools such as social media have a potential – with or without outside interference – to erode social trust and increase political fragmentation in (democratic) societies. The use of new socio-technical tools, however, is not predetermined, as Jasmin Haunschild, Marc-André Kaufhold, and Christian Reuter demonstrate in their chapter (Haunschild et al. 2022). This means, they argue, that new socio-technical countermeasures can be designed and developed that ameliorate the potentially negative effects of social and political bots. New technologies can be used to increase social cohesion or to exploit existing grievances. And while tech race dynamics can be strong – for example, between automated bot configuration and automated bot detection – social intervention will remain decisive. Their chapter highlights that the micro-politics of business and civilian actors designing the right social-technical tools might be as important for the resilience of democratic societies against disinformation campaign as the macro-political responses of state (security) organizations.

The effectiveness of foreign disinformation and propaganda is linked to the exploitation of preexisting social distrust and political grievances. On this, the authors of Chapters 3 and 4 agree. Successful disinformation campaigns exploit existing vulnerabilities of the public discourse and as such must be reduced from within, Schünemann notes. Uncertainty about the potential negative effect of foreign disinformation, he concludes, "must not let us stumble into a new phase of international threat politics and of securitisation of cyberspace with potentially detrimental effects on liberal democratic values and international peace" (Schünemann 2022: 33). Increasing the resilience of democratic societies against foreign disinformation campaigns remains a shared responsibility of civil society, the private and the public sectors.

Emerging technologies and the future of cyber security politics

Ever since cyber security issues have appeared on the agenda of national and international politics, Jon R. Lindsay (2022) argues in his chapter on the ambiguity of a cryptologic advantage, two analytically distinct perspectives have informed the debate about their relevance for cyber security politics. A first perspective builds on the premise that technology determines politics. Anticipating the transformative potential of emerging technologies, this view tends to extrapolate dramatic consequence for security politics. We have already reviewed early expert assumptions along the line that the nature of cyberspace is destabilizing and favors the offense. A second perspective starts from the opposite end of the relationship and assumes that politics determines technology. Such an analytical perspective translates into expectations that the sociopolitical context mitigates the supposed advantages of cyber offense and reinforces established power relationships (cf. Dunn Cavelty and Wenger 2019).

We argue throughout the volume that a perspective that combines the two views and unpacks the co-constitution and co-dependency of technology and politics provides a more productive analytical lens for studying the ambiguous implications of rapid technological change on cyber security politics and vice versa. Within this context, the chapters in this volume discuss three key insights on the interrelationship between emerging technologies and the future of cyber security politics. A first subsection concentrates on tech race dynamics as drivers of cyber threat perceptions. The focus here is on the interplay between global market and geopolitical dynamics under multidimensional uncertainty and how these dynamics feed into threat narratives. A second subsection highlights that the sociopolitical context conditions the strategic utility of emerging technologies. Here the focus is on how social and institutional factors shape the influence that emerging technologies have on the balance between the offense and the defense. A third subsection deals with the growing role of private actors in digital innovation in general and in securing cyberspace more specifically. The focus here is on how the multiplication of actors increases the socio-technical uncertainty and the sociopolitical ambiguity of the governance space around emerging technologies.

Tech race dynamics as drives of cyber threat perceptions

The dynamic and emergent trajectory of technology development is a key factor shaping the interplay between technology and politics. Multidimensional uncertainty – about the scope and tempo of the technological development and about market dynamics and social acceptance – is a key driver of the innovation process (see Figure 16.1). Technology firms are exposed to market pressures and driven by profit. They make their design and development decisions, including complex trade-offs between the performance and the safety and transparency of their products and services, in the shadow of a potential first-mover advantage and the promise of huge economies of scale. Conversely, governments influence the innovation process via the formulation and implementation of technology strategies that specify national levels of ambition. Such strategies aim at incentivizing the domestic uptake of new technologies and creating a regulatory environment that fits their societies' institutional and normative contexts while positioning their countries in the best possible way in the emerging global innovation space (Bonfanti 2022).

As new technological possibilities – linked to the development of artificial intelligence, quantum computing, or space technologies – appear on the horizon, both governments and corporations focus on their potentially transformative capacities, and, more specifically, anticipate what role these technologies will play in shaping cyber security. Most technologies discussed in the chapters of this volume are dual-use technologies and as such might influence the global economic *and* military balance. As a consequence, great powers tend to treat such technologies as a potential strategic resource. Out of these technical, economic, and (geo)political dynamics an ambiguous political interaction dynamic evolves that fits the logic of the security dilemma (Jervis 1978): The means – in this case maneuvring to attain or sustain an advantage in critical technologies – by which a state tries to maximize its national interests and security threatens the interests and relative security of other states.

From a political perspective, it is problematic if the technology development process is dominated by only a few dominant economic (global tech firms) and political actors (great powers). A concentration of technical resources in the hands of a few actors might affect the global distribution of economic and military power and create or deepen asymmetric economic and political dependencies. A context of an intensifying technology competition creates incentives for states to influence the innovation process and the proliferation of new technology in their narrow national interest (Fischer and Wenger 2019). Conversely, technology race dynamics act as drivers of national threat perceptions and tend to feed doom scenarios. State actors see themselves increasingly caught in a global race for AI or quantum dominance (Lindsay 2022; Bonfanti 2022). From the perspective of science and technology studies, such threat narratives are co-constituted by the micro-politics of design decisions in competitive global markets and the macro-politics of great powers that act strategically in a competitive international system (Fischer and Wenger 2021).

The strategic utility of emerging technologies depends on the sociopolitical context

The insight that the balance between offense and defense in intelligence has always depended more on institutional factors and strategic context than on technological architecture represents the key message of Chapter 6 in this volume. Analyzing the tumultuous relationship between cryptologic technology and political advantage, Jon R. Lindsay (2022) highlights the fundamental political paradox between cryptography (code-making) and cryptanalysis (code-breaking): They must cooperate to compete and respect the constraints of a cooperatively produced cryptosystem. As a consequence, cryptology turns into an organizational contest and as such heavily depends on social factors. It does not come as a surprise against this background that one of the central insights of cryptologic history is that "gullible humans are the Achilles Heel of classical cryptology" (Lindsay 2022: 89). This again, Lindsay argues, makes it reasonable to expect that humans "will also be the undoing of quantum cryptology" (Lindsay 2022: 89).

A working quantum computer should be able to crack the current cryptographic protocols that are vital for cyber security. Anticipating a one-sided technological breakthrough easily translates into fear that a breakthrough in quantum computing might compromise the existing public key infrastructure. As China began to heavily invest into quantum technology, a threat narrative evolved in Western states that perceived the great powers to be locked into a global race to gain a quantum advantage. A quantum breakthrough would have major repercussion for security and defense, so the arguments went, since one's own intelligence would be locked out while the first-movers' communication would become impenetrable. Should this indeed happen, policymakers and strategists feared, global stability could be at risk.

Yet the implications of the interaction between technology and politics will likely be more ambiguous, Lindsay argues. First, such a perspective overlooks that the search for quantum safe protocols begins parallel to the development of a quantum computer that would be able to break the current cryptographic protocols. Second, quantum computing would not change the reliance of cryptology on social factors. Intelligence remains fundamentally a contest between human organizations. The current golden age of cyber espionage was not enabled by a mathematically and technically weak public key infrastructure. It can be traced back to an overly complex organizational setup of the infrastructure and poor cyber hygiene among computer users. Third, even if one side in a geopolitical contest would develop a cryptographic advantage, how this advantage would translate into a political outcome is not predetermined by technology. Rather it would be contingent on the overarching strategic context and the specifics of institutional decision-making. A cryptanalytic success, Lindsay notes, can make a bargain more likely or a surprise attack more attractive, and it may even provide a false sense of security.

In his chapter, Matteo E. Bonfanti (2022) in a similar vein discusses the implications of emerging AI technologies for the offense–defense balance in cyber security. These implications are difficult to predict, he argues, because the context is characterized by widespread uncertainty and ambiguity. Most AI tools can be used in support of both cyber defense as well as cyber offense. AI-based cyber capabilities will affect both the logical (software) dimension as well as the semantic (content) dimension of cyberspace. That AI will have major implications for cyber security is undisputed among experts. Yet who will be the winner – offense or defense, states security agencies or private threat intelligence firms, democracies or autocracies – remains to be seen. The eventual outcome of the integration of AI technologies into cyber security depends on the strategic and sociopolitical context and the risk-benefit calculations of many different public and private cyber security stakeholder.

Private actor innovation increases socio-technical uncertainty and sociopolitical ambiguity

The growing role of private actors in cyber security and in the digital innovation process is noted in most chapters of the book. Big technology companies make key contributions to the development and operation of cyberspace. Private companies act as operators of networks, designers of products and suppliers of services (Eggenschwiler 2022). Small and large technology companies drive the AI innovation process (Bonfanti 2022). Private actors make smaller and more efficient satellites and have turned into key players in the integration of cyberspace and outer space. The growing role of private actors in outer space was enabled by legal changes in the United States and other states that in the context of a neoliberal vision of state-business relationship opened dual-use space projects to private investment and research and development (Erikkson and Giacomello 2022).

Over the past 30 years, the global technology innovation system has increasingly been shaped by the twin forces of globalization and commercialization. While during the Cold War, the development of nuclear, chemical, and biological dual-use technologies was dominated by state investment and national security concerns, the tide began to turn toward a private sector lead as the development of digital technologies began to take off during the 1990s when the first mobile phones and the internet were made available to the broader public (Fischer 2021). The multiplication of actors in digital innovation and cyber security had ambiguous implications, as the incentive structure of widely heterogonous and increasingly transnationally active technology companies increased the prevailing socio-technical uncertainties. Private technology firms are primarily driven by profit and economies of scale. Although their collective business success depends on high levels of social trust in digital technologies and infrastructures, individual firms have a structural motivation to protect their trade secrets and not to fully disclose all their data and algorithms.

Private actors are not only a key innovator of digital technologies, but they have also dramatically expanded their role in securing cyberspace. Brenden Kuerbis, Farzaneh Badiei, Karl Grindal, and Mitlon Mueller (2022) show in their chapter that private threat intelligence firms have turned into key attribution actors. The forensic capabilities of some of the bigger transnational firms are more advanced than those of many states. Yet their attribution claims lack transparency and public legitimacy (Egloff and Wenger 2019). Moreover, it is unclear why they would contribute to a transnational attribution authority, Kuerbis et al. (2022) note. Conversely, the average dependence of critical public security services on private technology companies providing specialized services in the area of big data analytics and AI-based automated evaluation and assessment will likely grow in the future. Already today, technology consultancy firms provide critical services for states' intelligence services, military (cyber) commands, and national police forces. All of these systems need to be maintained and further developed on a continuous basis. As a consequence, specialized private firms will be drawn ever deeper into the operational work of state security services, further increasing sociopolitical ambiguities.

During the golden years of globalization, liberals hoped that global technology norms and regulatory standards would increasingly converge. But while the technology innovation space increasingly expanded around the globe, alternative technology norms and regulatory standards began to emerge in the 21st century, based on a different vision of state-business relationship. China heavily invested in so-called national technology champions, installed a "Civil Military Fusion" mechanism (Bitzinger 2021), and began to actively influence the development of international technology standards (US-China Business Council 2020; Li and Chen 2021). As Western states increasingly perceived China as a geopolitical competitor, they began to set up foreign direct investment screening mechanisms and broadened their dual-use export control systems with the aim of limiting China's access to the West's technology innovation space. In parallel, they began to look for new ways of how best to secure their states' – and especially their security services' – access to their national technology base. As Danny Steed (2022) argues in his chapter, the Snowden revelations substantiated the extent to which Western technology firms shared data with the US state in the name of national and international security.

The upshot of these developments is that the governance space around emerging technologies has become increasingly fragmented and plagued by socio-technical and sociopolitical ambiguity. Cyberspace was originally created as a politically open space with governance structures limited to its technical architecture. As Steed notes in his chapter, the existing sovereignty gap in cyberspace "is not the source of fragmentation, it is the growing [geopolitical] competition to fill the gap that is". The same applies to the growing interconnectedness between cyberspace and outer space, as Johan Eriksson and Giampiero Giacomello (2022) show in their chapter. Private actors increasingly drive the space technology innovation process, as an increasing number of (cyber) infrastructures depends on space-based satellite services. Yet at the same time, state militarization and politicization of outer space accelerates, as an ever-growing number of states use satellite technologies to modernize their security services. The coming together of these two trends creates new vulnerabilities and new types of treats (e.g. anti-satellite weapons, space debris). At the same time, it increases political fragmentation. The diversification of private and state actors raises the old question with new urgency if and how public-private partnerships can secure technological reliability and long-term investment.

Strategic stability under multidimensional uncertainty

The assumed revolutionary potential of cyberspace, Miguel A. Gomez and Christopher Whyte (2022) note in their chapter, was the product of the twin uncertainties about the scope and tempo of the technical innovation and the related social and political responses. As new technological possibilities emerged, politics began to catch up in a process of sociopolitical normalization. As a consequence, state behavior evolved over time. In the absence of a demonstrable strategic utility of cyber operations and a strategic context characterized by a puzzling co-existence of restraint at the high end of conflict and persistent low-level cyber conflict, key states started to increasingly move away from deterrence to cyber conflict management. In 2018, the United States issued a new cyber strategy signaling a shift to persistent engagement and defend forward. The logic of the new approach emphasized that the characteristics of the operational environment in cyberspace – a space of constant contact – demand a continuing engagement and degradation of adversarial cyber capabilities and operations wherever they were found (US Cyber Command 2018; US Department of Defense 2019).

This shift away from deterrence might be premature and underestimate the potential of (unintended) escalation, Gomez and Whyte argue. Moreover, it is still unclear why states invest substantial technical, financial, and organizational resources in using the domain offensively if cyber operations are indeed of limited strategic utility only. Within this context, the chapters in this volume focus on three interconnected aspects of upholding strategic stability under multidimensional uncertainty. A first subsection concentrates on the micro-dynamics of decision-making that might drive escalation under uncertainty and ambiguity. The focus here is on how prior beliefs and cognitive biases might influence the response decisions of elite stakeholders in varying national strategic cultures. A second subsection deals with the ambiguities of attribution as a precondition for a credible deterrence threat. The focus here is on how policymakers perceive cyberspace as a completely human-built domain and how this translates into political apprehension about the applicability of deterrence in cyberspace. A third subsection analyzes the growing role of intelligence in cyberspace. The focus here is on how the digitalization of intelligence changed its strategic and operational role and what (un)intentional consequences this had for cyber insecurity, on the one hand, and for great powers' views on (un)acceptable behavior of intelligence services in cyberspace, on the other.

Escalation: The micro-dynamics of decision-making in varying sociopolitical contexts

Precisely because it is difficult to control the strategic effects of cyber (influence) operations, more research is needed on the micro-dynamics of decision-making that may drive unintended escalation. Contributing to the behavioral turn in cyber security research, Miguel A. Gomez and Christopher Whyte (2022) investigate the effects of uncertainty on judgment in the context of (crisis) decision-making under cyberattack. In such situations, the ambiguity of diffuse actors and malicious actions increases the uncertainty of decision-makers about both the intent behind and the consequences of cyber (influence) operations. The authors use war gaming as a pseudo-experimental method to determine if and how decision-makers use well-known heuristic mechanisms such as prior beliefs and analogical reasoning to discern intent and consequences behind cyber operations. The authors find distinct evidence in support of the notion that decision-makers, when faced with digital insecurity and the use of adversarial cyber operations, fall back on non-cyber situations to make their task simpler.

The degree to which heuristic shortcuts interfere with objectivity and results in more or less severe responses depends on distinct national (strategic) cultures. Gomez and Whyte discuss evidence of cross-national cultural variations influencing the response decision among elite stakeholders. The socio-institutional correlates of civil–military relations in a given democracy stand out to have a unique impact on decision-making processes. Based on their observations from cross-national war games, they conclude that the interaction between the micro-foundations of decision-making in a given cultural and institutional setting "might ultimately have some effect on the strategic calculations states make around signaling and adversary behavior" (Gomez and Whyte 2022: 125). The fact that unintended escalation due to prior beliefs, cognitive biases of decision-makers, and/or bureaucratic politics cannot be excluded in strategic context characterized by uncertainty and ambiguity highlights the advantage of deterrence as a conflict management tool: As a theory of interdependent decision-making, it might prevent militarization and escalation (Schelling 1966).

Deterrence: The ambiguity of attribution in the context of cyber conflict management

Over the years there has been considerable work invested at the science-policy interface in adapting deterrence to the ambiguous context of cyberspace. The scope of the practical applicability of the tenets of deterrence to cyberspace is considerably more limited than in more traditional conventional and nuclear deterrence settings (Soesanto and Smeets 2020). At the same time, deterrence attempts in cybersecurity and cyber defense span a wide spectrum of threats, including cybercrime, cyber espionage, and operational cyberattack.

From a conceptual point of view, the attention at the lower end of conflict shifted to criminological conceptions of deterrence and from punishment to denial mechanisms converging on target hardening through cyber resilience (Wenger and Wilner 2021). In such settings, though, deterrence approaches are typically integrated with other coercive and non-coercive tools into a broader conflict management strategy. Conversely, at the higher end of conflict the attention of strategists has shifted to the concept of cross domain deterrence (Lindsay and Gartzke 2019). The focus here is on adversaries that apply ambiguous "gray zone" strategies that integrate military and non-military coercive instruments while evading attribution. Cross domain deterrence tends to include both positive inducements and negative threats and brings the concept of deterrence "back to the broader coercive diplomacy literature from which it originally emerged" (Sweijs and Zilinick 2021: 152).

In his chapter on the limited reliance of Israel on cyber deterrence, Amir Lupovici (2022) explores how new digital technologies enter into doctrine and strategy. Acknowledging the methodological difficulties of studying cyber deterrence, he deliberately shifts the focus from studying what makes deterrence effective in a given strategic context to analyzing how the cyber domain is embedded in Israel's strategic culture and identity. From such a viewpoint, Lupovici argues, it is puzzling that Israel has so far not developed a clear cyber deterrence strategy, given the prominent role deterrence has played in Israel's strategy and the country's "deterrer identity" (Lupovici 2016). Israeli policymakers, he concludes, seem to recognize the uncertainty and ambiguity involved in establishing a deterrence balance in cyberspace and consequently shy away from formulating a declaratory cyber deterrence strategy.

From an operational point of view, Lupovici (2022) argues, Israel's repeated use of offensive cyber operations against the Iranian and Syrian nuclear programs have been interpreted by some experts as attempts to establish cumulative deterrence through the actual use of force, a concept which is deeply ingrained in Israeli strategic culture (Adamski 2021). Yet the effectiveness of such a strategy remains in dispute, Lupovici insists, and whatever deterrent threat might get through to the adversary is communicated in an indirect and implicit way only. From a conceptual perspective, the US strategy of persistent engagement and defend forward seems to share some of the tenets of the Israeli concept of cumulative deterrence (Tor 2015; Kello 2017). Yet the concept of cumulative deterrence was customarily rejected by most US strategists and policymakers, since in the context of nuclear deterrence the use of force was seen as a symptom of deterrence failure, signalizing a shift from a policy of influence to a policy of control (Adamsky 2021).

It is quite telling that two of the leaders in thinking about and in practicing deterrence in their different strategic contexts have come to accept the limits of deterrence in cyberspace. The way US and Israeli policymakers and strategist conceptualize the cyber domain – as an operating environment with a high degree of technical interconnectedness (increasing uncertainty) and constant political contestation (increasing ambiguity) – seems to be part of the explanation why they, respectively, moved away from cyber deterrence (United States) and never declared a clear deterrence strategy (Israel). Although cyberspace is conceptualized as the fifth domain of warfare, its structural characteristics differ from the other four domains. Cyberspace is completely human-built, shaped by technology companies, and operating in it will always be hard and only partially under control of any one actor (Seebeck 2019). Precisely because cyberspace is completely designed by humans, states can shape it according to their interest. Yet as in cryptology they must cooperate to compete and accept the constraint of a cooperatively produced network of networks.

The economic and political logic of cyberspace as something completely designed by humans might explain why states seem to perceive cyberspace as a domain of intelligence rather than warfare. As discussed above, the fact that setting up cyber exploitation is more expensive than countering released exploitation translates into an incentive to keep the target at risk. From a political point of view, transparent attribution as a precondition of a credible deterrence threat is difficult. Relating an intrusion set to a politically responsible party, Kuerbis et al. (2022) argue, remains challenging because it includes a judgment about the relation between victim and adversary. As such, it should be interpreted as "a product more of political science or intelligence studies than computer science" (Kuerbis et al. 2022: 222).

Intelligence: The growing operational role of intelligence as a source of cyber insecurity

In the context of the multidimensional uncertainty prevailing in cyberspace, intelligence agencies have turned into one of the most dominant actors in this human-built domain (Buchanan 2020; Egloff 2022). Their role in cyber conflict is a paradox and highly ambiguous one: They represent both the biggest threat and the most capable provider of security and safety. Such an outcome is not without irony, because the technical transformation from an analog to a digital world exposed them to a mortal threat: going dark. In his chapter on the consequences of the digital disruption of the second oldest profession, Danny Steed (2022) discusses how US and British intelligence "mastered the internet". In the process, he concludes, they not only transformed their role in security and defense, but unintentionally exacerbated cyber insecurity.

As global information flows began moving into fiber optics, US and British intelligence adapted their skillset to one that could penetrate digital codes and infrastructure (Buchanan 2020). Exploiting the sovereign geographic access to the submarine cables through which the bulk of the internet traffic traversed, was a key factor for success, as was a close partnership with numerous technology companies that facilitated access and sharing of meta-data. The solution to the old intelligence adage – to find the needle in the haystack – was found in technical innovation, as Steed explains: The two intelligence services temporarily collected the whole haystack in a buffer system, which allowed them to sort out relevant information and meta-data via automated analysis. This unique access to large volumes of internet traffic created intelligence dependencies even among close allies, as Stefan Steiger (2022) shows in his chapter on Germany's cyber security politics. Once the Snowden leaks highlighted that foreign intelligence was an accepted state practice even among allies, the German government in a partnership with Brazil invested into a new submarine cable across the Atlantic.

Intelligence services are the most purposefully ambiguous tools of statecraft. The legal ambiguity of intelligence in domestic and international law was for a long time based on the reciprocal assumption of great powers that intelligence services would help decision-makers guard against a military fait accompli and uphold strategic stability. The purpose of the limited intrusion into the sovereign affairs of another state was to provide enough transparency to avoid rapid escalation. In the context of their digital transformation, Danny Steed (2022) contends, their strategic relevance increased considerably. At the same time, their operational focus increasingly shifted from assessing uncertainty to eliminating uncertainty. The shift to a more operational role needs to be seen in the context of a unipolar world, in which the management of transnationally networked threats – terrorism, extremism, organized crime, cyberattacks, WMD proliferation – dominated Western policy and strategy. In the post-9/11 context, operational intelligence and close (bilateral) cooperation among asymmetrically dependent intelligence services played a preeminent role in the global management of the then dominant security challenges.

With the return of geopolitical rivalry between great powers and in the context of the pro-active use of intelligence and cyber (influence) operations by rising powers, international disagreement about what should be considered acceptable use of espionage began to multiply, as noted above in section one. From the perspective of great power politics, it seems essential that states sort out the difference between mutually acceptable espionage in support of strategic stability and inacceptable meddling in the internal political and economic affairs of another state. The 2015 mutual agreement between China and the United States, in which both states committed to not conducting or supporting economic cyber espionage (Baezner and Robin 2017), and the recent agreement between Biden and Putin to conduct "experts-level talks" on red lines for cyberattacks on "critical" sectors (Hirsh 2021), might be read as early beginnings of a long haul toward a tacit understanding of acceptable behavior of intelligence services in cyberspace.

It seems highly unlikely, however, that talks at the diplomatic level will result in a breakthrough any time soon. For this to happen, the differences of acceptable surveillance at the domestic level are simply too big. Societies need to know how their intelligence services work in cyberspace, because their tools and practices set practical norms with far-reaching effects on state, society and economy (Georgieva 2020). For authoritarian states, the priority is to control citizens' access to information, while for democracies the priority is to protect individual privacy and intellectual property rights. Questions about privacy, security, information are at the heart of the political struggle about cyber security and this makes the quest for global norms of responsible behavior in cyberspace a slow and difficult one.

The manner in which intelligence services mastered the internet, Danny Steed (2022) convincingly argues, created additional socio-technical uncertainty and exacerbated the cyber security challenge. Digitalization made intelligence more visible, because unlike in an analog world spies now worked within the same digital infrastructure as all other social, economic, and political actors. As a consequence, intelligence intrusion could be exposed much faster than before, which made intelligence far more visible. When whistle-blowers brought their activities into the spotlight, domestic and international political contestation about their role multiplied. As a corollary of the exposure of intelligence methods, intelligences services turned into inadvertent proliferators of malicious code and zero-day exploits. As a consequence, more people were enabled to use intelligence tools for malicious purposes – compared to intelligence services, with no oversight whatsoever. Some of these tools were later deployed in two global malware attacks – WannaCry and NotPetya – further increasing the ambiguity of action in cyberspace and the uncertainties of attribution.

Emerging governance responses: Policy coordination and norms formation

The socio-technical expansion of cyberspace is led by private technology firms, yet state actors shape the tighter coupling of technical systems with sociopolitical institutions. This in turn means that governments share the responsibility to secure cyberspace with actors from the economy and society. In the process of these socio-technical and sociopolitical transformations, emerging cyber governance responses unfold in an increasingly transnational and trans-sectoral policy space. The vision of a wireless, satellite-based internet accessible to everyone propagated by private business actors and the parallel reality of state actors that are increasingly politicizing and militarizing outer space is set to further expand cyberspace as a transnational policy space. As a network of interdependent information technology infrastructures, cyberspace is connected across state borders and through global satellite-based communications services. At the same time, cyberspace as a trans-sectoral policy space also expands rapidly. The tighter coupling of ever more socio-technical systems increases the interconnectedness of cyberspace. As a consequence, cyber security affects a rapidly growing number of different policy fields.

The key governance challenge in cyberspace is how to overcome fragmentation of authority and accountability. Within the context of a trans-sectoral and transnational policy space, the chapters in this volume highlight three aspects of the ongoing re-negotiation processes among state, society, and economy about their roles and responsibilities in cyberspace. A first subsection deals with the significant expansion of state responsibilities in cyberspace over the past decades. The focus is on how state actors fine-tuned their multidimensional role across different policy fields in a process that was influenced by distinct patterns of interaction between domestic contestation and international orientation and dependence. A second subsection concentrates on the increasingly prominent role of private and civil society actors in the search for new forms of transnational governance in cyberspace. The focus here is on the norm-based activities of big tech companies, on the one hand, and a series of proposals for a global platform for transnational attribution, on the other. A third subsection brings the attention back to state actors, shedding light on the critical role of intelligence services in (in)securing cyberspace. As long as great powers disagree about what constitutes acceptable behavior of intelligence services in cyberspace, the systemic levels of insecurity in cyberspace will likely not materially decrease.

Growing role of governments: Shifting patterns of domestic and international governance

The tech pioneers had built the internet based on the vision of an open technical governance infrastructure with minimal involvement of government. Yet as cyberattacks were becoming more persistent, more targeted, more expensive, and more disruptive, governments began to significantly expand their roles and responsibilities in cyberspace. Ever since states find themselves in the midst of two interlinked re-negotiation processes of their roles and responsibilities in (securing) cyberspace. While at the level of domestic politics they renegotiate their role in securing cyberspace as a shared responsibility with society and industry, at the level of international politics they renegotiate the patterns of international governance with states, private and civil actors.

In his chapter, Stefan Steiger (2022) analyzes how Germany's cyber security policies evolved over time, shaped by the complex interactions between domestic and international negotiation processes. He employs a role theoretical two-level game to analyze how domestic and international factors influenced the development of German cyber security policy. Isolating four interconnected policy domains – critical infrastructure protection (CIP); law enforcement; intelligence services; military – he discusses how varyingly fragmented national and international actors reached four distinct, but still connected policy outcomes. The CIP and law enforcement domains of German cyber security policy comprise the most distinct international and regional cooperation patterns, Steiger concludes. In the CIP domain, domestic CIP policies emerged first, based on a model of public-private partnerships that delegated the primary responsibility for cyber security to the private sector. Over time, however, the federal government strengthened its supervisory role considerably. The German government promoted the protection of critical infrastructures also internationally, primarily in the EU and the OSCE, reflecting the physical interconnectedness of critical infrastructure across borders. In the domain of law enforcement, EU members successfully harmonized criminal law, without however weakening the central authority and sovereignty of the (German) state.

The intelligence and military domains of German cyber security policy remain intergovernmental policy domains, in which the German government accepted no self-binding regulations. The intelligence domain exhibits the most paradoxical interaction patterns between national and international re-negotiation processes, Steiger notes. On the one hand, Germany's early call for international restraint in cyberspace was facilitated by the intelligence dependence on the United States. Once the Snowden revelations showed that digital surveillance was an accepted state practice even among allies, the role of intelligence was hotly contested at the domestic level. As a consequence, Germany expanded the legal basis for foreign surveillance, began to stockpile zero-day exploits, and expanded its access to the transatlantic internet traffic. In parallel, this expanded foreign mandate of German intelligence was balanced with stronger domestic control mechanisms and special protection rights for German and EU citizen. In the military domain too, Germany, because of its commitment to NATO, began to move away from international restraint, established a cyber-command, and prepared for the use of offensive cyber capabilities.

Chapters 11 and 12 in this volume offer two additional case studies discussing the cyber security policies of two states that are located at the periphery of Europe and want to move closer to Western institution. The evolution of their cyber security policies too is characterized by distinct patterns of interaction between domestic institutional transformation and international orientation and dependence. We have already discussed the case of Ukraine above. Ukraine represents the extreme case of a small state with weak cyber capacity that sits on the geopolitical fault lines between Russia and the West. Exposed to persistent Russian cyberattacks and massive information operations, the country recently lived through a domestic revolution linked to an abrupt reorientation of its foreign policy alignment from Russia to Europe and the West.

In his chapter, Aaron Brantly (2022) shows that the pattern of domestic contestation and international reorientation resulted in a fairly successful response of the country to Russia's information warfare, aimed at undermining the social and political fabric of Ukraine. He explains this as the result of a combination of a series of top-down government initiatives – including restrictive moves against Russian-dominated web platforms and broadcast channels and the introduction of a Ministry of Information Policy – with a series of bottom-up initiatives by journalist and externally sponsored NGOs – focusing on fact checking, disclosure of foreign propaganda, and the training of journalists and civil society. Less successful, however, were the country's efforts to increase its resilience against cyberattacks. Although the country aligned the legal and organizational foundations of its cyber security policies with EU and NATO standards, the new cyber security structures are not yet functional on their own, Brantly concludes. He points to the dominance of old bureaucratic cultures – especially in the security services – and dependence on external assistance and funding as the two main reasons for weak policy implementation.

Albania represents another interesting case of a small state with weak cyber capabilities that is transforming toward democracy and wants to move closer to Western institutions. In his chapter, Islam Jusufi (2022) discusses how both the cyber threat frames and the policy responses visible in Albania's policy documents diffused from the international level – especially from US, UK, EU, and NATO sources. This policy diffusion process to the national level had two notable consequences, the author argues: First, cyber security was preemptively upgraded to a national threat level, i.e. not in response to national incidents. Second, the new policy introduced the concept of multi-stakeholder governance that represented a shift from Albania's traditional state-centered governance model. In combination, these two developments resulted in a somewhat paradoxical outcome: While the dependence of a technologically weak state on foreign actors increased, the introduction of new international policy concepts augmented the fragmentation of domestic authority in cyber security. Moreover, this outcome highlights a certain time-inconsistency problem in international policy coordination. It is not without irony that Western states in parallel began to reclaim authority and sovereignty in certain policy domains – as demonstrated in the German case above – and expanded the protector role of the government in cyberspace.

Toward new forms of transnational governance: Norms and institutions

The search for new forms of transnational governance reflects a realization that digital technologies and the services they provide are increasingly connected across state borders and into outer space. Why do private and civil society actors play an increasingly prominent role in the development of norms and institutions that aim to regulate human behavior in cyberspace? First, cyber norms and institutions remain contested at the level of international politics. The inability of states to make progress in the direction of a common understanding of cyber norms, especially at the United Nations, provided the context for a growing engagement of non-state actors. Second, a series of large-scale data breaches and malware strikes undermined social trust – a critical success factor for the business models of transnationally operating tech firms – in the socio-technical systems that constitute cyberspace. Third, the mostly private creators of cyber space possess key engineering expertise that is essential to ensure that new governance approaches are anchored in a tacit understanding of research and development and broader business practices. In turn, civil society has the potential to provide additional benefits in terms of transparency, privacy, and equality.

In her chapter, Jacqueline Eggenschwiler (2022) evaluates the norm-based activities of big tech companies, including Kaspersky Lab, Siemens, Telefónica, and Microsoft. She introduces norms approaches as appropriate regulatory approaches to tackle the contextual ambiguities of fast-moving environments, which preempt costly – and from the viewpoint of tech firms unwanted – changes to legal frameworks. With their voluntary engagement in support of the development of cyber security norms of responsible behavior, technology firms aim to define responsible product development and engineering practices and establish trust in social interactions enabled by digital technologies. The norm-based activities of big tech have been partially successful insofar as they have converged on a number of widely shared normative ideas and design principles and injected these ideas and principles into a number of regional and international political processes. The procedural effects of a greater inclusion of private and civil society actors in norm development processes will likely be enduring, Jacqueline Eggenschwiler concludes. Yet big tech's push for cyber security norms has not resulted in a substantial reduction of cyber insecurity.

Not only the development of cyber security norms will be a long process, the same is true for the institutionalization of a recognized transnational attribution process, Brenden Kuerbis, Farzaneh Badiei, Karl Grindal, and Milton Mueller (2022) argue in their chapter. Cyber attribution as a socio-technical and highly interdisciplinary endeavor is a precondition for the deterrence of cyberattacks and a precursor for stable social relations in cyberspace. The current attribution claims of threat intelligence firms and national security services are however often based on limited evidence and the reputation of the attributing actor, and, as a consequence, lack transparency and credibility. However, new advances in attribution that combine better algorithm-driven technical attribution with better understanding of the institutional condition under which attribution might occur, Kuerbis et al. note, may in the future improve the baseline for institutionalizing transnational attribution.

The chapter discusses various proposals from private actors and academic institutions on how a global platform for transnational attribution could be set up and what the scope of its activities should be. The following two major challenges on the way toward implementation stand out in most of them: A first key question is how to ensure the technical independence of such a platform and the professionalism of the participants. There is still a lot of research needed to define the scientific and methodological standards, including transparency, reproducibility, and falsifiability, of the practice of attribution. In addition, it remains unclear why private tech firms with advanced forensic capabilities would participate in such a platform. A second key question is how to guarantee the judicial independence of such a platform and what governance form would be effective in aligning the participants' incentives. The spectrum of conceivable solutions ranges from hierarchically organized institutions to loosely organized forms of networked governance. In the final analysis, however, the success of private and civil sector–driven cyber security norms processes as well as of initiatives aimed at the institutionalization of transnational attribution critically depend on the political will of state actors, especially great powers, to agree upon norms of responsible behavior as the ultimate enforcer.

Great powers as ultimate enforcers: Re-negotiation, the ambiguous norms of espionage

States cannot govern cyberspace on their own, they need to integrate economic and social actors into a wider cyber security governance framework. Yet no stable cyber security governance framework will evolve without greater convergence among great powers on responsible state behavior as ultimate enforcers. It is therefore vital for non-state and state actors to work closer together and aid one another in their behavior-shaping efforts in order to decrease the systematic levels of cyber insecurity, Jacqueline Eggenschwiler (2022) argues in her chapter. As long as emerging (information) technologies are perceived as a geopolitical battleground, limited progress will be possible. States need to negotiate a tacit understanding about what constitutes a mutually acceptable balance between restraint in and exploitation of cyberspace. As discussed above, a critical component of such an understanding is linked to the behavior of state intelligence services in the digital domain. The great power's views on what forms of espionage and interference in the political processes and socioeconomic activities of other societies through cyberspace are acceptable need to converge before the systemic levels of cyber insecurity will materially decrease.

Conclusion

The chapters in this book discussed the ambiguity of current cyber security politics in an uncertain context characterized by rapid socio-technical transformation and increasing fragmentation of political authority. In this concluding chapter, we highlighted four key debates in current thinking about cyber security, all of them linked to the interplay between technological possibilities and political choices in cyberspace. An analytical perspective that emphasizes the co-constitution and co-dependency of technology and politics provides an especially productive lens for studying the complexities and paradoxes of cyber security politics. The key reason for this is found in the nature of cyberspace as a domain completely designed and built by humans – with a high degree of technical interconnectedness and constant political contestation. As a consequence, state, economy and society must cooperate to compete in cyberspace and accept the constraints of a cooperatively produced network of networks.

A key insight that such an analytical perspective offers is that both evolving cyber threat narratives and emerging cyber governance responses are co-produced by state and non-state actors in a rapidly changing trans-sectoral and transnational policy space. Emerging cyber threats are co-constituted by the micro-politics of technology design decisions in competitive global markets, the meso-politics of technology norms choices in competitive regulatory environments, and the macro-politics of great powers that act strategically in a competitive international system. Within this broader context, the chapters in this book highlight a series of interaction mechanisms between technology and politics that influence cyber threat politics in different strategic contexts: Tech race dynamics around emerging dual-use technologies clearly leave a mark in the national threat politics of great powers. Actors in "gray zone" conflicts attempt to manipulate the opaqueness of cyber (influence) operations. And in democracies policymakers are increasingly concerned about the asymmetrical vulnerability of their socio-technical public sphere to foreign disinformation and cyber influence campaigns.

That cyber threat perceptions are co-constituted by technology and politics also means that their realization is not predetermined. Both state and non-state actors can contribute to a decrease of the level of insecurity in cyberspace. States need to establish red lines, uphold strategic stability, and develop norms of responsible state behavior in cyberspace. Actors from society and economy need to develop norms of responsible behavior for the creators and users of emerging technologies as the bedrock of societies' trust in socio-technical systems. Yet the effectiveness of their individual responses to cyber threats depends on their mutual interplay. States and societal actors need to negotiate how public authority is exercised in cyberspace. A stable governance framework for cyber security can only emerge if great powers develop a tacit understanding on what represents a responsible use of cyber operations in state interactions, and societal actors successfully navigate the normative space around technology, information, privacy, and security.

Researchers can contribute to the search for a functioning governance framework: They can highlight the less visible actors in cyberspace, design and evaluate new socio-technical institutions to secure cyberspace or monitor, and analyze publicly available data about cyber operations. A key conceptual challenge for cyber security research is linked to the integration of theoretical knowledge from different disciplines that allows to analyze the many interactions between the international dimension of cyber *security politics* and the broader dimension of cyber security *politics* (Dunn Cavelty and Wenger 2019). Those who study the former tend to build on approaches from IR, security, and intelligence studies, but increasingly recognize broader contributions from critical security studies and practice theory. Those who study the latter, leverage an even broader array of theoretical perspectives including approaches from IPE, governance studies, and the IR norms literature.

A practical challenge is how to overcome the dominance of Western perspectives both in politics as well as in academia. We tend to see only the peak of an iceberg of malicious activities in cyberspace that is linked to the political and economic interests of Western states and threat intelligence firms. The empirical focus of most chapters in this book is informed by the geostrategic rivalry between Western democracies and Russia and China as their main authoritarian contender. It is this strategic context and the differences in the domestic institutional setup of the leading great powers that guide large parts of the analyses of cyber conflict in this volume. Yet at the same time, individual chapters point to interesting variances in the cyber security policies among traditional (United States, Israel) and aspiring (Albania, Ukraine) democracies, on the one hand, and to the important role of cross-national cultural variations in cyber decision-making, on the other. Cyber security is increasingly negotiated at the global level and this is why we need to better understand how different regions and cultures think about the interplay of technology and politics in cyberspace.

Bibliography

All links checked on September 3, 2021.

Adamsky, D. D. (2021). Deterrence by Denial in Israeli Strategic Thinking. In A. Wenger and A. Wilner (eds), *Deterrence by Denial: Theory and Practice*. Amherst, NY: Cambria Press, 163–190.

Baezner, M. (2018). *Hotspot Analysis: Synthesis 2017: Cyber-Conflicts in Perspective*. Zurich: Center for Security Studies (CSS).

Baezner, M., and Cordey, S. (2022). Cyber in the Grey Zone: Influence Operations and other Conflict Trends. In M. Dunn Cavelty and A. Wenger (eds), *Cyber Security: Socio-Technological Uncertainty and Political Fragmentation*. London: Routledge, pp. 17–31.

Baezner, M., and Robin, P. (2017). *Hotspot Analysis: Strategic stability between Great Powers: the Sino-American Cyber Agreement*. Zurich: Center for Security Studies (CSS).

Bitzinger, R. A. (2021). China's Shift from Civil-Military Integration to Military-Civil Fusion. *Asia Policy*, 28(1): 5–24. https://doi.org/10.1353/asp.2021.0001.

Bonfanti, M. E. (2022). Artificial Intelligence and the Offence-Defence Balance in Cyber Security. In M. Dunn Cavelty and A. Wenger (eds), *Cyber Security: Socio-Technological Uncertainty and Political Fragmentation*. London: Routledge, pp. 64–79.

Borghard, E. D., and Lonergan, S. W. (2017). The Logic of Coercion in Cyberspace. *Security Studies*, 26(13): 452–458.

Brantly, A. (2022). Battling the Bear: Ukraine's Approach to National Cyber and Information Security. In M. Dunn Cavelty and A. Wenger (eds), *Cyber Security: Socio-Technological Uncertainty and Political Fragmentation*. London: Routledge, pp. 157–171.

Buchanan, B. (2020). *The Hacker and the State: Cyber Attacks and the New Normal of Geopolitics*. Harvard: Harvard University Press.

Cavaiola, L. J., Gompert, D. C., and Libicki, M. (2015). Cyber House Rules: On War, Retaliation and Escalation. *Survival*, 57(1): 81–104.

Chesney, R., and Smeets, M. (2020). Roundtable: The Dynamics of Cyber Conflict and Competition. *Texas National Security Review*, 3(4): 4–7. https://doi.org/10.26153/tsw/10964.

Chesney, R., and Smeets, M. (forthcoming). *Deter, Disrupt or Deceive: Assessing Cyber Conflict as an Intelligence Contest*. Washington: Georgetown University Press.

Clarke, R. A., and Knake, R. K. (2010). *Cyber War*. New York: Ecco.

Devanny, J. (2021). 'Madman Theory' or 'Persistent Engagement'? The Coherence of US Cyber Strategy under Trump. *Journal of Applied Security Research*. Retrieved August 19, 2021, from: https://www.tandfonline.com/doi/abs/10.1080/19361610.2021.1872359.

Dewar, R. S. (ed.). (2018). *National Cybersecurity and Cyberdefense Policy Snapshots*. Zurich: Center for Security Studies (CSS).

Dunn Cavelty, M. (2008). *Cyber Security and Threat Politics: US Efforts to Secure the Information Age*. London: Routledge.

Dunn Cavelty, M. (2015). The Normalization of Cyber-International Relations. In O. Thränert and M. Zapfe (eds), *Strategic Trends 2015: Key Developments in Global Affairs*. Zurich: Center for Security Studies (CSS), pp. 81–98.

Dunn Cavelty, M., and Egloff, F. J. (2019). The Politics of Cybersecurity: Balancing Different Roles of the State. *St Antony's International Review*, 15(1): 37–57.

Dunn Cavelty, M., and Wenger, A. (2019). Cybersecurity Meets Security Politics: Complex Technology, Fragmented Politics, and Networked Science. *Contemporary Security Policy*, 41(1): 5–32.

Dunn Cavelty, M., and Wenger, A. (2022). Introduction: Cyber Security between Socio-Technological Uncertainty and Political Fragmentation. In M. Dunn Cavelty and A. Wenger (eds), *Cyber Security: Socio-Technological Uncertainty and Political Fragmentation*. London: Routledge, pp. 1–13.

Eggenschwiler, J. (2022). Big Tech's Push for Norms to Tackle Uncertainty in Cyberspace. In M. Dunn Cavelty and A. Wenger (eds), *Cyber Security: Socio-Technological Uncertainty and Political Fragmentation*. London: Routledge, pp. 186–204.

Egloff, F. J. (2020a). Contested Public Attributions of Cyber Incidents and the Role of Academia. *Contemporary Security Policy*, 41(1): 55–81. https://doi.org/10.1080/13523260.2019.1677324.

Egloff, F. J. (2020b). Public Attribution of Cyber Intrusions. *Journal of Cybersecurity*, 6(1): 1–12. https://doi.org/10.1093/cybsec/tyaa012.

Egloff, F. J. (2022). *Semi-State Actors in Cybersecurity*. Oxford: Oxford University Press.

Egloff, F. J., and Dunn Cavelty, M. (2021). Attribution and Knowledge Creation Assemblages in Cybersecurity Politics. *Journal of Cybersecurity*, 7(1): tyab002. https://doi.org/10.1093/cybsec/tyab002.

Egloff, F. J., and Wenger, A. (2019). Public Attribution of Cyber Incidents. In F. Merz (ed.). *CSS Analyses in Security Policy, 244*. Zurich: Center for Security Studies (CSS), pp. 1–4.

Eriksson, J., and Giacomello, G. (2022). Cyberspace in Space: Fragmentation, Vulnerability, and Uncertainty. In M. Dunn Cavelty and A. Wenger (eds), *Cyber Security: Socio-Technological Uncertainty and Political Fragmentation*. London: Routledge, pp. 95–107.

Fischer, S.-C. (2021). *The Mobilization of Commercial Technology Companies: Explaining the Pursuit of U.S. Technological Superiority vis-à-vis China in a Private Sector-Driven and Globalized Innovation System.* Unpublished PhD Manuscript. Zurich: Center for Security Studies (CSS).

Fischer, S.-C., and Wenger, A. (2019). A Politically Neutral Hub for Basic AI Research. *CSS Policy Perspectives*, 7(2). Zurich: Center for Security Studies (CSS).

Fischer, S.-C., and Wenger, A. (2021). Artificial Intelligence, Forward-Looking Governance and the Future of Security. *Swiss Political Science Review*, 27(1): 170–179. https://doi.org/10.1111/spsr.12439.

Gartzke, E. (2013). The Myth of Cyberwar. Bringing War in Cyberspace Back Down to Earth. *International Security*, 38: 41–73. https://doi.org/10.1162/ISEC_a_00136.

Georgieva, I. (2020). The Unexpected Norm-Setters: Intelligence Agencies in Cyberspace. *Contemporary Security Policy*, 41: 33–54. https://doi.org/10.1080/13523260.2019.1677389.

Gomez, M. A., and Whyte, C. (2022). Cyber Uncertainties: Observations from Cross-National Wargames. In M. Dunn Cavelty and A. Wenger (eds), *Cyber Security: Socio-Technological Uncertainty and Political Fragmentation.* London: Routledge, pp. 111–127.

Harknett, R. J., and Smeets, M. (2020). Cyber Campaigns and Strategic Outcomes. *Journal of Strategic Studies*, Ahead of Print: 1–34. https://doi.org/10.1080/01402390.2020.1732354.

Haunschild, J., Kaufhold, M.-A., and Reuter, C. (2022). Cultural Violence and Peace in Social Media: Technical and Social Interventions. In M. Dunn Cavelty and A. Wenger (eds), *Cyber Security: Socio-Technological Uncertainty and Political Fragmentation.* London: Routledge, pp. 48–63.

Healey, J. (2019). The Implications of Persistent (and Permanent) Engagement in Cyberspace. *Journal of Cybersecurity*, 5(1): tyz008. https://doi.org/10.1093/cybsec/tyz008.

Healey, J., and Jervis, R. (2020). The Escalation Inversion and Other Oddities of Situational Cyber Stability. *Texas National Security Review*, 3(4): 30–53. https://doi.org/10.26153/tsw/10962.

Hirsh, M. (2021, July 8). Putin Is Testing Biden's Cyber Resolve. *Foreign Policy*. Retrieved August 19, 2021, from: https://foreignpolicy.com/2021/07/08/putin-biden-cyber-security-attacks-ransomeware/.

Jervis, R. (1978). Cooperation under the Security Dilemma. *World Politics*, 30(2): 167–214.

Jusufi, I. (2022). Uncertainty, International Obligations, Fragmentation and Sovereignty: Cyber Security in Albania. In M. Dunn Cavelty and A. Wenger (eds), *Cyber Security: Socio-Technological Uncertainty and Political Fragmentation.* London: Routledge, pp. 172–185.

Kello, L. (2017). *The Virtual Weapon and International Order*. New Haven: Yale University Press.

Kostyuk, N., and Zhukov, Y. M. (2017). Invisible Digital Front: Can Cyber Attacks Shape Battlefield Events? *Journal of Conflict Resolution*, 63(2): 317–47.

Kuerbis, B., Badiei, F., Grindal, K., and Mueller, M. (2022). Understanding Transnational Cyber Attribution: Moving from 'Whodunit' to Who Did it. In M. Dunn Cavelty and A. Wenger (eds), *Cyber Security: Socio-Technological Uncertainty and Political Fragmentation.* London: Routledge, pp. 220–238.

Lewis, J. A. (2018). *Rethinking Cyber Security: Strategy, Mass Effects, and States.* Washington, DC: Center for Strategic and International Studies.

Li, X., and Chen, D. (2021, April 15). Should the West Fear China's Increasing Role in Technical Standard Setting? *The Diplomat*. Retrieved from: https://thediplomat.com/2021/04/should-the-west-fear-chinas-increasing-role-in-technical-standard-setting/.

Lindsay, J. R. (2013). Stuxnet and the Limits of Cyber Warfare. *Security Studies*, 22(3): 365–404.

Lindsay, J. R. (2014/2015). The Impact of China on Cybersecurity: Fiction and Friction. *International Security*, 39(3): 7–47.

Lindsay, J. R. (2017). Restrained by Design: The Political Economy of Cybersecurity. *Digital Policy, Regulation and Governance*, 19: 493–514. https://doi.org/10.1108/DPRG-05-2017-0023.

Lindsay, J. R. (2020). Cyber Conflict vs. Cyber Command: Hidden Dangers in the American Military Solution to a Large-Scale Intelligence Problem. *Intelligent and National Security*, 36(2): 260–278. https://doi.org/10.1080/02684527.2020.1840746.

Lindsay, J. R. (2022). Quantum Computer and Classical Politics: The Ambiguity of Cryptologic Advantage. In M. Dunn Cavelty and A. Wenger (eds), *Cyber Security: Socio-Technological Uncertainty and Political Fragmentation*. London: Routledge, pp. 80–94.

Lindsay, J. R., and Gartzke, E. (2019). *Cross-Domain Deterrence: Strategy in an Era of Complexity*. Oxford: Oxford University Press.

Lupovici, A. (2016). *The Power of Deterrence. Emotions, Identity, and American and Israeli Wars of Resolve*. Cambridge: Cambridge University Press.

Lupovici, A. (2021). The Dog that Did not Bark, the Dog that Did Bark, and the Dog that Should Have Barked: A Methodology for Cyber Deterrence Research. *International Studies Review*, viab032. https://doi.org/10.1093/isr/viab032.

Lupovici, A. (2022). Uncertainty and the Study of Cyber Deterrence: The Case of Israel's Limited Reliance on Cyber Deterrence. In M. Dunn Cavelty and A. Wenger (eds), *Cyber Security: Socio-Technological Uncertainty and Political Fragmentation*. London: Routledge, pp. 128–140.

Maschmeyer, L. (2021). The Subversive Trilemma: Why Cyber Operations Fall Short of Expectations. *International Security*, 46(2): 51–90.

Maschmeyer, L., Abrahams, A., Pomerantsev, P., and Yermolenko, V. (forthcoming). Donetsk Don't Tell. Hybrid War in Ukraine and the Limits of Digital Influence Operations.

Poznansky, M., and Perkoski, E. (2018). Rethinking Secrecy in Cyberspace: The Politics of Voluntary Attribution. *Journal of Global Security Studies*, 3(4): 402–416. https://doi.org/10.1093/jogss/ogy022.

Rid, T. (2012). Cyber War Will Not Take Place. *Journal of Strategic Studies*, 35(1): 5–32.

Rid, T., and Buchanan, B. (2015). Attributing Cyber Attacks. *The Journal of Strategic Studies*, 38(1–2): 4–37.

Rovner, J. (2019, September 16). Cyber War an Intelligence Contest. *War on the Rocks*. Retrieved August 19, 2021, from: https://warontherocks.com/2019/09/cyber-war-as-an-intelligence-contest/.

Schelling, T. C. (1966). *Arms and Influence*. New Haven: Yale University Press.

Schulze, M. (2020). Cyber in War: Assessing the Strategic, Tactical, and Operational Utility of Military Cyber Operations. In *2020 12th International Conference on Cyber Conflict*. Retrieved August 19, 2021, from: https://www.ccdcoe.org/uploads/2020/05/CyCon_2020_10_Schulze.pdf.

Schünemann, W. (2022). A Threat to Democracies? An Overview of Approaches to Measuring the Effects of Disinformation. In M. Dunn Cavelty and A. Wenger (eds),

Cyber Security: Socio-Technological Uncertainty and Political Fragmentation. London: Routledge, pp. 32–47.

Seebeck, L. (2019, September 5). Why the Fifth Domain is Different. *The Strategist*, ASPI (Australian Stratic Policy Institute). Retrieved from: https://www.aspistrategist.org.au/why-the-fifth-domain-is-different/.

Slayton, R. (2017). What is the Cyber Offense-Defense Balance? Conceptions, Causes, and Assessment. *International Security*, 41: 72–109. https://doi.org/10.1162/ISEC_a_00267.

Smeets, M. (2018). The Strategic Promise of Offensive Cyber Operations. *Strategic Studies Quarterly*, 12(3): 90–113.

Smeets, M. (2022). *No Shortcuts: Why States Struggle to Develop a Military Cyber-Force*. London: Hurst Publishers.

Soesanto, S., and Smeets, M. (2020). Cyber Deterrence: The Past, Present, and Future. In F. Osinga and T. Sweijs (eds), *NL ARMS Netherlands Annual Review of Military Studies 2020*. The Hague: T.M.C. Asser Press. https://doi.org/10.1007/978-94-6265-419-8_20.

Steed, D. (2022). Disrupting the Second Oldest Profession: The Impact of Cyber on Intelligence. In M. Dunn Cavelty and A. Wenger (eds), *Cyber Security: Socio-Technological Uncertainty and Political Fragmentation.* London: Routledge, pp. 205–219.

Steiger, S. (2022). Cyber Securities and Cyber Security Politics: Understanding Different Logics of German Cyber Security Policies. In M. Dunn Cavelty and A. Wenger (eds), *Cyber Security: Socio-Technological Uncertainty and Political Fragmentation.* London: Routledge, pp. 141–156.

Sweijs, T., and Zilincik, S. (2021). The Essence of Cross-Domain Deterrence. In F. Osinga and T. Sweijs (eds), *NL ARMS Netherlands Annual Review of Military Studies 2020.* The Hague: T.M.C. Asser Press. https://doi.org/10.1007/978-94-6265-419-8_8.

Tor, U. (2015). 'Cumulative Deterrence' as a New Paradigm for Cyber Deterrence. *Journal of Strategic Studies*, 40(1–2): 92–117.

US-China Business Council (USCBC). (2020). China in International Standards Setting. USCBC Recommendations for Constructive Participation. Retrieved from: https://www.uschina.org/sites/default/files/china_in_international_standards_setting.pdf.

US Cyber Command. (2018). Achieve and Maintain Cyberspace Superiority: Command Vision for US Cyber Command. Retrieved from: https://www.cybercom.mil/Portals/56/Documents/USCYBERCOM%20Vision%20April%202018.pdf?ver=2018-06-14-152556-010.

US Department of Defense. (2019). Cyber Strategy 2019: Summary. Retrieved from: https://media.defense.gov/2018/Sep/18/2002041658/1/1/1/CYBER_STRATEGY_SUMMARY_FINAL.PDF.

Valeriano, B., and Maness, R. C. (2015). *Cyber War versus Cyber Realities: Cyber Conflict in the International System*. Oxford: Oxford University Press.

Wenger, A., and Wilner, A. (eds). (2021). *Deterrence by Denial: Theory and Practice*. Amherst, NY: Cambria Press.

Index

Note: Page numbers in *italics* indicate figures, **bold** indicate tables in the text, and references following "n" refer endnotes.